LYNNE ALVAREZ
Collected Plays Volume I

LYNNE ALVAREZ

Collected Plays Volume I

CONTEMPORARY PLAYWRIGHTS
SERIES

SK
A Smith and Kraus Book

A Smith and Kraus Book
Published by Smith and Kraus, Inc.
PO Box 127, Lyme, NH 03768

Copyright ©1998 by Lynne Alvarez
All rights reserved
Manufactured in the United States of America
Cover and Text Design by Julia Hill

First Edition: June 1998
10 9 8 7 6 5 4 3 2 1

The Guitarrón © 1982 by Lynne Alvarez.

Hidden Parts © 1983 by Lynne Alvarez.

The Wonderful Tower of Humbert Lavoignet © 1984 by Lynne Alvarez.

Don Juan of Seville by Tirso de Molina, translated by Lynne Alvarez. © 1990 by Lynne Alvarez.

Thin Air: Tales from a Revolution © 1989 by Lynne Alvarez.

The Reincarnation of Jaime Brown by Lynne Alvarez. © 1994 by Lynne Alvarez.

Eddie Mundo Edmundo © 1996 by Lynne Alvarez.

On Sundays © 1981 by Lynne Alvarez.

The Library of Congress Cataloging-In-Publication Data

Alvarez, Lynne.
[Plays. Selections]
      Collected plays / Lynne Alvarez. —1st ed.
      p. cm. — (Contemporary playwrights series)
      ISBN 1-57525-146-9
      I. Title. II. Series.
      PS3551.L846A6   1998
      812'.54—dc21   98-24129
                       CIP

CONTENTS

FOR MY HUSBAND—THE BEAR

FOR MY BELOVED PARENTS

AND MY BEAUTIFUL DAUGHTER

PREFACE

"He grabbed me by the shoulders and showed me things...unbelievable things...the veins of silver in the ocean, sea creatures buried on the mountaintops, nations asleep with dreams drifting up like swirls of smoke. I saw fingers and eyes and a million hearts beating..."

These are the words of Humbert Lavoignet, an unemployed mailman created out of the endlessly abundant and complex imagination of Lynne Alvarez, in her play *The Wonderful Tower of Humbert Lavoignet*, one of eight plays included in this collection of stylistically and thematically diverse works for theater. And *for* the theatre, they are. Rich with language, they are not some kind of contemplative "poetic drama" that cannot survive beyond the page, Alvarez's plays fill the theater with living images—people, worlds, visions that are indelible and potent and, always, theatrical. Humbert is describing a transforming experience in the hands of his God, but this speech could also describe what can happen to an audience member watching one of Alvarez's plays. Lynne has the ability to take her audiences by the shoulders, lift them up and show them many amazing, terrifying, painful things and then drop them deftly and thrillingly into the laps of ordinary people struggling, with great humor and candor, in the complex political, spiritual, and emotional reality of day-to-day living. This gravity-defying feat is done with theatrical muscle, a sophisticated worldview (tempered by a lifetime of experience in, at least, two cultures), and an open, yet wary eye, on the murky past, the fluctuating present, and the tempting—and also terrifying—future.

From the darkly humorous presentation of a callow "brat-pack" young *Don Juan of Seville* in her new translation/adaptation of this UR-Don Juan story (based on the original play written in 1350 by Tirso de Molina) to the heartbreakingly candid revelations of an equally young, but sensitive Eddie in *Eddie Mundo Edmundo*. Alvarez takes her audiences into worlds of layers of feeling, points of view as diverse as our complex world deserves. *The Wonderful Tower of Humbert Lavoignet* lands us in the middle of a rural farm community where a miracle has happened—there's been a visitation by God to a postman, a tower is built of junk, and the future generation, in the body of a young boy, manages to see—to behold—the natural world for the first time. *The Guitarrón* allows us to live on the beach outside Veracruz in Mexico while we are surrounded by characters speaking a vernacular English with Spanish slang. Filled with passion and violence, *The Guitarrón* explores the strength of the artistic impulse, in the face of a crippling poverty. *Hidden Parts* takes us to the Midwest where a family has settled for the wrong dark secret and Alvarez paints this landscape like a sinister Grant Wood, with the language rhythms of rural Michigan. *The Reincarnation of Jaime Brown* introduces us to an ingenious young New Yorker who talks directly to the audience as she experiments with love and reincarnation in the streets and bus stations of a confusing and ever-threatening urban spectacle.

The greatest play, in my opinion, in this collection is burned indelibly in my imagination. *Thin Air: Tales from a Revolution* is a magnificent play that moves from dream to reality with breathtaking shifts and spillovers of image that are always wide-awake to the nightmare of revolution and the people who disappear into it. In this play, as in all her work, Alvarez creates a huge score of human emotions and story of operatic scope—and all through real characters who are simultaneously three-dimensional and universal. Although the variety of these works make generalizations difficult to come by, musical terms like opera and score are good "batons" with which to touch the plays of Lynne Alvarez. Although not through-composed musically, as opera is, the plays are through-composed with a musicality—of language and musical referencing. More even than a characteristic, music is almost a character. The use of two genres of piano music in *Hidden Parts,* the use of song throughout all the plays in this collection, even the frequent presence of musicians as characters show the intrinsic nature of music to the creation of her worlds.

But it's important to remember that however rich they are in music and language, these plays are not just accomplished aural events. Alvarez uses the unique ability of the theater to present and lay with a concrete world—of cultural, metaphorical, symbolic—even literal and, sometimes, just humorous physical images. From the lifting of roses off a dead body to reveal wounds underneath to the lowering of columns of the New York City Port Authority on top of a character, Alvarez uses the physical world of the theater in moving, startling, often humorous, and always amazing ways. In the short play, *On Sundays,* a young dancer lives one day of her life *in a transparent box* while, outside, her admirer lives out his Sundays until he's an old man. The fact that Alvarez can make all this happen in front of an audience shows how she, as playwright, has the imagination and artistry to create a metaphor that is not only concrete and beautiful, but *three-dimensional.*

The main characteristic all these plays share is their diversity—of setting, of character(s), of tone, of point of view, of theatrical language. It seems we live in an age where the society is supposed to be diverse, but its artists, particularly its writers, are supposed to pick a culture, gender, sexuality, ethnicity and stick to it. This rigid identity, meant to express some genuine specificity, instead can become a form of packaging, a box and even a prison for the writer's vision. Alvarez has characters in her plays called San Bot Lhu, Humbert, Juan, Anya, Calorías, Wilson, Jimmy, Jaime. Born in Portland, Oregon, of Argentinian parents, Alvarez grew up in Michigan. Later, she lived, married and had a child in Mexico, and this seminal experience is central in her work. She speaks English with a Michigan accent and Spanish with a Mexican accent. To me, she is an *earthling,* and the identity she most identifies with is the one we share—as writers. I'm honored to be related to her by this, most ancient, blood:

> *"Bearing witness, you know.*
> *Persisting for years beyond all odds."*

Alex, in *Thin Air: Tales from a Revolution.*

Constance Congdon
Amherst, Massachusetts
May 1998

THE GUITARRÓN

ORIGINAL PRODUCTION

Guitarrón was originally produced at the Theatre at St. Clement's, New York, in June 1983. Artistic director was Anita Khanzadian, producing director was Stephen Berwind with the following cast:

CALORÍAS . . . . Manuel Yesckas
JULIO . . . . Joseph Montalbo
MAESTRO . . . . Erick Avari
GUICHO . . . . Lionel Piña
MASTER BUILDER . . . . Paul Butler
MICAELA . . . . Elizabeth Peña

CHARACTERS

CALORÍAS, a firty-five-year-old fisherman, powerful
JULIO, Calorías' friend and lover, high-strung
MAESTRO, an eminent cellist
GUICHO, seventeen-year-old fisherman and boat builder's apprentice
ANTONIO, twenty-eight-year-old street beggar, crippled, brash
MASTER BUILDER, sixty-year-old alcoholic Cuban boatbuilder
MICAELA, seventeen-year-old prostitute

PLACE

Along the beach, Veracruz, Mexico

TIME

1970s

ACT I
SCENE ONE

It is just before dawn on the beach of Veracruz in a makeshift fishing camp. The moon is out. We hear the waves.

Julio is squatting stage right looking offstage expectantly. We can barely make him out.

Suddenly the Maestro, an elderly cellist, is spotlighted on an elevated wooden square. He is in full concert attire. There is a music stand and a chair. Thunderous applause. He bows and smiles. He sits carefully in profile at first and tunes and adjusts his cello. There is a slight pause. He turns full face and begins to play.

After a few moments of vigorous playing, the lights come up on Julio. The sound of the sea becomes increasingly loud and Calorías emerges dripping wet. He has just stepped out of the ocean. He is laughing and slapping himself, shaking off the water.

JULIO: Well? Well, mano?

CALORÍAS: There's thousands of them. Thousands!

JULIO: Ahhhuuuuua!

CALORÍAS: *(Shaking water on Julio.)* The sea's black with fish!

JULIO: Watch it!

CALORÍAS: Coward!

JULIO: Bastard!

CALORÍAS: Coward!

JULIO: It's cold.

CALORÍAS: *(Licks the salt from his skin.)* I love the salt from the sea.

JULIO: And the sea—what did she say?

CALORÍAS: She said albacore, tuna, bonito, bunker, snapper…sharks and dolphins swimmin' side by side…

JULIO: We'll be rich.

CALORÍAS: You'll keep quiet.

JULIO: We'll be first. But if they see us leave?

CALORÍAS: I'll leave at night. I'll fill the trawlers with ice in Alvarado.

JULIO: And where will you find the fish?

CALORÍAS: At Villahermosa. They'll be at Villahermosa in three days.

JULIO: The sea tells you the time too, eh mano?

CALORÍAS: Idiot. The sea tells me everything.

JULIO: You were born in the sea.

CALORÍAS: I was born in the sea.
> *(The Maestro's music is heard sharply. Calorías looks around.)*

CALORÍAS: What's that?! *(He shivers.)*

JULIO: Are you all right?

CALORÍAS: Yes!

JULIO: Are you cold?

CALORÍAS: I'm not cold you fool.

JULIO: Sí.

CALORÍAS: The sea keeps me warm. She loves me.
> *(Julio lights a cigarette and hands it to Calorías, who smokes.)*

JULIO: And me?

CALORÍAS: Don't be jealous of the sea.

JULIO: You're shaking.

CALORÍAS: Come here. *(He throws the cigarette into the sea.)*

JULIO: Don't throw out the butts.

CALORÍAS: Cigarettes are for women. We'll buy black cigars as big as this. *(He holds himself and laughs.)*
> *(Julio echoes his laugh, nervously. Calorías suddenly shivers.)*

CALORÍAS: It's cold. Come here.

JULIO: I'm here.

CALORÍAS: Good. *(He reaches out for him.)* Kiss me.
> *(They kiss. The light on them fades. The Maestro turns his back.)*

SCENE TWO

It is dawn the following morning. We hear gulls and the lighter sound of the morning tide.

A pair of feet stick out from underneath a large nearly finished shrimp boat on wooden barrels. There are tools scattered near it.

Guicho stumbles onstage, barely awake. He is wearing only a pair of dark trousers held up by a cord and rolled to the knee. He is dragging a net. He drapes it over a series of posts and examines it for holes. He takes out a needle and some thread and mends the holes.

Antonio enters in his cart, which is decorated with hubcaps and bottle caps. It is equipped with a horn and a handbrake. His hat is pushed back on his head. He checks under the boat, then wheels over to Guicho.

ANTONIO: Pssst.

(Guicho doesn't hear.)

ANTONIO: Psssst. *(Honks his horn.)*

GUICHO: Jesus Christ, Antonio! *(Indicates the boat.)* Shut up.

MASTER BUILDER: *(From under the boat.)* Goddammit it, motherfuckers, shut the fuck up!

ANTONIO: Whew!

GUICHO: I knew it. So you're grinnin' like an alligator. What's up?

ANTONIO: I did it mano… *(Waits dramatically.)*

GUICHO: Sure. Great. All right. What did you do?

ANTONIO: Why Guicho. I did just what I promised. Sí señor. I've done the impossible!

GUICHO: Micaela!!

MASTER BUILDER: Will you two shut up!

GUICHO: Just ignore him.

(From under the boat a hand appears patting the ground. It finds a bottle and pulls it under.)

GUICHO: But what'd she say!

ANTONIO: She says she'll see you. Right now!

GUICHO: Right now?!

ANTONIO: You got it mano.

GUICHO: Right now…right now. Jesus. How can I thank you. Right now?! You are terrific…superb—

ANTONIO: Excellent. I am excellent, right? *(Beaming.)* Sí señor. Micaela took pity on this poor ruined street beggar.

GUICHO: Wait a minute. What do you mean she took pity on you?

ANTONIO: Well…I shouldn't tell you.

GUICHO: Wait a minute now—

ANTONIO: Well ya see…I was in the portales, making my rounds as usual, right?

GUICHO: Yeah, yeah. Go ahead.

ANTONIO: And Micaela was sittin' at that first table at the Diligencias where she always sits…so anyways, I made a sign to her that I wanted to talk…I kinda winked—

GUICHO: Coño, Antonio. Hurry up!

ANTONIO: So we went around the block and I tell her you want to fuck her, right?

GUICHO: Did you have to put it that way?!

ANTONIO: And she said no…but—

GUICHO: No?!

ANTONIO: Let me finish my story, coño! So she says no and then I give her my sorrowful look...ya know...like this... *(He gives a very convincing sorrowful look.)* And then...
(Long pause.)

GUICHO: I don't want to hear this.

ANTONIO: So we did it mano. She thought I was a virgin, so she only took half my bag...fifty pesos, mano... *(Holds up his money bag.)* I spent fifty pesos, a whole evening's work...all for you mano!

GUICHO: What do you mean all for me! How could you of done somethin' like that!

ANTONIO: Oye. She's gonna do it to you for nothin'! Free. You're a saint, mano...a saint makin' miracles.

GUICHO: What are you talkin' about. You knew how I felt about her. I mean, I thought it would be somethin' different. Special maybe...but shit. I'm not standin' in line for love...What kind of friend are you anyways! *(He walks away angrily.)*

ANTONIO: I'll tell you what kind of friend I am, little brother! You listen to me, 'cause I keep you from gettin' hurt! Do you hear?! I mean the world's like that. If Micaela's a pro, she's a pro. There's ways to enjoy that too. Do you hear me, little brother?

GUICHO: Yeah.

(The Maestro has appeared suddenly on a dune. He is playing in a short-sleeved shirt and wearing a straw hat. It is about eight o'clock in the morning. He plays, stops, tunes and then plays again.)

ANTONIO: Don't feel down 'cause it ain't the romance of the century, right? So go on. Get ready...change your shirt or somethin'... *(He catches a glimpse of the Maestro.)* Will you get a load of that.

GUICHO: What?

ANTONIO: That old músico up there.

GUICHO: We got music while we work.

ANTONIO: *(Inspecting closer.)* Hey no kidding. That old man's famous. His picture's plastered all over the zócalo, sí señor. That guitarrón must be worth a bundle. Yes indeedee. *(Fishes around in his pockets.)* Speaking of which, manito. *(He pulls out some bills.)* No woman'll look at you twice if you don't got money in your pockets.

GUICHO: Heyyy.

ANTONIO: Take it!

GUICHO: But I'll pay you back! I'm good for it.

ANTONIO: Yes sir, when the fish come in, right?

GUICHO: I mean it.

ANTONIO: Forget it.

GUICHO: You're a good friend, mano.

ANTONIO: Get outta here!

(*Guicho leaves. Antonio wheels closer until he is looking straight up at the Maestro. The Maestro nods and smiles. Antonio nods and smiles.*)

ANTONIO: (*Waving and smiling, but talking to himself.*) You got a real nice guitarrón there, señor. Real nice.

(*Antonio leaves. The Maestro plays. Lights dim.*)

SCENE THREE

The Maestro is seen playing in his shirtsleeves on a dune, but he is almost offstage or behind a scrim. His music cannot be heard.

Micaela is sitting on the beach as if taking some sun. Her skirt is rolled up to her thighs and she is barefoot. Her shoes, pink high heels, are placed carefully next to her.

Guicho enters. When he catches sight of her he tries to appear nonchalant.

MICAELA: Hey Guicho…Hi. How're ya doin'?

GUICHO: Oh hi, Micaela.

MICAELA: Lookin' for me?

GUICHO: Yeah sure…why not. (*Looks around.*) Waitin' for…uh…someone special?

MICAELA: Of course.

GUICHO: Okay then…well… (*He starts to leave.*)

MICAELA: I don't believe this. I'm waitin' for you. Didn't you talk to Antonio?

GUICHO: Yeah, I talked to him.

MICAELA: So? Well come on over.

GUICHO: Sure. (*He looks around nervously and sits down. He makes a grab for her and tries to kiss her.*)

MICAELA: (*Slapping him hard.*) What's the matter with you. Animal! (*She stands up almost in tears.*) You creep! I thought you were different from the rest!

GUICHO: Yeah. Well I sure as hell didn't think you were such a whore… Makin' it with a cripple for Christ's sake!

MICAELA: Is that what Antonio told you?

GUICHO: Yeah. What'd you think? He'd keep it a secret? He's my friend you know.

MICAELA: Well your friend made it up. *(Pause.)* Really. *(Pause.)* All I did was give him a kiss…on the cheek…I was real glad you wanted to see me.

GUICHO: Yeah?

MICAELA: Yeah. I always thought you were cute.

GUICHO: I messed everything up, right?

MICAELA: So you were jealous?

GUICHO: Not jealous.

MICAELA: *(Touching his arm seductively.)* You were jealous and you haven't even laid a finger on me…You are going to be some lover…ummmhmmm…

GUICHO: Look. Never mind.

MICAELA: What's the matter Guicho. Come on tell me. Am I so bad?

GUICHO: I just don't understand. One minute you're cold 'n then you're all over me. Forget it.

MICAELA: You're scared.

GUICHO: Look. You're not dealing with…with a novice, you know. Chelito and I…

MICAELA: You don't got to be embarrassed with me, nene. Antonio told me everything.

GUICHO: I'll kill him.

MICAELA: Hey Guicho. It's simple. You're cute. You need a good woman to start you out. You get the wrong one manito and it'll put you off fucking for life. Believe me…I've seen a few and no matter what I've done…

GUICHO: Just don't talk about it.

MICAELA: *(Giggling.)* Oh yeah. You get jealous.

GUICHO: I ain't jealous. I just don't want you to be a—

MICAELA: A whore, right?

GUICHO: Not with me.

MICAELA: Oh I can see it now. Pretty soon, you'll say not with anyone else neither. You're really something.

GUICHO: Jesus. This definitely ain't going the way I thought. We'll do it another time. Okay?

MICAELA: Not so fast Guichito. You were my present too, you know. My special celebration. I had you all saved up. Somethin' sweet to remember when I go into La Falana's next week.

GUICHO: I've heard of her.

MICAELA: We don't got much time. Only a week.

GUICHO: I'll go see you there.

MICAELA: With all your money, right?

GUICHO: Right.

MICAELA: She's real expensive, Guicho. *(She looks into his eyes.)* You'd pay to see me?

GUICHO: Yeah.

MICAELA: You don't have to pay now. *(They kiss.)*

GUICHO: Don't go in. Stay like you are.

MICAELA: It's a big house. And she don't take just anyone, you know. She's got to send for you. Oh and you should see her, Guicho. She's got nails this long. And she's fat. But she smells like flowers. Doesn't use perfume either. They say her smell drives men crazy. They come and ask her to sleep on handkerchiefs and sheets for them.

GUICHO: Can you have a boyfriend?

MICAELA: You should see the dance floor. It's got beautiful tiles and there's jasmine and framboyán and little tiny lights laced through 'em enough to make you dizzy just standing there...

GUICHO: Come meet me outside. *(He kisses her again.)*

MICAELA: And don't think for a minute I don't got a real future. 'Cause I do. I got it all planned out. I'm going to be a singer. La Falana likes my voice, she says I can sing sometimes.

GUICHO: I guess that's great Micaela.

MICAELA: Anyways, I'll leave there whenever I want to. You believe me don't you?

GUICHO: I believe you. *(He takes her hand.)* Micaela can we go for a walk? I had it in my mind, we'd walk around or somethin'

MICAELA: Sure. *(She stops.)* Hey Guicho?

GUICHO: What?

(Micaela hugs him tightly. Lights dim.)

SCENE FOUR

An afternoon. Master Builder and Guicho are sanding the hull of the boat. Maestro is playing, but only a few notes can be heard now and then. The sea is loud.

Guicho puts down his tools and starts toward the Maestro.

MASTER BUILDER: *(Sharply.)* Where are you going, chico?

GUICHO: Can't hear the music.

MASTER BUILDER: What, you think this is a dance floor? Get back here and work.

GUICHO: It's weird ain't it. Sometimes I catch a note and it sounds like a human voice.

MASTER BUILDER: Don't give me your back when I'm talking to you.

GUICHO: You said there's no hurry. I want to see where he's from, an old man like that.

MASTER BUILDER: He's from his mother's gut like the rest of us, chico. Now do me a favor and give the molding some blows around the rudder, eh? *(Guicho hesitates.)*

MASTER BUILDER: You can't hear this human voice neither?

(Guicho snatches the mallet sullenly and goes under the boat.)

MASTER BUILDER: Nothing weird about that. Just a guitarrón, the back's a little flat, uglier than most. Hey chico, go tell that músico I can make him a mother guitarrón with inlay and mother-of-pearl. You should go tell him that.

(Master Builder looks through his bottles as he talks, holds them up, sniffs them. Finally he douses his face and head with the contents of one. Guicho is striking the boat.)

MASTER BUILDER: Okay, okay chico, don't put a hole in her bottom!

(Guicho comes out scowling and hands him the mallet.)

MASTER BUILDER: Don't be looking at me like a chicken at a snake, boy. This is water, see! *(Pours some on him.)*

GUICHO: You know how I feel about this.

MASTER BUILDER: No, no, no, no. Come here. Take a good look at her. She's a beauty…a beautiful seafarin' boat livelier than the fish theirselves. Damn! Once she hits the water, she'll be tight as a virgin… *(Ruefully.)* A virgin. Shit. I don't even remember. *(He laughs.)*

GUICHO: Calorías been by today?

MASTER BUILDER: This boat'll never be for Calorías!

GUICHO: Keep it down, old man. He paid for the wood and the parts.

MASTER BUILDER: I can tell you where he can go with the wood and the parts! Wood and parts. Shit. I put life into them. Just look at her, the Seahawk. She'll swoop down on them fish like a wild thing. No way this'll be for Calorías, he's no fisherman. None of you Mexicans can fish…This here masterpiece will be… *(Thinks for a moment.)* for the Japanese, chico. Those motherfuckers know how to fish. They'll go clear to India for a catch. Not like you people, last as long as the weed does. Dope fiends!

GUICHO: So let's go. Let's leave, Chinche. Take the damn boat and sail away. I hate it here.

MASTER BUILDER: What's gotten into you?

GUICHO: I'm seventeen. I got my whole life jumping inside of me and I ain't spendin' it here stinking of fish gut!

MASTER BUILDER: Well sure boy...sure, we'll leave... *(He looks around for a bottle with rum in it. He tries one and spits it out.)* Acchhh. Water! *(He finds some rum, drinks and sighs.)* You think I'm going to spend the rest of my life here. I'm with you, boy. Just you wait...we'll head off to Mother Cuba, yes we will and we'll find you a dark fragrant lady with sturdy legs. Wrap them around you till you forget your own name... ummhmmmm. And we'll take the bus to the Esquina del Pecado where the wind gusts in from the ocean...and we'll make this woman walk along in front of us. *(Laughs.)* And you'll see how this famous wind makes the simplest man into a poet.

GUICHO: You're crazy, Chinche.

MASTER BUILDER: No. No. I tell you, the finest poets in all Havana line up along the malecón and say sweet things to women as the wind blows and...lifts their skirts! *(Takes off his hat, as if he were bowing to a passing woman.)* Blessed be the earth where they planted the seed...

GUICHO: *(Joins in.)* ...the seed from which the tree was born that was used to make the cradle of this beautiful Cuban rose...olé!

(They laugh and end with a flourish. The Master Builder takes a drink.)

MASTER BUILDER: You should have known me in better times. I was a man.

GUICHO: Don't drink.

MASTER BUILDER: No business of yours. A man's the master of his own body.

GUICHO: *(Watches him.)* You're right.

MASTER BUILDER: What?

GUICHO: A man's the master of his own body.

MASTER BUILDER: Right.

GUICHO: I'm leaving.

MASTER BUILDER: What are you talking about?

GUICHO: I'm leaving...I'll climb that dune if I want to. *(Indicating the Maestro.)* And keep going.

MASTER BUILDER: You got another job?

(Guicho shakes his head.)

MASTER BUILDER: A woman? That's it, some woman put her spell on you... right, chico? Opened her legs and your brains fell out. I knew something made you lose your quiet. It'll pass.

GUICHO: I want to take her somewhere you know. Somewhere new, fresh, clean. You came from Cuba. Crossed the whole fuckin' ocean and never looked back!

MASTER BUILDER: But I was twenty-three. I was a master builder with eight boats to my name. I wasn't a punk kid chasing skirts. I sailed out of Havana with two shrimp boats and a fine blue boat to fish red snapper… I built them with these very hands…with not a single nail…every part cut and fitted from the finest woods…I was a master builder and only twenty-three…But this rotten port…achhh…everything rots here… We'll go back to Cuba, sí señor. We'll finish this Seahawk and sail back to Cuba…I'll take you down to the Esquina del Pecado and the Monument to Madrid…

(Calorías enters.)

GUICHO: You'll never leave.

CALORÍAS: Who's leaving? *(Looks the boat over.)* You're not done yet. But almost, eh? Another week should do it. What do you say, old man?

MASTER BUILDER: Maybe a week. Maybe more. Depends on the weather.

CALORÍAS: Maybe it depends on the bottle too? I want this in the water in two weeks.

MASTER BUILDER: *(Drinks.)* Creditors chasing you, eh chico?

CALORÍAS: *(Snatches the bottle from his hands.)* I want to take a pleasure cruise up the Papaloapán—so don't drink yourself to death before you finish!

GUICHO: Give it back to him Calorías. He ain't a child.

CALORÍAS: And you neither.

GUICHO: I work like a man, I am a man. Give it back to him.

CALORÍAS: *(Pats the three knives at his belt.)* When I was sixteen, I was a man too. Had two of these three knives. Took each one from a dead man. Yes I did. *(Hands Guicho the bottle.)* So man to man—I leave him in your hands. Take care of him and we can all take a joyride and I'll buy barbacoa and mangoes and we'll dive for sweetwater clams. I like you Guichito. You're a good kid. *(To Master Builder.)* And you, make me my Seahawk with wings spread out like so—and I'll rule the fuckin' ocean and you'll have money jingling in your pockets.

MASTER BUILDER: No fish. No money. No boat.

CALORÍAS: I heard them sliding through the sea.

MASTER BUILDER: Well I know the sea whispers her secrets to you before she tells the rest of us…but I'm a practical man and the fact is…I ain't seen full payment on this boat and until I do, it's mine.

CALORÍAS: It is?

MASTER BUILDER: You gave me a pile of sticks. I made the boat.

(Calorías calmly walks over to the boat. For a moment it seems he is caressing the hull, but he is looking for the edge of a plank. He finds one and suddenly pulls on it mightily until it comes off.)

CALORÍAS: You're right. The boat is made of wood. The wood is mine. *(He takes off another plank.)*

MASTER BUILDER: No!

GUICHO: *(Grabs Calorías's arm to stop him.)* Bastard!

CALORÍAS: *(Shucks Guicho off easily.)* I'll take it down to killing, boy. Don't start what you can't finish. *(To Master Builder.)* And if you want to see any money—have this ready soon. *(He leaves.)*

MASTER BUILDER: How could I let someone speak to me like that? How? *(He picks up one board and tries to hold it to the hull, put it back. It slips. He tries again.)* How have I come to this? Me? I thought this port would make me a millionaire. Three times a year I watched it fill black with fish. The air filled with birds…and I bought two new motors for my magnificent boats. I could go farther out to sea than anyone in Veracruz and I was only twenty-three! But now it's his turn. God toyed with me. I was his joke. The first school of fish never came and me waiting like an idiot…and so I lost one motor because I couldn't pay and then when I had no money to buy more marijuana for my crew—those perverts sank my other motor one night off the Bay of Tampico…But I was a big man then and strong…and I jumped into the bay with one man under each arm. And I held them under until they *died!* They died.

(The boards keep slipping as he tries to fit them back into place. Guicho comes to help him.)

GUICHO: Not now, Chinche. Later.

MASTER BUILDER: You! Go on. Leave. Go where you like. You treat me like he does. I don't exist. You don't hear me. You look through me.

GUICHO: No Chinche. Hey.

MASTER BUILDER: Maybe I ain't here no more. What do I know. Those men took part of me down with them…in this bottle…and this…and hundreds more. They're trying to drown me too!

GUICHO: *(Kneels near him.)* And are you drowning, old man?

MASTER BUILDER: Shit, chico. I have my boat. It's become my lifeboat.

(Lights fade.)

SCENE FIVE

That night. Calorías is asleep. He cries out, thrashing.
The Maestro is playing, spotlighted on a wooden square. He is in his
tuxedo. He nods and smiles at Calorías as he plays. This time, he is so close
they could almost touch him.
The Maestro stops playing and comes over with detached curiosity. He
nudges Calorías with his bow several times.
Calorías moans louder.
Julio sits up and lights a cigarette. The lights around them brighten. Julio
moves to Calorías and kneels by him, stroking his head as if he were a child.

JULIO: Calorías. *(Calorías moves restlessly.)* Wake up mano. Calorías.
(Calorías sits up suddenly. The Maestro returns to his seat, satisfied.)
CALORÍAS: Julio mano, is that you?
JULIO: Sí. Calm down…quiet.
CALORÍAS: Jesus Christ. Are we home?
JULIO: You're all right mano.
(The music rises menacingly. Calorías jumps to his feet and pulls a knife. He
stands right below the Maestro.)
CALORÍAS: Where is that motherfucker?
JULIO: It was a dream.
CALORÍAS: Shut up! *(He listens.)*
JULIO: What is it?
(Calorías looks all around him. It's as if he looks through the Maestro.)
CALORÍAS: Shut up! Listen.
JULIO: I don't hear nothin'.
CALORÍAS: You idiot. Listen.
JULIO: It's the sea.
CALORÍAS: No! I'll find the motherfucker!
JULIO: Come on back, it's another dream. *(Looks around.)* There's no one here.
CALORÍAS: I can hear it.
JULIO: *(Listening.)* Only the sea. Tell me the dream.
CALORÍAS: What's that?
JULIO: The sea.
CALORÍAS: *(Squatting.)* Ahhhhhh.
JULIO: Your dream's stuck in your head. Get it out.
CALORÍAS: It was nothin'.
JULIO: Dreams mean somethin'…now tell me your dream, mano. You tell me

'cause it'll hit the air and eeeeva-po-rate... *(Whispers.)* You keep it in and you go crazy.

CALORÍAS: Is that so? *(Laughs.)* It's the waitin's got me crazy.

JULIO: The dream.

CALORÍAS: Massage my shoulders...There...ahhhhh...It was only a stupid old man.

JULIO: *(Massaging.)* Yeah?

CALORÍAS: He had a stick that he moved. It made music.

JULIO: That's nothin'.

CALORÍAS: But every time he moved this stick, it went into my heart and come out with blood on it...Blood poured out *all over!*

JULIO: *(Chanting.)* Aserrín, aserrán
Los maderos de San Juan...

CALORÍAS: It's a bad dream. Something's wrong.

JULIO: Blood from the heart means a loss. It's bad luck. You'll lose something close to your heart.

CALORÍAS: Is it death?

JULIO: No but maybe you should stay.

CALORÍAS: Then I'd lose for sure. I'm leaving today...with that Japanese captain...Kirasawa...Kirasuga...on the other trawler...I can trust him...

JULIO: *(Chanting.)* Piden pán
No les dán
Piden queso
Les dan un hueso...

CALORÍAS: You wait for me in two days with ice...five tons...anchored offshore...don't tip off the bastards at the market...we'll sell straight from the boat. Ahhh...I feel better.
(The Maestro has stopped playing. He is rosining his bow and listening to the conversation.)

JULIO: But something's wrong.

CALORÍAS: The sea don't lie.

JULIO: No.

CALORÍAS: I feel empty. *(Presses his hand to his heart.)*

JULIO: *(Massaging his shoulders.)* Piden queso
Les dan un hueso
Para que se rasquen
El pescuezo.
(Lights out.)

SCENE SIX

The next morning. Fresh, early. The Master Builder is working hard repairing the boat. He and Antonio are talking.

Guicho walks out whistling, happy. He is carrying a bucket, a minnow net, and a hand net he can throw from shore.

ANTONIO: Hey there Guichito, going to the river?

GUICHO: Ain't no fish in the sea.

ANTONIO: *(Outlining a woman's body with his hands.)* I hear the fishin' on land's been pretty good lately, right? *(He starts up after Guicho.)* Hey wait up mano...wait up.

(Guicho waits for him.)

ANTONIO: Bet you're going to get oysters and clams. Am I right?...eh? Help you keep up with Micaela, right?

GUICHO: *(Playfully tilting Antonio's cart.)* I don't need no fish to keep up with her...

ANTONIO: Ooooooo manito's in love.

GUICHO: *(Tilting the cart more.)* You think so, eh?

ANTONIO: *(Real fear.)* Quit it. Quit it! Don't do that. I hate that.

GUICHO: I'm sorry.

(The Maestro appears suddenly on the dune. He is playing in his shirt-sleeves. The music is very distant.)

ANTONIO: It's okay.

GUICHO: *(After an awkward silence.)* Friends, right?

ANTONIO: Right. *(Pause.)* Listen.

GUICHO: What?

ANTONIO: I need your help.

GUICHO: Sure, Antonio.

ANTONIO: You see that Maestro up there? The papers said his guitarrón's worth more than ten thousand dollars. And he's got maybe three or four of them someplace.

GUICHO: Yeah? So.

ANTONIO: Well, little brother. Obviously God planted him here on this beach for a purpose.

GUICHO: No schemes, Antonio. Absolutely not.

ANTONIO: All I need is a couple thousand pesos, that's it and I'll be set up.

GUICHO: Forget it.

ANTONIO: You'll get half.

GUICHO: No.

ANTONIO: Three-quarters. Hey manito. He wouldn't miss one. He got lots of them. We won't hurt him, an old man like that. You could just grab it away from him, push him over or something. Look. I know a politician's daughter who'd pay a lot for a guitarrón like that. One of his, you know. They don't grow on trees. Manito honest, he has at least eight or ten. He's world famous, little brother. He'll never miss it. I promise. I swear to God.

GUICHO: Fishin' don't hurt nobody.

ANTONIO: Yeah. But it don't help nobody either, right? Sweating in the sun just to get up and do the same thing day after day.

(Guicho starts to walk away.)

ANTONIO: Hey wait. Just do a little research. Talk to him, mano. Look at that thing he's playing and tell me if it's in good shape. Look if you think he'd get hurt, I'd just forget about it. Guichito, put my mind at rest, talk to him. It won't hurt to talk to him. He looks like a nice man.

GUICHO: I'll talk to him. That's it though.

ANTONIO: Sí señor. Whatever you say. *(Salutes.)*

(Guicho climbs the dune and approaches the Maestro, who stops playing.)

GUICHO: Good morning.

MAESTRO: Good morning. *(He fishes in his pockets and pulls out some coins, holds them out.)* Here you go.

(Guicho looks to see what they are, puzzled.)

GUICHO: I don't want your money.

MAESTRO: Is it too little?

(Guicho reaches out shyly to touch the cello.)

MAESTRO: So you came to steal my cello, eh?

GUICHO: What? *(Retracts his hand quickly.)*

MAESTRO: Well you certainly want something. You and your friend there. Unsightly bunch.

GUICHO: Ah, you saw us.

MAESTRO: Oh I see everything from here. The island there…

GUICHO: La Isla de Sacrificios.

MAESTRO: Yes, yes, and you people down there. I picked you out right away. Oh don't feel special now, you look just like the rest to me, you know. Perhaps I knew you'd be the one to come up. They always do.

GUICHO: Who?

MAESTRO: The natives. Great curiosity. But not for the music. Could you hear it?

GUICHO: No. A little sometimes. The wind brings it…like a voice.

MAESTRO: A voice, you say.

GUICHO: I seen a lot of músicos...the marimba in the plaza...the Indians come and fiddle during Carnaval by the docks...and play tin horns... but this guitarrón...

MAESTRO: It's a cello. A cello. This cello...

GUICHO: This cello, cello...has a human voice.

MAESTRO: Would you like to hear it talk? *(He plays a popular tune.)*

GUICHO: Hey, I know that one.

MAESTRO: That's why I played it.

GUICHO: That was real nice and all...but there's something else I'd like to hear.

MAESTRO: Oh there is, is there?

GUICHO: Could you make it say a person's name? Like really talk.

MAESTRO: What name?

GUICHO: Micaela. Mii-caaa-ee-laaa.

MAESTRO: A musical name. Let me see. *(He tries one way and does it.)*

GUICHO: Shit.

MAESTRO: I'll show you how to do it.

GUICHO: Me?

MAESTRO: Why not?

GUICHO: Sure.

MAESTRO: Your friend will think you've got me now.

(He gets up and gives the cello to Guicho, who sits with it.)

GUICHO: Antonio don't mean nothing by it. He's always looking for a break, but he don't hurt nobody. He's got a good heart. *(He tries to hold the cello.)* He says you're famous.

MAESTRO: *(Adjusting Guicho's posture.)* Yes. Now grasp it between your knees so it doesn't move...

GUICHO: Why're you here then?

MAESTRO: Practicing. Now this is the bow...Hold it...like so...

GUICHO: I mean here, on this beach.

MAESTRO: Oh, I have friends... *(Waves vaguely indicating the shore.)* Now the trick is to be gentle, but firm...there is a trick you know. These are the notes...

(The Maestro moves Guicho's hand over the open strings, guiding the bow. They play three notes.)

MAESTRO: Now let's add a little rhythm. Say the name again.

GUICHO: *(Concentrating on moving the bow with the name.)* Mi-ca-e-la.

(The Maestro guides his hand.)

MAESTRO: There.

GUICHO: It's not the same as when you did it.

MAESTRO: Ahhhh, but this is a way you can do it. *(He moves Guicho's arm again.)* Do you see. These three strings and back to the first. Try it alone. *(Guicho tries but the bow wobbles hopelessly. The Maestro grabs his arm.)*

MAESTRO: No. No. You'll strip the bow. Relax. Shoulders down. Smoothly. *(They do it again.)*

MAESTRO: Fill it with something beautiful. That's the trick. *(The Maestro frees Guicho's arm. Guicho tries it alone. He does it fairly well.)*

GUICHO: Shit. I did it! *(He hands back the cello gingerly.)*

MAESTRO: Now you know what you're stealing. It's not just a piece of wood.

GUICHO: I am good with my hands.

MAESTRO: Yes. You are. *(Sits and adjusts the cello.)* Mi-ca-e-la.

GUICHO: I could bring her by…Maybe I could show her what I did?

MAESTRO: I don't think so, young man.

GUICHO: Antonio'll be pissed. But don't worry.
(Guicho waits for a second. The Maestro is absorbed in his playing. Guicho starts off. Lights fade.)

SCENE SEVEN

Later that day. Guicho is lying on the beach. Micaela enters carrying her high heels and a large radio.

GUICHO: It's about time.

MICAELA: How do you like the radio?

GUICHO: Come here.

MICAELA: I thought we could dance. I like to dance. Don't you?
(Guicho gets up and kisses her. They remain locked like that for a moment.)

GUICHO: Your hair smells like cigars.

MICAELA: Isn't it awful. Mmmmm you smell like the sea.

GUICHO: You've been drinking. I could taste it.

MICAELA: I stopped to get this radio. *(She finds a station she likes.)*

GUICHO: You had a drink.

MICAELA: Yeah.

GUICHO: Where?

MICAELA: Villa del Mar.

GUICHO: Shit!

MICAELA: Let's dance. Can you dance?

(She takes his arm, but he won't move.)

MICAELA: Oh come on. Don't spoil this.

GUICHO: I just got to know.

MICAELA: I met a friend. He had a radio. I asked if I could borrow it. He said never mind, keep it.

GUICHO: Quite a friend.

MICAELA: Yeah? Well, he's an old friend. Okay now. Let's dance.

(She turns up the radio. They dance together. He puts both arms around her. They kiss.)

MICAELA: Hey the kid can dance!

GUICHO: What'd you think.

MICAELA: You are toucheeee.

GUICHO: You think I'm a dumb kid who doesn't know what the fuck's going on, ain't that right?

MICAELA: Hey Guicho. Don't get your macho all riled up.

GUICHO: I know how you got that radio.

MICAELA: I thought we'd have fun. You know, dancing on the beach. I know you don't got any money.

GUICHO: Jesus!

MICAELA: I can't do anything right, can I?

GUICHO: You do everything right. That's the trouble. I get sick when I think of you with other men.

MICAELA: I warned you this would happen, didn't I?

GUICHO: I can't help it.

MICAELA: You're not like other men, mi amor. Believe me. You're special. My celebration. Anyways I told you this week was just for you. No one else.

GUICHO: Okay. All right. *(He fiddles with the radio.)*

MICAELA: What're you doin ?

GUICHO: Finding something romantic…There.

(He sits. She sits next to him.)

MICAELA: You want to go swimmin'?

GUICHO: No.

MICAELA: It's really a pisser…oh sorry. I mean it really gets me. I'm always near the ocean, but I never go in. Men always bother girls alone. I can't stand it.

GUICHO: I'll watch you if you like.

MICAELA: That's okay.

(They sit for a moment.)

GUICHO: So…how old are you?

MICAELA: You've been wanting to ask, right?

GUICHO: Yeah.

MICAELA: Why?

GUICHO: Well, I want to know something about you. I've seen you around but—

MICAELA: I'm seventeen.

GUICHO: Oh. I thought you were older.

MICAELA: I look that bad, eh?

GUICHO: No. You're beautiful. You just look…older.

MICAELA: More mature?

GUICHO: Right. *(Pause.)* You know you could get married at seventeen. Even younger…Does your father or brother think you should get married already?

MICAELA: *(Laughs loudly and then stops.)* I shouldn't laugh should I?

GUICHO: I just want to find out about you.

MICAELA: No brothers and my father put me on the streets.

GUICHO: I'm sorry.

MICAELA: It's okay.

GUICHO: I was thinking…look there's no fish now and I'm broke. I live with an old man on the beach. He found me wandering around when I was four or five. I don't really know how old I am…Maybe I'm eighteen already and don't know it…but I feel…I feel it's time I left. I feel like I'm on my way someplace. I don't know where exactly. Near the sea. I can fish and I'm good with my hands. When I leave I want you to come with me.

MICAELA: Seriously?

GUICHO: Yeah.

MICAELA: You don't know me. Maybe you wouldn't like me…after a while.

GUICHO: You're crazy. Kiss me. Come on.

(She gives him a quick shy kiss.)

GUICHO: That's the way you kiss a kid. Kiss me like you kiss the men.

MICAELA: I don't kiss them.

GUICHO: A real kiss then.

MICAELA: All right. You asked for it. Here. *(She kisses him hard.)* This time open your mouth.

GUICHO: *(Pulls back startled.)* You put your tongue in my mouth?

MICAELA: *(Giggling.)* What a bobo. Now put your tongue in my mouth.

(They kiss.)

MICAELA: Did you like that?

(Guicho grabs her and kisses her. They fall to the ground and sit there laughing and out of breath.)

GUICHO: I'll see you every day, right? Then we'll go away together.

MICAELA: You're really sweet, Guicho. But I'm going to be a singer.

GUICHO: I take my hands wherever I go. You take your voice. You can sing anywhere.

MICAELA: I want to be a famous singer on the radio. I want men to... *(She thinks for a minute.)* to fall dead in their tracks when they see me. I'm young now. Someone'll give me a break. I can't wander around little adobe villages. I got a future now. Pretty dresses. I won't even have to cook.

GUICHO: Just lie on your back.

MICAELA: We can get together after I make it. *(She turns the radio up.)*

GUICHO: Sure.

MICAELA: Let's dance. Hold me close.

GUICHO: Would it make a difference if I had money?

MICAELA: Yeah. Maybe. *(She dances by herself.)*

GUICHO: You're real pretty, Micaela. Beautiful.

(She gets shy and stops dancing.)

GUICHO: Some man'll give you a break. You can bet on it. I better go.

MICAELA: Hey. We got time.

GUICHO: No. Life's too short.

MICAELA: Take the radio. I brought it for you.

GUICHO: I don't want your fuckin' radio! *(He turns away from her, wanting to go but unable to move.)*

MICAELA: See, you're acting like a kid. You are a kid. I bet you're sixteen. Not seventeen. Christ. I couldn't just pick up and leave with a kid! *(She starts to stomp off with the radio on her shoulder blaring some popular instrumental the Maestro played.)*

GUICHO: Micaela.

(He takes the radio from her and turns it off. He places it on the ground. He takes her arm and pulls her stage right. Lights dim.)

SCENE EIGHT

It is a few days later, late morning. We hear the sea.

    The Maestro is playing softly, his back to the audience. As the scene progresses he turns more and more toward the audience, and the sound of the sea recedes as the music rises.

Julio is smoking nervously, cigarette after cigarette, staring out to sea. Calorías comes up the beach toward him and stops some distance away. He is unkempt and obviously exhausted. Julio feels his presence.

JULIO: Calorías, mano! What happened? You're three days late.
(Calorías stands staring at him.)
JULIO: I waited like you said offshore. But the ice melted in the sun.
(Calorías comes toward him.)
JULIO: And the fish? Mano? Were you wrong?
CALORÍAS: I wasn't wrong. Fool! Idiot. The fish were there. Give me a smoke.
(Julio hands him a cigarette and lights one of his own.)
CALORÍAS: The sea doesn't lie. We sailed to Punto Verde. Nothing. The same at Boca Andrea. Rocks and water. But at Villahermosa, yes, we sighted them, just as she said! The sea was black with 'em. Bonitos, red snappers, sharks 'n dolphins swimmin' side by side! *(He yells out.)* Maldito sea. It was just like she said. But she betrayed me! They didn't come up the coast. They turned east at Villahermosa and swam toward Cuba!
JULIO: Nooo!
CALORÍAS: She turned her back on me like I was a stranger, so I plowed the boats into the stream of them. We were three boats and we turned into the swarm of 'em, trying to turn them back, back to shore. And bone and gristle flew in our faces and we lost one motor and one boat sank, sharks diving after the men like they was tasty minnows. God, there was blood. *(Covers his face. Regains his composure.)* They hauled me to Alvarado and I walked three days to get here.
JULIO: We'll lose everything.
CALORÍAS: I walked day and night, thinking Why?
JULIO: They'll repossess everything.
CALORÍAS: No. I will not let this be.
(The Maestro is now facing the audience, playing rapturously the music Calorías heard in his dream. Calorías is silent for a moment, listening.)
CALORÍAS: *(Gripping Julio.)* That's it! Do you hear it?
JULIO: I hear what you're talkin' about. I hear a lot of things.
CALORÍAS: The music. I heard that music before! *(He pulls out his knife.)*
JULIO: *(Jumps Calorías to restrain him.)* Oh no you don't, mano. You're crazy. You can't be crazy now, you hear?! We got to do somethin' to protect ourselves, you know. We can grease the motors and sink 'em off port for a couple months. We can save them, right mano?
(Calorías struggles free and Julio grabs him again.)

JULIO: No, Calorías!

CALORÍAS: Idiot. Fool. Imbecile. He's toying with me. He's come here to laugh at me!

JULIO: I'm telling you, you're crazy.

CALORÍAS: I ain't crazy. I heard that music before. That man was in my dream!

JULIO: He's just some old músico.

CALORÍAS: He plays and she dances. But I challenge him! I challenge him!

JULIO: Fuck. You're getting me angry. Take a good look at him. Go on. Why're you botherin' with a pale skinny old músico like that? Eh?! We got things to do before the news comes in. We got to take the boat up the river to San Rafael, right?—'n sink the motor 'n keep good and clear so we can keep whatever the fuck we got!

CALORÍAS: Her sides heaved up like an animal under my boats. She cast me off! I swear. I swear to God. He played and she danced. Yes. *(Starts up the dune.)*

JULIO: *(Forces him to his knees.)* Listen to me, mano! You are not going crazy on me Not now! Not ever!

(Julio massages him Calorías lowers his head.)

JULIO: Aserrín, aserrán

Los maderos de San Juan

Piden pán

No les dán

Piden queso

Les dan un hueso

Para que se rasquen

El pescuezo

Aserrín, aserrán… *(Keeps repeating the chant.)*

CALORÍAS: You're right. Okay. Okay. I just got thoughts, that's all. Just thoughts. *(He is quiet for a moment.)* You got good hands, mano. I trust your hands.

JULIO: Aserrín, aserrán

Los maderos de San Juan…

CALORÍAS: And don't worry. I'm fine. I'll take care of everything.

(The Maestro gets up, walks right by Calorías and Julio, looking at them curiously. He exits.)

JULIO: Piden pán

No les dán

Piden queso

Les dan un hueso

(He fades out.)
Para que se rasquen
El pescuezo.
(Lights out.)

End of Act I

ACT II
SCENE ONE

Guicho is sprinting along the beach after seeing Micaela. He can hardly contain his excitement.

The Maestro is playing on top of a dune. It is midnight.

We can't hear the Maestro at first, but as Guicho approaches him the sound increases in volume. When Guicho addresses him, the Maestro stops.

GUICHO: Maestro.

MAESTRO: Oh it's you.

GUICHO: An old man like you shouldn't be out here on the beach alone.

MAESTRO: And a young man like you?

GUICHO: This ain't a tourist beach. You could get yourself into trouble.

MAESTRO: Oh there's always the police, don't you think? I imagine a scream or two would bring them running.

GUICHO: The police won't come here. It's a federal zone. Only the army can come and they don't bother with us…unless they want dope. What you doing out here anyways? It's dangerous.

MAESTRO: I agree. But it wouldn't be quite so beautiful without danger, don't you think? Soft waves, a sea breeze, salt in the air…utterly forgettable without that sharp edge of malice. Brings me alive, reminds me one never knows what will happen next! Delightful.

GUICHO: I'll walk you to the street if you like. I ain't tired at all.

MAESTRO: And I'm not tired either. We're in the same mood, no doubt. In love.

GUICHO: You got a girlfriend?

MAESTRO: Don't be so incredulous, young man. *(Holds out the cello.)* Isn't this shaped like a woman? And I make her tremble when I touch her so. *(He passes the bow over the strings.)*

GUICHO: I thought you were talking about a girl…a woman.

MAESTRO: There are loves beyond women.

GUICHO: Not for me, señor. And it's more than love. It's passion!

MAESTRO: Passion. Of course, she's beautiful, wonderful, a cornucopia of delights!

GUICHO: She can kill me with a look!

MAESTRO: Well, well, well, we have a common language. Passion is my daily bread.

GUICHO: An old man like you.

MAESTRO: I measure passion by foolhardiness, young man. And what could be more foolhardy than a rich old man sneaking out to play alone at midnight on a beach infested with…criminals! You may feel you're risking your heart for a mere glance from this girl, but I am risking my life for one moment of beautiful music on a beach at midnight! That's passion. *(Guicho laughs and sits down at the Maestro's feet.)*

GUICHO: You can keep playing if you like. It's nice out.

MAESTRO: You'll stand guard, eh?

GUICHO: Sure.

MAESTRO: Thank you. But you had better leave.

GUICHO: I like it here.

MAESTRO: It's dangerous.

(Guicho laughs.)

MAESTRO: I'm dangerous.

GUICHO: Are you kidding? I could snap you in two like a twig, old man…

MAESTRO: Of course, you see danger as clubbing someone on the head, don't you. Go away and be happy with your young woman!

GUICHO: There's no way you could be dangerous to me. No way!

MAESTRO: Then why are you up in arms, your back bristling, your heart pumping fire? *(He laughs.)* When I say something you don't understand, you feel threatened, look at you.

GUICHO: I was just wondering.

MAESTRO: You'll do more than wonder. You'll remember.

GUICHO: How do you know? You can't see into my mind. You got no idea what I'll remember. You ain't no witch.

MAESTRO: Of course I'm a witch and music is my magic. I wave my magic bow like so… *(He draws it across the strings.)* and the stars appear…
(The stars become bright. Guicho looks up startled.)

MAESTRO: Like so… *(He plays again.)* and the tides rise up…
(The noise of the sea increases. Guicho looks out to sea.)

MAESTRO: And sooo…

GUICHO: Don't joke like that!

MAESTRO: Ahhhh you're superstitious. I'm sorry. I'm just a crotchety old man on the beach and this is just a bow. Here. Take it.
(Guicho steps back.)

MAESTRO: Are you afraid?

GUICHO: *(Grasps it too quickly.)* No!

MAESTRO: Do you want to play again? Perhaps the name of your young woman…Micaela…is that correct?

GUICHO: *(Hastily returns the bow.)* No.

MAESTRO: I'll tell you what, I'll play it, then.

GUICHO: No. *(He reaches out to stop him.)*

MAESTRO: You needn't worry. Nothing will happen to her. Well then I'll play something soothing. Do you care for merengues? I especially like those huazteco songs, don't you?

GUICHO: That's okay. *(Starts to leave.)*

MAESTRO: I thought you wanted to stay.

GUICHO: I've changed my mind.

MAESTRO: You mean *I've* changed your mind.

(Guicho exits. Maestro lifts his bow to play.)

MAESTRO: And so it goes.

(The Maestro plays sonorously. Lights out.)

SCENE TWO

It is a nice hazy morning along the beach. Perhaps we see the edge of some moorings in the background.

The Maestro seems to be very far away stage left. We cannot hear him and can barely see him.

Julio and Calorías are moving a huge object, one of their new motors wrapped in canvas and tied to some poles in sledlike fashion. Julio pulls from the front and Calorías pushes from behind. It is slow difficult work.

JULIO: *(Stumbling.)* Hey, hey, hey. Watch it. You're runnin' me over. Shit! That's it. I quit. *(He sits.)* Let them have their fuckin' motor.

CALORÍAS: What are you talkin' about. It's almost paid for. I'd slit their throats before I'd let them take it back. For three payments, you fool.

JULIO: Okayyyy. Okayyy.

CALORÍAS: Now get movin'. The sun's up!

JULIO: I'm resting.

CALORÍAS: *(Paces.)* Fuckin' delicate. I want this sunk and us halfway up the river before noon!

JULIO: *(Looks toward the sun.)* They ain't even dreamin' about getting up yet. *(Antonio wheels in, out of breath.)*

ANTONIO: Hey there. Good morning. Good morning. How do you do, gentlemen?

JULIO: I need a drink.

ANTONIO: Well what do you know, señor. I search around in my magic box and...

(He feels around, pulls out a bottle. Julio pounces on it.)

ANTONIO: Burn a hole in your brain and let the sunlight in, señor.

CALORÍAS: What do you want, cripple?

ANTONIO: What makes you think I want somethin'? Perhaps I only wanted to greet you fine gentlemen.

CALORÍAS: Don't bullshit me, cripple. I ain't in the mood.

ANTONIO: Fine, right, correct. Well now. Down to business. I hear you and Julio are skipping off.

CALORÍAS: You're wrong.

ANTONIO: I see. *(He turns to go.)* Well then I'll just keep my little going-away present. *(He holds up two bags of marijuana.)*

JULIO: I'll just keep mine, little brother. *(He giggles and holds up the bottle.)*

CALORÍAS: *(Laughs and steps in front of Julio.)* If it happens that we were going on a little trip, what did you want from us?

ANTONIO: There is a trip, right?

CALORÍAS: Let me see what you got. *(He opens one bag, smells and tastes the contents.)*

ANTONIO: Well let me tell you about these two bags. They are worth four, sí señor. The finest dope, straight from Sonora with a little mixed in from Guatemala. It got two tribes of Indians high just picking it. And all for the slightest favor.

CALORÍAS: We're in a hurry, cripple.

ANTONIO: Barely a moment out of your way.

CALORÍAS: So?

ANTONIO: You see the Maestro there?

CALORÍAS: What about him?!

ANTONIO: I need his guitarrón.

JULIO: It's too big for you, mano. You need a fiddle.

CALORÍAS: The Maestro, eh?! Why do you want it?

ANTONIO: I like music.

CALORÍAS: Fuck you.

ANTONIO: I got a friend who likes music. A lady. I want to impress her, all right?

CALORÍAS: I don't believe you.

ANTONIO: Just grab it. What can he do? You could snap him in half.

JULIO: Snap him in a minute, like dry wood. Must be close to a hundred years old.

ANTONIO: You'll do it?

CALORÍAS: For you? Of course. I'd be glad to pay my respects. *(Holds out his hand.)* The dope.
ANTONIO: You forget. I'm a businessman. A paid musician plays a bad tune.
CALORÍAS: *(Holds Antonio easily while he takes the other bag.)* And you forget, mi cuate. You ain't a businessman. You're a cripple. *(Opens the second bag and tastes the dope.)*
ANTONIO: You bastard.
CALORÍAS: Don't worry, little brother. I'll take care of it for you.
JULIO: Me too.
CALORÍAS: Andale, Julio. You idiot. Let's sink the motor. Move it!
(Julio and Calorías move off. Antonio wheels in the opposite direction. The Maestro turns to face the audience, enraptured in his music. Lights fade.)

SCENE THREE

Another part of the beach later that morning. The Maestro is seated far away, stage right. We can hear only trails of music now and then, as if carried by the wind.
Guicho and Micaela enter. Guicho is carrying some varnish. Micaela is fanning herself.

GUICHO: I like the way you look with nothing on your face.
MICAELA: Thanks.
GUICHO: Without all that gook you look seventeen like you said.
MICAELA: Fifteen.
GUICHO: I thought you said seventeen.
MICAELA: Oh no. Fifteen.
GUICHO: Well whatever. You look like a kid. And you love me.
MICAELA: Uhmmmm.
GUICHO: Amazing. I can hardly believe it. Go ahead. Say it. Look straight in my eyes and tell me.
MICAELA: *(Mugging, putting her face next to his.)* I love you.
GUICHO: Amazing.
MICAELA: I told you you were my celebration.
GUICHO: Yeah, I know.
(They walk a little.)
GUICHO: Don't think I forgot about our future. I got it all figured out.
MICAELA: By yourself?

GUICHO: Come on Micaela. I don't like it when you make fun of me. You got to stop being fresh like that.

(Micaela walks away. The music comes up. She is irritated.)

MICAELA: I wish that old man would get out of here. He gets my nerves on edge.

GUICHO: Listen to me. I'll go to Villahermosa and get a job in the oil fields. They give you a brick room and a stove of your own...if you're married.

MICAELA: Great.

GUICHO: It ain't that I'm putting pressure on you. I just mentioned it.

MICAELA: It sounds nice.

GUICHO: There's thousands of people. French, gringos. You could sing there.

(Micaela takes out a mirror and puts on rouge and then lipstick.)

GUICHO: Why're you putting that stuff on?

MICAELA: Well, you got to work, right?

GUICHO: Yeah.

MICAELA: My brother's going to give me a loan.

GUICHO: I thought you didn't have any brothers.

MICAELA: A half brother. My dad got around.

GUICHO: Micaela.

MICAELA: You got to look good. Can't look like you need it too bad.

GUICHO: I'll meet you this afternoon. When the varnish is drying?

MICAELA: You got any money? If you had, it would sure save me a trip.

(Guicho can't look at her.)

MICAELA: I'll see you.

GUICHO: This afternoon.

MICAELA: I do love you.

(Guicho holds her and kisses her. She walks away, swaying on her heels. Lights dim.)

SCENE FOUR

The Maestro is drinking water from a thermos and cooling off. Antonio is trying to get the Master Builder up.

ANTONIO: Hey old man. Your luck's changing. Get up!

MASTER BUILDER: You're right chico. My luck's changing. I dreamt the sea was black and there was music, Cuban music, far away.

ANTONIO: This boat'll be yours, señor. Can you hear me? Julio and Calorías are leaving.

MASTER BUILDER: They'll be back.

ANTONIO: Finish this and you can sail awaaayyyy.

MASTER BUILDER: I'll be gone. Give me a drink.

ANTONIO: But keep it quiet. Not a word about it. Keep the lid on and the water won't boil away, right? Hey are you okay?

MASTER BUILDER: I can't see anything. Are my eyes open, chico?

ANTONIO: They're closed, old man.

MASTER BUILDER: Give me a drink. I can't see.

ANTONIO: You stupid old man. You don't want a drink. *(He looks through the bottles.)* How will you work on your boat? I'll get you some water. *(He opens a bottle and smells it.)* You got any water here?

MASTER BUILDER: A man like me shouldn't be reduced to drinking water.

ANTONIO: Here. Try this.

(Antonio tries to make the Master Builder drink but he spits out the water.)

ANTONIO: Don't be so stubborn. An old captain like you ain't afraid of a little water.

MASTER BUILDER: *(Grabbing Antonio's hand.)* I feel very bad.

ANTONIO: *(Afraid himself and looking around for someone.)* Where's Guicho? *(The Master Builder makes a weak gesture.)*

ANTONIO: Has he seen you like this? You're overworking, my friend. Do you need more water?

MASTER BUILDER: I need all the water this alcohol has sucked from me these thirty years…an ocean of water… *(His mind wandering.)* beautiful seafaring boats.

ANTONIO: What?

MASTER BUILDER: Guicho?

ANTONIO: No. It's me. Antonio. *(Giving him more water.)* Hey. That's better. You kept some water down. Sí señor.

MASTER BUILDER: My feet are swollen. I can't walk. I'm dying.

ANTONIO: No you ain't. You're just tired. Just tired. *(Tries to soothe him.)*

MASTER BUILDER: Guicho?

ANTONIO: I ain't Guicho.

(Calorías and Julio enter. The Maestro plays Calorías's theme.)

CALORÍAS: Hey there cripple. Master Builder. Hot today.

JULIO: Hey there Chinche. *(Kneels next to the Master Builder.)*

(Calorías shades his eyes and studies the Maestro, who nods at him.)

CALORÍAS: He's nodding at me. He knows.

ANTONIO: Not a hint. He's smiling.

CALORÍAS: Well. I'm a man of my word.

(Calorías strides up the dune. The Maestro watches his approach nodding and smiling.)

MASTER BUILDER: Is that Calorías? *(He reaches out for Antonio's hand.)*

JULIO: Calorías and me, Julio.

ANTONIO: Don't worry, Chinche.

MASTER BUILDER: He wants the boat!

ANTONIO: He don't want nothing with you. It's okay. Everything's fine. Don't you worry, right?

(Calorías stands by the Maestro.)

CALORÍAS: *(Softly.)* It's time for you to go now.

MAESTRO: *(Stops.)* Ahh well. *(Irritated, he looks up but has to shade his eyes.)* Step over here. I can't see you.

CALORÍAS: Why don't you tell me who you are, eh?

MAESTRO: You are a perfect stranger.

CALORÍAS: Who are you?

MAESTRO: An old man.

CALORÍAS: I saw you before.

MAESTRO: There are so many posters.

CALORÍAS: No. Not that way.

MAESTRO: *(Tiredly.)* I have been here for days and days. An eternity. It's very hot. *(He wipes his face with a kerchief.)* I must be going.

CALORÍAS: You were in my dream.

MAESTRO: Perhaps you are right. It's time to go.

CALORÍAS: It was you in my dream and your music. You know me, don't you?

MAESTRO: I know many men.

CALORÍAS: You played with that…thing and my blood spilled and my boats sank! You sank my boats! You'll pay!

MAESTRO: I've annoyed you, haven't I? *(He stands carefully and turns out his pockets.)* I don't have any money. Nothing. Look!

CALORÍAS: You were in my dream…and the guitarrón.

MAESTRO: *(Holding the cello.)* This? You want this then?

CALORÍAS: *(Jumping back.)* Don't wave that thing at me.

MAESTRO: *(Gathering his things.)* It's beautiful here. The sea. But I'll leave.

CALORÍAS: Give me the guitarrón.

MAESTRO: No.

CALORÍAS: A simple request, old man. The guitarrón.

MAESTRO: I'm sorry. I can't do that. *(Holds it tightly.)*

CALORÍAS: You're stronger than you look, cabrón.

MAESTRO: And you're weaker. You see, I'm still a man of pride. I know what matters.

CALORÍAS: So you want it man-to-man…eh?

(He pulls harder, but the Maestro clings to it.)

CALORÍAS: Idiot! Imbecile! Don't cross me! *(He pulls out his black knife.)* Not man-to-man. See this? This is my gutting knife…Black and silver. See it? Now let go of that guitarrón before I cut you away from it.

MAESTRO: Man-to-man? Not with a knife. You are a beast and an animal. *(He starts to leave.)*

CALORÍAS: *(Grabbing him.)* Give me that guitarrón. Give it to me! Give it to me!

(They struggle.)

CALORÍAS: Hijo de la chingada…give it to me…No old man is going to get the best of me!

(Calorías grabs the Maestro by the hair, pulls back his head and slits his throat.)

CALORÍAS: Not *me!*

(Julio runs to the top of the dune.)

ANTONIO: *(Seeing what Calorías has done.)* No! No! Nooo.

MASTER BUILDER: What? What is it?

JULIO: Oh my God. What have you done?

CALORÍAS: *(Staggering with the cello and bow.)* I don't know. I'm sticky.

JULIO: Let's go…

(Calorías looks back.)

JULIO: Drop that thing. *(Pulls Calorías down the dune.)*

CALORÍAS: I can't.

ANTONIO: Calorías, mano… *(Going to him.)* You didn't have to kill him.

CALORÍAS: But I did.

JULIO: God help us.

ANTONIO: The guitarrón. *(He clings to Calorías.)* Give it to me.

CALORÍAS: *(Tips Antonio over.)* Stupid! *(Throws him the bow.)* Here.

ANTONIO: Puto, bastard!

MASTER BUILDER: What is it? What's he done?

JULIO: Let's go. Let's get outta here. Now! Andale!

(Julio and Calorías run offstage.)

MASTER BUILDER: What?

ANTONIO: He killed the old músico. Bastard! Help me! Help me!

(Master Builder struggles to get up but can't. Lights fade.)

SCENE FIVE

A short while later. The Master Builder is asleep. Antonio is sprawled, exhausted from trying to pull himself into his cart, which is turned over on its side, some distance from him.
Guicho enters near the dune. He sees the overturned chair and crumpled figure of the Maestro. He climbs up and stands looking down at him. He kneels, touches him, takes off his shirt and covers his face. He stands up and looks down at Antonio and the Master Builder, then out along the beach. Antonio catches sight of him.

ANTONIO: Guicho. Guicho mano. Guicho, help me.

GUICHO: He's dead. Poor old man.

ANTONIO: Guicho.

GUICHO: Poor old man.

(Guicho starts searching near the boat and finds a knife, examines it for sharpness and slips it through his belt. Master Builder stirs.)

MASTER BUILDER: Is that Calorías?

ANTONIO: Hey mano, what you doin'? Help me will you. Guicho. Hey mano, don't make me beg. *(He is almost crying.)*

GUICHO: *(Helping Antonio into the cart.)* It was Calorías, wasn't it?

ANTONIO: He didn't have to kill him. My God.

MASTER BUILDER: Guicho?

ANTONIO: He stole the guitarrón.

MASTER BUILDER: I can't see. I've gone blind.

GUICHO: Did they go to the river?

ANTONIO: Leave them alone. They're gone.

MASTER BUILDER: What are you doing? Are you going after them? Chico? *(He is guiding himself along the boat toward the voices.)*

GUICHO: Yes.

ANTONIO: *(To Master Builder.)* He's got a knife. But you ain't goin' to use it, right little brother? Correct? That would be highly stupid.
(Guicho starts off. The Master Builder catches hold of him.)

MASTER BUILDER: Stay here, chico. Calorías likes to kill. He's crazy. Don't go. Think about me too.

GUICHO: Let me go, old man.

MASTER BUILDER: He's a stranger, an old man ready to die. What do you care about a stranger?

GUICHO: He was old. But he was a man. To get what he loved away from him, they had to rip open his throat!

(Guicho pushes the Master Builder away. The Master Builder stumbles.)

GUICHO: And you? You fall away like rotten fruit.

MASTER BUILDER: I am a man!

GUICHO: Would a man let them walk away with his boat and fish? Would a real man let them smile and fuck him over again and again as if nothing happened? Shit. *(He leaves.)*

MASTER BUILDER: *(Sits on the sand.)* I am a man. Still. Inside.

ANTONIO: *(Finds the bow and holds it up examining it for cracks.)* Ahhhhhh.

MASTER BUILDER: Guicho?

ANTONIO: You okay, old man?

MASTER BUILDER: Go in my shoe, Antonio. Under the boat. I got some money there.

(Antonio looks, finds it.)

ANTONIO: Twenty-five pesitos, manitos. Not much.

MASTER BUILDER: Get me a pint or two of something…anything…that won't kill me right off.

ANTONIO: Not me. I ain't going to help you kill yourself, old man. *(He wheels away.)* Get some sleep. *(He exits.)*

(The Master Builder sits and then drags himself to his boat. He finds some iron tools, gets a long one and sticks it under a board like a lever. With great effort, he pries a board loose. He tries another.)

MASTER BUILDER: Ah my beauty, my Seahawk. I won't betray you. No. I am a man. See. I am a Master Builder with forty boats to my name, shaped and fitted from the finest… *(He loosens another board.)* woods! Did you think I would finish you and make you go to Calorías? My beauty? My masterpiece…My lifeboat?

(Lights dim.)

SCENE SIX

It is nearly dusk. The sound of the sea is strong. Guicho is sitting on one of several huge cement breakwaters. They are shaped like giant jacks thrown up against the shore.

Micaela climbs out to Guicho.

MICAELA: There you are. *(She sits with him.)* You okay?

(He's silent.)

MICAELA: Talk to me.

GUICHO: What do you want?

MICAELA: You can hide with me for a few days. I heard about Chinche…and that Maestro. I'm sorry.

GUICHO: Go away.

MICAELA: I can help you, you know.

GUICHO: I just let things pass. Everything. So I got nothing.

MICAELA: Let me hold you. I can help.

GUICHO: I don't get it Miki. I can't seem to do nothin' I want, but Calorías, he can do anything he fuckin' likes. I'm a coward. *(Takes out the knife.)* You know, I ain't stuck anyone in my life.

MICAELA: *(Caresses his arm, takes the knife from him and puts it down.)* I was thinking. The oil fields might not be too bad. I could just not show up at La Falana's tomorrow morning. Pack a few things. Like an adventure, you know. Maybe I'll learn to say something in French or something. I'd like that. *(She holds him.)*

GUICHO: It'll be the same there.

MICAELA: Oh no, manito. Americans, French, Arab people. All different. Everyone likes oil. I could learn all different kinds of music. That might make me famous. "Micaela of the thousand tongues," how does that sound? *(Laughs.)* They might get the wrong idea from "tongues" though. Right? Hey Guicho, come on. Laugh a little.

GUICHO: I can't.

MICAELA: Forget Calorías. He's crazy.

GUICHO: He has the guitarrón—its wood's so thin, delicate, like you. Not glittery. And it sings…like you…it makes your name sound like music. I'll play your name for you, Micaela.

MICAELA: Make love to me.

GUICHO: I'll get it back.

MICAELA: *(Picks up the knife.)* With this? I heard they slit the Maestro's throat. Antonio told me.

GUICHO: *(Takes it back.)* With this, if I have to. *(He studies it, puts it away, takes a moment preparing himself and gets up.)* Okay, so I'll see you later.

MICAELA: Stay here with me. Let me make you feel better.

GUICHO: If I stayed, you wouldn't love me.

MICAELA: I do love you.

GUICHO: If he ever did anything to you, you'd want his heart out.

MICAELA: But he didn't. He hasn't. He won't. Guicho, Guichito. This is different.

GUICHO: I'll be back.

MICAELA: I see. You'd rather kill than make love. Is that it, little brother? You want to kill, like Calorías. Feel that thrill of a knife entering. Muy macho. Go around with knives in your belt. I've seen it a thousand times. Yeah. You pull out a knife—and guys turn cold…and girls turn hot. Is that it?

GUICHO: Don't talk like that.

MICAELA: Why? You want me to always talk sweet poetry to you? I can do that, if that's what you want. Maybe you want me to act like a hooker, maybe that's what you really want, right? Say all those phony things to you. I was mistaken. I thought I could act like myself with you. Say what I really feel.

GUICHO: Miki—don't take it like that. We'll talk later.

MICAELA: No. You'll be different later. Listen to me now. I'm telling you, we can leave. You and me. Go away. We'll be so sweet together. *(She starts kissing him.)*

GUICHO: I got too many things in my head.

MICAELA: You don't got to do nothing with your head. *(She tries to pull him down.)* I'll make you forget the old man, Calorías, knives, everything. Come here.

GUICHO: I can't do it, Micaela. I can't.

MICAELA: You can do it, papacito. Mi amorcito. You're young, healthy, handsome, strong. And I'll do everything for you. Anything you want…papacito.

GUICHO: Not that way. Not like a fucking whore! *(He breaks free and exits.)*

MICAELA: Don't you dare look down on me. Not with blood dripping off your knife. Stinking lousy fisherman. Don't you ever come near me. Do you hear. Idiot. My last free night and I waste it on this idiot! *(She is crying. She starts after him.)* Hey Guicho. What's the matter? *(She stops.)* Don't you like me? Don't you like me?
(Lights dim.)

SCENE SEVEN

The stage is empty except for a few pale stars. Calorías and Julio enter. Calorías carries the cello on his shoulder.

GUICHO: *(Out of sight.)* CA-LO-RÍÍÍÍAAS! CAAA-LOOOO-RÍÍÍÍAAS!

(Guicho appears over a dune. Calorías and Julio stand looking at each other. Guicho takes out his knife.)

JULIO: Hey Guichito.

CALORÍAS: Why Guicho, you comin' with us?

GUICHO: No.

CALORÍAS: Ah yes. I see now. You have a knife. *(Approaching.)* Perhaps you're angry. Did I hurt a friend of yours? *(He laughs.)* Have you come to kill me, little boy?

(Guicho shakes his head. He is terrified.)

GUICHO: I want the guitarrón.

JULIO: Ay Guichito. Go away.

CALORÍAS: *(Picking up the cello.)* This. Ah yes. It is this you want.

GUICHO: Just give it to me.

CALORÍAS: If only it were so simple…eh? But I can't give it to you. I have to destroy it.

(Calorías turns toward the fire that Julio is building.)

GUICHO: Please Calorías.

CALORÍAS: Please? *(He laughs.)*

GUICHO: *You animal!*

JULIO: Leave him alone, Guicho.

GUICHO: Give me the guitarrón, Calorías.

JULIO: *(Trying to keep Guicho from approaching.)* Manito. You got to understand. Calorías he got a thing about it. I'm beggin' you.

GUICHO: Turn and look at me Calorías. *(He brushes by Julio.)* You killed the Maestro! *You slit his throat!*

(Guicho lunges at Calorías, who turns. The knife is imbedded in Calorías's shoulder. He staggers with the blow. He drops the cello. Julio rushes to pull the knife out.)

CALORÍAS: Stay away you fool. If you take it out, I'll bleed to death!

JULIO: *(To Guicho.)* Run. Shit! Get away from here.

(Guicho is too frightened to move.)

CALORÍAS: You see Guichito. You see why I must burn this guitarrón. You see how it works little brother? It has changed everything, everyone. Even you. *(He takes out his black knife.)* Now I have to kill you too.

(Julio stands blocking Calorías.)

JULIO: What terrible luck. Guicho run, for God's sake. *(He throws up his hands to Calorías.)* Remember your dream. The blood!

CALORÍAS: Burn it!

JULIO: Throw it into the ocean, mano.

(Calorías is trying to stalk Guicho.)

JULIO: Then I'll throw it away for you. I'll break it into a thousand pieces. Let's get out of here.

(Calorías slashes Julio across the hands.)

CALORÍAS: Move!

JULIO: Ayyyy, my hands. My hands.

(Calorías walks toward Guicho.)

GUICHO: You can't kill me, Calorías. Look at you. You're a dying man.

CALORÍAS: It takes more than a little boy's knife to do me in. *(He starts circling.)*

GUICHO: I'll never let you keep that guitarrón, Calorías.

CALORÍAS: Ay Guichito. Why have you done this? Eh? When I love you. If you go now…I might let you leave.

GUICHO: I want the guitarrón.

(He tries to get it and Calorías blocks him laughing.)

CALORÍAS: You don't even have a knife now, Guichito.

GUICHO: *(Circling him.)* And if I reach out and take back my knife? You'll spill your blood all over the sand.

CALORÍAS: You won't…

(Guicho lunges and taps his knife hard. Calorías shudders.)

GUICHO: You see how easy?

CALORÍAS: Ayyy.

GUICHO: Shall I do it again? And you'll shake and bleed? *(He taps it again.)* See?

(Calorías shudders violently in pain. Julio approaches with one hand bound in his shirt.)

GUICHO: Give me the guitarrón.

JULIO: Andale…give him the pinche guitarrón, mano. We'll leave…go to Villahermosa…andale.

CALORÍAS: *(Bellows.)* NOOOOO!

GUICHO: Give me that guitarrón!

JULIO: *(Picks up the cello and holds it above his head.)* You two is crazy. Fightin' about a fuckin' piece of wood. Will you die for a lousy piece of wood?!

CALORÍAS: There's death in its stomach!

GUICHO: There's life. I felt it.

(Calorías lunges at Guicho and nearly lands a blow with his knife.)

GUICHO: And I will feel it whenever I want! *(He grabs the handle of the knife in Calorías's shoulder and pulls it out with great effort.)*

JULIO: Dios mio.

(Calorías staggers. Julio drops the cello and catches him, desperately trying to stop the bleeding.)

CALORÍAS: Julio...Julio...Take me to the sea.

JULIO: Quiet. Quiet.

(Julio leads Calorías offstage. Guicho slowly picks up the cello. He places it on its metal tail and sinks to the ground center stage. The cello remains upright above him. The light darkens gradually. The stars shine. Blackout.)

SCENE EIGHT

Very early the next morning. There is still a moon. We hear the ocean. Guicho is sitting as before. He has fallen asleep with the cello propped upright.

He is dimly spotlighted so that we can only just make out his shape. Antonio wheels in. He approaches cautiously, not sure if Guicho is alive.

ANTONIO: *(Whispering.)* Guicho? Hey manito?

GUICHO: *(Stirs.)* What?...Ay. It's only you.

ANTONIO: Are you all right?

GUICHO: No. *(He sighs.)* Yes.

ANTONIO: I see you got the guitarrón...Way to go, mano... *(He looks around curiously. He finds Calorías's knife and holds it up.)* And Calorías?

GUICHO: I don't know...yes. He went *(Motions.)* to the sea.

ANTONIO: You all right, manito?

GUICHO: Yes. *(He gets up.)*

ANTONIO: Heyy okayyyy... *(He pauses.)*

(Guicho shakes the sand from his clothing. He examines the cello.)

ANTONIO: Nice instrument, right?...Well. Guess what I have for you, little brother?

GUICHO: What?

ANTONIO: Look! *(He pulls out the bow from his cart.)* I kept the little stick that goes with it!

GUICHO: That's great Antonio! I didn't even have time to think about it. You are excellent, su-perb!

ANTONIO: Wait a minute. It's mine now too.

GUICHO: What do you mean "yours"?

ANTONIO: I saved it for you didn't I?

GUICHO: What are you talkin' about?

ANTONIO: We're partners, ya know. Part of the guitarrón belongs to me.

GUICHO: What the fuck are you talkin' about?! I'm the one who was close to the Maestro. I'm the one who played the fuckin' thing!

ANTONIO: I'm not talkin' about playin' it, manito.

GUICHO: I'm keepin' it with me.

ANTONIO: Well now Guicho. I'm goin' to do you a favor, see? I'm goin' to teach you a little business sense. We're goin' to sell this guitarrón for a few hundred pesos, right, mano? And then we're goin' to buy some grass and double our money. Go into business.

GUICHO: Sell the Maestro's guitarrón for grass? What the fuck do you think I am?

ANTONIO: You can buy a little prime time with Micaela, right? The full treatment!

GUICHO: You mean, all you can think of is to sell this for a fuck and a ten-minute smoke for some hijo-de-puta murderer?! I got stupid bloody death hangin' all over me and that's all you can think of?!

ANTONIO: Hey mano. Cool down a minute. I got to think about my future. Yours too.

GUICHO: Don't bother.

ANTONIO: Oh, I see. You're going to give concerts on the street, right. Shit. You can't play that thing and the Maestro's gone. He's dead as lead, señor.

GUICHO: I'll get him back. With a wave of that little stick.

ANTONIO: You ain't no músico, little brother. 'N no magician neither.

GUICHO: Well I ain't no street beggar. That's all you are…a beggar!

ANTONIO: I do what I can, mano. You forget, I'm a cripple.

GUICHO: You never said that before!

ANTONIO: Why do I have to say it? Don't you got eyes, manito? Didn't you see me turned on my back like a fuckin' turtle? I couldn't get up without your help.

GUICHO: I never thought of you as a cripple before.

ANTONIO: Well my head ain't crippled, right? I can make my way good enough.

GUICHO: *(Snatches the bow from Antonio.)* No. Not good enough!

ANTONIO: Oye!

GUICHO: Not everythin' in this world is ugly!

ANTONIO: Part of that guitarrón is mine!

GUICHO: How could it ever be yours! You don't even know its fuckin' name. It's a cello! A cello! Do you hear me?! *(Menaces Antonio.)* Now get outta here before I turn you over again! *(He walks toward the cart.)* Andale!

ANTONIO: *(Leaving.)* You'll be alone. You'll see!

GUICHO: I am alone.

(Guicho sits for a moment. The light brightens. It is noon. It fades to late afternoon. Then, three bright stars appear. The Maestro walks out. He watches Guicho curiously. His shirt is stained with blood.

Guicho walks a bit with the cello and finds one of the giant jacks. The Maestro follows.

Guicho sits on the breakwater and checks the cello. He tightens the strings. We hear the ocean crash. Guicho strokes the cello, looking out to sea. Then the boy sits in imitation of the Maestro and places the cello between his knees. He holds the bow crudely.

The Maestro takes off his shirt, cleans himself off, rolls up his pant-legs, removes his shoes, puts on a bandanna. He looks like a fisherman.

Guicho moves the bow across the strings. They are out of tune and the bow bounces on them or makes them squeal.

Guicho stops. He tries again, this time trying for the rhythm of Micaela's name. The sounds are terrible. He tries again slower—it is worse—then faster. He rests his head against the neck of the cello.)

GUICHO: Maestro?

(Light comes up on a place above Guicho, perhaps on a breakwater situated higher up. The Maestro walks there. He finds a net and examines it, getting comfortable with it.)

GUICHO: Micaela. Mi-ca-e-laa.

(Guicho accompanies the name with the bow across the strings. He does it lightly but successfully. He does it harder. We hear the waves. The stars glitter. The sounds are off-key. He continues one more time with the full rhythm and then finds the last note and plays it over and over again. The Maestro casts the net. He gathers in the stars and the lights dim, then black out.)

END OF PLAY

HIDDEN PARTS
A Comedy

ORIGINAL PRODUCTION

Hidden Parts was originally produced at Primary Stages, October 1983. Artistic director was Casey Childs, producing director was Susan Gregg, with the following cast:

THOMAS .... Leon Russom
CYNTHIA .... Joan Grant
JUSTIN .... Christopher Fields
DARIA .... Cara Buono

CHARACTERS

In order of appearance:

THOMAS ARN, retired farmer, sixty-two

CYNTHIA ARN, wife, fifty-seven, a keen eye, secretive mind, plays piano, pastes paper butterflies on her walls

JUSTIN ARN, twenty-one, son, concert pianist, obsessive

DARIA ARN, fifteen, niece, living with her aunt and uncle, she refurbishes old umbrellas and paints them with fantastical plants and animals

TIME AND PLACE

All action takes place during five days in the present in and around a cornfield on a farm in the Midwest.

ACT I
SCENE ONE

First day. Everything is oversized and more brightly colored than real life. Stage left is taken up by an eight-foot-high cornfield—rough, fibrous, the color of straw. It is October. We can see some portion of the sky—a light vibrant blue now, as it is late afternoon. In one part of the cornfield, far stage left, is a cleared area in which we see various umbrellas in different stages of repair. They are opened and laid out over the cornstalks to dry. Some are painted with brilliant, fantastical birds and suns and plants and fish. We cannot see behind them.

Stage right is the wing of a white farmhouse. The top story consists of a porch where Thomas Arn, dressed in work clothes, is peering through a telescope on a tripod, scanning the field. There is a rocking chair and a rifle.

The bottom room is Cynthia's bedroom. It is painted light yellow and has exaggeratedly large windows with shutters that reach floor to ceiling. When they are opened, the whole interior is visible. There is a piano and stool and a vase with flowers.

Cynthia is in the yard, which is center stage. A table is covered with a red paper tablecloth, and streamers of red crepe paper and red balloons are hung for a party. The table is set for three. Cynthia is blowing up balloons and tying them to the crepe paper. She is in a bright cotton dress.

THOMAS: There he goes! There he goes! *(Grabs his rifle.)* I betcha he's a big one, doggone it.

CYNTHIA: Don't swear, dear.

THOMAS: You call that swearing. Women don't know what real cussin' is. *(Takes aim.)* Hope your heart's with God, 'cause your body belongs to me! *(He fires.)* Gotcha, ya bugger.

CYNTHIA: I do wish you wouldn't kill those animals, dear. I hate killing.

THOMAS: What is the matter with you. That old fox must've eaten fifteen chickens. Left nothing but their heads. How's that for killin', eh?

CYNTHIA: Killing's natural for a fox, dear.

THOMAS: Well damn it, Cynthia, if God was so set against us killin', he wouldn't have given us rifles.

CYNTHIA: You have a foolish sense of humor. *(Pause.)* Well, aren't you going to bury the poor thing?

THOMAS: Let 'im rot.

CYNTHIA: I can't stand how close we are to nature sometimes.

THOMAS: Picker'll come along in a couple weeks and squish him all up anyways. Should make for a nice green spot when the grass comes up in the spring.

CYNTHIA: I won't react. I know you're doing it for effect. If I could see your face right now, you'd be grinning ear to ear.

THOMAS: You could see my face. Right now, if you wanted. Just step out in the yard and look up. *(Pause.)* Hell I've changed quite a bit in twelve months. I'm completely bald and have whiskers to my knees. Why I'm standin' up here stark naked.

CYNTHIA: Just tell me when Justin turns down the road.

THOMAS: Justin! *(He looks through his telescope.)* Well, lookee there!

CYNTHIA: Is that him?

THOMAS: Jericho boy's peein' in the middle of the road.

CYNTHIA: That's too much. Put that thing away and leave people their private moments.

THOMAS: Peein' in the middle of the road ain't what I'd call private.

CYNTHIA: You're a pervert, peeking around with that thing all the time.

THOMAS: I ain't a pervert. I'm a student of human nature. I know more about the insides of folks from watching their outsides. Take the Jericho boy for instance. Got a real sense of humor. *(Follows with his telescope.)* Up... down...you should see that boy take aim.

CYNTHIA: I don't want to hear your filthy thoughts!

THOMAS: There's no end to what you can tell from the littlest nastiest detail. Aha! He better put his thingy away...here comes Daria with a load of those damn umbrellas. She looks like hell these days and the boy can't take his eyes off her. Must be true love. Uh-oh-oh...watch it there buddy. *(Reaches for his rifle.)* Not too close.

CYNTHIA: What are you doing? Daria won't get near him. You took care of that!

THOMAS: What's bred in the bone comes out in the flesh. She's got gypsy blood and she's dark and flirtatious like her mother.

CYNTHIA: She's our niece! *(She rushes to her room, slams the shutters and plays "Moon over Miami" on the piano.)*

THOMAS: *(Yelling.)* Cyn! Cyn! Justin's here!

CYNTHIA: *(Comes out quickly, aflutter.)* Yes?!

THOMAS: *(Looks at her for a moment.)* I lied.

CYNTHIA: I can't stand it.

THOMAS: I just wanted to see you.

(Justin enters in his performing tuxedo. His arms are full of fragrant flowers—roses, lilies.)

JUSTIN: Surprise.

CYNTHIA: Oh God, you lied about lying.

THOMAS: How did he do that? *(Checks his telescope.)*

JUSTIN: *(Hugging Cynthia.)* Something for the senses.

CYNTHIA: Oh honey. I can barely believe it. *(She hugs him, takes the flowers.)* They're just beautiful. Aren't they, Thomas? Sweet, sweet flowers. They make me dizzy.

THOMAS: That comes from blowin' up all those balloons. *(To Justin.)* Your mother's spent quite some time on the decorations.

CYNTHIA: They'll need their water, won't they? I'll be right back. *(Indicating the table.)* You see we've made a party for you. A celebration, at last! *(Exits to house.)*

JUSTIN: *(Walks around the table studying the decorations a bit too carefully, avoiding his father.)* They're great. You did a terrific job, Mom.

THOMAS: Hope you like red. *(Pause.)* Good to see you, son.

JUSTIN: Hi Pop.

THOMAS: I'd come hug you too. But I'm in exile. I ain't allowed below the fifteenth step while there's a woman on the premises. What do you think of that?

JUSTIN: Beats jail.

THOMAS: So how you doing, sonny? Tired? Why don't you sit right down and wipe the manure off your pointy shoes?

JUSTIN: Pop. I beg you. Make this visit tolerable.

CYNTHIA: *(Reenters with a platter.)* How handsome you look. So handsome. It breaks my heart. Mere appearance shouldn't do that, should it?

THOMAS: You were right not to be a farmer, son. Only wholesale business where you got to buy everythin' retail. Besides, we don't dress too well. As a matter of fact, I'm giving it up myself. Another couple weeks and everything you see'll be silage. I'm leasing the land to the Jerichoes. Now those four boys know how to get their hands dirty.

CYNTHIA: Let's seee… *(Studies the table.)*

JUSTIN: Where's Daria?

THOMAS: Watch her run out of that field like fool's fire.

(Justin rings the bell.)

THOMAS: She knows you're coming…

CYNTHIA: What she does with old tattered umbrellas is nearly a miracle. Wait until you see. She's so talented. Like you. She's only fourteen, but she has quite a special gift. Don't you think, Thomas? *(Exits to house for more food.)*

THOMAS: Oh yes. We get all kinds of geniuses out here in the sticks. There's Chester down the road. He's a genius whittler. He whittled a wagon and a team of horses last week. He whittled a fiddler and he makes elephants with flippin' ears too. Then there's Daria painting old umbrellas…and you of course…

JUSTIN: Shall I go get her?

CYNTHIA: *(Enters with more food.)* Oh, no—she'll be out in a minute I'm sure. She gets all caught up in what she's doing. I worry about her getting curvature of the spine, hunched over painting all day. Her bones aren't all formed yet, are they? She's only fourteen. Let's see what we're missing. *(Daria stomps out of the cornfield. Her hair has been hacked short. She wears an oversize dress, a sweater and men's shoes.)*

DARIA: Well, goddammit. Here I am.

JUSTIN: Jesus Christ.

CYNTHIA: Is that how you greet your cousin?

DARIA: Sure as hell is. *(Softer.)* Hi there, Justin.

JUSTIN: Hey there, squirt.

(He goes to hug her. She sticks out her hand.)

DARIA: Let's shake.

(They shake hands.)

DARIA: Hey, you look like a million bucks.

THOMAS: How's your art, sweetheart?

JUSTIN: What happened to your hair?

DARIA: What do you think? Got it caught in a combine. *(To Cynthia.)* Do we got any—

CYNTHIA: Have any.

DARIA: Orange drink?

THOMAS: Your language is going to hell in a bucket, girl.

CYNTHIA: Sit down and I'll see.

(Justin holds out chair for Daria, who sits.)

CYNTHIA: I think I've brought everything out. Funny. Now that I look at it, I made all sweets. There's a cobbler and cookies. That's green tomato pie.

DARIA: *(Grabbing food.)* Ugh.

CYNTHIA: It tastes just like apple. You make it with brown sugar and cinnamon. It probably has a lot of Vitamin C. Nutrition was never my strong point, but I do know some things. I made tea also, with milk or lemon. Like the English serve, I hear. Or do they use cream? Well, we'll do the best we can. I have beer inside too, if you want. Justin, hand me your plate.

JUSTIN: Is this the punk look or something?

DARIA: What?

JUSTIN: In England, kids rip their clothes and put safety pins through their ears and chop their hair off.

DARIA: That's weird!

THOMAS: So how long are you stayin', son?

DARIA: Don't answer him. I haven't talked to him in a year.

JUSTIN: I've got to leave in…about an hour. I have to see what kind of an instrument they've dug up for me at the station. I think there's an interview.

CYNTHIA: We're such strangers. *(She touches his hair.)* A beautiful stranger. So beautiful. I've missed you terribly. I sent you away too young.

DARIA: Oh God, Auntie. *(She hands Cynthia her napkin.)* Here.

JUSTIN: I will be staying a week.

CYNTHIA: A week. *(She cries harder.)*

JUSTIN: Five days really.

DARIA: *(Gets up abruptly.)* Well goddammit to hell!

JUSTIN: Look it was hard to manage five days. I have a million concert engagements to fulfill. Well, ten at least.

CYNTHIA: Justin's famous now. Time is like pure gold, isn't it?

JUSTIN: Not quite famous, Mother. We have yet to find hordes of teenage girls lining up to put atonal music on the charts.

CYNTHIA: Daria, sweetheart. Let's try this again, shall we? We'll all sit down. *(They sit.)*

DARIA: What's atonal music?

JUSTIN: That's what I play. Music of the twentieth century…very tricky stuff indeed. Did you know I have to open the top of the piano and pull out the strings?

DARIA: You do not.

JUSTIN: You should come see.

DARIA: Goddamn it. You do not.

CYNTHIA: I don't feel like sweets. I'd like a tuna fish sandwich. *(She gets up and exits.)*

JUSTIN: I wonder…would you prefer *Pierrot Lunaire* or *Wozzeck?* I think you'd like Berg. He suits you. He was handsome, poetic.

DARIA: Like you.

JUSTIN: Exactly!

THOMAS: I think that's close enough.

JUSTIN: Why don't you come and see for yourself? You could wear headphones and wave a baton at the quartet—four seriously unwashed music majors I'm sure.

THOMAS: I wouldn't like to see you touch her again.

JUSTIN: Of course, you could sit backstage and smile just for me.

DARIA: I got school.

CYNTHIA: *(Enters eating.)* You haven't been to school in a year. *(Silence.)* Well, it's true. It is. It's a sin and a shame. *(She sits.)*

THOMAS: What did I say about familiarity, son?

CYNTHIA: Really. Justin and I have always been touchy people. It's a sign of affection.

JUSTIN: You know, it doesn't bother Daria half as much as it bothers you, Pop. Why is that? Daria knows who I am, right?

DARIA: Right. Goddamn Justin.

CYNTHIA: Her vocabulary is more and more like Thomas's.

DARIA: It is not!

JUSTIN: *(Quieting her.)* Your goddamn cousin? Is that who I am?

DARIA: Goddamn right.

(They both laugh.)

JUSTIN: So. Therefore. I can... *(Moving suddenly the way you do to surprise a child.)* touch your elbow and your knee and your nose.

DARIA: Justin!

(Thomas fires a shot. Daria and Justin both jump up.)

DARIA: Jerk! I told you he's a jerk. What a jerk!

JUSTIN: For Christ's sake, Pop!

CYNTHIA: Daria, sweetheart. Calm down. Thomas! Justin, dear. I'm sorry.

DARIA: What a jerk. He don't have to worry about me keeping men away. I swore when he raped me that no man would lay a hand on me without getting something worse back! And no one, not him, not even his son will take advantage of me again unless I so desire. And he can be damn proud of himself 'cause he taught me desire was a curse!

(She runs into the field. Some umbrellas fly up from the field like startled birds.)

JUSTIN: You crazy lunatic.

THOMAS: Keep away from her. It gets her upset.

CYNTHIA: Don't be ridiculous, Thomas. Put that gun away. I refuse to put up with this foolishness another instant.

THOMAS: *(Retires grumbling.)* Women always come to your aid. Ever since you was a kid. I bet they made your career, didn't they, son? *(He retires from view.)*

JUSTIN: Why haven't you had him put away?

CYNTHIA: He's your father.

JUSTIN: That's utterly depressing.

CYNTHIA: I'm not protecting him. Think of me. Think of Daria. Imagine the talk. The looks. The scorn. The derision.

JUSTIN: Things are about to change. Mother. I promise. Why do you think I came? *(He kisses her and exits into the field.)*

CYNTHIA: Step out of the shadows, Thomas. And don't shoot. That's our only son cutting through the field.

THOMAS: *(Steps into view.)* I know. Contrary to what you think. I ain't stupid.

CYNTHIA: Then you must be crazy.

(She waits. Thomas rocks in his chair, silent.)

CYNTHIA: You could answer. You could say something. Explain yourself.

(We hear only rocking.)

CYNTHIA: You needn't be rude to me. We all have our crosses to bear. I try to live a blameless life and here I suffer for it.

(Cynthia goes into her room and slams the shutters. We hear "Blue Moon." The lights suddenly change. It is dark. Stars appear and a small bright moon. Thomas goes to his telescope and looks into the field.)

SCENE TWO

First evening. We hear "Blue Moon" from a great distance. We are in the clearing in the cornfield where Daria works. Several open umbrellas, a cot, a moon overhead. A lantern. Daria is stripping a frame. Rustling in the field. Daria stops. She slowly rises to get an umbrella, which she holds as a weapon.

DARIA: Okay now…all right, boy…come here…here, boy…here, boy…

(Justin bursts through the corn. His coat covers his face. He looks like a giant crow.)

JUSTIN: Jesus, how do you expect anyone to find you. It's a maze in there. *(He laughs.)*

DARIA: What the hell are you laughin' at?

JUSTIN: Maize corn, maze labyrinth. A play on words. *(Pause.)* I made a joke.

DARIA: I thought you were a goddamn dog. *(She puts her umbrella away.)* I got to work.

JUSTIN: Umbrellas!

DARIA: These umbrellas sell like goddamn hotcakes. I'm making a lot of money. Charlie takes them to fairs and bazaars for me, that sort of thing.

JUSTIN: Charlie?

DARIA: Jericho.

JUSTIN: Ahhh yes, those sweaty, hardworking Jericho boys.

DARIA: I made forty-six bucks last week plus I got a big order from a lady in Brighton who wants three wedding shawls. I already got the idea for them. All fish and seaflowers 'cause her daughter's a Pisces.

JUSTIN: I see everything's under control, eh?

DARIA: Sure.

JUSTIN: Nice place you got here.

DARIA: I love nature.

JUSTIN: Spartan, but peaceful. Beats the madhouse back there.

DARIA: The house?

JUSTIN: Yes. The mad-angry, mad-crazy house.

DARIA: Stop it!

JUSTIN: Come here little one.

DARIA: I hear you're going to England. They say it rains a lot there. *(She presents him with a closed umbrella.)* I made you a present. What do you think?

JUSTIN: Give me a minute. *(He opens it.)* It's amazing. I can't believe a squirt like you made this.

DARIA: I didn't make the frame. Charlie found it. You know Charlie.

JUSTIN: Um-hmm.

DARIA: I thought of every mean creature I possibly could. Hawks and eagles and sharks. But look at this. *(She turns it for him.)* Ain't this a bitch? The dragon! If you turn it, the wings sparkle. Crushed the mother-of-pearl myself. That's seashells, you know. And look at his fangs and the fire rolling out. I think he's goddamn beautiful. Fierce, breathin' fire. So fierce…and he's beautiful…like you. You like it?

JUSTIN: Are you kidding? Of course I like it. I love it.

DARIA: Cross your heart?

JUSTIN: Cross my heart. Hope to die.

DARIA: I think artists can carry it off, right?

JUSTIN: Right. Tell me how you're doing? Really.

DARIA: Every time you open it, you'll be someplace beautiful and you'll think of me.

JUSTIN: Then I don't need to open it now, do I?

DARIA: Justin, you're a jerk.

JUSTIN: Like Pop?

DARIA: No.

JUSTIN: Do you think all men are like Pop?

DARIA: Do you think all girls are like me?

JUSTIN: I take it that was a stupid question.

DARIA: Yeah.

JUSTIN: Tell me how to talk to you then. I don't know how anymore.

DARIA: If you were here for more than fifteen seconds you would.

JUSTIN: I'll make it up to you.

DARIA: It's beautiful out here. I seen spring and summer. It's fall. Winter's comin'. Do you think I can get out of here, Justin? I don't have much time. Winter's comin' early this year. I can tell. See over there. The trees are full of sparrows. Hundreds of 'em. They're going south already. The geese are leavin'. The leaves are gone, the grass is white. It's gonna be cold and I don't want to go back to that house again...Justin, I think this is a desperate situation.

JUSTIN: Not so desperate. I can help.

DARIA: No one can help.

JUSTIN: I'll subsidize you. I'll buy all your umbrellas—past, present, and future.

DARIA: It's like I can't move. My goddamn heart weighs a million pounds.

JUSTIN: A heavy heart, eh? Weighted down by your long dark past.

DARIA: Why are you laughing? It is dark. And I need something dark to get rid of it. *(She shivers.)* I scared myself. *(She lights her lantern.)* Look at that fire. Pretty little dancing thing.

JUSTIN: So you are a gypsy after all. Fire, mystery, romance. What would a gypsy be without a long dark past. That shouldn't stop you. We all have our troubles, sweetheart, I left when I was your age.

DARIA: You weren't raped!

JUSTIN: Don't ever say that again! We've all had our troubles!

DARIA: Yeah, well you had scholarships, and teachers and places to go.

JUSTIN: Sure, I had music. I could pull it out like a pocket mirror and blind folks with the flash...but of course, I also had a heavy heart.

DARIA: It was different for you.

JUSTIN: All right. No parallels there. Let's find another example then. Closer to home. Your mother. Nothing stopped her. She left. Seventeen, husband dead, living with strangers, a babe in arms and then...then what? She left. Whatever happened to her, whatever made her leave suddenly without a word, without a warning. Whatever dark and painful thing happened to her didn't weigh her down. It freed her. She left. She left a trail for you to follow.

DARIA: She didn't leave a trail. She left me! She's dead as far as I'm concerned.

JUSTIN: I don't want to get you upset. I just don't want to come back in a year and find you angry and bald and swearing like a sailor.

DARIA: You're never goddamn serious.

JUSTIN: Aren't I? Listen to my concert tomorrow night and you'll hear serious, I assure you. Boulez at nine. The university station.

DARIA: FM right? All goddamn culture's on FM.

JUSTIN: And wait up. I want to see you. I'll quiz you on the program notes.

DARIA: What?

JUSTIN: *(Opens the umbrella.)* Great umbrella. Just great. Wait here tomorrow. And no bullshit. *(He exits whistling.)*

DARIA: *(Calls after him happily.)* You got bullshit on your shoes, farmboy! *(Lights fade.)*

SCENE THREE

Later the first evening. Lights dim over the cornfield. Thomas scans the skies. Cynthia is playing softly, her shutters nearly closed.

THOMAS: Sweet Jesus, I can see Antares, red as a drunkard's eye. *(Swings the telescope around.)* 'N Aldebaran…'n Arcturus, shining like a pot of gold! Cynthia, if you'd only come out here. *(Pause, louder.)* Cynthia.

CYNTHIA: *(Stops playing.)* Yes, dear?

THOMAS: Cynthia, come out here.

CYNTHIA: What do you want? *(She opens one shutter and stands there.)*

THOMAS: You play like an angel.

CYNTHIA: Shall I play "Blue Moon" for you?

THOMAS: Well, now…

CYNTHIA: Yes?

THOMAS: What would you say if I asked to come down to you tonight?

CYNTHIA: I'd have to say no, Thomas.

THOMAS: Of course.

CYNTHIA: Why do you keep asking? Does it make you feel better getting hurt all the time? I think it's perverse.

THOMAS: Don't think I don't know what you're getting at. I read them magazines too. I guess I'm just a sad old masochist.

CYNTHIA: You old fool. You mean a sadomasochist.

THOMAS: I know what I mean!

CYNTHIA: You're impossible! *(She slams the shutter shut.)*
(Stage darkens. End of day one.)

SCENE FOUR

The second evening, at dusk. The moon has risen. Daria brings a chair from the house and places it in the yard in preparation for the concert. She reaches in her pocket, pulls out a butt, and lights it. Cynthia's shutters are closed, but we hear a radio faintly within and lights are on in the house. The radio is turned up. Cynthia throws open the shutters. She is dressed in an elegant black evening dress that reveals her shoulders. Her hair is upswept and she has on evening makeup. Daria quickly drops the cigarette and tries to put it out without letting her aunt see.

CYNTHIA: Daria, honey. It's almost nine. Justin should be on any minute.

DARIA: God, Auntie. You look beautiful.

CYNTHIA: And do pick that cigarette up. I hate those butts lying around the yard. They attract all kinds of filth. That's a darling.

DARIA: Shit. *(She puts it back in her pocket.)* I never seen you so dressed up before, Auntie. You look great!

CYNTHIA: I always dress for special occasions. It's just we've had so few. No weddings, no dinners. Life has become quite sad. *(She dabs her eyes with a lacy handkerchief she pulls from her bosom.)*

DARIA: Don't cry. This is gonna be great! *(She sits on the chair with her feet up.)*

CYNTHIA: *(Still crying.)* I can't help it. This is my wedding dress! *(She adjusts the station.)*

DARIA: Are you kiddin? It's black!

CYNTHIA: Hush!

(They listen for a moment. The announcer is speaking about something else.)

CYNTHIA: Not yet. What did you say, dear?

DARIA: Why did you choose black for a wedding?

CYNTHIA: I was an individualist. I wasn't going to marry in white in the month of June like all those twenty-year-old ninnies from town. I married in January and I was twenty-five. I knew my mind. I thought I did. *(The tears flow.)* Oh, your uncle really fooled me. He was so good-looking. I just loved having a good-looking man on my arm. I felt like someone. And we had such fun. Thomas laughed when he saw my dress. Everyone else was shocked, but he grabbed my arm and we laughed right down the aisle. Thomas has such a good laugh. Straight from the heart. That's why I married him. He was straight from the heart. It goes to show you, doesn't it. Blind as I was at the time, you could say I was unusually farsighted. Black has proven quite appropriate for our marriage!

(The piano starts—something by Boulez. She turns it up abruptly.)

CYNTHIA: Oh, this is him.

DARIA: Will he give a dedication or something?

CYNTHIA: These programs don't have dedications, dear. Hush.

(Daria listens. The music is extremely dissonant.)

DARIA: Oh, my God. What is that?

CYNTHIA: It's by some Japanese person, I believe.

DARIA: I like dance music better.

CYNTHIA: Shhhh. You should learn to sit still.

DARIA: You know I can't. I got to move around. It's in my blood.

CYNTHIA: It's just manners. You can learn manners like anyone else.

DARIA: No. Certain things are just in you. I bet I'd like gypsy music if I heard it. *(Pause.)* I bet I would.

CYNTHIA: What, dear?

DARIA: Gypsy music. I bet I'd have a natural liking for it.

CYNTHIA: Because your mother was a gypsy?

DARIA: Yeah. Like you and Justin. You play the piano and Justin plays.

CYNTHIA: That was influence, dear, not birth.

DARIA: Bred in the bone?

CYNTHIA: Oh, listen. He's playing something romantic, an arabesque by Schumann. You'll like this one. It always makes me cry. It's quite romantic. *(She cries.)*

DARIA: I'm destined to be like my mom. I'll probably wander all over the place.

CYNTHIA: Sweetheart, that's just not so. *(She starts to embrace Daria, but then is distracted by the music.)* Every note sparkles so. To think a son of mine can play like that. Isn't it a miracle? To play so strangely and beautifully. It comes out of nowhere.

DARIA: Auntie, I don't belong here, but I can't leave. I ain't brave like my mother.

CYNTHIA: Oh, you never know what a teenager is thinking, do you?

DARIA: Did my mom leave 'cause Uncle Thomas raped her?

CYNTHIA: My God! How can you possibly think that?

DARIA: Well, why the hell else did she just up and leave all of a goddamn sudden? Something sent her off.

CYNTHIA: Of course, something did. Of course. But she was always unhappy. Who knows what little thing broke the camel's back so to speak. Why, she was surly most of the time. She wouldn't lift a finger to help. She'd lay on her bed spreading out her gypsy cards again and again. God knows what she thought she saw.

DARIA: It could have been Uncle Thomas.

CYNTHIA: It was no such thing. I would have known.

DARIA: You didn't like her, did you?

CYNTHIA: Of course I did. It was a bit difficult I admit. We were thrown together suddenly. Thomas's brother died in the war and of course we had to bring her in. She had you. Where else could she go? To a gypsy caravan? I thought she was...an interesting person, but Thomas changed around her. I resented that part. When I was alone with him, he was so... it's not immediately apparent, but he was quite intelligent and friendly. But around her he became crude, a bully. Perhaps he thought that was how such women were handled. Who knows. But he didn't rape her. He never laid a hand on her. I would have known. Women have a sixth sense where that's concerned. No. I just think she decided to leave. It was a pretty day. Clear. She walked down the road quite calmly. She even waved to me. I thought she was going for the mail. They say she went west somewhere. Took a ride with one of the dairy trucks. To Missouri perhaps. She couldn't stand being cooped up in one place, I suppose.

DARIA: I don't believe that. She left her baby. Something happened.

(They listen to the music.)

CYNTHIA: Yes, things do happen. But the world is full of beauty. It's full of love and music. I believe that. Certain little things allow me to believe that. Like this music. Like this moment when all of Justin's goodness comes pouring through his music.

(They listen to the music.)

DARIA: Do you know the most disgusting thing, Auntie?

CYNTHIA: What, dear?

DARIA: When he was all done, he kissed me right here. *(Touches her neck.)* Why would he do that?

CYNTHIA: Maybe he was sorry, dear.

(Cynthia turns up the music. It ends sweetly. Lights dim.)

SCENE FIVE

Later the second evening. The yard and house are dark. We hear crickets. Justin appears. He is in his suit, but his collar is loosened, his tie is in his pocket. He carries a bottle of wine and is flushed and happy. He looks around the yard, settles himself and takes a drink from the bottle.

Thomas steps into view on the porch with his rifle.

THOMAS: One shot through the wrist'd be the end of your career.

JUSTIN: Hello, Pop.

THOMAS: All those years of training and then "ka-boom." Funny, ain't it?

JUSTIN: Yeah, it's a riot.

THOMAS: Your mother don't like my sense of humor neither. *(Puts his rifle away.)* I don't like prowlers.

JUSTIN: You must have seen me coming.

THOMAS: Yep.

JUSTIN: At least I know you're not going to shoot me. *(Waits for an answer. There is none.)* I played a concert tonight.

THOMAS: I know.

JUSTIN: Did you hear it?

THOMAS: Your mother had the darn radio on.

JUSTIN: Well, come on, Pop. What'd you think?

THOMAS: You sure you want to know?

JUSTIN: Sure. *(Drinks from the bottle and corks it again.)*

THOMAS: I thought it was crazy. Terrible. Especially the last one.

JUSTIN: You mean the *Quartet for the End of Time?*

THOMAS: If that was the last one. *(Pause.)* Everyone's asleep.

JUSTIN: I'm staying here tonight. I'm going to hit the sack myself pretty soon.

THOMAS: Not me. Ain't you going through the field?

JUSTIN: No. Why?

THOMAS: Do you want to know why I'm still up?

JUSTIN: What?

THOMAS: Don't you want to know why I'm standin' here when it's so god-damned late?

JUSTIN: Sure, Pop. What are you doing up so late?

THOMAS: Can't sleep. *(Pause.)* Jericho boys say a wild dog's loose. Been tearing out the throat of some calves round here.

JUSTIN: Bucolic country life, right?

THOMAS: What?

JUSTIN: Nothing.

THOMAS: Nothing? That's just what I'm plannin' to do. Last crop'll be out. Rent out the land. I'll be makin' more money collectin' rent than I ever did breaking dirt. More predictable. I guess I never really understood the way of things. I'm trying to though. The natural order and such. And you?

JUSTIN: I'm learning Takumisu's *Opus Thirteen.*

THOMAS: Don't be a smart ass. I want to know if you understand the natural order.

JUSTIN: Pop…

THOMAS: I got a theory.

JUSTIN: I'm too tired to discuss the finer points of farm philosophy with you right now.

THOMAS: This is important. Why, this could save your life. Son. You see, nothing's really unpredictable. Crops, weather, people. We're just too close to see the patterns. Things seem sudden to us—like a hailstorm breaking—but they've really been comin' for a long, long time. We just need a little distance and everything makes sense.

JUSTIN: *(Drinks.)* You want some wine?

THOMAS: What do you think of my theory?

JUSTIN: It's Chardonnay. From California, but what can you do? *(He corks the bottle and holds it up.)*

THOMAS: You never did know how to be generous.

JUSTIN: Now where the hell did that come from?

THOMAS: Your smile says one thing, but your body gives you away every time.

JUSTIN: Christ.

THOMAS: You offer me a drink, but you cork the bottle.

JUSTIN: I can't win with you, can I?!

THOMAS: I'm a student of human nature and I see what I see, and I know why you came.

JUSTIN: I came to take all your money, Pop. What do you think?

THOMAS: You don't want my money. You got enough money. I can see your clothes and that silky yellow tie you got tucked in your pocket 'n I can see that fancy black car you left by the road shining like a hearse. So it ain't money you came for. You've come to take my family right out from under me.

JUSTIN: That's ridiculous.

THOMAS: I'll fight you all the way, boy.

JUSTIN: What can I say? I can't turn myself inside out like a pocket so you can see my intentions, now can I? You obviously made up your mind about me a long time ago. You've hated me since the day I was born.

THOMAS: Hated you? Hated you? Why I was so happy the day you were born, I ran stark naked through the cornfield. That's probably when I got my bad reputation and folks started believing everything they heard about me.

JUSTIN: We've all heard quite a bit about you, Pop. Was it the full moon that made you go crazy and rape a thirteen-year-old girl?

THOMAS: You really think I did it? She never saw his face. He come up behind her and threw her down.

JUSTIN: You confessed.

THOMAS: Yep. I did do that. *(He takes his telescope and scans the field.)* So, you want a first-hand account.

JUSTIN: No, thanks. I got one from Daria.

THOMAS: Ain't you curious? You are curious. I know that much about you. *(He turns his telescope on Justin and watches. Justin turns and their eyes meet.)*

THOMAS: Gotcha! Well now, there I was, about this time last year, fixin' the fence this side of the river bed, and the barbed wire sprung back on me 'n scratched me up bad. Almost took out an eye. Hurt like the dickens. And there I come walking out of the cornfield expecting some sympathy, and what do I find? My niece is raped and my wife hates me for life.

JUSTIN: It's hard to believe that's what really happened.

THOMAS: It's harder to believe what I saw returnin' home, son.

JUSTIN: What was that, Pop? *(He takes some wine.)*

THOMAS: Well now, the corn'd dried out last year, remember? When you moved through it, it crackled like fire. And comin' home I saw a young man, all flushed 'n dirty in the face, runnin' like hell through the cornfield.

JUSTIN: Well, shit. Why didn't you say something?

THOMAS: 'Cause I thought it was you, Justin.

JUSTIN: Isn't that just like you.

THOMAS: Was it you, son?

JUSTIN: You cowardly son of a bitch.

THOMAS: Be a man and tell me the God's truth.

JUSTIN: You know damn well it wasn't me!

THOMAS: I'll forgive you anything, son.

JUSTIN: Christ, Pop. I don't know whether to call the county jail or the county hospital.

THOMAS: Don't call no one. I'm a vigilant person by nature. And whoever that was I saw, he won't have a chance to do harm around here, again.

JUSTIN: The harm's been done. You've ruined everything.

THOMAS: *(In a deep oratorical voice.)* "In all your life have you ever called up the dawn or shown the morning its place? Have you taught it to grasp the fringes of the earth and shake the Dog-star from its place? Have you entered into the springs of the sea or have you walked in the recesses of the deep? Have the gates of death been revealed to you?" I wouldn't be so pessimistic, son. One good thing has come of all this. It drove me straight to the Bible. Memorized the entire Book of Job. Now there's a man who didn't know what hit him! God gave him one hell of a lesson on perspective. "Can you bind the Cluster of the Pleiades or loose

Orion's belt? Can you bring out the signs of the Zodiac in their season or guide Aldebaran and its train?" *(He laughs.)* And I can find 'em all now. Every single star in the Zodiac. There's Aldebaran itself, the pink star over your head. Aldebaran's the eye of the Bull, you know. *(Pause.)* You should learn about the stars, Justin. They're far enough away so you can see their patterns.

JUSTIN: If I take the top off this bottle, maybe you might like me to leave it on the back stairs?

THOMAS: That would be nice. Put it on the fifteenth step.

(Justin throws the cork away flamboyantly and puts the bottle on the stairs.)

JUSTIN: I'm turning in.

THOMAS: Don't tell your mother what I said.

JUSTIN: About the boy in the field?

THOMAS: Yep. She'd be pretty upset to know the fella's still on the loose. *(Pause.)* Poor fella, he don't know that if you go against the natural order, it'll spring right back in your face. Take out an eye. Eye for an eye. Wild folks never think it applies to them. Good night, son.

JUSTIN: Good night.

THOMAS: Daria's lantern's still lit.

JUSTIN: Take care, Pop. *(He retires.)*

THOMAS: I will.

(Thomas starts down the stairs. We hear his slow steps descending. The stage is empty. Lights dim.)

SCENE SIX

The third day. Afternoon. Thomas is rocking on his chair on the porch. Justin is playing George Crumb in Cynthia's room, but the shutters are closed and we hear it faintly. He is practicing certain parts over and over again. Cynthia is in the yard with a small rickety table piled high with colored paper butterflies. Daria is stage left in the cornfield examining the umbrellas she is selecting and making into a bundle to be taken and sold.)

CYNTHIA: I remember when he couldn't reach an octave. I'd hold up his little hands and press down the webs between his fingers, so they'd grow long and slim. Little duck webs, I'd call them. Do you remember, Thomas?

THOMAS: Nope. That was your private world.

(Justin plays a long lyrical passage and then slams both hands down on the

keys. He flings the shutters open and the butterflies fly off the table and all over the yard.)

CYNTHIA: *(Hurrying to pick them up.)* What's wrong, dear? What is it?

JUSTIN: It's nothing, Mother. Don't worry about it. A fit of artistic temperament.

CYNTHIA: Yes, I suppose. These things come up suddenly. Why, look at these poor butterflies blown all over the yard. Come help me.
(He does.)

CYNTHIA: Aren't they marvelous? Daria makes them for me. I want to cover the walls with them. I do love butterflies. They have such brief beautiful lives. *(She is crying.)*

JUSTIN: Mother? Are you crying?

THOMAS: She's always crying. "Weeping" she calls it.

CYNTHIA: I'm so glad for you, Justin. Things have progressed, haven't they? You lead a wonderful life, full of music and ease. *(Cups his face in her hands.)* Isn't that true?

JUSTIN: Yes. It's more than true. It's a wonderful life. Really splendid. I'm just preoccupied. I have a concert later. I better go.

CYNTHIA: Yes, of course.

JUSTIN: *(He kisses her hands.)* You're wonderful, Mother. I'll see you…tomorrow. Yes?
(Justin heads for the field. Thomas springs up and grabs his rifle.)

THOMAS: Where you going, son?

JUSTIN: Daria's out there, isn't she?

THOMAS: Yep.

JUSTIN: See you, Pop.
(Justin enters the field. Thomas watches. It grows dark suddenly. The moon appears. Daria has opened the umbrellas over her and lit a lantern.)

CYNTHIA: I'm glad they have each other. It's a shame they're cousins. I look at them and think they would be a beautiful couple, just beautiful. They're both so artistic. But then, their children might be born monsters. *(She goes into the house. She plays* Claire de Lune.*)*

JUSTIN: Hello, Daria.

DARIA: Don't it look like a Chinese lantern?

JUSTIN: Japanese. Balinese, perhaps. Something delicate.

DARIA: Do you got a match?

JUSTIN: Are we planning a conflagration?

DARIA: What are you talkin' about?

JUSTIN: A fire, a marshmallow roast, a barbecue, pray tell? Actually that's not what I'm talking about.

(Justin hands Daria a match. She lights a cigarette.)

DARIA: Why do you do that?

JUSTIN: A smoke screen. *(Laughs.)* It's a little song and dance because you won't talk to me.

DARIA: I'm talking.

JUSTIN: No, you're not. What about last night? Are you angry, hurt, disappointed? Relieved I didn't show up? Indifferent?

DARIA: I'm used to you being gone.

JUSTIN: I brought you some wine. Then I left it for Pop. I meant to come find you and talk all night long—but I crawled into bed and didn't think of you at all. What do you think of that?

(Daria shrugs.)

JUSTIN: I had a little heart-to-gunbarrel talk with Pop last night. It really got to me.

DARIA: He got to me too, remember? But I never forgot you.

JUSTIN: I see we can't talk. Well, I just came to say good night.

DARIA: Okay.

JUSTIN: I'd like to stay.

DARIA: You got more concerts I suppose.

JUSTIN: One. At the high school. Maybe I'll play hooky.

DARIA: You?

JUSTIN: Why not? Everything's perfect. Being here with you on a country night. The corn leaves smelling as sweet as flowers, the stars so big and close, it seems we're standing on the edge of the world and all we have to do is jump off and fly.

DARIA: That's pretty. You always have pretty things to say.

JUSTIN: Are you glad I'm here?

DARIA: Shhhh. Can you hear your mom?

JUSTIN: Yes.

DARIA: Do you like that kind of music too?

JUSTIN: Yes. That kind too.

DARIA: I do love you, Justin. I miss you. It gets goddamn hard to bear, you know. Here. Alone. The only thing that saves me are these stupid old umbrellas. Believe it. I love to make them new again. It mends my heart. They got so many little rods and things. It makes me think of tiny bird skeletons. They look so wounded. So when I find one, I strip it and straighten out its little bones and cover them with silk. Then I paint them with everything I've ever seen—horses with curly manes and wild swans and colored fish. And dragons. I especially love dragons 'cause they're fierce and fly away.

JUSTIN: Fly away with me.

DARIA: Sure.

JUSTIN: I mean it. I'm leaving and never coming back.

DARIA: Me too.

JUSTIN: Come with me then. I'm serious. Meet me tomorrow. We'll watch your sparrows circle off and we'll follow up and off until we disappear. What do you say?

DARIA: You always sound like you're quoting something. Like your dad.

JUSTIN: I need you.

DARIA: I don't know what's going to become of me, Justin.

JUSTIN: Come away with me. You'll have bushels of umbrellas. I'll buy you paints and seashells and books, a thousand books of colored pictures to give you ideas. We'll see dragons in China, go to lost islands and see Gila monsters and palm trees.

DARIA: I can't. I want to, but I can't.

JUSTIN: Yes, you can.

DARIA: No. Not til your dad knows how bad he hurt me. I want him to feel it and drag it around with him like a...like a stone, like I do. I ain't talked to him in a year, I ain't looked at him once. But before I leave, I want him to see my eyes. I'll look at him and I hope his soul freezes right up in his goddamn body and he drops dead. I just can't look at him yet.

JUSTIN: You won't leave. Pop has a hold on you.

DARIA: He does not!

JUSTIN: Why else would you stay?

DARIA: Ain't you heard a thing I said?

JUSTIN: "Ain't you heard a thing I said?" Stop talking like that, will you! You don't have to talk like a hick. You know better.

DARIA: Yeah. I know better. I talk this way on purpose. It's tough.

JUSTIN: It's not tough. It's pitiful. The way you look, the way you act. It's fucking pitiful.

DARIA: Where did all of that come from? What is the matter with you?

JUSTIN: I'm dying. Can't you see? I need you. Christ!

DARIA: But everything's going great. Your music. All those prizes. And I seen pictures in magazines with beautiful women smiling up at you.

JUSTIN: Not at me. Not me at all. You're so innocent. They're looking at the music. Beau-ti-ful music. That's me. All lit up alone on stage. How easy.

Everyone is so appreciative. A little music, a little kindness. Be kind to them, Justin. Smile, listen, say something complimentary, understanding. They'll love you for it. Be kind. Women are always so hungry for kindness. So hungry. *(He pulls Daria roughly to him.)* And you know what, little gypsy?

DARIA: *(Pushes him away.)* Don't.

JUSTIN: I'll tell you a secret. If that fails. Be cruel. They'll love that too!

DARIA: I don't like you when you talk that way.

JUSTIN: I told you.

DARIA: Do you take advantage of people like that?

JUSTIN: It's cold, isn't it?

DARIA: Yeah, it is.

JUSTIN: It's cold and I'm freezing to death!

DARIA: I'm sorry.

JUSTIN: Come with me, then. Remind me who I am. I'll show you places— New York, Chicago, Paris, Berlin, Strasbourg, Copenhagen, London, Dublin, Helsinki—the goddamn Republic of Chad!

DARIA: I'm scared, Justin.

JUSTIN: That's not it.

DARIA: Yes, it is.

JUSTIN: Maybe you liked what he did. Is that true? Is that why you're staying? Did you like it? Are you waiting for more?

DARIA: Shut up, Justin.

JUSTIN: *(Pacing.)* You know, I wasn't going to tell you this…But I think you should know. Maybe you won't have so much trouble leaving.

DARIA: What?

JUSTIN: Do you know what Pop told me during our little heart-to-heart last night?

DARIA: No.

JUSTIN: Well, I'll tell you, little cousin. He confided in me. He thought it would bring us closer. Do you know what he said? He said he couldn't help himself. He said he'd see other men look you over and he'd get hot. He said he couldn't get you out of his mind the way your clothes stuck to your breasts when you got wet. He said he'd wake drenched and smelling like a bull after he'd dreamt of holding you and spreading your thighs!

DARIA: *(Hitting him.)* Shut up! Shut up! Get away from me. I don't want to hear anymore. Please! *(She holds her ears and rocks herself.)*
(Cynthia opens her shutters. Thomas comes out on the porch with his rifle.)

JUSTIN: *(Dims the lantern.)* Shhhh now. Shhhh. Nothing's going to happen. It's all right. I promise. Nothing's ever going to happen. Cross my heart, hope to die. Stick a needle in my eye, remember? There, you see, you're smiling.

DARIA: I hate it here.

JUSTIN: I know. Sweetheart I know. It's okay. We'll leave tomorrow. We'll go far away. We'll start over again. I promise.

(Lights on Justin and Daria fade. Thomas and Cynthia stand—Cynthia in her room with the shutters wide open, Thomas on the porch with his rifle— each unaware of the other listening.)

THOMAS: Hello? Anyone there?

CYNTHIA: Daria?

THOMAS: Cynthia?

CYNTHIA: It's me, Thomas.

THOMAS: Cynthia, is that you?

CYNTHIA: Yes.

THOMAS: I heard a shout.

CYNTHIA: I was dreaming.

(Thomas relaxes, lowers his rifle.)

THOMAS: Matter of fact, I was dreaming too. Could be we were dreaming the same dream.

CYNTHIA: I doubt that, Thomas.

THOMAS: *(Clears his throat.)* To tell you the truth, I was dreamin' about love.

CYNTHIA: There! You see. I was dreaming about something entirely different. I was dreaming about a pair of birds with tiny curved bones. They were magical birds with great fearless hearts. They only stayed here for a while—circling, circling, and then, all of a sudden they left! They dove straight up—oh it hurt the eye to follow them—they dove straight up into the brightest part of the sky! *(She is crying.)* Oh, good night, Thomas! *(She closes the shutters.)*

THOMAS: Aw shit!

(Blackout.)

End of Act I

ACT II
SCENE ONE

Fourth day. Morning. It is quite early and the sky is changing from rose to light gray. Cynthia is pasting butterflies on her walls. The shutters are wide open. Daria comes out of the house with a bundle of umbrellas under her arm. She has made some effort to clean herself up. Her hair is combed, her face is clean. She wears a cardigan over her dress.

DARIA: Hey, Auntie!
  (Cynthia turns.)
DARIA: Shhhh. Auntie, listen. You got to give Justin a message for me.
CYNTHIA: I don't "got" to do anything. *(Pauses to look at her.)* My, don't you look nice.
DARIA: Okay, Auntie, will you please give Justin a message for me.
CYNTHIA: Yes, of course.
DARIA: Actually, when he gets up, he won't say nothing for a while. You know, he won't ask for me directly. You'll just see him gettin' worried. Well, you tell him I'll be back this afternoon. Now he's going to be a little excited by that, but you just slow him down. Just ask him if he don't...if he doesn't have something to tell you about me and him.
CYNTHIA: What do you mean about you and him?
DARIA: Uncle's out back, right?
CYNTHIA: Yes, but what about—
DARIA: *(Going into the field.)* I'll take the shortcut.
CYNTHIA: Where are you going? Surely you can tell me.
DARIA: I'm sellin' umbrellas, okay? But don't tell no one. Bye now. *(She exits.)*
CYNTHIA: Why people feel so lighthearted about leaving trouble in my hands I'll never know.
  (Cynthia returns to her work. Justin walks in, very elegant and cool. He is holding down his excitement, however.)
JUSTIN: Hullo, Mom. Any coffee?
CYNTHIA: Back in the kitchen. I'll get it for you if you like.
JUSTIN: That's all right. *(He paces.)*
CYNTHIA: You're up awfully early. All dressed up and smelling like lavender, I believe. *(She steps to the window to inhale.)* Is it lavender? So sensual. *(She goes about her pasting.)*
JUSTIN: Is Daria up yet?
CYNTHIA: Oh, she's gone.

JUSTIN: Gone! How could she be!

CYNTHIA: Perhaps I put it a bit strongly. She's only gone to sell umbrellas. Oh, there it is. I told you. She made me promise not to say—please make believe I didn't say a word. I'm no good at secrets.

JUSTIN: What do you mean she's gone to sell umbrellas? She's supposed to be here. I'm ready to leave.

CYNTHIA: But you never told me. Oh, I thought we had days yet. We haven't even had a chance to sit down together. Were you going to just leave like that?

JUSTIN: When did she say she'd be back?

CYNTHIA: Were you going to just leave?

JUSTIN: Mother, please! When will she be back?!

CYNTHIA: I wish you wouldn't be so petulant, dear. I don't deserve it. All these poor butterflies have fallen and I'm having the worst time trying to match them to their tiny antennae.

JUSTIN: Shit!

CYNTHIA: Oh my, darling. You do look upset. Daria warned me. She shouldn't be long. She'll be back by nightfall, I'm sure. My, I wonder if she went to town. Wouldn't that be wonderful. Maybe she finally went into town. Oh, Justin!

JUSTIN: How could she do this?

CYNTHIA: She also said that there was something you would want to tell me about you and her?

JUSTIN: What did she mean?

CYNTHIA: Well, that's for you to say, dear. I haven't a clue.

JUSTIN: Well, we can't have you walking around without a clue, can we? That would be cruel. *(He studies her for a moment.)* I've asked Daria to leave with me. Today. Just like you said—without a word.

CYNTHIA: Oh.

JUSTIN: It's not what you expected, is it? I'll tell you something else. I love her.

CYNTHIA: You can't love her, Justin.

JUSTIN: Because she's my cousin? That's ridiculous!

CYNTHIA: She's fourteen. She's a wounded child, dear. You can't just…

JUSTIN: Just what? Take her? Use her? Violate her? I wouldn't hurt her for the world.

CYNTHIA: Does she have any idea how you feel?

JUSTIN: Not exactly. But she must sense it. Yes, she senses it.

CYNTHIA: And she's agreed to go away with you?

JUSTIN: Yes.

CYNTHIA: It's wrong, son. It is. There's something primitive about it.

JUSTIN: Good. You can read about it in *National Geographic*. I'm going for a walk.

CYNTHIA: No, wait. Please. I'm not only afraid for her. You're my son. She'll break your heart. She's a gypsy, you know. I love her very much. I do. But gypsies do wander. Your father has a saying, "What's bred in the bone..."

JUSTIN: "Comes out in the flesh." Yes, I know that one. And you believe that crap, don't you?

CYNTHIA: I don't know. I believe...Oh, I believe that there is much more to things than I ever imagine. Such terrible things happen. Mothers walk out on their babies. Decent men are beasts underneath. The world's a mystery.

JUSTIN: Voilà. A revelation! *(He turns to go.)*

CYNTHIA: Be disdainful if you like. There are things I know about you I never guessed before.

(He stops cold.)

CYNTHIA: I favored you and shut your father out. You were such a charming little boy. You had the brightest eyes. To think you were mine alone for nine months, your heart a tiny echo of my own. And for all that, you've turned out like your father.

JUSTIN: That's hogwash.

CYNTHIA: You do have quite a bit of him. That terrible will, that terrible solitude. I never saw it. Sometimes I think that's it, all this trouble is my own making. I never saw things. I always was a bit distracted, wasn't I? Perhaps if I were a more perceptive person, more aware, if I had only noticed certain attractions, perhaps we never would have had a tragedy like we did. I think of that, you know. It haunts me.

JUSTIN: It's different now. You know about "certain attractions."

CYNTHIA: Yes, I do.

JUSTIN: And you can help.

CYNTHIA: I'm not sure.

JUSTIN: You can. You don't want another tragedy, do you?

CYNTHIA: I need to understand, Justin. I can't act until I understand.

JUSTIN: You could never understand!

CYNTHIA: How can you say that?!

JUSTIN: Because I know!

CYNTHIA: You see, you're like your father. All pronouncements. No explanations!

JUSTIN: Daria's mine. She was meant for me. You had Pop and Pop had you.

CYNTHIA: *(Laughs.)* Honey, Daria had her mother—

JUSTIN: Yes indeed, you're right. For a while Daria had her mother and Pop had her too, didn't you know? I saw it. She was in the barn. Nursing. He touched her breast. Then he stood behind her and kissed her...right here. *(He touches his mother on the back of the neck.)* She liked it.

CYNTHIA: You can't shock me. I sensed it all. It comes as no surprise. I'm short of breath. *(She sinks into a chair.)* Perhaps I drove her to it. Do you think I did? I was so cold to her.

JUSTIN: I didn't do anything about it. I'm sorry. I wanted to jump out of the dark and pull his hand away, but I didn't. I just stood there like a jackass.

CYNTHIA: You were a child.

JUSTIN: But you know what? A miracle. It was all for the best. Because the next day, she left. Walked away. And you had Pop. And Daria was left for me.

CYNTHIA: That's how you saw it as a child. It was nothing. A moment of no special weight. It has such slight importance, the tiniest transgression, and look what came of it.

JUSTIN: There's nothing wrong now. We'll have a wonderful life. Believe me. Full of music and ease. I promise.

CYNTHIA: I don't know.

JUSTIN: You don't want her to stay here with Pop, do you? Mom, give us a chance to get the hell away from here. *(Pause.)* Pop can't know until we've left.

CYNTHIA: Don't ask me to keep secrets. I've never kept anything from him.

JUSTIN: Maybe it's time you did. Would you rather he shot us?

CYNTHIA: He's not a murderer. He just waves that rifle around.

JUSTIN: Are you sure?

CYNTHIA: No.

JUSTIN: And don't tell Daria we talked.

CYNTHIA: Shhh. No! No more secrets. I can't abide secrets. They're dangerous. They rise up suddenly and betray you like a beast in the field. No more secrets!

(Cynthia goes into her room, closes the shutters and plays Claire de Lune. *Lights dim.)*

SCENE TWO

Fourth evening. It is nearly twilight. A pale moon rises suddenly, awkwardly. Daria enters, coming from the fair. She carries a large bag full of old umbrellas to be fixed. She looks around the yard and finds a lantern. She lights a match, watches it, lights another and another, watching them burn. She's waiting for Justin. Cynthia is playing "Moon over Miami." Thomas stands with his hands clasped, looking up at the stars.

THOMAS: Nice evening, ain't it? Makes you feel closer to the stars. My, my, I can almost see Alpha Centauri. Sirius'll appear right over there.

(Daria glances up involuntarily and quickly looks down. She lights another match and watches it.)

THOMAS: Now why things're so orderly and predictable up there and so downright sloppy down here, I'll never know. *(He leans over to watch Daria.)* What're you going to do with that fire, honey? Burn me up? *(Waits.)* It's a shame to feel hatred on a night like this. With a silvery moon and stars as big as my fist. I could reach right up and pluck one down for you if you wanted. *(He waits again.)* How can you stare at matches when God's filled the skies with fire!

(Daria turns and stares at Thomas. He meets her gaze and looks away. Daria lights her lantern and enters the field. Thomas calls after her.)

THOMAS: If I were Justin now, we'd be having one hell of a conversation, wouldn't we? Wouldn't we?! WOULDN'T WE?! AAAAAAAAAAAAAA-AAAAAAAAAAAAAAAAAA!

(Cynthia quickly opens the shutters.)

CYNTHIA: What's wrong? What is it?

THOMAS: AAAAAAAAAAAAAAAAAAAAAAAAAAAAAAAAAAAA!

CYNTHIA: What is it? Thomas? Are you having a heart attack?

THOMAS: "I tell you God Himself has put me in the wrong. He has drawn the net around me. If I cry 'Murder,' no one answers"!

CYNTHIA: Are you having a fit, dear? Maybe I should come upstairs.

THOMAS: No. No. Don't come near me! I've done a terrible thing. I can't stand it any longer. "O earth, cover not my blood and let my cry for justice find no rest. For look! My witness is in Heaven."

CYNTHIA: *(Overlapping.)* Are you quoting the Bible again? Honestly! Thomas, please. Tell me what is wrong?

THOMAS: I can't stand the hate anymore. I can't stand the loathin' and the bitterness. I can't stand the loneliness 'n the house in pieces. I want this all to heal!

CYNTHIA: I hardly know what to say. It's a pity. It really is. But I believe we're past healing, Thomas.

THOMAS: There's still hope for us.

CYNTHIA: No, Thomas.

THOMAS: Are you about to leave me too?

CYNTHIA: No.

THOMAS: Any particular reason?

CYNTHIA: I'm your wife.

THOMAS: In name only, and hell, you could change your name again.

CYNTHIA: After all these years?

THOMAS: They do it all the time, I hear.

CYNTHIA: I wouldn't recognize myself Besides, we have a solid marriage. Not a good marriage. But solid. We have a child we've seen to manhood. We have a house and land. I fix meals and you eat them. I play the piano and you listen. We talk.

THOMAS: But that's all.

CYNTHIA: I suppose so.

THOMAS: I thought, after all these months, we'd find something beautiful again in the sameness 'n the solitude out here. But I was wrong.

CYNTHIA: You were wrong. *(Pause.)* I will tell you something, Thomas. I would like to see you redeem yourself. You see I had a talk with Justin.

THOMAS: I talked with the boy too.

CYNTHIA: And…well, you can appreciate that Justin is afraid of you.

THOMAS: The boy's always been afraid of me. Ever since he was a little one. Made me afraid to even pick him up.

CYNTHIA: Well, there you were, gritty from the fields, and always staring at him with those hawk's eyes of yours.

THOMAS: Well, damn my eyes then! I can't help it if I got hawk's eyes.

CYNTHIA: Justin is still afraid of you and you haven't helped it any, waving your gun in his face and threatening him like a bully. He's still very concerned about Daria, and you can see why!

THOMAS: I know why!

CYNTHIA: And he wants me to help him steal Daria away.

THOMAS: I knew it! I knew it!

CYNTHIA: He only said that because he's so awfully frightened of you, Thomas Arn. But I can't do things that way. Secretly. Therefore, I am appealing to your better judgment. And now that you are talking of healing, well, I want you to let them go off together without a fuss. With your blessing.

THOMAS: Over my dead body, they will!

CYNTHIA: Justin's going to take her all over the world and offer her an education. She would feel like part of the human race again. *(She takes out a handkerchief and dabs her eyes.)* She'd let her hair grow and clean her face and wear beautiful clothes. Justin would buy her beautiful clothes, I know he would.

THOMAS: I can't let them.

CYNTHIA: You're completely hopeless!

THOMAS: "I tell you God Himself has put me in the wrong. He has drawn the net around me. If I cry 'Murder,' no one answers."

CYNTHIA: You quoted that once already today! Anyway to hear you quoting the Bible is blasphemy! *(She is crying.)*

THOMAS: I will never consent to them bein' together and that's that! I got good reason.

CYNTHIA: That's all you'll say?

THOMAS: That's it!

CYNTHIA: This hurts me terribly. I don't know why. I certainly shouldn't have any feeling left for you. But I do. I do. *(Straightening herself.)* However, I'm letting you know. If you so much as threaten those two beautiful young people, I'm leaving you and you'll never see me again! *(She slams her shutter and starts playing "Moon over Miami.")*

THOMAS: I knew it! Damn! *(He paces.)* Cynthia, angel…Cynthia. Come out. *(Cynthia stops playing to listen.)*

THOMAS: Come out. I have something to tell you.

CYNTHIA: *(Opens the shutter.)* All right, Thomas. What do you have to say?

THOMAS: Step outside the window. I want to look at you. I want you to see my face.

(Cynthia steps out and faces Thomas.)

CYNTHIA: God knows why. Here I am.

THOMAS: You're a beautiful woman. I'd almost forgotten.

(She starts to leave.)

THOMAS: No. No. I didn't mean to offend you. I'm just nervous. Can't even find a quote from Job to cover it. Well…I'll never let Justin walk away with Daria. Maybe since you're standin' there, maybe you'd better sit down on something.

CYNTHIA: Will you get on with it! You're driving me crazy!

THOMAS: All right. Justin raped Daria and I'll kill him before I let him get near her again.

CYNTHIA: What possible reason do you have for saying that?

THOMAS: I know you don't believe what I say. I don't blame you. I've lied once already and sullied my credibility. But I swear on the Holy Bible. I swear on…on Aldebaran 'n Arcturus. I swear on my love for you. Justin raped Daria 'n I never told you 'cause I couldn't bear to see the look on your face I'm seein' right now.

CYNTHIA: *(Steps out of sight.)* Don't look at my face then. Say what you need to.

THOMAS: I saw Justin scratched and running through the field. His face was red and his clothes was tangled. And when I walked out of the corn, I saw Daria scratched, like me, caked with dirt, and she was grabbing your hand and crying, crying so hard no tears would come, crying so very hard I had to turn away. And in that moment, you blamed me. I saw it. And I thought Justin was young and foolish. I thought he'd got outta hand. Oh, I was a stupid man. I thought rape was no more than a cow bein' bothered by a bull she didn't want. I thought Justin was your special boy and gettin' him you didn't need me no more. I thought ten million thoughts in that one second. But Justin did a terrible thing and I let him go. And I let you despise me. And I can't tolerate it. I thought I could. I can tolerate almost anything. Great heat. The bitterest cold. And in my heart I thought Justin would come back and beg my forgiveness. But he didn't and I can't tolerate it! And if I so much as see Justin brush that girl's cheek, after all these months and months without you, I swear I don't know what I'll do.

(Cynthia comes into the yard and faces Thomas again.)

CYNTHIA: You wouldn't kill him?

THOMAS: Now that I see you standing right before me, all I want is for you never to go away. I won't kill Justin. If Daria knows it was him 'n still loves him, I'll let them leave—if that's what you want. Whatever your choice is, I'll abide by it.

CYNTHIA: Oh, Thomas. How will I know? I recall that Justin left a week before the rape and when we called him in Chicago with the news, he sobbed so hard he could barely speak.

THOMAS: You believe what you want. I watch people. Always have. I watched our son since the day he was born 'n I know how he runs 'n I know how he cries 'n I know he was wearin' the same blue suit we bought for his concert. *(Pause.)* I'll tell you something, Cynthia, if that boy had been overcome by passion 'n if he had come to me cryin' 'n beggin' for mercy, my heart would have gone out to him. But he planned it 'n he stalked that little girl 'n he never said a word.

CYNTHIA: I'm going in now, Thomas.

THOMAS: Do you believe me?

CYNTHIA: Let me alone for a while. I have to gather my thoughts.

(Cynthia climbs through the window and slowly closes the shutters. The lights dim.)

SCENE THREE

The fifth day. Late afternoon. Daria is waiting for Justin. She holds one large black umbrella over her head or perhaps it floats there. The clearing is clean. Daria is dressed neatly, a Sunday quality to her appearance. Justin appears.

JUSTIN: All right. We're even. You paid me back. I stood you up and now you've stood me up.

DARIA: I thought you'd left.

JUSTIN: I should have.

DARIA: You didn't come by last night. I waited up for you. You were pissed, right?

JUSTIN: Not really. However, it did take quite a while to change the car rental, the plane tickets, the hotel reservations, a couple of taping sessions, and a rehearsal.

DARIA: I'm sorry.

JUSTIN: Good.

DARIA: You were plenty mad at me, weren't you?

JUSTIN: Yes, I was. Actually, I was more hurt than mad. But I'm over it. Cool, calm. *(Holds out his hands.)* See? *(Roughly.)* Let's go.

DARIA: There's more to say.

JUSTIN: In the car.

DARIA: I am leaving. I can't tell you how glad I am. Everything's over. Look at those old witchy trees across there. I didn't even see the sparrows leave. Did you? The geese even took off. You can still hear them calling to each other. We all should leave, don't you think?

JUSTIN: Is there a bag or something?

DARIA: Not really. I sold all my umbrellas. Look—I made a hundred and fifty-eight dollars yesterday. I wanted to leave with money, you know?

JUSTIN: You're scared, aren't you, little gypsy? You don't have to be scared. I'll take care of you. You are pretty. I don't think I've ever seen you so pretty.

DARIA: That's a real compliment when you say it. You have lots of experience. Charlie says it too, but he's never had a girlfriend so I don't think he knows what he's talking about.

JUSTIN: Why are we talking about Charlie? I don't really feel like talking about Charlie. I arrange to come halfway across the continent—I insist on these stupid broadcasts to corn pickers and dairy farmers—just to see you and you're off with Charlie. You can't even see your way to meeting me on time! Well, I apologize. I really do. I thought I was just a wee bit more important to you. Well, I'm sorry. My mistake.

DARIA: Justin, that's not it.

JUSTIN: And there I was, packed and nervous like some idiot teenager, waiting for you—and you're off selling these *(Grabs her umbrella.)* ridiculous umbrellas—

DARIA: Hey careful!

JUSTIN: —with some local hick! Jesus!

DARIA: I thought you weren't mad.

JUSTIN: I'm not.

DARIA: Oh yeah?

JUSTIN: I'm not. I'm furious!

DARIA: Did you really come here just for me?

JUSTIN: Yes.

DARIA: That's the sweetest thing anyone's ever done.

JUSTIN: "I am no pilot, yet wert thou as far as that vast shore wash'd with the furthest sea, I would venture for such merchandise…"

DARIA: That's the Bible, right?

JUSTIN: It's Shakespeare. *Romeo* to *Juliet.*

DARIA: I'm leaving, but I'm not going with you, Justin. Charlie's offered to drive me to Missouri to see if I can locate my mother. I want to see what she's like. I want to see if she has gypsy hair and gypsy eyes. You were right again, see? She left a trail and I want to follow. I want to see her, Justin. And it isn't as crazy as it seems. We're going to hit all the flea markets along the way and the county fairs. This is the season. My mom might be at one of the fairs reading cards. She'd be easy to spot. There can't be too many gypsies in Missouri.

JUSTIN: A lovely girl like you. Of course you'd have someone. How stupid of me! You should have told me sooner. You let me go on and on like a fool!

DARIA: Not you, Justin. You could never be a fool. You're wonderful. So cool and handsome. Trailing secrets. I know you think you've come all this way for nothing, but you don't know how much you've done for me. You don't know. I couldn't do any of this without you. You brought the world to me. I was as stuck here as some dumb old crow in a cornfield. I couldn't step through the open door of a public bus, never mind ride in a truck alone with a boy. But you came here so cocky and sure of yourself, I thought, nothing's stopping him, right? Well, nothing's stopping me neither. It was my thoughts all along, just like you said. And you know what, I bet that's just how my mother felt too. Free. Walking down the road to who knows where.

JUSTIN: For God's sakes, Daria, you're not going to leave me for an eighteen-year-old boy!

DARIA: You're not taking this right.

JUSTIN: You know what the trouble is? You don't know what the fuck you're doing. You never have. You don't have a clue about other people's intent or your effect on them, and that's going to get you into a mess all over again. Now, let's look at this rationally, okay? Okay?

DARIA: Okay. But you're mad.

JUSTIN: No. I'm not. Now look, this Jericho boy, who the hell is he?

DARIA: Charlie.

JUSTIN: This Charlie kid, he's taking you around the country for free because he's such a kind, generous person. Is that right?

DARIA: It isn't free. I'll pay him for gas and stuff.

JUSTIN: But what does he really get?

DARIA: I guess about full value for gas and oil.

JUSTIN: Don't play the hick with me, little one.

DARIA: He gets my friendship. That's what he gets. He's helping me out.

JUSTIN: People don't do things for nothing. You're helping him out too, aren't you?

DARIA: Don't say it like that. You make it sound dirty and nasty. Like I'm selling myself or something.

JUSTIN: Do you love him?

DARIA: It's nothing like that!

JUSTIN: It's something! There's something. What is it? What's the matter?

DARIA: Your questions make me feel like a criminal.

JUSTIN: You're hiding something. Don't hide things from me.

DARIA: You get mad now. You never used to get mad.

JUSTIN: You're right. I won't get mad.

(Daria looks at him skeptically.)

JUSTIN: I won't. Cross my heart.

DARIA: I asked Charlie to lie down on top of me to see if I could get near a man. But I couldn't do it. As soon as I felt him pinning me down, I wanted to scream and tear his eyes out. You should have seen him jump back.

JUSTIN: Daria, you just can't do those things.

DARIA: I'll never be a proper woman.

JUSTIN: You are a proper woman. You're perfect.

DARIA: I'm going with him anyways. He thinks we'll try again, I can tell.

Maybe I should. But inside me, I don't know. But you would know, Justin. Tell me, am I doomed? Will I ever be like any woman with any man?

JUSTIN: Yes, yes. Of course you will.

DARIA: Maybe I'll always feel pinned down. Maybe I'll always feel that terror in my chest. Maybe every man who lies on top of me will be the man who raped me cold in that field.

JUSTIN: Charlie's virtually a stranger. You can't jump into bed with a stranger.

DARIA: Yeah, you should talk. You've had lots of girls, right? I bet you don't even remember half of their names?

JUSTIN: Girls and girls and girls.

DARIA: And they didn't make you want to scream, did they?

JUSTIN: Are you so sure? Are you so very sure, little one? What about my first love? Surely you remember. She was such a lovely girl. I was as close to her as I've been to any human being in my life. But she was young, wasn't she? That was a problem. She didn't know what she was doing. She sure was pretty. She had long silky hair, beautiful hair that fell smooth as water along her face. But she tortured me. Never gave it a second thought. She'd look at me with those black eyes and tell me about the boys she wanted to kiss. We'd go for walks—she'd take my hand and look up at me and ask if she'd ever "really, truly" fall in love. Can you imagine? With me standing there half dead on my feet for her? It killed me. I hated her. I tore up everything she ever gave me—cards, photos, little presents. She gave me a baby field mouse once, and I drowned it!

DARIA: Why I…gave you a baby field mouse…

JUSTIN: But every conscious moment of my life, I've been bound to her. And it's very ironic, Daria. I must tell you how ironic it is. It didn't destroy me. I've become a big success! I use it. Endlessly. In my music. That fury slices through me so I bleed in public until they applaud. It all comes from her, isn't that funny? And I've become quite well known. And it doesn't matter! Because no matter how many thousands and thousands of people sit at my feet, no matter how many lights burn over me on stage, it's always dark and cold and I'm alone.

DARIA: That girl you're talking about is me, isn't it?

JUSTIN: Yes.

DARIA: I don't want that girl to be me.

JUSTIN: It just happened. I couldn't help it. But I swear. I promise you. I can make things better. I swear. It won't be like Charlie or whatever his name is. You'll make love again. Under the sky with the stars spinning. I swear to God.

DARIA: I don't want it this way.

JUSTIN: Yes you do.

DARIA: No I don't, Justin.

JUSTIN: Everything about you tells me you do. The way you move, the way you take my hand and laugh, the way you swear—even your goddamn swearing. Christ! I miss your hair though, your long beautiful hair like a rippling stream along a smooth white shore. *(He touches her neck.)*

DARIA: Don't do that. Hell, Justin. It was you. It was. Why did it have to be you?

JUSTIN: Wait. Listen to me, Daria. Please!

(Daria turns and runs through the field to the farm. Justin pursues her. It is suddenly evening, large pale stars appear. Thomas holds his rifle and stands on the porch.)

DARIA: UNCLE THOMAS! *(She emerges into the yard.)* Uncle Thomas!

THOMAS: Yes, Daria.

(Justin comes out of the field, sees Thomas and starts back in.)

DARIA: Uncle Thomas.

THOMAS: Come out, Justin.

JUSTIN: Pop?

THOMAS: That's fine.

DARIA: I hate you. As much as I ever loved you. I hate you. *(She exits down the road.)*

JUSTIN: She doesn't mean that, Pop.

(Justin starts after Daria. Thomas readies his rifle. Cynthia comes out. Her words overlap with Thomas's.)

THOMAS: Son. Please.

CYNTHIA: Thomas, what is all this shouting about? Can't you two get along for one minute, honestly! Why, Justin honey, why are you standing there so pale?

THOMAS: Can't you admit it, son? Here between us? For God's sake, show me some sign of your goodness and contriteness—hell, of your decency as a human being. Say it, son. Say you raped Daria and you can't contain the sorrow you feel. That's all I need to hear.

CYNTHIA: Where's Daria? Is she all right? Thomas?

JUSTIN: I don't know what you're talking about, Pop.

CYNTHIA: Thomas?!

THOMAS: She's fine. Go back to bed!

CYNTHIA: There you go. Orders, pronouncements. Enough! I won't let this continue. Put that damn rifle away, Thomas, and stop persecuting your son. Do you enjoy terrorizing children? Is that it? *(She is in tears. She steps between Justin and Thomas.)*

THOMAS: Cynthia, you know that ain't true.

CYNTHIA: Who can believe a crazy old hermit who greets visitors down a rifle barrel, who's an unrepentant philanderer, a man who would kill his own son.

THOMAS: "I tell you God Himself has put me in the wrong. He has drawn the net around me."

JUSTIN: *(Puts his arm around his mother.)* That's Job, isn't it? Well, you're fooling yourself, old man. God hasn't drawn the net around you. You have. You did it all by yourself.

THOMAS: *(Turns to leave.)* You know, you better leave. For good. 'Cause I will kill you if I catch you here when I get back.

JUSTIN: Where are you going?

THOMAS: If you ever get within a mile of Daria, I'll put a bullet straight through your heart. Maybe I should use a silver one, 'cause I ain't sure you're human. *(He exits.)*

JUSTIN: I'm human. I'm your son. You won't kill me!

(Justin starts after Thomas. Cynthia puts her hand on Justin's arm.)

CYNTHIA: Where are you going?

JUSTIN: You're not going to let him get to Daria, are you?

CYNTHIA: Yes, I am. *(She touches his hair and face.)* My sweet son.

JUSTIN: Pop's crazy.

CYNTHIA: I'm extremely sad. My heart is breaking in two. I want you to leave.

JUSTIN: Daria loves me, you know.

CYNTHIA: Oh, son. I love you. Who loves you more than I do? Did you rape her? I have to know. I'm your mother. You grew inside me like a little hothouse plant. Is that where it all began? Was it there inside you, bred in the bone? Was it something I did? You're not listening, are you? You're all tensed up like an animal about to spring. What shall I do?

JUSTIN: Forgive me.

CYNTHIA: I can't. I'll listen to your music wherever you go. Always. I'll fill scrapbook after scrapbook after scrapbook. Just leave. Please.

JUSTIN: I told you you'd never understand! I can't leave her. I was the first man she ever had and she'll never forget me!

CYNTHIA: Then I do understand. *(Suddenly weary, she goes to her window.)* Must this go on and on? Are you waiting for my permission like a dutiful son? Well, I won't give it. Leave the poor girl alone. But your life's your own now. I wash my hands of you. I'm suddenly so tired. *(She climbs into the window.)* Perhaps God, if there is a God, will work it all out. But it's your choice. You can walk down the road and climb in your beautiful black car and drive away. But you want her, don't you? So there's always the shortcut through the field—and perhaps Daria, waiting there for you on the other side.

(Cynthia doesn't watch. Justin runs into the field. We hear Thomas mumbling, climbing slowly to his room.)

CYNTHIA: I never believed in destiny. My father was a pioneer. He always said, "Character is Destiny." Perhaps that's true. Perhaps.

(Cynthia closes the shutters. Thomas reaches the porch. He is out of breath. He looks into the yard and smiles. Cynthia plays "Blue Moon" and then stops. A large clear moon is overhead. The sky is filled with stars. The stage is bathed in moonlight.)

THOMAS: Cynthia? Cyn? You managed him. You always could. Thank the Lord. I hope he's on his way to fame and fortune. *(Pause.)* Daria didn't come back with me. But not for what you think. She don't hate me now. Not that you'll believe me. I let her go. Jericho boy pulled up in his pickup—damn if he ain't a big boy for eighteen, maybe I just don't remember. He leaned over and opened his door for her. I could've stopped her, but I figure it was better with a boy like that. She was off anyways. Got it in her blood, I suppose. *(Spots a movement in the field.)* Great God Almighty! *(He grabs his rifle.)* Look at the size of him! *(He takes aim.)* Steady now. Steadyyyy. *(He shoots once.)* Send your prayers to heaven, fella, your chicken-thievin', calf-killin' days are over! *(He fires again and again.)* Damn! Gotcha, ya ole bugger!

(Cynthia flings open the shutters. She is dressed in her black wedding dress.)

CYNTHIA: Oh Lord, Thomas! Did you shoot him?

THOMAS: Goddamn. I've done it. Shot the wild dog, dead in the field.

CYNTHIA: Oh my.

THOMAS: Size of a horse, I swear. Excuse me for going on. I know how you hate to hear about killing. But I must say, took three shots to get him down. He must've been a fierce creature. Fierce.

CYNTHIA: Yes. He must have been quite fierce. Oh, Thomas.

THOMAS: For a minute it felt so queer.

CYNTHIA: What?

THOMAS: Nothing I guess. I felt such sadness for a minute there. *(Shakes the feeling from himself. Gets the telescope and gazes at the stars.)* Look at them stars. Like the eyes of children up there. Huge, gentle creature children, bending over us, blinking their eyes. I ain't religious, but it looks so joyous

up there, and hopeful. But I can't live up there, can I? *(He puts his tele-scope away carefully.)* My heart's so full tonight, Cynthia...
(Cynthia has walked out into the yard. She brings two chairs and places them center stage. She sits on one, waiting in the moonlight.)
THOMAS: Never mind. Well. Best be getting to the field.
CYNTHIA: There'll be time enough for going into the field.
THOMAS: Cynthia, can I...? Shit.
CYNTHIA: Why Thomas, there's nothing I would like better, than for you to come down and sit with me here in the moonlight.
(Cynthia settles herself. Thomas starts down. Blackout.)

END OF PLAY

THE WONDERFUL TOWER
OF HUMBERT LAVOIGNET

ORIGINAL PRODUCTION

The Wonderful Tower of Humbert Lavoignet as originally produced by Capital Repertory Company in Albany, N.Y., opening on 12 April 1985 with the following cast and creative contributors:

JOHNNY SNOWALKER . . . . Maury Cooper
HUMBERT LAVOIGNET . . . . Barry Snider
CONSTANCE LAVOIGNET . . . . Phyllis Somerville
ARNOLD TYLER . . . . Richard Zobel
MICHAEL LAVOIGNET . . . . Michael Dolan

Director . . . . Susan Gregg
Scene and lighting design . . . . Dale F. Jordan
Costume design . . . . Lloyd Waiwaiole

CHARACTERS

JOHNNY SNOWALKER, itinerant Indian fiddler, seventies
HUMBERT LAVOIGNET, unemployed postal worker, opinionated, late forties, dreamer of unmanageable dreams
CONSTANCE LAVOIGNET, determined, sensual, direct, Humbert's wife, early forties
ARNOLD TYLER, telephone lineman, midthirties, dreamer of manageable dreams
MICHAEL LAVOIGNET, teenage son, athletic, high-strung

TIME AND PLACE

The play takes place over a few years in a small Midwest township.

SCENE ONE

Johnny Snowalker walks down a road playing "The Yellow Rose of Texas" on his fiddle. We also hear faint thunder. Johnny is quite old. He is wearing a cotton plaid shirt, a leather vest, Levis, boots. All are very worn. He has on a sweat-stained, wide-brimmed hat covered with metal pins from county fairs, ballparks, circuses, and so on. His fiddle case is strapped to his back and contains his belongings.

    Thunder, lightning. We hear a car approach, headlights. Johnny tries to hitch. The car whizzes by. Thunder, lightning. In a flash of lighting, we see Humbert Lavoignet, sitting on the porch of a small wood frame house. He is staring straight ahead and dressed in an undershirt and boxer shorts. Johnny catches sight of him.

JOHNNY: Well I'll be. *(Approaching.)* You sure spooked me, But then again, I never did see a ghost in skivvies. *(Humbert sits rigidly.)* Don't mean to be pushy but it's late, it's goin' to rain, and embarrassin' as it is—I'm lost. I mean, I been a trapper, a tracker, an escap-ee—yessir. And you can take my word for it, this is the first time I've been lost. Johnny Snowalker's the name *(Holds out his hand.)* and I'd be obliged if you would point me to the nearest town—one with a bar in it. This ain't a dry county, is it? *(He waits. Moves his hand before Humbert's unblinking eyes.)* I see you're lost yourself. Well, sorry to bother you. *(Passes his hand before his face as before.)* Maybe you'd like a song. Somethin' to cheer you up.
    (He plays "The Tennessee Waltz." Humbert stands up and starts turning around.)

JOHNNY: I'll be damned. A music lover.
    (When Johnny stops playing, Humbert stops turning. Johnny plays again. Humbert turns around and around. Johnny stops. Humbert stops. Johnny plays again, just a little bit longer than before.)

JOHNNY: *(This time, when Johnny stops, Humbert continues.)* Thatta boy. You should take up an instrument.
    (We hear a car approach. Headlights approaching.)

JOHNNY: I better get a move on. This'll be my ride.
    (Johnny holds out his thumb. All of a sudden the car turns on a red light, a siren. Johnny takes off. Car follows.)

JOHNNY: Aw shit!
    (Connie comes to the door and turns the porch light on.)

CONNIE: Honest to God, Humbert, what are you doing out there naked as a fool?! *(She puts on a faded cotton robe and comes out.)* Do you think you're dancing to music? That's thunder Humbert. Thunder and lightning. *(She goes out to fetch him.)* All right honey. Come on now. Let's get a move on.

(He resists.)

CONNIE: I'm serious.

(He keeps turning arms outstretched. Connie has to duck.)

CONNIE: For Christ's sakes, will you stop turning like a goddamn weather vane.

(He continues. She retreats to the porch.)

CONNIE: All right. You stay there and freeze to death. See if I care. Probably be better if you died anyways, what good are you like this! *(She watches him.)* Two years, Jesus, no one else goes to pieces 'cause they lose their job. I think this is just an excuse to sit around the house. I do. It was a crummy job, anyways. A mailman is not a big deal in the scheme of things Humbert. Not a speck in the eye of God. Why you just froze up like this because they replaced you with a truck, I'll never know. You always complained about your bicycle. Hell, I can't stand it. You look like an idiot.

(She is determined, and goes out to get him again. This time he marches stiffly, with Connie pushing. He gets up the porch.)

CONNIE: Good. Good. This is really exciting. What fun. Now sit, Humbert—sit! *(She whacks him at the waist so he bends and she can seat him.)* Fine.

(She wipes him off and wraps him in a blanket. It is raining. We hear it. Connie wipes herself off and lights up a cigar. She stares into the rain. An echo of Johnny's fiddle.)

CONNIE: March. Winter's tail end, winter's hiney. And where are we? You, well, just look at you…And me? I'm forty. Halfways to heaven. *(She sighs and smokes.)* You know, you're right, Humbie. The rain does sound like music. Like music and I want to dance.

(She watches the rain. Faint thunder. Faint lightning. Sound of rain. We hear a police siren. Lights dim.)

SCENE TWO

It is a Sunday morning in June, bright, sunny. We see the exterior of a modest frame bungalow. Humbert is seated on the porch wearing a cap, and a plaid shirt partially tucked into his jeans. He is barefoot and sits rigidly as before. Stage right is a small fruit and vegetable stand with a large sign that reads "HOMEMADE BREAD, FRESH DAILY." The stand has melons, cucumbers, beans, etc. A bag full of empty cans lies near the porch. Center stage, Connie and Arnie are finishing a poker game. Connie is dressed in her Sunday best, which includes a small hat. Arnie has on work clothes.

ARNIE: *(Happily.)* Okay. *(Lays down his hand with a flourish.)* Full house!

CONNIE: Royal flush!

ARNIE: Shit!

CONNIE: You owe me twenty dollars!

ARNIE: Well, goddamn, monkey-screwing son-of-a-bitch!

CONNIE: Arnie. You swear too much.

ARNIE: *(Getting his money out.)* I can't help it. My mother always swore.
  (Mike jogs in, checks his watch, and keeps jogging in place.)

CONNIE: *(To Mike.)* Hi, sweetheart.

ARNIE: Hey there, Mikey.

MIKE: Mike.

CONNIE: Run your ten miles?

MIKE: Almost.

ARNIE: Wish you'd come over here and play a hand or two with us.

MIKE: Runners in my bracket don't sit around playing cards.

ARNIE: We need a man here.

CONNIE: Amen.

ARNIE: I'm serious. I don't feel the right kind of satisfaction if I win from a woman.

CONNIE: Win! Cross that bridge when you come to it.
  (Car horn honks.)

CONNIE: Mikey, will you get that? Bread's at one-fifty. Cuke's four for a dollar.
  (Mike grabs a loaf from the stand and runs offstage. Connie clears the table.)

ARNIE: I don't know how you do it all, honey. You're a miracle worker.

CONNIE: I'm just a worker. Miracles bring in more than one-fifty a piece.

ARNIE: *(Counting through a wad of bills.)* You know, I'm stringin' these here telephone cables like they was party ribbons. Three-hundred-fifty new lines in the next three weeks…Township's really growing. I figure civilization's fillin' up my pockets…so I might as well spread it around a little.

CONNIE: We don't take charity.

ARNIE: Long-term loans?
  (Connie shakes her head. Humbert seems to twist in his seat, groans.)

ARNIE: You're a hard woman to please.

(She goes and sits next to Humbert.)

ARNIE: I said, she's a hard woman to please, old buddy. *(He sticks some money in Humbert's pocket. To Connie.)* All right. All right. We'll stick to Sunday poker.

(Mike comes in and hands her some change. He checks his watch and jogs in place.)

MIKE: I can take care of Dad now. You can still make the eleven o'clock service.

CONNIE: I suppose so. What time is it?

MIKE: Ten forty-five and forty-three seconds.

CONNIE: Don't give me the seconds. You make me feel rushed.

ARNIE: I'll run you over in my sexy white van.

MIKE: You don't have to. She's got time.

ARNIE: No trouble.

MIKE: I don't think it's necessary…

CONNIE: Stop acting like a pill, Mikey.

MIKE: Mike.

CONNIE: Honestly, I don't know what's gotten into you. I liked you better when you were a swimmer.

ARNIE: Shaved his head— *(Laughing.)* Bald as a baby's butt.

CONNIE: Oh my God. *(She is laughing too.)* Everyone thought he had ring-worm.

MIKE: Yeh? Well, it worked. I won two all-state trophies.

CONNIE: *(Laughing.)* I know. I know.

MIKE: Mom, quit it!

CONNIE: I'm sorry. It was funny. *(She continues laughing as she enters the house.)*

ARNIE: Still workin' off those hormones, eh, old buddy? *(Grabs Mike playfully.)*

MIKE: *(Getting free and stopping his watch. He's not jogging.)* I don't see why you guys still play poker. Must be boring. Just the two of you.

ARNIE: Nope.

MIKE: I bet my mom thinks it's boring.

CONNIE: *(Comes out with her purse and gloves.)* Let's get a move on. *(Kisses Mike.)* Love you, sweetheart.

MIKE: That perfume's awful!

CONNIE: You'll like it better when you're older! *(She pinches his cheek.)* Get all those cans together, hon. Arnie'll cash them in for us.

MIKE: Yes, Ma'am.

CONNIE: 'Bye, Humbert, I'll pray for you.

(Humbert twists in his chair but quiets down right away.)

ARNIE: See ya, Mikey.

(They exit. We hear the van pull away.)

MIKE: Mike. Goddamn it.

(Thunder rumbles. Humbert twists in his chair. Mike studies the sky and then watches his father.)

HUMBERT: Uhhhhh.

MIKE: Yeh, I think so, too. *(Bends close to him.)* Dad? Can you hear me?

HUMBERT *(Agitated, jerky movements.)* Uh! Uh!

MIKE: Aw, don't worry, Dad. It won't rain. It's only thunder. Summer thunder—not a cloud in the sky.

(Humbert is quiet. Mike sets his watch and starts jogging in place again near his father. After a while he sits down next to him.)

MIKE: You know, this really isn't a great time in my life, I don't know why…I grew two inches this month—that should make me feel good—guess I'm about as tall as you now—probably won't grow much more… School's out—that's okay—not a lot of kids around though, but runners in my bracket don't have time to hang out anyways. I'm up to ten miles a day—they say that's about as much as you should train… *(Pause.)* But I don't know, maybe I could push it. I never trust those experts anyways—one year they tell you ten miles the limit, the next year they're swearing twelve is better, or two. I hear it all the time on the radio, the final ultimate word, "Take this drug and save your life." Six months later they're back with emergency bulletins telling you, "This drug is a hazard to your health." I don't know what to think, Dad…things are getting to me…Even running. I like to be out there all alone, but then sometimes it gets lonely. I miss people, you know? Dad? *(He peers into his face, expectantly. Gets up again, checks his watch, and starts jogging.)* Another two-tenths of a mile.

(Thunder.)

MIKE: What do I know, maybe it will rain, right?

HUMBERT: Sounds like rain.

MIKE: Dad?

HUMBERT: Son, do you have any idea what time it is?

MIKE: Dad?! Oh, my God! *(He hugs him.)*

HUMBERT: *(Laughs.)* Calm down there. *(Patting him.)* Hey now, what is it? What's all the ruckus, boy?

MIKE: Wait 'til Mom hears about this.

HUMBERT: *(Testing his arms and legs.)* Funny, I feel like a bike that's been left out in the rain... *(Makes creaking noises and puts on an old man's voice.)* You better give me a hand, Son. I've aged overnight.

MIKE: Overnight? Are you serious?

HUMBERT: Sure. Why?

MIKE: Dad, you've been sitting there for six months!

HUMBERT: *(Sits back down.)* Holy Jesus! Connie! Connie!

MIKE: Mom's at church. I'll go get her.

HUMBERT: No, wait. Six months?

MIKE: Yeh.

HUMBERT: No shit. Six months. What did I do?

MIKE: Nothing.

HUMBERT: Did I say anything?

MIKE: Not a word.

HUMBERT: Six months.

    (Thunder rumbles.)

MIKE: *(Hugs him.)* I can't believe you're okay.

HUMBERT: *(Addressing the sky.)* Wouldn't let me up for air, would you, big fella? You sure as hell drive a hard bargain.

    (Thunder again.)

HUMBERT: Sorry.

MIKE: *(Pulls away.)* Who're you talking to?

HUMBERT: God.

MIKE: *(Backs farther away.)* Oh no.

HUMBERT: Hey, Mikey. Don't worry.

MIKE: Don't be crazy now. Please.

HUMBERT: I did talk to God, Son.

MIKE: Don't say that.

HUMBERT: All right. *(Long pause.)* But I did. I have a lot to tell you.

MIKE: Just don't.

HUMBERT: Hey there, kiddo, only an act of God could keep me away from you and your mother. You know that, don't you?

MIKE: For a minute I thought you were all better.

HUMBERT: He wants me to do something! He had a voice like...like a scathing flash of lightning and He let me see...everything! Lit up the world like a light bulb! Wonderful. It was wonderful! God told me to do something wonderful! *(Pause.)* You say it was six months?

MIKE: Yeh.

HUMBERT: Six months. Say, you know what?

    (Mike shakes his head.)

HUMBERT: I saw you. You spend too much time alone, Son. Running down those roads.

MIKE: Runners in my bracket have to be alone. Inner concentration.

HUMBERT: I see.

MIKE: I got the urge to go running right now.

HUMBERT: Michael.

MIKE: What?

HUMBERT: I'm not crazy. I can prove it. Sort of a cheap trick, though, like pulling a rabbit out of a hat. *(Pause.)* Okay. *(Takes a deep breath.)* You won three marathons. *(Waits. No effect.)* Not bad for a skinny fifteen-year-old kid.

MIKE: Thanks.

HUMBERT: I saw you run them, Son.

MIKE: Bullshit.

HUMBERT: I was there.

MIKE: You were here!

HUMBERT: Okay, by your own reckoning I was sitting here like dead wood for six months, but I'm going to tell you some things no one could possibly know, unless they were right there with you, looking out from your very own eyes...now just let me see...Aha! There was the tri-county high-school marathon in...in...what month are we in now?

MIKE: June.

HUMBERT: Right! Then the marathon must have been in April. I'll just picture it a minute. *(He closes his eyes and concentrates.)* It was April nineteenth in Ann Arbor. You pulled a muscle in your groin, hurt like hell, but you still qualified in two hours and forty minutes as I recall.

MIKE: Hey!

HUMBERT: Number twenty-one, right? Blue shorts, grey shirt. At twenty-one and-a-half miles you dropped five yards off the front pack, that muscle again. You thought you'd lost it for sure and then you did a mile in... *(Concentrating.)* four minutes forty-nine seconds and sprinted in first.

MIKE: That's right.

HUMBERT: I was real proud of you, Son. Hold on a second. There's more...

MIKE: How'd you really know that?!

HUMBERT: Mysterious are the ways of the Lord, eh, buddy boy? The next race was in Evanston, Illinois, by special invitation, no less...hmmnnn...and there was this guy you were real worried about...Roland...

MIKE: Roland Summers!. That's right!

HUMBERT: You'd heard he'd run the course in two hours thirty-five minutes and you just expected to shadow him, jack up the pace a bit, am I correct?

MIKE: Yeh. Absolutely!

HUMBERT: He snapped a tendon. *(Snaps his fingers.)* Just like that and you finished the race in two hours forty-two minutes twenty-six seconds... coming in first again!

MIKE: That's amazing! Fucking amazing!

HUMBERT: Damn straight it is! Amazing? I mean there I was, no job, no education to speak of. What could a man like me possibly do in the world? But He showed me. He grabbed me by the shoulders and showed me things...unbelievable things...the veins of silver in the ocean, sea creatures buried on the mountaintops, nations asleep with dreams drifting up like swirls of smoke. I saw fingers and eyes and a million hearts beating...I saw beating hearts! God wouldn't let me go.

MIKE: What does He want you to do?

HUMBERT: I don't know.

MIKE: A miracle?

HUMBERT: *(He roams around the yard, picking up things and discarding them.)* I don't know.

MIKE: Did He give you a hint?

HUMBERT: No. He took a poor, dejected human being and lifted me up... up... *(Pause. He looks up.)* Well, I'll be damned.

MIKE: What?

HUMBERT: I mean, He took me waayyyy up. Changed my perspective, so to speak. Made me smaller and bigger at the same time. *(Looks up.)* He lifted me up...hmmmmmmmm. *(He goes to the cans and opens the bag.)*

MIKE: What're you doing?

HUMBERT: Instead of a little fool with little dreams, He made me into a little fool with big dreams!

MIKE: Yeh?

HUMBERT: Son, I'm going to build the tallest, most beautiful damn tower you ever saw. A tower so high, it'll take your breath away...and woven...out of things...everything...a filigree tower. We have the makings right here! *(He pours out the bag of cans and goes through them.)* The silver ones here. Gold ones here! Silver ones here! Gold ones here! We'll need thousands of these. Scour the neighborhood!

MIKE: The town!

HUMBERT: The entire state!

MIKE: We'll need millions!

HUMBERT: That's a boy!

(They sort through the cans. We hear fiddle music, faintly: "The Yellow Rose of Texas." The lights turn blue.)

MIKE: Jeez, Dad, how did you know it was God? I mean, did He come right out and say *(Lowering his voice.)* HEY, MAN, THIS IS GOD?! I mean this is amazing. Fucking amazing. *(Pause.)* I didn't even think God worked this way anymore!

(Lights out.)

SCENE THREE

The stage is dark except for a spot on Johnny, far right. He is dressed as before, but we see him through the bars of a jail cell.

JOHNNY: I ain't a vagrant. Vagrants got no folks and no place to go. I know jest where I'm goin'. Got people there, too, and my people's people. Yessiree, I got an e-xact destination. Don't know the precise name, but I got an e-xact picture in my mind. There's a meadow with yeller grass up to my hip and a stream rollin' through to one side of the foothills of a two-peaked mountain. Snow line's pretty low. I like snow. Johnny Snowalker's the name. And I ain't no vagrant. My pa was a red-haired cowboy from Bisbee, Arizona, but my ma was a full-blood Laguna Pueblo. So I got people. I got resources too. You caught me a little short at the moment, but I'm a travelin' fiddler. What'd y'all like to hear? "The Tennessee Waltz?" "The Yeller Rose of Texas?" I play other states, too, "Arkansas Traveler," "Oklahoma," "Mississippi Mud!" For two bits I'll sing you a chant that'll make your corn grow right past your eye-brows...or what you got around here...deer?...moose?...I got an old Cree song good for moose. And that ain't all. In case of emergency, lookee here. Can you see my gold tooth? Yessiree like money in the bank. So though I'm very much obliged to ya fer the meals and the roof over my head, you can let me out now. I'm rested and I got to get goin'. Got plenty of ground to cover. *(Waits, paces.)* I really got to get a move on. Did you hear me? *(Shakes his head, gets out his fiddle, and tunes as he talks.)* I'll tell you what. I'll play ya a little refrain while you're thinkin it over. One, two, one, two, three, and... *(He sings, sometimes just fiddling, sometimes only singing the words to "Goin' Down this Road Feelin' Bad.")*

SCENE FOUR

It is late evening a week later. Stage right is lit with a blue light. Stars are out. We hear night sounds, crickets, etc. We can barely make out Mike filling the yard with row after symmetrical row of cans that gleam faintly to gold and silver in the starlight. The rows begin to look like the long, faceless lines of graves in an Army cemetery. Stage left is the darkened interior of Connie and Humbert's bedroom, now lit by starlight and perhaps porchlight. The room has dark walls and there is a bedside stand, a flower print on the wall. The paint is peeling. Humbert is wearing shorts and stands near the window. Connie lies in bed in a nightgown.

CONNIE: Humbert?

HUMBERT: Shhhhhhhh.

CONNIE: He can't hear us.

HUMBERT: I hope not.

CONNIE: ...and he can't see us...

HUMBERT: Bet he knows what's going on though.

CONNIE: I hope the whole wide world knows... *(She stretches languorously.)* Mmmmmmm. Come on back to bed, honey.

HUMBERT: You bet!
    (He jumps in bed. They kiss.)

HUMBERT: Lord, I wish I was a pervert!

CONNIE: Humbert!

HUMBERT: Well I do.

CONNIE: What are you talking about?

HUMBERT: If I were a pervert, we could do all kinds of things...Grrr... *(He tickles her.)*

CONNIE: You fool.
    (They kiss.)

CONNIE: I love you.
    (They kiss again.)

HUMBERT: Wait just a minute there! *(He bolts out of bed and runs offstage.)*

CONNIE: Honest to God, Humbert, where are you going?! *(She waits. He doesn't answer. She stretches again, gets up, and goes to the window.)*

HUMBERT: *(From offstage.)* Get back in bed. Quick!

CONNIE: Okay. Okay.
    (Connie gets into bed. Humbert rushes back in, carrying a beer can on a

plate. A flower is stuck through the opening. He presents it to her with a flourish.)

HUMBERT: You see, I didn't forget just what you like after a good…

CONNIE: Humbert!

HUMBERT: After a good Humbert!

(Humbert gets into bed. They sit there, sipping beer for a moment.)

CONNIE: I can barely believe we're lying here together again.

HUMBERT: I know.

CONNIE: I thought I'd lost you forever. I'm telling you, I can't believe it. *(She tries to hug him. It is awkward because of the beer.)* Put that thing on the floor a minute.

(He does.)

CONNIE: Now hold me.

(He does.)

CONNIE: Tighter, tighter.

HUMBERT: Do you believe it now?

CONNIE: Not yet. Tighter. Tighter. There!

(Humbert kisses her.)

CONNIE: You taste like beer. But I like it…and the sheets smell like you…. MMmmmmmm. I'm going to leave them on this bed 'til they fall apart. Then I'll be sure you're back for good.

HUMBERT: Of course I'm back for good. I couldn't stay away from a woman like you.

CONNIE: Well, it happened once.

HUMBERT: You're a good woman, Con.

CONNIE: Not always.

HUMBERT: Always.

CONNIE: There were times…

HUMBERT: Shhhhhhh.

CONNIE: You should know.

HUMBERT: I know.

CONNIE: Humbert…

HUMBERT: I know. You mean times at the Strathmoor Lounge? There you were, silver earrings, low-cut dress, soft blue lights, slow sulky music. You were dying to dance and a whole lot more.

CONNIE: *(Nervous. Lights a cigar.)* Who told you.

HUMBERT: I just know.

CONNIE: People can't wait to talk, can they?

HUMBERT: It's behind us.

CONNIE: Sure, just like your "trouble."

HUMBERT: It's all behind us.

CONNIE: I wish I could say I'm sorry.

HUMBERT: I know.

CONNIE: It's been worse for Mikey. He's quiet. But he's loyal to you. Men with the men, you know. He's trying real hard to be a man—for you.

HUMBERT: Don't smoke…

CONNIE: You should talk to him, Humbie. He wants so much to please you. He shouldn't drop everything like that, though. Cans, cans, cans. We can't live off five-cent deposits!

HUMBERT: Put out that cigar, please.

CONNIE: Can't live off my breads and pies either.

HUMBERT: Did you hear me?

CONNIE: The cigars? Yes, I heard you.

HUMBERT: I don't like to see you smoking a cigar.

CONNIE: Really? Well, that's just why I started. I figured you'd get pissed off and wake up.

HUMBERT: You can stop now.

CONNIE: Now I like 'em.
   (Silence.)

CONNIE: Bought them with my own money.
   (Pause.)

CONNIE: When it's your money again, I might consider stopping. *(Show-blows out a long stream of smoke.)*

HUMBERT: I see. *(Gets out of bed.)*

CONNIE: You've been up and around a week now.

HUMBERT: I know.

CONNIE: *(Just about in tears.)* Humbie, I don't want to argue about this. Not now. But it's spilling out of me. I can't help it. I've been so worried.

HUMBERT: I know.

CONNIE: Stop saying that. You don't know.

HUMBERT: *(Looking out the window.)* Just believe in God, honey.

CONNIE: What?

HUMBERT: Trust in the Lord. Isn't that how they say it? God? Lord? The Almighty?

CONNIE: I don't believe my ears. You telling me to believe in God! That's a laugh. I'm the one who goes to church and talks to Him every damn week.

HUMBERT: I know.

CONNIE: There you go again. Mister Know-it-all.

HUMBERT: JUST BE-LIEVE IN GOD!

CONNIE: Don't you dare stand there yelling at me about God! You coward, you took the easy way out. Sitting there paralyzed while I slaved myself to death! God! You can't put everything on God! Next you'll be telling 'em it was God's will you sat there for six months like a bump on a log. Wouldn't that be convenient!

(Humbert hangs his head. Connie goes to him and brings him to the bed.)

CONNIE: Oh, Humbie, it wasn't God who kept you away from us, it was your own fear of facing the present.

HUMBERT: I would never do anything to hurt you and Mikey if I could help it.

CONNIE: I forgive you. It's only human to want to escape. And I'll tell you a secret. Something you don't know, Humbie. That very evening before you opened your eyes, I was out riding with your best friend, and I opened the window wide and let the wind blast through, and I turned up that radio loud as I could and I watched the lights fly by and I put my foot right on top of Arnie's on the gas pedal and pressed down until we were going one hundred ten miles an hour. And the world sped by and there was music and the warm body of a man next to me. Let me tell you, Humbert, I thought I was close to God too. But it wasn't God in me. It was only me, not wanting to face what was back here.

HUMBERT: I'm prepared to face whatever I have to.

CONNIE: Are you going to look for a job tomorrow?

HUMBERT: Connie...

CONNIE: Are you?

HUMBERT: Connie, I love you.

CONNIE: And?

HUMBERT: And I can't make things better. *(He gets up and walks out into the yard.)*

CONNIE: Humbert. You have to. Humbert. Do you hear me? Humbert. Oh, Humbie. You bastard! *(She starts ripping the sheets off and throws them on the floor.)*

HUMBERT: *(Goes to Mike and puts his hand gently on the boy's shoulder.)* Hello, Son.

MIKE: Hey there, Dad.

HUMBERT: What're you doing?

MIKE: I don't know. I just felt like seeing them all spread out. Like a design.

HUMBERT: Standing in a row.

MIKE: Yeh. Kinda like soldiers. *(He salutes Humbert.)* Right?

HUMBERT: *(Sadly, salutes him back.)* Right.

(Lights dim.)

SCENE FIVE

It's a cool October day. Downstage in a spot is Humbert in fall work clothes hauling a large, unwieldy sack of bottles and cans. He is awkwardly carrying some window screens under his other arm. Johnny Snowalker enters and heads right over.

JOHNNY: Howdy there, Mister. Need some help?

HUMBERT: Think you can handle it?

JOHNNY: Ain't as puny as I look. Johnny Snowalker's the name.

HUMBERT: Guess I could use a hand. Thanks. It's only a few steps.

JOHNNY: *(Taking the sack. It's heavier than he thought.)* You must be the fella is building the tower.

HUMBERT: What makes you think that?

JOHNNY: Fellas over to the bar was arguin' 'bout you haulin' garbage on foot.

HUMBERT: Garbage, eh?

JOHNNY: Ain't too many folks on foot around here. Mostly cars zoomin' by.

HUMBERT: Arguin'…eh?

JOHNNY: Some said you was makin' art. Some said it was a pile of junk and a public nuisance. Figured I'd like to see for myself. So I been lookin' fer you.

HUMBERT: Well, I'm the one you're looking for, for all that's worth. Humbert Lavoignet's the name.

JOHNNY: Like to climb the tower.

HUMBERT: It's hardly built yet.

JOHNNY: How high you plannin' to go?

HUMBERT: That's a good question.

(They arrive at the yard. Lights up. We see one huge foot of the base of the tower, taller than the house, rising out of sight. It is made of cable, window frames, bottles, and cans. The stand has pumpkins, squash, apples. In addition to the bread sign is a smaller sign that reads, "HOMEMADE PIES.")

HUMBERT: Well…here we are… *(Sardonically.)* That's my wife's thriving business over there and this is my wonderful tower.

JOHNNY: *(Goes over to it.)* Beautiful piece of work.

HUMBERT: How about a slice of pie and some coffee?

JOHNNY: Much obliged. Sure would like to climb the tower.

HUMBERT: Help yourself. *(He goes in for some pie.)*
(Johnny makes his way up the tower.)

HUMBERT: *(Comes out with the food.)* How're you doing up there?

JOHNNY: Can't see far enough yet. *(Comes down.)*

HUMBERT: What're you looking for?

JOHNNY: Some of my people.

HUMBERT: I know the area fairly well. So if you tell me where they're staying…

JOHNNY: Don't reckon I know its name now. But I can describe it to you. *(Pause.)* There was a meadow, violets mixed with the grass. When I saw 'em, children was playin' tag. The men was fishin' 'n drinkin' beer by a little runnin' stream that come down from the mountain. A two-peaked mountain. The wimin was makin' fires and gossiping. I could see it so clear. I was climbing up to the snowline. Always loved the snow, seemed like magic to me, 'cause I was born on the desert. I was so high I could see my friend lyin' with a pretty little woman in the tallest part of the grass, yesiree. I can still picture it in my mind, clear as can be.

HUMBERT: When were you there?

JOHNNY: 'Bout fifty years ago.

HUMBERT: I see. *(Pause.)* And you think they're still at this place?

JOHNNY: Not this place e-xactly. Place like it though. That two-peaked mountain'd be easy to spot.

HUMBERT: There's no mountains for at least two hundred miles.

JOHNNY: If the tower was high enough now…

HUMBERT: Maybe you wouldn't recognize your people. The children would be all grown and your friend with the woman would be an old man by now.

JOHNNY: Oh, no. They'd be e-xactly the same. See, I saw it all so clear, way up there by the snowline. I saw those ranchers pull up with their trucks. I saw 'em pour kerosene on the grass and light it with torches. Didn't take to Indian people camping there, see. A wall of fire flew up and my people burned and the men were gunned down in the stream. So I know they never got old. They're the same. Only I got old. I'm alone now, so I been lookin' fer them.

HUMBERT: But, old man, they died.

JOHNNY: Oh, no. I don't believe in death. Live things always spring back. Just in a better place. Each according to its nature. If they lived in woods, it's woods. If they lived on the plains, it's grass rollin' forever under their feet. *(Pause.)* Tell you what. Winter's comin'. I'll stay 'n help you build that tower high as you like. By spring maybe I could see clear to the Pacific Ocean.

HUMBERT: I'd really like to do that for you, but we're barely scratching through here ourselves.

(Car horn honks.)

JOHNNY: I'm a hard worker, if that's what you mean.

(Car honks impatiently.)

CONNIE: *(Comes onto the porch.)* Aren't you going to get that! Bread's one-fifty and pie's sixty cents a slice. That'll be sixty cents for you too, Mister.

JOHNNY: *(Jumps up.)* I'll git that, Missus. *(He goes offstage.)*

CONNIE: Humbert?

HUMBERT: It's all right, Con. *(Pause.)* His name's Johnny Snowalker. Tells quite a tall tale.

(Johnny runs back onstage without saying a word and strikes a blatantly corny pose next to the tower. He runs offstage again.)

CONNIE: Birds of a feather!

JOHNNY: *(Reappearing.)* Got two-fifty fer the bread and sold a whole pie. Got one-fifty fer the photo, too. So here's your sixty cents, plus some extra.

CONNIE: I can't believe my eyes.

JOHNNY: Hope you don't got nothin' against Indians, Missus. 'Cause I was tellin' your husband here I'm hard up fer a wintering place.

CONNIE: It's awfully small here, Mr. Snowalker.

JOHNNY: I'm clean 'n I get up early. Hardly eat a thing. You can see I'll earn my keep and put money in your pocket. *(Pause.)* Tell you what. If I don't work out, you can kick me out in the middle of a snowstorm.

CONNIE: *(Laughs.)* I like the way you talk.

JOHNNY: You bet. I'm a real entertainer. I've fiddled for every kind of person, junkie to gentleman.

HUMBERT: He'd help with the tower.

CONNIE: Don't talk to me about that damned tower!

HUMBERT: I'll finish it faster, Con.

CONNIE: *(Pause.)* Guess you have a deal, Mr. Snowalker. Mr. Snowalker can share the living room with you, Humbert, so you won't have to sleep alone anymore.

JOHNNY: Much obliged.

CONNIE: *(Starts in and then comes out again.)* Can you play dance music, Mr. Snowalker?

JOHNNY: Sure can.

CONNIE: How about hymns?

JOHNNY: Got just the one!

CONNIE: Why don't you come play your fiddle back by the kitchen for a while. I sure could use the company.

(They walk around back. We hear Johnny tuning. He begins "Amazing Grace" and goes to "Will the Circle Be Unbroken." We hear it faintly. Humbert climbs the tower.)

HUMBERT: Quite a view. Township's growing. People are spreading over the hills like molasses. There's ole Arnie stringing up a pole. Working like a son-of-a-bitch. Hey there, Arnie! Over here, old buddy! *(Waits.)* Guess not. *(Turns.)* Look at that stretch of maple. Sugar maple, black maple, silver maple, red maple, mountain maple, maple paradise...Uh...there's the highway crew struttin' around...Think they're hot shit...Hey, isn't that Mikey smoking near the trailer?! Michael! Son! Up here! Heyy! Smoking'll slow you down! Hey there. Look up! *(Pause.)* He'll look up. They all will. You just wait. This tower will stop people dead in their tracks. Pink in the morning and orange in the evening. When the sun hits this tower, it'll look like a pillar of fire.
(Lights out.)

SCENE SIX

It is midwinter and Connie and Arnie are driving along in the van. Arnie has on a plaid lumberjack's jacket. Connie is loosening her winter outer clothing. Perhaps a screen projection behind gives the impression of driving through a winter forest.

CONNIE: I'm halfway to heaven, Arnie.
ARNIE: *(Pats her leg.)* Thanks, darling. I like to be with you too.
CONNIE: Halfway to heaven means I'm forty, Arnie.
ARNIE: Oh.
CONNIE: It means one foot in the grave!
ARNIE: It ain't that bad.
CONNIE: Oh, yeh? How old are you?
ARNIE: How old do I look?
CONNIE: Thirty-eight, thirty-nine, maybe.
ARNIE: Thanks a lot. I'm thirty-six.
CONNIE: There! You see, forty's old!
ARNIE: Not on you.
CONNIE: You better pull over.
ARNIE: You ain't mad, are you?
CONNIE: Find a nice, quiet spot. I want to talk to you.
ARNIE: We're talking.
CONNIE: I want to be still...and talking.
ARNIE: Sure thing. *(He continues driving.)*

CONNIE: Well, not next year.

ARNIE: Hold your horses. I don't want Humbert peering down at us from his goddamned tower and gettin' the wrong idea. *(He pulls over.)* There. You see. Open the window a little so you can breathe some fresh air. *(They sit in silence. Arnie whistles to himself.)* Well, not next year, honey. What do you got on your mind?

CONNIE: I don't know where to begin.

ARNIE: I do. *(He pulls her toward him and kisses her.)*

CONNIE: Arnie!

ARNIE: Shit!

CONNIE: *(Laughs.)* What're you swearing for?

ARNIE: I surprised myself. I've been thinking about doing that for so long. I'm sorry. I'm sorry. *(He looks around guiltily.)* I don't know what got into me. I apologize.

CONNIE: Fine.

ARNIE: You looked so soft and sad there. Really, I'm sorry. *(He kisses her again.)* I can't help it.

CONNIE: Have you lost your mind?

ARNIE: Yep. *(Pause.)* Hey, wait. Why aren't you fighting me?

CONNIE: Why should I?

ARNIE: What about Humbert?

CONNIE: It's got nothing to do with him. This is between you and me.

ARNIE: Hey. That ain't right. You're married.

CONNIE: You fool. You were the one who kissed me.

ARNIE: But you know my reputation.

CONNIE: Yes. I do.

ARNIE: Well?

CONNIE: You're perfect. *(Silence.)* What's wrong?

ARNIE: *(Suspicious.)* No woman ever called me perfect before.

CONNIE: You are for me. Perfect. A light-hearted lover, nothing heavy, nothing serious.

ARNIE: Just a beam of light in the darkness.

CONNIE: So what do you think?

ARNIE: Well, shit, I dunno. *(Pause.)* Do you like me?

CONNIE: Honestly, Arnie. Of course I like you. I like your shiny hair, I like your big old hands. *(She kisses him.)* And I like your warm, warm heart. *(They kiss.)*

CONNIE: Well?

ARNIE: Just so you keep in mind how I am with women.

CONNIE: Right.

ARNIE: Can't settle down.

CONNIE: That's a good thing.

ARNIE: I really like you, Connie. I think you're real pretty. Sexy too.

CONNIE: You too.

ARNIE: And you can forget about this halfway to heaven bit, darlin'. 'Cause we're talkin' all the way.

> (He laughs. They kiss.)

ARNIE: But about Humbert…

CONNIE: Let's get this straight once and for all, Arnold Taylor, I don't want to leave Humbert. I just want to love you.

SCENE SEVEN

> It is a late morning in May. Johnny is taking down the "HOMEMADE BREAD" sign. He props it against the porch. Then he nails up a sign that reads "TOWER PHOTOS $2.50." Humbert stands in the yard, ripping a dress of Connie's into long strips. Mike enters with a window frame.

HUMBERT: Arnie Taylor for Christ's sake!

MIKE: Hey, Dad. What're you doing?! That's Mom's!

HUMBERT: So what. She didn't want it. She left it behind. She left behind everything she didn't want, didn't she?!

> (Mike is silent.)

HUMBERT: No use letting it go to waste. (He wraps a strip around his hand and flexes it.) Helps my grip. It's like grabbing hot pokers up there. We'll have to start working late again.

> (Mike takes the cloth and holds it for a moment and gives it back.)

HUMBERT: You could have gone with her. But you didn't, Son. Man with the men, right?

MIKE: Right.

> (Car horn honks. Johnny runs out.)

MIKE: Maybe you could've explained things to her.

HUMBERT: And have her take me for a madman?!

MIKE: She took you for a fool!

HUMBERT: Watch your mouth, young man.

JOHNNY: (Returns.) We got pickled watermelon rind?

HUMBERT: I think we're out? Mikey?

(Mike shrugs.)

JOHNNY: *(Grabs some jars from the stand and rushes out.)* That's okay!

HUMBERT: Look. Things happen for a reason. It's painful, but we had to learn the difference between a church-going and a God-fearing woman! Where did church-going get her anyways? For a ride in Arnie Taylor's van, that's where! Arnie Taylor for Christ's sake! Jesus! *(He grabs the rags and goes up the tower.)*

JOHNNY: *(Reenters.)* Wanted green tomatoes, but I sold 'em three jars of strawberry jam fer four-fifty!

MIKE: Great.

JOHNNY: We're scrapin' by with grace 'n promise.

MIKE: Grace and promise isn't enough. I want money.

JOHNNY: We'll be okay.

MIKE: I don't think so. *(Pause.)* Hey, Johnny?

JOHNNY: Yep.

MIKE: I've been thinking of digging ditches.

JOHNNY: Fine occupation.

MIKE: The guys said I could lay blacktop too…I'd make enough money to live on.

JOHNNY: So you're thinking of leaving?

MIKE: I'm almost sixteen…It'd be a good thing.

JOHNNY: Hard to tell what's a good thing.

MIKE: You don't seem to have much trouble. You found the tower and figured that was a good thing…

JOHNNY: Maybe so. Maybe-not. Can't judge the end from its beginning. You just got to wait around and see.

MIKE: Don't give me one of those Indian answers.

JOHNNY: I ain't dodgin', if that's what you mean. I have learned that from personal experience, Sonny. Take a tornado for instance.

MIKE: Oh, come on.

JOHNNY: No, listen now, would you say that's a bad thing? Yes or no?

MIKE: Never seen one.

JOHNNY: I seen a lot. Looks plenty bad up close. The air goes green, then black. Makes a grindin' noise like a freight train passin' overhead. It'll flatten your refrigerator and wrap it around a tree; lift a man from his living room chair, break every bone in his body and set him down again…now that's pretty bad, ain't it?

MIKE: Yeh, I guess so.

JOHNNY: But then again… A tornado brought my uncle a pony once…all saddled up and everything, a real pretty little thing. Landed right in the front yard. He rode it around for two years; set up a little pony ride for kids; did well; bought his wife a hair dryer and added on to the house. That little pony brought him nothin' but luck. So now, would you still say that tornado was a bad thing?

MIKE: Not for him.

JOHNNY: Maybe. Maybe not. 'Cause later some rich man pulled up in his Chevrolet and called that little pony by its rightful name. It sped right out from under my uncle; broke two of his vertebrae, lost his business, and ended up spending five years in a wheelchair.

MIKE: Oh, God.

JOHNNY: See what I mean? You got to wait around.

MIKE: No way! Look what happens if you wait around! Disaster! You got to take things into your own hands. Nature's too unpredictable.

JOHNNY: What is there besides nature?

MIKE: Man.

JOHNNY: Man's different than nature, eh?

MIKE: Yeh, man can take things into his own hands. He can build something good and it's good and it makes him happy and he can add on to it piece by piece. And each piece he adds gets better and better…unless he fucks up. Take this, for example. *(He indicates the tower.)* The higher we go, the darker it gets.

(Humbert jumps down from the tower, agitated.)

HUMBERT: Johnny, step over here a minute, will you? Now take a good look. *(He indicates a place on the tower. They stare at it for a moment.)*

JOHNNY: I don't see nothin' much.

HUMBERT: Does that tower look shorter to you?

MIKE: Shorter?

HUMBERT: Yes, shorter! Where's the tape!

(Johnny hands it to him. Humbert goes up the tower.)

HUMBERT: Maybe I am a stark-raving, senile, paranoid, hallucinating maniac, but goddamn it, Johnny, I could have sworn we added three feet to that center section yesterday!

JOHNNY: I reckoned we did too. Maybe we should write down jest how high we built, so it won't trouble us.

(Humbert comes down again.)

HUMBERT: It's shorter and the top bolts are wobbling around like an old man's tooth. The wind wouldn't have done that.

JOHNNY: No wind last night.

MIKE: Neighborhood kids.

HUMBERT: Why would they do a thing like that?

JOHNNY: Pranks maybe.

MIKE: Johnny, do you got a wrench?

HUMBERT: Well, that does it.

JOHNNY: Sure thing. *(Gives it to him.)*

HUMBERT: We'll work nights. Right, Mikey?

MIKE: Right. *(Starts up.)*

HUMBERT: It's awful hot up there. You want these? *(Starts to unwrap rags.)*

MIKE: No.

HUMBERT: *(Watching him, to Johnny.)* Will you look at him. Physical. That boy is physical. *(To Mike.)* We'll work nights like we did last summer. That was fun, wasn't it?

(Mike is silent.)

HUMBERT: We had a good time. It was like a party. Wasn't it like a party, Mike? The stars sparkling overhead, trucks and vans and cars pulling up. Just like a drive-in movie. They'd have a beer, watch, make out. *(He laughs, but it turns sad.)* I really liked that. Connie'd make pies and cakes. We'd turn on the radio. The pies and cakes and music and Connie. Just like a party, wasn't it, Johnny?

JOHNNY: Yessiree.

HUMBERT: Goddamn party. *(Angrily removes the rags, almost in tears.)* I need a break. Johnny, let's go. Mikey!

JOHNNY: We could hit them two bars down the road. They got plenty of bottles and cans and I know for a fact they'd give us a beer or two fer a coupla my songs.

HUMBERT: Get your fiddle and let's get a move on. You coming, Mikey?

(Johnny gets his fiddle and begins to tune it.)

MIKE: I'll just tighten these bolts.

HUMBERT: Don't get yourself a sunstroke.

MIKE: You guys go ahead. You need it.

HUMBERT: We do indeed.

JOHNNY: Ready?

HUMBERT: Yep.

(Johnny starts off. Humbert hesitates.)

HUMBERT: Mike!

MIKE: Yeh?

HUMBERT: I'll bring something back for you.

MIKE: That's okay.

HUMBERT: I'd like to.

MIKE: Do what you like.

HUMBERT: *(Can't bring himself to leave.)* Yeh. Okay. Take it easy.

MIKE: I will.

HUMBERT: Keep an eye out.

MIKE: Good-bye, Dad.

(Humbert leaves. Everything is quiet. Perhaps we hear birds or traffic far away, that's how still it is. Then we hear loud banging and wrenching. Pieces of the tower shower down. Humbert reenters, guiltily.)

HUMBERT: Hey, Mikey, I can't leave you up there alone.

(A big chunk of the tower falls, just missing him. Humbert falls back.)

HUMBERT: Hey!

(Mike scrambles down the tower and runs to him. He helps his father up.)

MIKE: Dad? Dad? Are you all right? You okay?

HUMBERT: *(Dusts himself off, shaken.)* I told you those bolts were loose!

MIKE: I'm sorry.

HUMBERT: Goddamn it! Look at the mess!

(They both look around. Pause.)

HUMBERT: Hey, wait. You weren't tightening those bolts, were you?

(Mike looks him dead in the eye but doesn't respond.)

HUMBERT: Tell me you were tightening those bolts. Please… *(Grabs him.)* Go ahead. Tell me! In the name of God!

MIKE: *(Takes his hands away.)* No. I wasn't tightening the bolts.

HUMBERT: What do you mean?!

MIKE: I wasn't tightening the bolts…I was loosening them.

HUMBERT: Michael. Son…why?

MIKE: It's junk, Dad. It's garbage. You've been burying us in a pile of junk, a garbage heap. The work of God! How could this be the work of God?

HUMBERT: Hey, now, just a minute. You believe me, you do, don't you, kiddo?!

MIKE: Nobody believes you. Nobody cares. People see me coming and won't open the door. I work my butt off for you. I make a fool of myself day after day. They laugh in my face and the kids…Forget it!

HUMBERT: Just wait, Mikey. It'll happen. Give me a few more days, another month!

MIKE: Another day, another month, another year, who cares?! In fifty years, a hundred people'll be zooming around in rocketships looking at the stars, and this? After all we've been through, this'll be gone, forgotten, buried under a forty-lane highway! And you'll be dead and me and Mom'll be dead and what will it all matter, Dad? Let's go and get Mom. Please. Let's bring her back and start over.

HUMBERT: I can't.

MIKE: Yes, you can! Dad?! *(Pause.)* What do you think you're doing anyways? You're just junking up the landscape. If you want people to see God so bad why don't you go plant a tree and have 'em file by to watch it grow?!

HUMBERT: Because one tree isn't enough! It's the forest they have to see before the Earth gets poorer and uglier and the wild animals disappear, and the sky's poisoned and the land stripped bare they have to see a hundred miles of trees! You think I'm a fool and a dreamer like your mother does, but I'm a realist! Mikey, we can't grab people by the scruff of the neck and make them stoop to see a tree—they'd just argue about the best bug spray... But we can lift them up to see a whole forest! We can! And what's more, if we have to, we can do it with what people don't want anymore—with what they leave behind. We'll take it all, Mikey, and we'll use it!

(Johnny reenters and scans the fallen pieces of tower.)

MIKE: We is one too many, Dad. *(Mike gathers some things to go.)*

HUMBERT: What're you doing?

(Mike leaves.)

HUMBERT: Hey! Wait a minute! *(To Johnny.)* Where is he going?! *(Starts after him.)* Michael! Wait!

SCENE EIGHT

It's an evening in July. Thunder. Lightning. The yard is empty of all debris. Everything has been used up. We see the house, the porch. Humbert sits glumly in his boxer shorts and undershirt. Johnny stands nearby, watching the sky.

JOHNNY: Storm'll be here in...oh I'd say about eight-and-a-half minutes.

HUMBERT: Please.

JOHNNY: When the storm leaves, maybe I should foller it.

HUMBERT: You mean leave?

JOHNNY: Can't see there's much for me to do. We're bogged down.

HUMBERT: It's a pause.

JOHNNY: A pause then. Still can't see much for me to do. Everything's used up, everyone's given up.

HUMBERT: It's a goddamn pause, I'll get it back. I always get it back.

JOHNNY: I can't pause.

HUMBERT: Now why can't you pause?

JOHNNY: I'll drop dead.

HUMBERT: I feel like a goddamn straight man here. Why will you drop dead?

JOHNNY: I'm old. Old people die. A chill, a dampness, the slightest breeze—why, anything can carry you off when you're old. Especially waiting.

HUMBERT: I'll go with you.

JOHNNY: Fine company. Not only don't you know where you're goin', you don't hardly know what you're doin'.

HUMBERT: God wouldn't have given me something impossible, would He?

JOHNNY: It's your vision, Sonny.

HUMBERT: The eternal optimist. The eternal optometrist. I need my vision checked.

(Thunder and lightning.)

HUMBERT: I looked for a sign, all right. What'd I get? Bottles and cans. Lighting flashed. Thunder rolled. They looked like gold and diamonds to me. That was my sign.

JOHNNY: Great Medicine is full of signs. The whole world speaks to you if it's truly great medicine.

HUMBERT: Is that so?

JOHNNY: Look for a sign.

(Humbert stumbles around the yard. He picks up a strip of metal. Shakes his head, drops it, picks up some newspaper.)

HUMBERT: Nawwww… *(Picks up a stick.)* Is this a sign?

JOHNNY: If it's a sign you know it.

HUMBERT: So what the fuck's your sign? Do you have one?

JOHNNY: Yep.

HUMBERT: Wordy old coot, aren't you? Well, what is it?

(Lightning flashes. A roll of thunder.)

JOHNNY: You. *(Gets up and dances.)* Hey-ya-ah-na-ah! Hey-ya-ah-na-ah!
Ku-ru-tsu-eh-ah-eh-na! Kuru-tsu-eh-ah-eh-na!
To the east below,
to the south below,
the winter people come.

HUMBERT: There's nothing left! NOT A WIRE, NOT A CAN. NOT A WINDOW FRAME!

JOHNNY: Hey-ya-ah-na-ah! Hey-ya-ah-na-ah!
Ku-ru-tsu-eh-ah-eh-na! Kuru-tsu-eh-ah-eh-na!

To the west below,
to the north below,
the winter people come.

HUMBERT: What are you doing?

JOHNNY: I'm helping. All medicine is connected.

HUMBERT: Maybe you can conjure Connie back then. Tell her the yard's all cleaned up. She'd like that. Nothing left but the house!

(Thunder and lightning. Thunder. Humbert shades his eyes and looks up.)

HUMBERT: Aw, shut up!

JOHNNY: *(Goes in the house.)* Porch door's comin' off.

HUMBERT: Well, I'll be. *(Rushes to the porch and takes the screen door off.)* Hey, Johnny. Come here!

JOHNNY: Want some coffee?

HUMBERT: Hey there, buddy. We still have the house.

JOHNNY: I see what you mean.

HUMBERT: Do you? Do you? There's window frames and aluminum siding. There's all that wiring too. A gold mine! *(He drags the door toward the tower.)* *(Thunder and lightning.)*

JOHNNY: Watch out for the lightning!

HUMBERT: Go ahead. Hit me. If I'm wrong, strike me dead right now!

(Thunder and lightning.)

SCENE NINE

Two areas of the stage are used. Downstage, Mike is digging, wearing a T-shirt and jeans. He is listening to a baseball game on the radio. In the second area, we see Humbert high in the tower. Johnny is at the base, his ear close to the radio, trying to pick up a tune on his fiddle. We can't yet hear what is on the radio. Arnie walks over to Mike. Mike is digging and doesn't notice him. Arnie turns off the radio.

ARNIE: How ya doin', Son?

MIKE: Turn that radio on!

ARNIE: Tigers losin' anyways… *(Looks around him.)* So, have a fight with the guys? *(Mike keeps on with his work.)*

MIKE: I like being alone.

ARNIE: Oh, yeh, that's right. I forgot. I thought maybe they were picking on you…We saw those articles about your dad in the paper last week.

MIKE: He's a freak.

ARNIE: Your mom and I kinda thought they made him into a celebrity.

MIKE: If you consider freaks in a sideshow celebrities. Him and Johnny posing and grinning with the house all torn apart.

ARNIE: Funny how those things go. All those people who pushed him down, now that he's down, can't do enough for him; leaving bags of bottles and scrap metal. Even donated butane and a blow torch. Show me the man who doesn't love an underdog...

MIKE: I don't

ARNIE: So...uh...you like living with those bozos?

(Mike doesn't respond.)

ARNIE: Starting to look like them...not bad. Turning into a real hunk. All muscle from the neck down. You're really growing up. Seems like I ain't the only one who's noticed. Certain girl came by and told your mom you've been acting pretty grown up with her.

MIKE: Yeh. So.

ARNIE: The girl's pretty unhappy about it.

MIKE: I didn't do anything to her she didn't want done.

ARNIE: Don't think that's acceptable, Mikey.

(Mike doesn't answer.)

ARNIE: Your mom wants to talk to you.

MIKE: She knows where I live.

ARNIE: She loves you. You're on her mind a lot.

MIKE: That's her problem.

ARNIE: Gentleman all the way down the line, ain't you...Well, sorry, that ain't acceptable neither...Mi-key.

MIKE: Mike.

ARNIE: You're actin' like a spoiled brat...Mikey.

MIKE: *(Threatens him with his shovel.)* Get outta here.

ARNIE: Mucho macho, eh.

MIKE: Look. I don't care what's acceptable to you. Screwin' my mom when she's married is acceptable to you! Breaking up my family is acceptable to you! Well, fuck you. Fuck all of you.

ARNIE: I'll say this for you. You got good comebacks. Fast. You think fast. Run fast. Fast with the girls. *(Slowly.)* You're faster than me, that's for damn sure. You're like your mom. *(Pause.)* That scares me.

MIKE: What?

ARNIE: Bein' fast. Move in fast. Move out fast. I don't know.

MIKE: If you got problems with my mom, don't come crying on my shoulder!

ARNIE: I can handle my problems. Now what should I tell your mother?!

MIKE: Tell her she's a slut.

(Arnie slaps him.)

MIKE: Tell her diggers in my bracket can't just walk off the job… *(He laughs ironically.)* …or they get fired.

(Lights down. Arnie leaves. Sound and lights up on Humbert and Johnny. We hear an overlay of "Georgia on My Mind" on the radio.)

JOHNNY: *(Singing along loudly.)* Georgia…Georgia … *(Takes up his fiddle, ready to play, but doesn't.)* Nice state. Think I'll add it to my collection. *(Music fades. We hear distant thunder.)*

HUMBERT: Do you hear thunder? Is that thunder? Anybody up there? Anybody home? Hello. Hello. You're not going to tell me it was all a goddamned dream, are you? A delusion, a dream, an hallucination, and now here I am stranded alone. God? God. *(He laughs.)* So here I am, twilight. Complete darkness out there except for one little porch light lost in the hills. Some poor bastard waiting out there for someone, anyone, a knock on the door, night closing in and what does that poor bastard have? A light as big as a fingernail…He should be up here with a thousand lights burning overhead and silver shining along the hills. Maybe he wouldn't be so goddamn lonely. Maybe, somehow, he'd see—what I know I'm finally going to see—just how everything fades away up here and is forgiven… *(Pause.)* Johnny! Hey, Johnnny!

JOHNNY: Yes?

HUMBERT: I can't build any higher.

JOHNNY: You sure?

HUMBERT: Yeh.

JOHNNY: Then I reckon it's done. *(Turns his music up.)* Now if I could jest get this song down.

(Strains of "Georgia on my Mind." Fade out. Lights down.)

SCENE TEN

Humbert is high in the tower, out of sight. The house is altered. Most of the porch is gone and there are piles of bottles and cans in the yard. The vegetable stand is empty. The sign now reads, "TOWER PHOTOS $5.00, QUESTIONS ANSWERED." Johnny, dressed for early fall, is giving a talk. We see the flash of flashbulbs occasionally as he talks. Connie approaches quietly and watches. She carries a red suitcase and a box; she wears a light sweater.

JOHNNY: Can't say as I ever heard of *(Mispronounces.) Zud Deutsche Zeitung* but we got lots of papers comin' 'round, *National Geographic* come by last month. Yessir. We been workin' here fer a year and a half now. Piece of history in the making. Tower's six stories high. You can see clear over the Great Lakes goin' both ways. We used two hundred forty-six thousand bottles and four hundred twenty-two thousand, six hundred fifty-seven cans. Some was sent from as far away as Orlando, Florida. We got three thousand miles of wire and cable and used four hundred seventy-eight storm winder frames. The bottom here *(He poses as he talks.)* spans forty feet and when she's finished, she'll be eight stories tall spannin' ten feet at the pinnacle. So do not neglect this opportunity, folks, to make your small contribution to history. Five bucks, if you please, more if you're willin'. Thank you, much obliged.

(Humbert is climbing down. He looks wild, dressed only in shorts. Connie gasps and starts toward him.)

JOHNNY: Sorry, Ma'am, no one's allowed on the premises but if you'd like to make a small…

(Connie puts the suitcase down.)

CONNIE: Johnny!

JOHNNY: Oh, Missus, Missus, I'm sorry.

(Humbert catches sight of her and is torn between wanting to run to her and away from her.)

HUMBERT: Connie.

CONNIE: So you did use the house like they said.

HUMBERT: Not your room. Not the kitchen. It's just as you left it. *(He brings a chair for her. He limps slightly.)* Here, make yourself at home.

CONNIE: Home. Thank you.

(They look at each other. Humbert is extremely self-conscious.)

CONNIE: Aren't you cold?

HUMBERT: No. Sun's hot up there….I…

CONNIE: Oh, Humbert, aren't you ashamed?

HUMBERT: I…look picturesque this way. People would rather contribute…if they think…

CONNIE: If they think you're crazy.

HUMBERT: Yes. *(He shifts from foot to foot uncomfortably.)*

CONNIE: What's the matter with your foot?

HUMBERT: I don't know. Nothing much.

CONNIE: Let me see.

HUMBERT: Connie…I…I need a bath.

CONNIE: Wouldn't be the first time. Now let me see your foot.

(He puts his foot in her lap.)

CONNIE: Honestly, Humbert, you have to keep your nails trimmed. They're cutting into your skin. Get a chair and stop hopping around.

(She goes in the house and gets some clippers. He gets another chair. He is very sad.)

HUMBERT: So. How've you been?

CONNIE: Fine. Just fine and dandy. Give me the other foot.

HUMBERT: Time passes. *(Pause.)* Leaves are falling from the trees.

CONNIE: I know.

HUMBERT: It's another world up there, Con.

CONNIE: It must be. Scampering around like a monkey in the treetops.

(Long pause.)

HUMBERT: You can scamper up there too…I built a little walkway for you, winds right up to the top. You can climb up and stand there looking out over the trees. It's wonderful, Con. Vast! Stretches of maple and birch and oak and sycamore, cottonwood, spruce, balsam, white pine, poplar, walnut.

CONNIE: *(Laughs.)* You always did know their names!

HUMBERT: Names?! You want names?! There's hickory and wild plum and ash trees and dogwood and crabapple and chokeberries and weeping willows by the streams.

CONNIE: *(Touches his face.)* I knew the birdcalls and you knew the trees.

HUMBERT: Connie, please come see it.

CONNIE: I don't need a tower to see.

HUMBERT: But you do. How else can you see the entirety—the whole thing, the dead trees standing with the living. Dead and alive together so straight they'll break your heart. You only know which are dead and which alive when spring comes again and the leaves open. Even the dead trees have dignity. A man falls down when he dies.

CONNIE: Why are you talking about death? Don't you feel well? Can't we talk about life or love or…aluminum siding… *(After a pause.)* or us.

HUMBERT: I am talking about us. I want you to believe me, Con. I'm not a madman, I did it. I'm right. I've done something wonderful. I recreated God's view of nature! The only thing you can't see from there—is the future!

CONNIE: Then it's not God's view. He can see the future.

HUMBERT: You don't believe me. *(Abruptly pulls his foot away and gets up.)* Are you through?

CONNIE: Honestly, Humbert. Give a body half a chance! We've got to get things back to normal!

HUMBERT: Normal? Why? I like my nails long and my hair long and my beard grown! I like what I'm doing and I like who I am.

(He gets very close to her and she backs away. He keeps approaching and she retreating.)

CONNIE: What's gotten into you?

HUMBERT: I like everything that's happening and everything that's happened. I am perfectly content. Ha-ha-ha.

CONNIE: Johnny! What's wrong?!

(Johnny comes over.)

HUMBERT: I am happy and you are happy. Blubba, blubba, blubba, blubba grrr-rrrrrrr. *(Tries to scare her away. Then he plops into a chair and freezes, staring straight ahead.)*

CONNIE: Johnny, what is it?

JOHNNY: *(Passing his hand before Humbert's eyes.)* I don't rightly know, Probably your visit just upset him a bit. He was fine before.

CONNIE: *(Sadly.)* I can't stop thinking about him. Can't eat. Can't hardly sleep. That's how he feels about the tower, isn't it? Great. I feel that way about him. He feels that way about the tower.

JOHNNY: You better sit down. You look peaked, Missus.

CONNIE: I'm just tired. I haven't slept all night and I'm not quite myself. *(Giddy.)* I'm somebody else someplace else. *(She lights her cigar.)*

JOHNNY: We got some cinnamon-walnut tea in the house. You want some?

CONNIE: Sure.

(Johnny exits. Connie paces, working herself up.)

CONNIE: You know what the trouble is, Humbert? It's not that you're crazy. I can handle you crazy—I did it before. It's that you're proud. You're so high and mighty you think only you have dreams and only your dreams matter. But I'll tell you, I have dreams too—a lot of them and not one includes you.

(Johnny enters.)

JOHNNY: *(Giving her a cup.)* Honey's already there.

CONNIE: I've been wanting to come for so long. *(She jumps up.)* But I can't stay here. Lord! Not one minute more!

(She takes the suitcase and runs. Johnny opens the box. Humbert comes over, very normal.)

HUMBERT: Do you think she was glad to see me?

JOHNNY: You acted like a fool.

HUMBERT: I think she would have stayed.

JOHNNY: Not with you actin' like a fool.

HUMBERT: *(Long pause, anguished.)* What else could I do? I have got to finish this tower and I would give up everything just to have her back with me. *(Lights out.)*

SCENE ELEVEN

It is a bright Saturday in November. Humbert is in the tower in shorts and a shirt. Johnny is in an old jeans jacket, perhaps with a scarf. He is sitting, putting finishing touches on a sign that will read, "GRAND OPENING THE WONDERFUL TOWER, NOVEMBER 5, FREE ADMISSION. PHOTOS $8.00. Humbert is throwing streamers of banners from different portions of the tower so he can string them across and decorate it for the opening. This is already partially done.

HUMBERT: *(Lets one loose.)* Yahoo! *(Throws another and watches it.)* This'll be a goddamn maypole!
(Car horn honks impatiently.)

JOHNNY: *(Crosses his arms on his chest.)* I ain't movin'.
(Car honks again.)

JOHNNY: Tomorrow. Come back tomorrow. Can't you read? *(Waves them away impatiently.)* You'd think those folks don't got eyes in their heads. I put five big signs along the highway sayin' the openin' is November Fifth clear as day!
(Humbert comes down, ties streamers in place.)

HUMBERT: Now all we need are the people and we're through, *(Steps back to examine it.)* finished. One year, six months.

JOHNNY: And twenty-two days.

HUMBERT: *(Drawing it out.)* One year—six months—and—twenty-two—days. *(Goes to the bottom of the tower.)* And what do you suppose they'll really see up there?
(Sound of a car driving up.)

JOHNNY: Uh-oh. We got company!

HUMBERT: *(Alarmed.)* Why the hell would these two be coming here!
(Mike and Arnie walk in, dressed for fall. Johnny goes to meet them. Humbert keeps his back to them.)

JOHNNY: Howdy.

MIKE: Hi, Johnny. *(Makes a beeline for the house. Ignores Humbert.)*

ARNIE: *(To Johnny.)* Hi there, pardner. *(Goes right to Humbert.)* Hello, Humbert.

HUMBERT: *(Follows Mike to the door.)* Mikey?

(Mike hesitates at the door. He is about to speak, doesn't, looks to Arnie for support.)

ARNIE: Don't worry about it now, Son. Just get the clothes.

(Puts his hand on Humbert's shoulder. Humbert moves away.)

ARNIE: Humbert.

HUMBERT: I guess you and him are pretty close? *(Laughs uneasily.)* Yes, well. He needs a friend. *(Trying to make conversation.)* Looks bigger…filled out around the shoulders…More like a man I guess. *(Laughs again.)* Time sure flies. I haven't seen the boy in…ok…

ARNIE: In seven months…

JOHNNY: And fifteen days.

HUMBERT: Right. It has been a while, hasn't it? *(Pause.)* Uh…you want something? Hey, Johnny, any Stroh's left? *(To Arnie.)* There isn't much. I don't stock up with just the two of us here and everything…Maybe we still have a Coke, or some coffee…

ARNIE: I know I should have come by sooner.

HUMBERT: You know, I really don't feel like offering you anything. I mean, if the truth be known, I don't even want to talk to you! *(He heads for the tower.)*

ARNIE: You got to listen to me.

HUMBERT: Piss off, Arnie.

ARNIE: Look, this is hard enough…

HUMBERT: What do you know about hard? You have your cushy little job, and a warm little woman waiting for you at home. We've got nothing to talk about…old buddy. *(Tries to go to tower.)*

ARNIE: We do, Humbert. Connie's dead.

(Silence; no one moves.)

ARNIE: I said…

HUMBERT: I know what you said!

ARNIE: I…I found her this morning in her chair by the window. Her magazine had fallen on the floor…the light was on…I guess she couldn't sleep. I did my best, you know? But she'd lost her peace. She'd just walk and walk and cry and walk. I tried everything I could. I'd hold her and rub her back but she'd just smile and pat my hand, and get up again…

HUMBERT: Arnie…

ARNIE: She used to tell me she was halfway to heaven…'Cause she turned forty, you know…And I'd tease her. I'd say, "Halfway ain't nothin', dar-lin'…Stick with me and I'll take you all the way…all the way…" Wasn't much of a joke, was it? *(Tries to say something, stops, goes on.)* I was never an exciting person to her, Humbert, but she was to me… *(Covers his face with his hands.)*

(Humbert starts toward Arnie, perhaps to comfort him. Mike comes out and Humbert retreats.)

MIKE: *(Has on a suit coat that is slightly small.)* The pants don't fit anymore. Do you think the jacket's okay?

ARNIE: *(Trying to compose himself.)* Sure.

MIKE: The pants don't fit anymore.

ARNIE: *(Puts his arm around Mike.)* It's okay. Jeans are dark.

MIKE: Mom wouldn't care.

ARNIE: It's just to show your love and respect.

HUMBERT: *(To Mike.)* Hey, kiddo.

MIKE: *(Makes a display of ignoring Humbert.)* There's some things of hers. I'll need a box. Johnny? Is there a box around here someplace?

JOHNNY: Eh?

HUMBERT: You can't take her things.

MIKE: Johnny?

(Johnny is undecided. Takes his cue from Humbert and stays back.)

HUMBERT: Leave her things.

MIKE: Why? So you can rip them up?

HUMBERT: She left them here. They are mine.

(Mike doesn't respond and looks around for a box. Humbert follows him.)

MIKE: There must be a box or a bag or something.

(Johnny rummages around with him.)

HUMBERT: If she wanted them, she would have taken them with her. She took everything else—pots, pans, sewing kit, nightgowns, pictures, sheets… even her goddamn garden trowel.

MIKE: Don't you curse when you mention her!

HUMBERT: I'll curse if I damn well please! This is my house, buddy boy, and she left! She walked out!

(Mike tries to avoid him, but Humbert follows.)

HUMBERT: She could have waited, tried to understand! How long did it take to do this—two years? Not even two years! What's two years in a life-time? There were years I didn't understand her either! Did I leave?! Did I walk out?! She could have had a fling with Arnie here, a little thing on the side, if she was so pissed off. She didn't have to go and leave me!

MIKE: I did too, remember?

ARNIE: Don't do this now.

HUMBERT: Stay out of this!

ARNIE: *(Puts his hand on Humbert's shoulder, trying to calm him and seek comfort.)* She's dead, Humbert.

HUMBERT: *(Strikes out blindly at him.)* Keep your hands off me!

(Arnie stumbles back. Mike grabs Humbert and throws him to the ground and stands over him. The three should be utterly surprised at this turn of events.)

MIKE: Leave him alone! *(Stands, straddling him.)* You freak!

ARNIE: *(Pulls him off toward the house.)* It's okay, kid. It's okay. Back off… That's it…back off.

(Arnie guides Mike into the house. Humbert sits up, dazed. Johnny approaches.)

JOHNNY: Things got a little out of hand.

(Humbert stands up unsteadily.)

JOHNNY: Maybe you should sit back down fer a minute here.

HUMBERT: I'm all right. *(He sits down anyway.)*

JOHNNY: *(Hesitantly.)* I'm sorry about the missus.

HUMBERT: She died thinking I was a fool.

JOHNNY: Guess she did.

HUMBERT: I robbed her of her home and her peace and she died knowing I was a fool. *(Goes to the tower.)* Pile of junk. God's view, my ass! God flicked his little finger and Connie died. That's God, life and death—not junk! *(He kicks it.)* Shit. *(He cries quietly.)*

JOHNNY: I'm really sorry. Wish I could help.

HUMBERT: *(Stares at him.)* Do you believe in everlasting life, Johnny?

JOHNNY: Yep.

HUMBERT: Are you born that way or can you learn it?

JOHNNY: I reckon you can't learn it like a fact. But if you see things right, you can understand it.

HUMBERT: I want to find Connie again. *(He jumps up suddenly, filled with energy, starts looking for his clothes.)* Do you got a comb, Johnny, I better neaten up!

(Johnny hands it to him.)

HUMBERT: Thanks. *(Starts getting dressed as he talks, with growing excitement.)* You said living things come back according to their nature, didn't you?

JOHNNY: Yep.

HUMBERT: If they lived in woods, it's woods… *(Pause, considering.)* Connie loves woods. But she likes neighbors. So she wouldn't be way out in the woods. She likes a couple shops too where everyone knows her and she can smoke those damn cigars...There'd have to be a house...a little one. She never did like housework...But there'd have to be a big stove... *(Starts getting dressed, adding shoes, shirt, and so on.)* And there'd be a garden with melon vines and tomato plants, wildflowers...nothing too tame, you know...Oh! We should look for one of those tall, white Anglican churches with stained glass and bells. The works! She likes to pray in style! *(Checks his appearance—hair, pants, shirt.)* Do you think I can find her with that description?

JOHNNY: Maybe so. Lots of places like that northwest of here. *(Smiles broadly.)* Fact is, the other day I thought I saw a two-peaked mountain northwest of here. Clouds come up and covered it, but it sure looked familiar. Like to go see it. How about you? I got five bucks. What you got?

HUMBERT: Three, three-fifty. *(Checking his pockets.)* I don't know.

JOHNNY: We don't need much.

HUMBERT: Hardly a thing.

JOHNNY: So?

HUMBERT: I'm ready.

(Johnny gets his fiddle and checks his equipment and hands Humbert a fistful of cigars.)

HUMBERT: Guess I almost forgot my peace offering!

(He scribbles something on a piece of paper and tacks it onto the tower. They start off.)

HUMBERT: Say, can you play the fiddle while we're walking?

JOHNNY: Sure can. *(Tunes it.)*

HUMBERT: Do you know... *(Pauses to consider.)* "Amazing Grace"?

(They walk off. Johnny plays "Amazing Grace." The yard is empty for a moment. Arnie comes out.)

ARNIE: Humbert? *(Calling.)* Humbert!

(He doesn't see anybody. It's very still. The note catches his eye. He goes to it and reads it. Mike comes out, some of Connie's clothes draped over his arm.)

MIKE: We can just carry it.

ARNIE: *(Takes the note off the tower.)* You got a note here, Son. *(Hands him the note.)*

MIKE: What?! *(Snatches it, reads it.)* Can you believe this?! "Dear Mike, I went to find your Mom. In the meantime, everything I have is yours. Signed Humbert Lavoignet. November 4, [current year]." *(Crumples the note.)* Dad! Dad! *(Starts searching frantically.)*

ARNIE: You know how he's been.

MIKE: He's not going to get away with this! I'll find him!

ARNIE: We can take the van.

MIKE: *(Goes to the tower and clambers up.)* I'll spot him from here. Catch him in his own trap! *(Climbs.)* Jerk! Coward! Thinks you can run away every time there's trouble! What's the matter with him? Why does he do it? Disappear! Every fucking time something's wrong—up the tower! Got a problem?—Up the tower. Need some help—up the tower. Need anything—up the damn tower!

ARNIE: Can you see him?

MIKE: Nope. *(Stops and looks.)*

ARNIE: Can't have gone far. Probably behind a tree or something.

MIKE: *(Cups his hands around his mouth and yells.)* Daaad? *(Quieter.)* Dad? *(Falls silent.)* I can't see him, Arnie, he's disappeared.

ARNIE: Hold on a minute.

MIKE: *(Climbs higher.)* Arnie?

ARNIE: Be patient.

MIKE: I can see for miles up here...miles and miles... *(Turns around in all directions.)* Miles and miles... *(He strains to locate him.)* He's gone.

ARNIE: Don't worry, kid, you'll find him.

MIKE: I don't know.

(Silence between them. We hear wind.)

ARNIE: Maybe it's time for you to come down now.

MIKE: *(Something catches his eye.)* Look at the damn highway crew struttin' their stuff. They think they're really hot shit—look like little roosters to me. Hey, guys. Heyyyyy.

(Perhaps we see Johnny and Humbert in silhouette. Perhaps we only hear a faint strain of "Amazing Grace," as if brought by the wind.)

ARNIE: Mike, we should go.

MIKE: You'd think I could see him from here. The land goes on forever.

(Lights slowly dim until Mike is isolated on the tower. The wind is blowing. We hear it. Mike raises his collar, peers into the growing darkness. We hear "Will the Circle Be Unbroken.")

ARNIE: Mike.

MIKE: There's a huge stretch of trees, Arnie. You should see 'em. Must be a million. One after another after another sooo straight... *(His voice trails off.)* Do you know what kind of trees those are? Lived around here all my life, but I never learned their names.

(Music up. Lights down. Blackout.)

END OF PLAY

DON JUAN OF SEVILLE
by Tirso de Molina
A Translation

ORIGINAL PRODUCTION

Don Juan of Seville was originally produced at CSC Repertory in March 1989. It was directed by Carey Perloff, composer Elizabeth Swados, scenic design Donald Eastman, costume design Gabriel Berry, lighting design Frances Aronson, movement Mark Taylor, production manager Jeffrey Berzon, Technical director David Brune, with the following cast:

DON JUAN . . . . Jeffrey Nordling
ISABELA. . . . . Denise B. Mickelbury
KING OF NAPLES . . . . Norberto Kerner
DON PEDRO . . . . Ron Faber
GUARDS . . . . Michael Jayce, Don Gettinger
OCTAVIO . . . . Jack Stehlin
RIPIO. . . . . Al Rodriguez
SERVANT . . . . Jill Williams
TISBEA. . . . . Kim Yancey
CATALINON . . . . Michael Perez
CORIDON . . . . Winter Mead
ANFRISO . . . . John Wendes Taylor
ANABELA . . . . Hope Nye
KING ALPHONSO. . . . . Ron Faber
DON GONZALO . . . . Robert Langdon Lloyd
COURTIERS. . . . . Sara Erde, Sarah Williams,
Royce M. Becker, Al Rodriguez,
Don Gettinger, Michael Jayce
DON DIEGO . . . . Norberto Kerner
MARQUIS DE LA MOTA. . . . . Al Rodriguez
SERVANT TO THE MARQUIS . . . . Sara Erde
DOÑA ANA . . . . Sarah Williams
AMINTA. . . . . Sara Erde
BATRICIO. . . . . Michael Jayce
WEDDING GUESTS . . . . Don Gettinger, Hope Nye,
Royce M. Becker, Winter Mead, Jill Williams
GASENO . . . . Norberto Kerner
BELISA . . . . Hope Nye
FABIO . . . . Don Gettinger
DON JUAN'S SERVANTS. . . . . Royce M. Becker, Jill Williams
DON GONZALO'S SERVANTS . . . . Al Rodriguez, Don Gettinger,
Winter Mead, Michael Jayce

CHARACTERS

DON JUAN TENORIO
DUCHESS ISABELA, a court of Naples
KING OF NAPLES
DON PEDRO TENORIO, Don Juan's uncle, Spanish ambassador to Naples
   from the court of Seville
DUKE OCTAVIO, court of Naples
RIPIO, Duke Octavio's servant
TISBEA, a fisherwoman
CATALINON, Don Juan's servant
CORIDON, a fisherman
ANFRISO, a fisherman
ANABELA, a fisherwoman
KING ALPHONSO OF SEVILLE
DON GONZALO DE ULLOA, Lord Commander, court of Seville
DON DIEGO TENORIO, Don Juan's father, High Chamberlain, court of
   Seville
MARQUIS DE LA MOTA, court of Seville
MARQUIS DE LA MOTA'S PAGE
DOÑA ANA, Don Gonzalo's daughter
AMINTA, a shepherdess
BATRICIO, Aminta's husband
GASENO, Aminta's father
BELISA, a shepherdess
FABIO, Duchess Isabela's servant
TWO SERVANTS TO DON JUAN
MUSICIANS, GUARDS, SERVANTS, COURTIERS, WEDDING GUESTS

PLACE

Naples, Seville, and many places on the road in between.

ACT I

A room in the palace of the King of Naples. Don Juan enters with his face muffled, accompanied by the Duchess Isabela.

ISABELA: This is the safest way to go, Duke Octavio.

DON JUAN: Again, Duchess, I swear to you, I'll live up to my sweet agreement.

ISABELA: So—I can glory in these oaths and promises, compliments, wishes and desires—because, of course, they'll all come true?

DON JUAN: Of course, my dear.

ISABELA: Let me fetch a light.

DON JUAN: But why?

ISABELA: So my very soul can take in this delight that I'm about to…

DON JUAN: I won't let you. I'll crush it.

ISABELA: My God man, who are you?

DON JUAN: Me? A nameless man.

ISABELA: You're not the Duke?

DON JUAN: No.

ISABELA: No?

DON JUAN: Wait. Stop.

Give me your hand, Duchess.

ISABELA: Soldiers, the palace guard!

Don't touch me you beast.

(The King of Naples enters with Guards, carrying a candle in a candlestick.)

KING OF NAPLES: What's this?

ISABELA: Oh no, not the King.

KING OF NAPLES: Who are you?

DON JUAN: Who do you think?

A man and a woman.

KING OF NAPLES: *(Aside.)* This calls for prudence.

(To the guards.) Guards, arrest this man!

ISABELA: I've been disgraced.

My honor's lost.

(Don Pedro Tenorio, the Spanish ambassador, enters with a Guard.)

DON PEDRO: I heard shots from your room, Sire.

What happened?

KING OF NAPLES: My dear Don Pedro Tenorio, how good you've come.

Why don't you take over.

Let me add. It might be smart to play dumb.

Take a look at who these two are…and

keep it to yourself that I was here

because if I see this

I'll have to notice it. *(He exits.)*

DON PEDRO: *(To guards.)* Hold him!

DON JUAN: All right—which of you will be first?

I may lose my life, but not cheaply.

Someone will pay quite dearly.

DON PEDRO: Kill him.

DON JUAN: Don't fool yourselves.

I'll die if I have to

because I'm a nobleman from the Spanish Court.

On guard then—and know

that in this sport I'm guaranteed

the right to fight you one-on-one.

DON PEDRO: Break it up. You.

All of you. Retire with that woman

to her chambers.

(Guards and Isabela exit.)

DON PEDRO: Now we're alone, young man.

And it remains for you to show your strength and skill.

DON JUAN: I'm strong enough, Uncle, but I won't use my strength on you.

DON PEDRO: Tell me who you are!

DON JUAN: I've just told you.

I'm your nephew.

DON PEDRO: *(Aside.)* Oh dear,

I fear there's trouble afoot.

(To Don Juan.) Enemy! What have you done?!

How did you get into this fix—

Tell me immediately what's going on you cheeky rebellious scum!

I'm about to kill you, so

out with it!

DON JUAN: Uncle sir…

I'm young.

You were young once and knew about love.

So forgive my love of love.

And, well, since you want the truth,

I'll tell you.
The truth is
I tricked Isabela, the duchess, and seduced her.
DON PEDRO: Stop. Don't go on.
How did you fool her?
Keep it low. Whisper.
DON JUAN: I pretended I was her duke.
DON PEDRO: That's enough. Quiet.
Don't tell me any more.
(Aside.) If the King knows this, I'm done for.
What should I do?
For such an important matter
I'll use my wits...
I must find some ingenious,
inventive twist...
(To Don Juan.) Tell me, you vile person,
wasn't it enough you fooled
and forced yourself on a noblewoman
in Spain?
Must you do it again?
In Naples as well?
In the royal palace?
With such an important woman?!
May God punish you.
Your father's already saved your skin.
He shipped you from Seville
to these foam-tossed Italian
shores hoping to be repaid
with gratitude or more,
and what do you do?
You dishonor his name
and deflower a lady!
But we're wasting time.
Look, what do you want to do?
DON JUAN: I won't ask for forgiveness.
That would be beneath me.
My blood is yours, sir.
Spill it and pay off the debt.
I'm at your feet, sir,
and here's my sword.

DON PEDRO: Get up.

> Show some courage.
> You've won me over with your humility.
> What do you say—could you jump
> from the balcony?

DON JUAN: Of course.

> Your favor's given me wings.

DON PEDRO: I'd like to help you. So, go to Sicily or Milan, where you can live incognito.

DON JUAN: I'm on my way!

DON PEDRO: To Sicily? To Milan?

DON JUAN: Don't worry. I'm gone.

DON PEDRO: My letters will tell you, then,

> how this sad affair, which you've initiated,
> will end.

DON JUAN: *(Aside.)* Sad?

> Happy for me, I'd say.
> *(To his uncle.)* Yes. It was my fault.

DON PEDRO: Your youth has led you astray.

> Here's the balcony. Jump!
> *(Aside.)* And pray.

DON JUAN: What a fine excuse—if you will—

> for me to return to my favorite haunts
> in Seville.
> *(Don Juan exits. The King of Naples enters. Guards reenter during the following dialogue.)*

DON PEDRO: As I was executing

> your orders, Sire, the man...

KING OF NAPLES: Died?

DON PEDRO: Escaped...from our sharpened blades.

KING OF NAPLES: How?

DON PEDRO: How?

> How.
> You had given the order—
> when in a flash
> he grasped his sword,
> wound his cape around his arm,
> and with daring quickness,
> fending off soldiers with great deftness,

searching for a way out from certain death—
he threw himself over the balcony!
Your men pursued him diligently.
But when they went out,
they found him twisting and untwisting about,
like a coiled snake.
And then—
He jumped up—
and as the soldiers shouted
GUARDS: "Die! Die!"
DON PEDRO: His face bathed in
blood—
he left—
with such heroic swiftness,
I was bereft
of any alternative.
And the woman—
who is Isabela—
I know that surprises you—
has now retired to her room.
She claims it was Duke Octavio
who stalked her, tricked her
and enjoyed her as a groom!
KING OF NAPLES: What was that you said?
DON PEDRO: I said, she herself confessed.
KING OF NAPLES: *(Aside.)* Oh poor honor.
If you are indeed
the soul of man,
why do they leave you
in the fickle hand
of woman?
(To guard.) Here!
GUARD: Your Excellency.
KING OF NAPLES: Bring that woman before me.
DON PEDRO: Your guards are bringing her already, Sire.
(The Guards bring in Isabela.)
ISABELA: *(Aside.)* How can I face the King?
KING OF NAPLES: *(To guards.)* Retire and guard the doors.
(To Isabela.) Tell me woman,

what drove you,
what angry star compelled you,
in my palace,
to profane its interiors
with your lascivious beauty, eh?

ISABELA: Sire…

KING OF NAPLES: Quiet.
Your tongue can't gild
the baseness of your offense.
That man was Duke Octavio?

ISABELA: Sire…

KING OF NAPLES: You'd think that guards, servants, locks,
bolts and battlement walls
would keep love out, and here
a mere boy penetrates it all.
Don Pedro Tenorio,
take this woman away immediately
and lock her in a tower
somewhere secretly.
Arrest the Duke.
I'll make him keep his word.

ISABELA: Your Grace,
please turn and look
me in the face.

KING OF NAPLES: You've offended me behind my back
and it's only right
I turn my back on you. *(He exits.)*

DON PEDRO: Let's go, Duchess.

ISABELA: My lapse may be inexcusable
but with the help of Duke Octavio
it could well become invisible.
(They exit. Duke Octavio and Ripio, his servant, enter.)

RIPIO: You're up so early, sir?

OCTAVIO: There's no rest
that can put out the fire
love burns in my breast,
since, in essence,
love is a child
who won't be beguiled

with a soft bed
regaled in linen
and covered with white ermine.
No, he lies down, but never rests,
always waiting to spring awake and play.
Ah, thoughts of Isabela
keep me at bay.
She lives in my soul,
but, my body suffers,
always guarding, it's true,
whether present or absent,
the castle of her virtue.

RIPIO: Excuse me, sir.
But your love seems ridiculous.

OCTAVIO: What did you say, you imbecile?

RIPIO: It's stupid to love the way you do.
Shall I continue?

OCTAVIO: Yes. Go on.

RIPIO: Continuing.
Does Isabela love you?

OCTAVIO: You doubt it, you dolt?

RIPIO: And you, do you love her?

OCTAVIO: Yes.

RIPIO: Well, wouldn't I be an ass,
albeit of distinguished class,
if I lost my mind with worry
over someone I love, who also loves me?
Now, if she didn't love you,
you should court her,
spoil, flatter, and adore her.
But if you love each other equally,
don't be silly—
How difficult could it be
to get married?

OCTAVIO: Nincompoop!
That's too easy.
Only lackeys and washerwomen get married that way!

RIPIO: And what's wrong with washerwomen?
All that washing and scrubbing,

defending and offending,
hanging up her underwear,
joking and giving—
I say "giving" because "to give"
is something great.
And if Isabela can't "give,"
see if she knows how to "take"!
(A Servant enters.)

SERVANT: The Spanish Ambassador is even now
making his way to our doorstep and has expressed
with a strange anger and ferocity
the necessity of speaking to you in person,
and if I didn't understand incorrectly
I understood he means prison.

OCTAVIO: Prison?
But what for?
Show him in.
(Don Pedro Tenorio enters with guards.)

DON PEDRO: Someone who can sleep so late without a care must have a
clear conscience.

OCTAVIO: It's not right that I sleep at all
when Your Excellency comes to call and honor me.
In fact, I'll stay awake the rest of my life.
Why have you come?

DON PEDRO: I've come because the King of Naples sent me.

OCTAVIO: If the King, my lord,
deigns to think of me
on this occasion
it would only be the right and proper decision to offer
him one's life.
Tell me sir, what glad star has guided me,
what happiness,
so as to be
remembered by the King?

DON PEDRO: It was rather your *unhappiness,* Duke.
I'm the King's ambassador and I've brought
you an embassy.

OCTAVIO: That doesn't bother me,
Marquis.
Go on. I'm waiting.

DON PEDRO: The King has sent me to arrest you.
　　Now, don't get all excited.
OCTAVIO: You've been sent by the King to arrest me?
　　Why?
DON PEDRO: You know better than I.
　　However, if that's mistaken,
　　listen to the explanation
　　and charge my King has sent me on.
　　(Pause.) Just at that moment when the giant negroes,
　　folding their dark tents, flee the dusk,
　　jostling each other as they run,
　　I was with His Highness in discussion
　　of certain matters of state—
　　you know how the powerful hate
　　the sun—
　　Just at that moment we heard a woman shout
　　whose fading echoes heard throughout the sacred
　　vaults and arches repeated—
　　"Help. Help."
　　The King himself ran toward the cries and noises
　　and he found
　　Isabela wound in the arms of some powerful
　　man—after all, whoever would aspire to such
　　defiance must indeed be a giant
　　or a monster.
　　The King ordered me to take him prisoner.
　　I remained alone with him, sir;
　　I approached.
　　I wanted to disarm him
　　But I swear the Devil took human form
　　because enveloped in smoke and fumes
　　he threw himself from the balcony down
　　to the roots of the vast elms
　　that surround
　　the beautiful turrets of the palace.
　　I had the Duchess arrested
　　I and in front of everyone she confessed it
　　was you, Duke Octavio,
　　who with a husband's hand…enjoyed her!
OCTAVIO: What was that you said?

DON PEDRO: I said—
   that what was so publicly declared...
   what is so clearly laid bare...
   what Isabela in a thousand ways has...
OCTAVIO: Enough!
   I don't want to hear about Isabela's betrayal.
   However—if that was her excuse...Go on!
   Tell it!
   Why are you so quiet?
   But wait—
   what if you're poisoning my steadfast
   heart
   and weakening my resolve?
   What does this involve?
   It makes me think perhaps
   you're a sly weasel
   expelling through the mouth
   only what you've received through the ear.
   Can this be what I hear—
   that Isabela, my love,
   has cast me off to kill me?
   Yes. Yes.
   Now I see the lies.
   Good arrives and evil flies.
   Although I am angry,
   my heart is enlightened
   and I'm no longer frightened of truly
   judging whether these are only
   flights of fancy.
   Sir, Marquis.
   Sir, can it be
   that Isabela truly deceived me?
   Mocked my love?
   It seems impossible.
   Utterly.
   Oh woman. Oh terrible reign of honor
   I had undertaken.
   But I was mistaken,
   and now, after this deception,

I'll no longer concern myself with her protection!
Last night, Isabela, with a man…in the palace…
I must be mad!

DON PEDRO: It's as true as the fact that birds
are carried by the wind,
that fish swim
in the seas,
that we share four elements,
that happiness dwells in heaven,
loyalty in a good friend,
betrayals in an enemy,
darkness in the night,
that day offers light,
that is how true my statement is!

OCTAVIO: Marquis, I don't want to believe you.
There's nothing worse,
nothing astounds me more than this—
that the woman I thought to be truest
of all
is, after all, only a woman.
Nothing remains for me but to…face it.

DON PEDRO: You're such a wise and prudent person.
I leave it to you to name the solution.

OCTAVIO: My solution is to disappear.

DON PEDRO: Well then, Duke Octavio.
You'd better hurry up.

OCTAVIO: I'll cast off for Seville and put my troubles behind me.

DON PEDRO: You can slip through the garden door.

OCTAVIO: Oh weathervane, oh bending reed,
you've made me flee
this deceit to strange lands.
Farewell homeland!
Isabela…with a man…in the palace—
I must be mad!

(They exit. Enter Tisbea, a fisherwoman with a fishing pole.)

TISBEA: I—of all the girls whose roselike, jasmine feet
are kissed on the ocean shores by fugitive waves,
I—am the only one exempt from love, whom love obeys.
I—alone am ruler of my fortune.

Here, where the sun touches the sleepy tides,
sparking sapphires where the shadows hide;
Here, by the finespun grains of sand—
like pearls at times, or tiny particles of sun;
Here, I keep from love's crazed grasp,
listening to the bird's love-cries,
or the sweet rasp and sighs
of the water on the rocks;
Here, on this sandy shoal
I amuse myself with this slender
fishing pole,
already bending with the grazing movement
of a little fish—
or with this net
in whose shaded depths
those who inhabit
the shell-filled deep are snared;
Here, I am confident, free, my spirit spared
the love serpent's poisonous fangs.
Here, in a tiny skiff with other girls,
tossed on the waves' white lacy caps,
their most desperate complaints of love
only make me laugh.
Oh, I'm the envy of all the rest.
I'm a thousand times blessed.
For
Love, you've pardoned me—
not that you look down entirely
on my humble hut crowned with
obelisks of straw and grass
where my virtue is conserved
like a delicious fruit
or the most delicate crystal glass.
Now let me see…
How many fiery
Tarragonian fisherman
who defend our silver coasts
from pirates boast
that I delight and disdain them—

deaf to their sighs,
merciless to their pleas,
stone to their promises,
but let me see...
Ah, there's also dear Anfriso—
prodigious in body and soul,
whom Heaven's powerful hand
has granted all its graces,
measured in his words,
generous in his works,
stoic in misfortune,
modest in his pleasures—
who, in rainy icy weather,
mends my thatched roof
every morning with loose green boughs
cut from elm trees,
fastened with praises, sweet
guitars, soft shepherd's pipes.
He phrases serenades for me.
But, none of that matters.
I live superbly controlled,
mistress of love.
I take pleasure in his pain
and glory in his torment
while all other girls die for him
in vain
and I?
Every hour I kill him with disdain.
Oh this is love's proper perspective,
to love when hated,
to scorn when adored,
if encouraged, to die,
if censured to enjoy—
in such happiness,
assured of my admiration I live.
Love won't spoil my youthful years.
How fortunate it is, love,
that at such a florid age,
I don't find your amorous nets

among the ones I hold.
And yet, what a stupid topic
keeps me from my activity
and bores me
with things that do not interest me.
I'd much rather
cast my fishing line
into the wind and hook
a little fish—but look—
two men have jumped from a ship
into the sea, before the ocean
swallows it, and can it be?
Here it comes
over the water and runs
foul of a reef;
and like a gorgeous peacock
the sea spreads its waves
like a tail.
And in its pride and splendor
it nearly splits the ship asunder
and makes it disappear;
one side takes water—
it's sunk and has left
only its topsail to spear
the mad howling wind
which has made its home in the lofty turret—
for it's always the madman who's
left in the garret.

DON JUAN: *(Offstage.)* I'm drowning.

TISBEA: One man is waiting for the other
who says he's drowning.
Manly courtesy—
he takes him on his shoulders—
Anchises and Aeneas
if the waves were Troy.
But no—swimming bravely
he cuts through the water to the beach.
Oh, I don't see anyone who can reach
and comfort them.

I'll shout.
"Tirseo, Alfredo, Anfriso—hey!"
The fishermen are looking this way.
I hope to God they hear.
But miraculously,
the two have come ashore.
The one who was swimming
out of breath
the one he carried, alive,
but limp and sore.
(Enter Catalinon carrying Don Juan.)

CATALINON: Well, praise my horse's ass,
    if that sea isn't salty!
    What a mess.
    If you really want to save yourself
    put your foot down right here.
    Out there, it's just ridiculous.
    The sea's brewing death.
    Pity—God didn't put as much wine
    as He did water out there.
    Salt water!
    What an awful substance
    for someone who doesn't fish.
    Water is bad enough fresh—
    but salt water…!
    Oh what I wouldn't give
    for a glass of wine
    no matter how bad.
    After all this water I've had
    I'll never drink water again.
    From now on, no water.
    Not even holy water. Amen.
    I just don't want to see it move.
    Oh sir
    damp and cold,
    has he died?
    The sea caused the trouble,
    but all the same
    I'll be the one to take the blame.

Cursed be whoever first planted
pine masts on the sea,
whoever measured its depths
with such breakable wood!
Cursed be the vile tailor
who sewed the ocean's seam
with his astronomical needle!
And cursed be Jason and Tifis
in the hereafter
for causing such a wretched disaster!
He's dead and who will believe me?!
Poor me, poor Catalinon.
What should I do?

TISBEA: You there.
What's put you in such a state?

CATALINON: Many bad things and the lack
of any good one.
Dear fisherwoman, do me a favor.
Look and see if my lord is dead.

TISBEA: No. He's still breathing.

CATALINON: Breathing? Where?
Here?!

TISBEA: Of course here.
Where else would he breathe from?

CATALINON: Who knows?
Let me kiss your ice-cold hand.

TISBEA: Why don't you go call the fishermen
who are all over there
in that hut.

CATALINON: If I call them, will they come?

TISBEA: Of course they'll come.
And quickly. Tell me.
Who is this nobleman?

CATALINON: He's the legitimate son
of the King's High Chamberlain
by whom, God be praised,
he'll be raised
to Count of Seville within a week,
which is where he was going

and where His Highness is waiting
and where, when all this ends,
I will be, that is,
if we're still friends.

TISBEA: What's his name?

CATALINON: Don Juan Tenorio.

TISBEA: Go call my people.

CATALINON: I'm on my way.

(Catalinon exits. Tisbea holds Don Juan on her lap.)

TISBEA: You splendid, stalwart, noble and gallant man.
Wake up, sir.

DON JUAN: Where am I?

TISBEA: Can't you see?
You're in a woman's arms.

DON JUAN: If I died in the waves,
I've come to life in your arms,
and the radiance of your charms
like the sun burning away the clouds
has dispelled the fears that shrouded me
in that hellish sea.
A horrible hurricane
swept up my ship
to hurl me at these feet I now embrace
as a port in the storm.
I was nearly lost,
but in your divine dawn,
I'm reborn.
But don't be afraid—after all,
the distance traveled is quite small.
A mere two letters between "lost" and "love."

TISBEA: Quite a bit of breath
from someone who could barely breathe.
You also seem quite relieved
for someone who's just been shipwrecked.
But perhaps—the sea being stormy
and its waves cruelly stung—
perhaps breaking the rigging
also loosened your tongue—
of course it could be allowed

that you're drunk
with all the salt water you've swallowed.
But actually
you said quite a bit
even when you weren't speaking
and when you washed up senseless
it seems you sensed
quite a bit of this meeting.
Pray to God you're not deceiving.
You seemed so much like
one of the gods of the Greeks
that the tides have deposited
at my feet.
And overcome by water
you still took fire.
And I inquire—
If you burn all wet
what will happen when you're dry?
You promise to be quite ardent.
I pray to God—this is not
all a lie.
Plega a Dios que no mintáis!

DON JUAN: Praise God indeed.
It pleased him to save me
so I could end up both sane and crazy
in your arms.

TISBEA: You have such fire.
Pray God I don't discover you're a liar.
Plega a Dios que no mintáis!
(Catalinon enters with Coridon, Anfriso, and Anabela.)

CATALINON: Well, they're all here.

TISBEA: Your master's already awake.

DON JUAN: Your presence brought me back to life.

CORIDON: How can we help?

TISBEA: Coridon, Anfriso, my friends...

CORIDON: We were just waiting for a chance like this.
Tell us what you want Tisbea, with those lips
like carnations.
We're here waiting to worship you

on the plains, in the hills and valleys,
in any way, shape or form.
I'll plough the sea, lay waste to the land,
step on fire, stop the wind…

TISBEA: *(Aside.)* How awful these flatteries seemed yesterday
but today,
I can see he's telling the truth.
(To her friends.) I was here, friends,
fishing on these rocks
and I saw a ship go under there
and swimming in the brine
two men, quite far away, entwined,
and feeling for them,
I shouted but no one heard.
They arrived with great difficulty
freed from the ocean's treacherous fury.
Lifeless on the sand, this one here
carried a nobleman
unconscious and so overcome
I sent for you.

ANFRISO: Well, we're here.
We'll do whatever you want,
although maybe we shouldn't.

TISBEA: I want you to take them to my hut.
We'll mend their clothes.
We must pamper them and please.
You know how my father
loves these pieties.

CATALINON: She's extremely beautiful.

DON JUAN: Psst.
Come here. Listen.

CATALINON: I'm listening.

DON JUAN: If she should ask who I am—
you won't tell her anything.

CATALINON: Me?
You're telling me what to do…?

DON JUAN: I'm dying for that gorgeous fisherwoman.
I'll enjoy her tonight.

CATALINON: How will you manage that?

DON JUAN: Just keep quiet.

CORIDON: Anfriso,
in an hour the fishermen will gather to sing and dance.

ANFRISO: Good. Tonight's the perfect chance
to knock about.

CORIDON: And knock some back!

DON JUAN: I'm dying.

TISBEA: Really?
You're walking.

DON JUAN: Just barely,
as you can see.

TISBEA: You talk a lot.

DON JUAN: You hear everything.

TISBEA: Plega a Dios que no mintáis!
(They exit. Don Gonzalo De Ulloa and King Alphonso of Seville enter.)

KING ALPHONSO: How did your mission go, my Lord Commander?

DON GONZALO: I found your cousin, the King of Portugal,
preparing thirty ships for his fleet in Lisbon.

KING ALPHONSO: Where are they bound?

DON GONZALO: He told me, Goa.
I think it will be Ceuta or Tangiers.

KING ALPHONSO: May God help him
and reward his zeal with fortune—
And what agreements did you make?

DON GONZALO: Sire. He asks for Serpa and Mora and
Olivencia and Toro.
In exchange he'll return Villaverde, the Almendral,
Mertola
and Herrera between Castille and Portugal.

KING ALPHONSO: The agreements should be signed immediately, Don Gonzalo.
But tell me, how did things go along the way?
You look rather tired and drawn.

DON GONZALO: I'm never tired of serving you, Sire.

KING ALPHONSO: Is Lisbon a good place?

DON GONZALO: It's the most splendid addition to your empire.
If you'd like me to describe what I've seen
I'd be delighted to paint a picture
for you, Sire.

KING ALPHONSO: Fine. I'd like to hear.
Bring me a chair.

DON GONZALO: Lisbon is the eighth wonder of the world!
From the lands of the Cuenca
the abundant River Tajo is born,
crosses half of Spain and flows
into the ocean
on the shores of this sacred city.
At its southern tip,
before it loses its brightness and distinction,
it forms a port between two hills—
which holds all manner of boats
and ships and caravels.
There are so many galleons and settees
that from land it seems
like some grand city
where Neptune reigns.
Two forts, Cascaes and St. John—
the strongest on earth—
guard the western side of the port.
And a little over a league away
lies Belen, the Convent of St. Jerome,
renowned for its lion guards and its stone.
This is where the Catholic kings and queens
have their eternal resting places
and in between,
Alcantara stretches a league to Fabregas,
a beautiful valley enclosed
by three slopes
which even the painter Apelles
had no hopes of capturing,
because seen from afar
it seems to hold clusters of pearls
suspended from the stars,
whose immensity would swallow up
ten Romes in convents, churches, and homes,
streets, buildings, lots, fields and farms,
in letters and arms.
The brotherhood of Misericordia
also honors its shores,
thus honoring all of Spain, and perhaps,

teaching her something more of honor.
And what is most amazing
about this superb city
is that looking in any direction
from the Castle
there are at least sixty
places where the sea laps the shore.
One of these is the Convent of Ovidelas—
which as I saw with my own eyes,
had six hundred thirty cells
where at least one thousand two hundred
nuns and monks dwell.
From there,
at only a short distance from Lisbon,
one thousand one hundred thirty farms,
that we from the province of Andalusia
would call granges—
all with their orchards, paths, fields, and ranges.
And in the center of the city,
a superb plaza called Rucio,
large, beautiful and well-planned,
where over a hundred years ago,
I hear, the sea bathed its sands,
but now between the square and its sea,
which has changed its course many times,
there must be
at least thirty thousand houses
spread along this strand.
It has a street called Rua Nova
or New Street we would say,
which outshines the Orient in
splendors and riches today—
so much so that your cousin
the King told me—
there's one merchant living there,
so rich he never counts his money
or wares
in anything smaller than bushels.
The Court, where the House of Portugal rules,

has an infinite number of ships docked
and mules
carrying wheat and oats from France and England.
The Royal Palace, that the River Tajo kisses,
is truly a building befitting Ulysses.
It is so grand indeed,
that when the city was founded,
it was called by those of the Latin tongue
Ulisisbona.
—And wait, I'm not done.
It has as a coat of arms—
a sphere bearing the red wounds
of King Don Alphonso the brave,
who sustained them in a great and bloody crusade
for Christ, His great Majesty.
And I'll tell you what else is outstanding and excellent—
You can eat at your table and if you wish,
you can see the fishnets, left out on
the open sea,
swelling with fish,
and what's more,
every afternoon,
one thousand boats
loaded with all kinds of goods come ashore—
carrying bread, oil, wine, wood, fruit of infinite
varieties and other niceties
including ice from the hills of Estrella,
which they will sell you
from baskets carried on vendors' heads
through the streets—
and I've hardly touched the surface—
for recounting all the details of the opulence
of this city would be to no purpose—
it would be like counting the stars
or each grain of sand.
It has one hundred thirty thousand subjects
and one monarch who salutes you and kisses your hand.
I'll tire you no more.
KING ALPHONSO: Don Gonzalo,

I appreciate your colorful succinct description
more than actually having seen Lisbon.
So thank you and by the way—
do you have any children?

DON GONZALO: My lord, I have a beautiful shapely daughter.
Her face is sublime. Nature outdid herself.

KING ALPHONSO: As a favor, I'd like to give her hand in marriage.

DON GONZALO: Just as you wish, Highness.
I accept on her behalf.
But who would be the husband?

KING ALPHONSO: He's from Seville.
He's called Don Juan Tenorio.

DON GONZALO: I'll go tell Doña Ana the news.

KING ALPHONSO: Yes. Go quickly as possible
and return with her answer.
(They exit. Enter Don Juan and Catalinon.)

DON JUAN: Get those two mares ready.
They look sturdy.

CATALINON: Steal those mares?
Why that's wrong.
I won't have the good name of Catalinon
associated with anything horrid.
I won't have people think I'm sordid.

DON JUAN: While the fishermen are celebrating,
borrow those two mares.
The success of our little gamble depends
on their flying feet.

CATALINON: So you do plan to seduce Tisbea?

DON JUAN: Why do you bother to ask?
You know that seduction is an old habit of mine.

CATALINON: I know you're a beast with women.

DON JUAN: I'm dying for that Tisbea.
She's a good woman.

CATALINON: You really know how to pay back her hospitality!

DON JUAN: Fool,
Aeneas did the same with the Queen of Carthage.

CATALINON: You wait.
I'm not lying.
The women you trick and seduce this way
will make you pay—by dying.

DON JUAN: It's quite a while until I die, you little shit.

CATALINON: Do what you like then.
I'll have none of it.
When it comes to seducing women,
I'd rather be Catalinon.
Here comes that poor unhappy girl.
Wait until she sees what goes wrong.

DON JUAN: Go on.
Get the mares.

CATALINON: Poor woman. I'm sorry.
You'll pay more than you think
for this little party.
(Catalinon exits. Tisbea enters.)

TISBEA: Even in the short time I've been
away from you
I'm not myself.

DON JUAN: How can I possibly believe these pretenses?!

TISBEA: What do you mean?

DON JUAN: Why all these defenses?
If you really loved me,
you'd avail yourself of my heart.

TISBEA: I'm yours.

DON JUAN: Why are you waiting?
Or perhaps, I should say,
why are you hesitating?

TISBEA: I'm hesitating because I've found love's punishment...
and I've found it in you.

DON JUAN: I love only you, my love.
I'll do anything for you.
I wouldn't stop at losing my life,
for you.
I've already lost it to you and
I promise to be your husband.

TISBEA: But I'm not your equal.

DON JUAN: Love is a King of great mettle
ruling us all—silk or sackcloth—
at the same level.

TISBEA: I almost want to believe you.
But you men are such traitors.

DON JUAN: Is it possible that
my loving conduct doesn't matter?
Today your lovely hair netted my heart.

TISBEA: I feel better
now that you've promised
to be my husband.

DON JUAN: I swear to you, beautiful eyes
that kill me with a glance,
I would never lose this chance
to be your husband.

TISBEA: Fine.
But I warn you, my love.
God exists and so does death.

DON JUAN: Death?
Why it's quite a while before I die
and while God grants me life,
I'll be your slave. I don't lie.
Here's my hand and my promise.

TISBEA: I won't pay you poorly.

DON JUAN: I can't wait.

TISBEA: Come.
We're going to a love nest,
our fire's bridal bower.
I'll hide you behind these straw walls
until our wedding hour.

DON JUAN: Where should I go in?

TISBEA: I'll show you where.
Don't worry.

DON JUAN: Thank God, my love.
Hurry.

TISBEA: Remember, your desire has obligations.
If not, God will require some payment
for your impatience.

DON JUAN: I still have quite a while
before that payment's due.

TISBEA: Plega a Dios que no mintáis.

(They exit. Enter Coridon, Anfriso, Anabela, and Musicians.)

CORIDON: Hey there—
call Tisbea and the other fellows
so our guests can see our court out here in the sticks.

ANFRISO: There's no one crueler.

    Whoever's caught like a lizard in her flame

    is sad and miserable.

    All the same,

    we should alert Tisbea before we dance.

ANABELA: Yes. Let's call her.

CORIDON: Let's go.

ANABELA: We're at her hut.

CORIDON: She's probably occupied with those fortunate guests

    of whom at least a thousand of us are jealous.

ANFRISO: Everyone's jealous of Tisbea.

ANABELA: Let's sing something until she comes out.

ANFRISO: How can I put to rest these cares that jealousy has aroused?

ALL: *(Singing.)* A pescar salió la niña

    teniendo redes;

    y, en lugar de peces,

    las almas prende.

    (Tisbea enters.)

TISBEA: Fuego! Fuego! Que me quemo,

    que mi cabaña se abrasa!

    Sound the fire bell, friends,

    My poor hut's another Troy in flames.

    But there are no more Troys to tame

    so Love stoops to burning huts.

    Oh hurry. Hurry!

    If love melts stone with great anger

    and strange fury—

    how can we keep mere straw and hay from burning?

    Fire, lads! Water. Water!

    Mercy love. Mercy. You're burning my heart.

    Fuego, fuego zagales, agua, agua!

    Amor, clemencia, que se abrasa el alma!

    Oh, you stupid hut.

    Vile instrument of my dishonor

    and my infamy.

    Wild cave of thieves

    that shelters injury!

    Rays of burning stars

    that fall in your tresses

so that they're charred
as if badly combed by the wind.
Oh false guest
that leaves a woman
dishonored and distressed!
Cloud that came out of the sea
to darken my heart!
I was the one who always disdained men,
and always the one who disdains
is disdained in the end.
He tricked me under word, oath, and faith.
He profaned my honor and my bed
and escaped!
He seduced me—and I myself
gave wings to his ardor
with two mares which he seized
and rode all the harder.
Follow him, all of you, follow him!
But if he's gone—I still want my vengeance.
I'll go to Seville,
to the King's royal palace.
Fuego, fuego, zagales. Agua, agua!
Amor, clemencia, que se abrasa el alma!

CORIDON: Follow that vile fellow!

ANFRISO: One who suffers silently is sad.
But thank God, through that fellow,
we've been allowed to get revenge
on that ungrateful wench.
But let's follow her. Sound an alarm.
She's feeling desperate
and could do herself harm.

CORIDON: This is what comes from pride, my friend.
Her trust and folly have brought her to this end.

TISBEA: *(At a distance.)* Fire! Fuego!

ANFRISO: She's throwing herself into the ocean!

CORIDON: Tisbea, wait! Stop!

TISBEA: Fuego, fuego, zagales. Agua, agua!
Amor, clemencia, que se abrasa el alma!

End of Act I

ACT II

Enter King Alphonso and Don Diego Tenorio.

KING ALPHONSO: What did you say?

DON DIEGO: I'm telling the truth, Sire.
  I've just received this letter from my brother,
  Don Pedro in Naples—
  Don Juan was discovered in the King's own
  rooms with a beautiful woman from the palace.

KING ALPHONSO: What sort of woman?

DON DIEGO: A duchess, Sire. Isabela.

KING ALPHONSO: Isabela?

DON DIEGO: Duke Octavio's fiancée.

KING ALPHONSO: What shocking temerity!
  Where is he now?

DON DIEGO: I can't hide the truth from Your Highness.
  He arrived in Seville last night with his manservant.

KING ALPHONSO: You know how much I think of you, Tenorio.
  Therefore, I'll let the King of Naples know
  as soon as possible that I'm marrying Juan to Isabela,
  thus returning peace of mind to poor Duke
  Octavio, the innocent victim.
  In the meantime, send Juan into exile. Immediately.

DON DIEGO: But where, Sire?

KING ALPHONSO: My anger certainly sends him out of Seville.
  Have him leave for Lebrija as soon as he can.
  And he should be very grateful
  that his father is such a worthy man.
  But tell me, Don Diego,
  what should we say to Don Gonzalo de Ulloa
  so as not to offend him.
  Now, there's no way I can marry off his daughter
  to Juan.

DON DIEGO: Well, my lord—
  why don't you order me to do something else
  in accord with the virtue and honor
  of this fine man's daughter?

KING ALPHONSO: There is one measure I can take to

assuage his anger.

I can make him Major Domo of the palace.

(Ripio enters.)

RIPIO: Scusate, è arrivato un gran signore staniere chi pretende
chiamarsi il Duco Ottavio.

KING AND DON DIEGO: Duke Octavio?

RIPIO: Yes sir.

KING ALPHONSO: Undoubtedly he's learned about Juan's excesses
and incited to vengeance, he's come to ask
my permission to challenge Juan to a duel!

DON DIEGO: My lord, my life is in your heroic hands.

My life also lives in the life of my
disobedient son, who—although he is a brave and
manly youth, some say the best of his generation,
the Hector of Seville,
if you will—
he has carried his escapades beyond reason.
If at all possible, don't permit this duel.

KING ALPHONSO: Enough. It's understood, Tenorio.

Have the Duke come forward.

DON DIEGO: At your feet, my lord.

How can I ever repay such kindness!

(Enter Duke Octavio in traveling clothes.)

OCTAVIO: This miserable wandering pilgrim,
my lord, anticipating in essence,
that my hardships are already
made lighter by your presence,
kisses your feet.

KING ALPHONSO: Duke Octavio...

OCTAVIO: I'm fleeing a demented wild woman
who has been the unforeseen cause of grief
for this nobleman who has come to beg at your feet.

KING ALPHONSO: I am already aware of your innocence, Duke Octavio.

I'll write to the King of Naples and see
that he reinstates you in your holdings.
You should know, however, it's a pity
that your absence
has made you seem rather guilty.
So with your license and permission,

I'll marry you in Seville, for I imagine
that although Isabela may be an angelic beauty,
after what she's done, she must now seem
quite ugly.
Don Gonzalo of Ulloa, High Chamberlain of
Caltrava,
has a daughter
whose outstanding virtue is
a dowry in itself, in addition to,
of course, her marvelous beauty.
In Seville, she's the sun of all the stars.
This is the woman I've picked to be yours.
OCTAVIO: Just knowing that I have pleased you,
    makes the whole journey and my life
    fortuitously fortunate.
KING ALPHONSO: Find the Duke some lodgings
    and make sure he lacks for nothing.
OCTAVIO: Whoever has faith in you, Sire,
    will be more than recompensed.
    You're first among all the Alfonsos
    although actually, you're eleventh.
    (The King and Don Diego exit. Ripio enters.)
RIPIO: What happened?
OCTAVIO: What happened?
    Why I accomplished exactly what I set out to do
    because what I did was well done.
    I spoke with the King. He saw me, honored me,
    I was Caesar with Caesar.
    I saw, I fought, I won.
    What's more, he'll help me find a wife
    by his own hand,
    and he'll soothe the King of Naples
    and repeal my ban.
RIPIO: I see why he's considered so generous in Seville.
    So—he did get around to offering a wife?
OCTAVIO: Yes, my friend, if
    you really want to know,
    a wife from Seville—the kind only Seville breeds.
    Once you hear, you'll be astounded

because if Seville engenders strong,
proud men,
the women are equally full and well-rounded,
a silken veil covering a pure sun
of dash and daring.
If not in Seville—where else would
you find such a pairing?
I'm so pleased, I've forgotten my pain.
(Enter Don Juan and Catalinon.)

CATALINON: Hold it, sir. There's that innocent Duke,
Isabela's Sagittarius—
although despite the month he was born,
we might better, now,
call him a Capricorn. *(Makes the sign of horns.)*

DON JUAN: Act at ease.

CATALINON: You betray those you flatter.

DON JUAN: So sorry, Octavio,
I left Naples in such haste,
having been called by the King of Seville
whose word is law,
that I couldn't pay my proper respects
to you at all.

OCTAVIO: Then how fortunate,
Don Juan, my friend,
that we've happened upon one another
in Seville.

DON JUAN: Yes,
who would have thought
I'd see you here
and greet you as I would have wanted.
So you've left behind Naples
and Puzol? It's just as well.
If you had to leave such excellent
places as these—that you left them
for the splendors of Seville.

OCTAVIO: If they heard that in Naples
they'd be amazed,
but seeing Seville myself
I can agree she's beyond

simple words of praise.

Who is that coming this way?

DON JUAN: That is the Marquis de la Mota.

(To Octavio.) Now I'll have to be rude.

OCTAVIO: Very well, if you need anything from me—

here—my arm and my sword at your service.

CATALINON: He may need to enjoy another woman

in your good name and reputation.

DON JUAN: I'm very pleased to have come across you like this.

CATALINON: And if you need any help, gentlemen,

you will always find Catalinon ready to serve you.

In the Blind Parrot—

a wonderful tavern!

(Duke Octavio and Ripio leave. Marquis de la Mota enters followed by his Page.)

MARQUIS DE LA MOTA: Don Juan, my friend,

I looked for you all over today, and here you are,

Don Juan, under my very nose, and I your friend,

suffering your absence.

DON JUAN: My God, man, why are you making such a fuss?

CATALINON: *(Aside.)* Why don't you simply hand over your girl

or anything else of value. You can entrust

it to him.

And if this seems a cruel condition

why—it's just the manner of being a nobleman.

DON JUAN: So what's new in Seville?

MARQUIS DE LA MOTA: The whole court has changed.

DON JUAN: The women?

MARQUIS DE LA MOTA: That goes without saying.

DON JUAN: Ines?

MARQUIS DE LA MOTA: She's leaving for Vejel.

It's a fine place I know.

DON JUAN: For someone born such a lady—

MARQUIS DE LA MOTA: Such a long time ago.

DON JUAN: And Constance?

MARQUIS DE LA MOTA: It's painful to see her

losing her hair.

DON JUAN: But surely—

you can still see a strand here and there?

MARQUIS DE LA MOTA: And Theodora?

DON JUAN: She was always a tease.

MARQUIS DE LA MOTA: She's sweating off the French disease.
But she's still young and tender.
Just today—she threw me a tooth
wrapped in a flower.

DON JUAN: And Julia from Candilejo?

MARQUIS DE LA MOTA: Still struggling with her mustache and gout.

DON JUAN: Does she still sell herself for trout?

MARQUIS DE LA MOTA: She's down to cod, I don't doubt.

DON JUAN: And what about—deception, seduction?

MARQUIS DE LA MOTA: Don Pedro and I have pulled off a good one.
The poor girl was truly a virgin.

DON JUAN: And tonight?

MARQUIS DE LA MOTA: I know some fine women.

DON JUAN: Good—there's a few nests I can put my eggs in?
What about finer courting? Moonlight serenades?

MARQUIS DE LA MOTA: I've given up those charades.

DON JUAN: What?

MARQUIS DE LA MOTA: I love someone unattainable.

DON JUAN: She doesn't reciprocate?

MARQUIS DE LA MOTA: Oh yes.
She favors me and holds me in high regard.

DON JUAN: Who is she?

MARQUIS DE LA MOTA: Doña Ana, my cousin who's just arrived.

DON JUAN: Why, where has she been?

MARQUIS DE LA MOTA: With her father
at the embassy in Lisbon.

DON JUAN: Is she beautiful?

MARQUIS DE LA MOTA: She's astonishing.
Nature outdid herself
with Ana of Ulloa.

DON JUAN: So she's that beautiful!
Good God. I've got to see this one!

MARQUIS DE LA MOTA: You'll see the most extraordinary beauty
the King has ever set eyes upon.

DON JUAN: This is extreme.
You better get married.

MARQUIS DE LA MOTA: We can't. The King wants to marry her off,
but we don't know to whom.

DON JUAN: She cares for you?

MARQUIS DE LA MOTA: Yes.

    She writes me.

CATALINON: *(Aside.)* I wouldn't go on, if I were you.

    Look who you're talking to.

    No prosigas, que te engaña

    el gran burlador de España!

DON JUAN: What can you possibly fear—someone as head-over-heels in love as you?

    Go on, seek her out, visit her, write her, trick her.

    Who cares if the world catches fire and burns?!

MARQUIS DE LA MOTA: I'm here now, waiting to see what the decision is.

DON JUAN: Don't lose time, man. Go inquire.

    I'll wait here for you.

MARQUIS DE LA MOTA: I'll be right back.

CATALINON: Mister Short and Mister Long,

    Say good-bye to Catalinon.

PAGE: Good-bye.

    (The Marquis de la Mota and his Page leave.)

DON JUAN: We're alone now, friend.

    Follow the Marquis.

    (Catalinon exits. A Woman speaks through the gate.)

DOÑA ANA: You there. You.

    Who are you?

DON JUAN: Who's calling?

DOÑA ANA: Shhh. Quiet. Be discreet

    and give this letter to your friend

    the Marquis.

    And careful,

    the well-being of a lady is wrapped in it.

DON JUAN: I swear I'll give it to him.

    I'm a friend and a gentleman.

DOÑA ANA: Good enough, stranger.

    Good-bye. *(She leaves.)*

DON JUAN: The voice has left.

    Doesn't this seem like magic?

    This paper would seem to have

    been delivered just so I can have it.

    Undoubtedly, it's from the woman

the Marquis has fallen for.
How lucky.
Gossip in Seville has it I'm a rogue beyond measure.
And yes, my greatest pleasure is
to seduce and abandon women.
Good God,
as soon as I leave this little plaza
I'll tear this one open.
But why be so cautious?
This makes me want to laugh—
the letter's open and sure enough
it's signed by Doña Ana herself.
It says:
DOÑA ANA: "My faithless father has
married me off behind my back,
so there's nothing I can do.
I can't live like this,
it's a death sentence.
But if you esteem me,
as I believe you do,
if you love me,
as I love you,
show it now.
You'll know how I care for you.
So come to my door tonight,
it will be open.
Come promptly at eleven.
Enter to fulfill your love.
And my darling,
wear a crimson cape
as a sign
for me and my maids.
I trust you completely, my love.
Farewell."
DON JUAN: Poor lover.
Have you ever seen such a thing?
I'm already laughing at her scheme.
By God, I'll seduce her
with the same trick and hoax I used for
Isabela in Naples.

(Catalinon enters.)
CATALINON: Here comes the Marquis.
DON JUAN: We both have a lot to do tonight.
CATALINON: You have a new scam.
DON JUAN: It's amazing.
CATALINON: I don't approve.
We won't get caught, you always claim,
but he who lives to fool
will end up damned.
And only a damned fool would risk his
soul again.
DON JUAN: So, all of a sudden, you've turned into a preacher,
you bastard.
CATALINON: Reason makes one brave.
DON JUAN: And fear makes a coward.
I want no suggestions.
One who's a servant should never
question.
Everything's in the doing
not the telling.
And don't forget—
you're serving but you've been
quite willing.
So, if you want to win—act!
For it's a fact—
in any game,
he who does more, wins more.
CATALINON: Then again,
he who acts and tells
ends up losing as well…
DON JUAN: Enough.
I'm warning you this time,
but I won't warn you again.
CATALINON: As I was saying…
from now on, whatever you tell me,
I'll do…I won't run from it.
I'll stand strong by your side—
like a tiger or an elephant.
Watch out, you priests!

You'll see,
if you order me to shut them up
or rough them up
I'll do it with no mercy,
my lord.

DON JUAN: Be quiet.
Here's the Marquis.

CATALINON: So, he's the one to be subdued.

(The Marquis de la Mota enters with his Page.)

DON JUAN: Marquis,
they handed me a message meant for you,
very discreetly, through the bars of the gate.
I couldn't see who passed it through.
I only knew it was a woman by her voice.
Succinctly, it said that you should go secretly,
at midnight,
to the door—
(Aside.) which will actually be open at eleven—
(To the Marquis.) where you'll enjoy your heart's desire
and passion,
and possess your love…and…oh—

PAGE: Ole!

DON JUAN: You should wear a crimson cape
as a sign for the girl and her maids.

MARQUIS DE LA MOTA: What was that?

DON JUAN: They passed me this message through a window
in the gate
and I couldn't see who brought it.

MARQUIS DE LA MOTA: You've brought such relief to my cares!
Oh friend,
you've reawakened my hope—
give me those feet!

DON JUAN: Listen, these are my feet not hers.
Get up.

MARQUIS DE LA MOTA: I'm so happy, I don't know what I'm doing!
Oh sun—hurry on your way!

DON JUAN: Don't worry, the sun's setting.

MARQUIS DE LA MOTA: Come on friends,
let's get away from here.

We'll set out tonight.

I'm going crazy.

DON JUAN: We well know

you'll go even crazier at midnight.

MARQUIS DE LA MOTA: Oh dear, dear, cousin. My priceless cousin!

How you reward my faith.

What a prize I've been given!

CATALINON: Dear God,

I wouldn't bet anything on this cousin!

(The Marquis and his Page exit. Don Diego Tenorio enters.)

DON DIEGO: Don Juan?

CATALINON: Your father's calling you.

DON JUAN: What would you like, good sir?

DON DIEGO: I'd like to see you

saner, better, wiser and with a good

reputation.

Is it possible that in every way, at every turn,

at every hour, in every situation,

you're trying to kill me?

DON JUAN: Why?

What's the matter?

DON DIEGO: Your behavior.

Your lunacy.

It's come down to the fact

that the King's ordered me to throw you out of the city.

Even though you've tried to hide it from me,

the King already knows about it in Seville

and the crime is so great, I don't even want

to say it out loud.

In the royal palace?...You actually betrayed a friend?!

Traitor! In time—mark my words—

God will punish you dearly for such a crime.

For even though it seems God protects you,

your punishment will come,

and when it does, it will surely be

a severe retribution.

Es juez fuerte

Dios en la muerte.

DON JUAN: When I die?

You've given me that long?
It's quite a stretch until I'm gone.
Don't you think?

DON DIEGO: It will seem quite short.

DON JUAN: And now,
what must I do to appease the King?
Will that take long as well?

DON DIEGO: You'll retire to Lebrija until you've satisfied
the grave injustice done to Duke Octavio.

DON JUAN: Does the Duke require
that I satisfy
him with a duel?

DON DIEGO: No, the King has
given you a light sentence
considering your treachery in Naples.
A wedding with Isabela will do
to settle your betrayals.
With everything I say, everything I do,
even this punishment doesn't affect you.
I leave your punishment to God! *(He exits.)*

CATALINON: He's crying.

DON JUAN: Being old is something to cry over.
Those tears are tears of old age.
Let's go find the Marquis.
It's growing dark.

CATALINON: Let's go.
So finally you'll enjoy this woman!

DON JUAN: This is going to be great sport.

CATALINON: What I don't understand is,
why, since it's common knowledge
that you're a beast that preys on
women,
they don't take heed and
when you're coming,
just make a public announcement
to all little maids, saying—
Watch out, be careful!
This man deflowers virgins
and leaves them in shame.

He's the worst scoundrel
in all of Spain.
No prosigas que te engaña
el gran burlador de Espana!

DON JUAN: What kind words.

(The Marquis enters with Musicians and his Page. It is night. They enter singing.)

MUSICIANS: El que un bien gozar espera
cuanto espera desespera.

DON JUAN: What's that?

CATALINON: It's music.

(The music ends.)

DON JUAN: Friend.

MARQUIS DE LA MOTA: Don Juan?

DON JUAN: Marquis?

MARQUIS DE LA MOTA: Who else would it be?

DON JUAN: I knew it was you
as soon as I saw the cape.

MARQUIS DE LA MOTA: Sing.
Don Juan is here.

MUSICIANS: El que un bien gozar espera
cuanto espera desespera.

DON JUAN: Whose house are you staring at?

MARQUIS DE LA MOTA: Don Gonzalo de Ulloa's. The palace of Alcazar.

DON JUAN: Indeed—the house of your dear cousin.

MARQUIS DE LA MOTA: You're right.

DON JUAN: And you'll stand there lovestruck until midnight?

MARQUIS DE LA MOTA: No, I'm off.

DON JUAN: Where to, my good friend?

MARQUIS DE LA MOTA: Why, where else—
To Lisbon.

DON JUAN: But you're in Seville.

MARQUIS DE LA MOTA: Yes, but the best women of Portugal
live in the worst part of Seville.

DON JUAN: And where is that?

MARQUIS DE LA MOTA: On Serpent Street—
where one suddenly becomes Adam
tempted by a thousand honied Eves,
offering tasty morsels which relieve
our hunger and our wallets.

CATALINON: I won't go down that awful street so late.

What's honey in daytime turns to shit at night.

And one night, unhappily,

I stepped in it

and found out just how sticky

those Portuguese are.

DON JUAN: While you're off,

I have my own schemes to carry out.

I'll let you go then.

MARQUIS DE LA MOTA: Yes.

DON JUAN: Well?

MARQUIS DE LA MOTA: My friend. Let's stay a bit.

DON JUAN: It's getting late.

MARQUIS DE LA MOTA: Friend.

DON JUAN: Yes.

MARQUIS DE LA MOTA: My friend—there's an angry pimp

waiting in my favorite house, perhaps…

DON JUAN: Allow me, sir, friend,

I won't let him escape.

MARQUIS DE LA MOTA: Go ahead.

Disguise yourself.

Put on my cape.

DON JUAN: Good idea.

Come and show me his house.

MARQUIS DE LA MOTA: While you're at it,

disguise your voice.

Do you see that window, with lattice?

DON JUAN: I see it.

MARQUIS DE LA MOTA: Go up and say "Beatrice,"

and enter.

DON JUAN: And Beatrice is…

MARQUIS DE LA MOTA: The maid.

DON JUAN: What kind of maid is she?

MARQUIS DE LA MOTA: An old maid.

I'll wait for you on the stairs.

DON JUAN: Good-bye Marquis.

CATALINON: Where are we going?

DON JUAN: Shut up you idiot.

Keep quiet.

We're on our way to execute my plan.

CATALINON: No one escapes you, do they?

DON JUAN: I love a challenge.

CATALINON: You've thrown your cape to the bull, I see.

DON JUAN: Actually, the bull has thrown the cape to me.

(Don Juan and Catalinon exit.)

MARQUIS DE LA MOTA: Beatrice will think he's me.

What a lovely trick—

How to hit the bull's-eye

while missing the target.

PAGE: No prosigas que te engaña

el gran burlador de España.

(They exit. Doña Ana is heard from within.)

DOÑA ANA: *(Offstage.)* Liar. You're not the Marquis.

You've tricked me!

DON JUAN: *(Offstage.)* But I am.

DOÑA ANA: *(Offstage.)* You treacherous thief. Liar, liar!

(Don Gonzalo enters with his sword drawn.)

DON GONZALO: That's Doña Ana's voice.

DOÑA ANA: *(Inside.)* Won't someone kill this traitor,

my honor's murderer!

DON GONZALO: Would someone dare?

She says she's been dishonored.

God, her tongue's so loud and loose—

a bell ringing out the news!

DOÑA ANA: *(Offstage.)* Kill him!

DON GONZALO: The tower of my honor has fallen!

(Enter Don Juan and Catalinon with drawn swords.)

DON JUAN: Who's here?

DON GONZALO: Traitor!

You've laid waste to my life's foundation!

DON JUAN: Let me by.

DON GONZALO: Let you by?

Certainly. Through the point of this sword.

DON JUAN: I'll kill you.

DON GONZALO: Honor is all.

DON JUAN: Look. I'll have to kill you.

DON GONZALO: Die, traitor!

DON JUAN: This is how I die!

CATALINON: *(Aside.)* If I get out of this,

I swear no more jokes or tricks, not
one hoax or party, no more drinks!

DON GONZALO: My God, you've killed me!

DON JUAN: You've killed yourself.

DON GONZALO: With my honor lost—what was my life worth?

DON JUAN: Get out of here.

(Don Juan and Catalinon flee.)

DOÑA ANA: *(Offstage.)* Father!

DON GONZALO: Traitor! You betray me because
you are a coward and a liar.
Traitor! Coward!
I may be dying alone and
cold but my spilled blood
runs hot like fire.
So beware, I warn
you. It's fire to my fury
and my fury will pursue
you.

DOÑA ANA: *(Offstage.)* Father!

(Don Gonzalo dies. Marquis de la Mota, his Page, and Musicians enter.)

MARQUIS DE LA MOTA: It'll strike twelve any minute
and Don Juan is late.
What a fierce prison it is to wait.

(Enter Don Juan and Catalinon.)

DON JUAN: Is it the Marquis?

MARQUIS DE LA MOTA: Is that Don Juan?

DON JUAN: It's me. Take your cape.

MARQUIS DE LA MOTA: And the hoax?

DON JUAN: To tell the truth—funereal, Marquis.
There's been a death.

CATALINON: Sir, you've escaped from death.

MARQUIS DE LA MOTA: So you carried it off?
What shall I do?

CATALINON: *(Aside.)* You're the one who'll be carried off.

DON JUAN: This hoax has cost me dearly.

MARQUIS DE LA MOTA: I'll be the one who pays for it, Don Juan,
because my woman will complain about me if I'm late.

DON JUAN: It's almost twelve.

MARQUIS DE LA MOTA: I want to enjoy this.
I hope morning never comes.

DON JUAN: Good-bye Marquis.

CATALINON: The poor fellow will find
    quite an opportunity.

DON JUAN: Let's get out of here.

CATALINON: Sir, I'll fly so fast, an eagle couldn't touch me.

MARQUIS DE LA MOTA: You can all go home.
    I should go alone.

PAGE: Good. God created night for sleeping.
    (All but the Marquis leave.)

VOICES INSIDE: This is terrible. Horrible.
    Have you ever seen anything worse?
    Have you ever seen more of a tragedy?

MARQUIS DE LA MOTA: My God.
    I hear shouts in the palace of Alcazar.
    What could it be at this hour?
    I feel ice in my heart.
    From here it looks like Troy burning,
    so many lights, such huge flames.
    A squadron of torches is approaching.
    Why is this fire imitating the stars
    dividing into points of light?
    I want to know what is going on.
    (Don Diego Tenorio and Guards with torches enter.)

DON DIEGO: Who's there?

MARQUIS DE LA MOTA: Just
    someone waiting to see what all this
    noise and tumult is about.

DON DIEGO: Arrest him.

MARQUIS DE LA MOTA: Arrest me? *(He puts his hand on his sword.)*

DON DIEGO: Don't draw your sword.
    It's wiser not to fight.

MARQUIS DE LA MOTA: How dare you talk to the Marquis de la Mota like
    that!

DON DIEGO: Give me your sword.
    The King has ordered your arrest.

MARQUIS DE LA MOTA: Good God!
    (The King and Courtiers enter.)

KING ALPHONSO: We'll search
    throughout Spain and even Italy—in case he fled
    to Naples.

MARQUIS DE LA MOTA: Your Highness,
    you've actually ordered my arrest?
KING ALPHONSO: Take him and hang his head from the ramparts.
    You dare to be in my presence?
MARQUIS DE LA MOTA: Oh the tyrannical wonders of love,
    so light in passing,
    so heavy in surviving.
    The wise men are right:
    A thousand things can come to pass
    before the lips can touch the glass.
    But the King's rage worries and surprises me,
    I don't know why I'm being arrested.
DON DIEGO: Who would know the cause
    better than you?
MARQUIS DE LA MOTA: Me?
DON DIEGO: Let's go.
MARQUIS DE LA MOTA: This is a strange confusion.
KING ALPHONSO: Try the Marquis immediately
    and cut off his head tomorrow.
    Bury the High Commander as befits a
    noble and
    holy person.
    In the most grand and solemn manner,
    make a tomb
    with his likeness
    in bronze and stone,
    and write about his vengeance on tiles
    in Gothic script.
    The burial, bust, the tomb, and crypt
    shall be ordered
    at my expense.
    Where has Doña Ana gone?
DON DIEGO: She sought refuge with your wife, the Queen.
KING ALPHONSO: This loss will be felt in all of Spain
    and all the Knights of Calatrava
    will mourn this fine captain.
    (*They exit. Batricio, his bride Aminta, Aminta's father Gaseno—an old
    man, Belisa, Shepherds, and Musicians enter.*)
ALL: (*Singing.*) Lindo sale el sol de abril

con trebol y toronjil
y aunque le sirve de estrella
Aminta sale más bella.

BATRICIO: On the flowered carpet—
where over frosty hills
the listless sun marches
with its newborn light—
sit down.
This inviting spot
will serve us as a bridal
plot.

AMINTA: Sing a thousand, thousand praises
to my sweet husband.

BATRICIO: *(Singing.)* Lindo sale el sol de abril
con trebol y toronjil
y aunque le sirve de estrella
Aminta sale más bella.

GASENO: You sing very well.
The Kyries in church aren't as
tuneful as that.

BATRICIO: The color and softness of your lips
make even the Tyrian purple lilies' tips
shamefully open to the April sun.

ALL: Salud!

AMINTA: Batricio
you are a flatterer and a liar.
But thank you for your
compliments.
Let the dawn sing to you
in subtle and soothing ways…
(All sing "Lindo sale el sol." Enter Catalinon traveling.)

CATALINON: Sirs,
This wedding party should have more guests.

GASENO: Everyone should take part happily
in this event. Salud!
Who else is coming?

CATALINON: Don Juan Tenorio.

GASENO: The old one?

CATALINON: Not *that* Don Juan.

BELISA: Then it must be his handsome son.
BATRICIO: This is a bad omen.

> Noble and handsome men
> detract from all the goings-on
> and cause jealousy.
> Who told them about my wedding?

CATALINON: We heard it on the way to Lebrija.
BATRICIO: I suppose the devil sent you.

> But then again, why should I worry?
> Come to my sweet wedding everyone.
> Then again,
> having a nobleman at this wedding
> is indeed a bad omen.

GASENO: Let the Colossus of Rhodes show up,

> the Pope, Prester John, Alphonso the Eleventh and his full court!
> They'll all see how spirited and brave
> Gaseno is.
> We have mountains of bread,
> Guadalquiviles of wine,
> Babylons of bacon
> and among the armies of cowardly birds
> we have basted
> chicken and dove.
> So.
> Let such a great nobleman come
> to Dos Hermanas today.
> That's fine.
> Let them honor these gray hairs
> of mine.

BELISA: He's the son of the High Chamberlain...
BATRICIO: It is still a bad omen—

> since they have to sit him
> next to my wife.
> I have not even begun to enjoy
> myself and if that's not enough,
> the heavens have condemned me
> to sit here jealously.
> Love, suffer and shut up.
> *(Enter Don Juan Tenorio.)*

DON JUAN: Passing by, I learned by chance that there's a wedding here.
And since I've been so fortunate
as to happen upon you...
I'd like to take part.
GASENO: Your Lordship has come
to honor and ennoble us.
BATRICIO: I, who am the groom,
say that you have shown
rather bad timing.
GASENO: Won't you make room
for this gentleman?
DON JUAN: By your leave,
I'd like to sit down right here. *(He sits down next to the bride.)*
BATRICIO: If you sit there, sir,
in front of me,
it will seem as if you are
the bridegroom.
DON JUAN: If I were, I certainly could have chosen worse.
GASENO: Of course, but he is the bridegroom.
DON JUAN: Forgive me my mistake and my ignorance.
CATALINON: *(Aside.)* Unlucky husband!
DON JUAN: *(To Catalinon.)* He's upset.
CATALINON: *(Aside.)* He's bullheaded
and I wouldn't bet
a bull's balls
on his wife or his honor.
But you're the more unfortunate one.
You're given over totally to Satan.
DON JUAN: Señora,
Can it be that I'm so fortunate?
Why, I'm already jealous of your husband.
AMINTA: It seems you are flattering me.
BATRICIO: I knew it was a bad omen.
to have someone
powerful at my wedding.
GASENO: Well, now, what do you say—let's eat.
Then His Lordship can rest awhile and sleep.
(Don Juan takes Aminta's hand.)
DON JUAN: Why are you hiding this?

AMINTA: It is mine.

GASENO: Hurry up!

BELISA: Sing again.

DON JUAN: What did you say?

CATALINON: Me?
I said, I'm afraid of the gallows,
a vile death at the hands of these rude fellows.

DON JUAN: Good eyes...white hands
they stir up all my fire.

CATALINON: Suck their blood
and throw them out.
Now there's four to worry about.

DON JUAN: Look, they're staring at me.

BATRICIO: At my wedding,
a nobleman is bad luck.

GASENO: Sing!

BATRICIO: I'm dying.

CATALINON: Sing now, because soon
you'll be crying.

End of Act II

ACT III

Gaseno's house in Dos Hermanas. Batricio enters pensively.

BATRICIO: Jealousy,
    clock of cares, and laments,
    every hour you ring in chaos
    and murderous torments.
    Jealousy,
    stop torturing me
    so thoughtlessly.
    I am an easy mark.
    Love gives me life
    and you want to kill
    me outright.
    What do you want, sir,
    that you torment me so?
    I was right when I saw him
    at my wedding and called him
    a bad omen.
    Is it not bad that he sits down
    to eat with my wife
    and would not let me touch
    one dish?!
    Every time I wished to reach
    for one, he moved it away,
    saying each time,
    "How crude, how vulgar."
    Then, when I tried to complain,
    people answered with disdain—
    "What are you complaining about?
    What does it matter?
    You have nothing to fear.
    Be quiet. It is only sport.
    It is just how they do things
    in court."
    Fine manners! Outrageous behavior!
    They would not act that way in Sodom—
    eating with another man's bride
    and letting the groom go hungry!

Hell, the other pretty boy
took everything he wanted.
"You do not eat this?"
he would ask.
"How foolish of you,"
he would say
and he would immediately
move it away.
It was obvious
this was not a wedding.
It was a flogging.
I cannot tolerate this
any longer.
Any Christian would be vexed.
And after eating with both of them,
what next?
He will go to sleep with both of us
and I bet
when I reach for my wife
he will say—
"How crude, how vulgar."
Then he will hold her.
Here he comes
I cannot stand it.
I want to hide, but I cannot.
I think he has already seen me.
(Don Juan enters.)
DON JUAN: Batricio.
BATRICIO: My good sir,
    what would you like?
DON JUAN: I'd like to let you know…
BATRICIO: *(Aside.)* Has he come to bring me misery?
DON JUAN: I want to tell you,
    Batricio,
    I've given my soul
    to Aminta,
    and I've enjoyed…
BATRICIO: Her honor?!
DON JUAN: Yes.

BATRICIO: This is clear and obvious proof
of what I have witnessed.
Even though she might have wished
he had never come—
of course, of course—she is a woman.
DON JUAN: Of course,
Aminta, jealous and perhaps
desperate that I'd forget her,
wrote me this letter—
calling for me.
With that—I swore to be honest
and enjoy what my heart
had already promised.
This is how it all came to pass. But
give yourself a chance—
because I warn you—
I'll kill whoever stands in my way.
BATRICIO: Well,
if you ask me to make a choice,
I will do as you like.
I will not be had,
for honor and women are bad
when gossiped about.
Women are like bells,
judged by their sound.
Everyone knows a woman's value goes down
when she sounds damaged.
And I certainly do not want a woman
like that in marriage!
So,
enjoy her a thousand years.
I would rather die undeceived
than live with deceit.
She is yours. *(He exits.)*
DON JUAN: I won, using his own sense
of honor against him.
Peasants always wear their honor
on their sleeves
and are always on watch

lest they be deceived.
I tell you,
and believe me,
honor has suffered so many lies
and insults in the city,
that it fled to the villages.
Before I go wreak havoc on the daughter,
I'll go speak with the father.
He can authorize my deception.
I must say—I'm manipulating
this one
rather well.
I hope to enjoy that girl
tonight.
Stars that shine down on me,
burn large and bright.
Make me lucky,
and if I get my just reward
when I must die,
keep death away
a long long time.
(Don Juan exits. Aminta and Belisa enter.)
BELISA: Listen, Aminta,
your husband's on his way.
Hurry up and get undressed.
AMINTA: I must say,
I do not know what I feel about this wedding, Belisa.
My Batricio has been bathed in melancholy
all day.
No one is amused.
Everything is jealous and confused.
What a terrible misfortune—
Tell me—
what kind of gentleman
has deprived me of my husband?
Shame has been turned into
nobility in Spain.
I am terribly worn.
Leave me alone. I am so upset.

How evil this nobleman must be
to deprive me of my happiness.
BELISA: Shhh.
I think Batricio's coming.
Listen.
No one will dare to step on
such a robust bridegroom!
AMINTA: Good-bye then, my dear Belisa.
BELISA: You'll soothe him in your arms.
AMINTA: I hope to God
my sighs act as endearments and my
tears as caresses.
(They exit. Enter Don Juan, Catalinon, and Gaseno.)
DON JUAN: God be with you, Gaseno.
GASENO: I'd like to go with you and congratulate my daughter
on her good fortune.
DON JUAN: You can do that tomorrow.
GASENO: You're right.
I offer you my heart through my daughter.
DON JUAN: You mean my wife.
(Gaseno leaves.)
DON JUAN: Saddle up, Catalinon.
CATALINON: Why?
Are we leaving?
DON JUAN: I'll be leaving here at dawn,
dying with laughter from this
little scam.
CATALINON: I hope you're not forgetting
out in Lebrija,
there's another wedding.
So we better leave this one in a hurry.
DON JUAN: This has got to be the best joke yet.
CATALINON: I just hope we both get
out of this one safely.
DON JUAN: What are you afraid of?
Isn't my father Chief Justice and privy to the King?
CATALINON: That doesn't mean a thing.
If crimes aren't punished by man,
God then takes a hand.

And believe me when everything crashes,
I don't want to be struck down by lightning
and turned into ashes!

DON JUAN: Go on.
Saddle up.
Tomorrow I'll be sleeping in Seville.

CATALINON: Seville?

DON JUAN: Yes.

CATALINON: Seville?
What are you talking about?
Look at what you've done.
Even the longest life
is only one
brief journey to death
and after death, there's hell.

DON JUAN: After death?
Since you've granted me such leeway—
more scams, more hoaxes,
more tricks to play…!

CATALINON: My lord…

DON JUAN: Go on.
You're starting to irritate me
with your stupid fears.

CATALINON: Well!
How brave we are!
Yes.
Strength to the Turks.
Strength to the Scythian,
to the Persian and the Lybian,
to the Galician, the Troglodyte,
the Japanese, the Germans, to the tailor
with the golden needle
in his hand,
imitating the Royal Purser
in the Pale Maid's tale! *(He exits.)*

DON JUAN: Night is spreading in dark silence
and now the Pleiades' little goats
tread the highest pole
among clusters of stars

in the airy cold.
But it's no time to be still.
Love takes me where it will.
No man can resist her.
I want to go to bed,
Aminta!
(Aminta enters.)

AMINTA: Who is calling Aminta?
Is it you, my Batricio?

DON JUAN: I'm not your Batricio.

AMINTA: Then who are you?

DON JUAN: Look around you and see who I am.

AMINTA: Oh no!
Now I am lost.
What are you doing in my room
at these hours?

DON JUAN: These are the hours I keep.

AMINTA: Go away.
Do not overstep the courtesies
that Batricio has extended to you.
I will scream.

DON JUAN: Just listen to two words.
Let me speak,
then hide within your heart
the scarlet blush
so rich and precious on your cheek.

AMINTA: Leave.
My husband will come.

DON JUAN: I am your husband.
Why are you so surprised?

AMINTA: Since when?

DON JUAN: Since now...

AMINTA: Who arranged it?

DON JUAN: My happiness.

AMINTA: And who married us?

DON JUAN: Your eyes.

AMINTA: With what authority?

DON JUAN: With a glance.

AMINTA: Does Batricio know?

DON JUAN: Yes.
    He'll forget you.
AMINTA: He'll forget me?
DON JUAN: Yes.
    Because I adore you.
AMINTA: How?
DON JUAN: With both my arms.
AMINTA: Get out of the way!
DON JUAN: How can I?
    I'm dying for you.
AMINTA: That is a terrible lie.
DON JUAN: Listen and know the truth, if you care to,
    the truth being a woman's best friend—
    I am a nobleman.
    Head of the Tenorios,
    ancient conquerors of Seville.
    And my father's will—
    after the King's himself—
    is revered and esteemed
    and at court,
    life and death hangs
    on his every word and deed.
    And traveling along this road,
    I saw you.
    Love led me.
    Perhaps some
    forgotten destiny.
    I saw you.
    I adored you,
    was caught up, so inflamed,
    that love has moved me
    to give you my name
    and marry you.
    Even if the whole kingdom
    murmurs against it;
    and the King himself forbids it;
    even if my father were angry and
    threatened to prevent it—
    I must be your husband.
    What do you say?

AMINTA: I do not really know what
     you are talking about.
     You wind your truths in poetical lies
     but there is no doubt
     I am already married to Batricio
     and the marriage is not absolved
     even if he desisted so...
DON JUAN: The truth being told—
     by not being consummated
     through reason or deception,
     it can be annulled!
AMINTA: Then Batricio is the one
     who has annulled it.
DON JUAN: Good.
     Now give me that hand
     and confirm your desire.
AMINTA: You are not playing a joke on me, are you?
DON JUAN: The joke would be on me.
AMINTA: Then swear to me
     you will keep your word.
DON JUAN: I swear on this hand
     to keep my word to you
     or suffer Hell's icy cold
     if you should ever find me untrue.
AMINTA: Swear that God will
     curse you if you fail.
DON JUAN: If by chance
     I fail in my word
     and don't keep faith with you,
     I pray to God
     that I be killed
     for perfidy and betrayal
     by a man...
     (Aside.) who is dead.
     Not a live one, heaven forbid!
AMINTA: All right.
     With that oath
     I am your wife.
DON JUAN: I offer you my heart
     in my arms.

AMINTA: My life and heart are yours.

DON JUAN: Ay,
  my lovely Aminta, tomorrow you'll
  walk on shoes with silver soles
  studded with golden nails from Tibar.
  Your alabaster throat will be clasped
  by jeweled chokers
  and your fingers in rings
  set with fine translucent pearls.

AMINTA: From now on, my husband,
  my desires follow your will.
  I am yours.

DON JUAN: *(Aside.)* Ah, my dear girl,
  how little you know
  the scoundrel of Seville.
  (They exit. Enter Isabela and Fabio on the road.)

ISABELA: *(Singing.)* He robbed me of my master,
  the jewel I most admired and desired.
  Oh rigorous demands of truth,
  night—day's disguise,
  shadowy antithesis of the sun
  and enemy of my dream
  of being a wife!
  (Speaking.) Where are we now?

FABIO: Tarragona.
  From here we'll shortly reach
  Valencia, a beautiful city,
  a palace for the sun.
  You'll amuse yourself there
  for a few days and then
  on to Seville,
  where you will see
  the eighth wonder of the world.

ISABELA: I thought that was Lisbon.

FABIO: And if you've lost Octavio,
  do you really care?
  Don Juan is more manly,
  and I hear
  the Tenorios have more land.

So why are you sad?
They say Don Juan Tenorio
is already a count.
The King himself has arranged the marriage
and his father is a favorite of his house.
ISABELA: I'm not sad because I'm marrying Don Juan.
    After all, it's well known
    he's nobility.
    My dismay is due to the rumors and gossip
    and loss of my honor—
    something I'll mourn for
    the rest of my life.
FABIO: Look.
    There's a fisherwoman
    weeping and sighing tenderly,
    crying so sweetly.
    Here she comes, undoubtedly
    trying to see you.
    While I go call your people,
    you two can lament together
    even more sweetly.
    (Fabio exits. Tisbea enters.)
TISBEA: Strong Spanish sea,
    waves of fire, fugitive waves;
    the Troy of my cabin—
    in seas of fire, in fiery kisses—
    was wrecked in its abysses.
    See how the ocean—with flames
    was to blame for creating more water
    in my eyes.
    Cursed be the wood
    that on your bitter crystal waves
    found its path to my abode.
    Cursed be Medea's whim,
    the first rope,
    the first linen
    sheet
    churned by the winds
    into cloths and instruments
    of deceit!

ISABELA: Handsome fisherwoman,
   why are you complaining so tenderly
   about the sea?
TISBEA: I have a thousand complaints for the sea—
   but how fortunate you must be
   seeing that you can laugh during this
   storm.
ISABELA: Oh, I have complaints about the sea.
   Where are you from?
TISBEA: From those huts
   wounded by the wind,
   so victorious among them...
   Among those thatched
   rooms,
   I was given a heart as pure and strong
   as diamonds.
   But certain events
   caused by an arrogant
   monster have softened me
   to the point
   where wax melting in the sun
   is even more robust and strong
   than I am.
   But you,
   are you the beautiful Europa?
   Are those great bulls carrying
   you and all your things?
ISABELA: They're taking me to Seville—
   to be married
   against my will.
TISBEA: If my troubles provoke pity
   and if the infamy
   of the ocean drives you mad,
   take me with you.
   I'd be glad
   to serve as your humble slave
   for I'd like, if the pain
   and offense don't put an end to me,
   to ask the King for justice

for a cruel hoax of evil intent;
Don Juan Tenorio arrived,
drowned and spent,
thrown by waters on these shores.
I helped him.
I sheltered him in obvious need,
and the vile guest,
a snake in the weeds,
with his word as husband
which he treated as a jest—
seduced me—oh yes.
Oh it goes badly
for a woman who trusts men.
Mal haya la mujer que en hombres fía.
In the end,
he went away and left me.
You tell me if you think it's fair
that I ask for revenge and some repair.

ISABELA: Quiet!
Cursed woman—you've killed me.
Leave my presence immediately!
But wait! Halt!
If pain incites you,
it's not your fault.
Go on with your story.

TISBEA: Happiness was mine.

ISABELA: Mal haya la mujer que en hombres fía.
Who do you have to go with you?

TISBEA: Anfriso, a fisherman; and my
poor father, witness to my troubles.

ISABELA: *(Aside.)* This vengeance fits my problem to a *t*.
(To Tisbea.) Come on then
in my company.

TISBEA: Mal haya la mujer que en hombres fía.
(They exit. Enter Don Juan and Catalinon.)

CATALINON: Everything's in bad shape.

DON JUAN: What do you mean?

CATALINON: They say…
Octavio already knows about your betrayal in Italy

and de la Mota, offended by you,
is justly and bitterly
complaining.
They say...
you lied and dissimulated the
message that his cousin sent
and, using the cape, you committed
the treason and betrayal that
has defamed him.
They say...
That Isabela is on her way
and that you'll be her husband.
They say...

DON JUAN: Shut up!

CATALINON: You've broken a molar!

DON JUAN: Blabbermouth.
Who told you so much nonsense?

CATALINON: Nonsense!
Nonsense!
It's true!

DON JUAN: I didn't ask if it's true or
not.
In any event,
when will Octavio kill me?
Am I helpless?
Don't I have hands too?
Where have you put me up?

CATALINON: Down the street in a church,
well hidden.

DON JUAN: Good.

CATALINON: Church is sacred ground.

DON JUAN: Yes.
You can't tell me they'll kill me
there in broad daylight.
So, did you see the bridegroom from
Dos Hermanas?

CATALINON: Yes.
I saw him anxious and sad from your hoax.

DON JUAN: And Aminta.

In these two weeks
she hasn't caught on to the joke.

CATALINON: She's so gullible,
thinking nothing's amiss.
She's going around
calling herself "Countess."

DON JUAN: God, what a great joke.

CATALINON: Great joke? Never!
This one will make her cry forever.
(They come across the tomb of Don Gonzalo de Ulloa.)

DON JUAN: Whose tomb is this?

CATALINON: Here's where Don Gonzalo de Ulloa lies buried.

DON JUAN: That's the man I killed.
What a grand tomb they've fashioned
for him.

CATALINON: The King himself
ordered it made this way.
What does this writing say?

DON JUAN: "Here lies a knight most loyal
waiting for God's
vengeance for his betrayal."
That's good for a laugh.
(Pulling on Don Gonzalo's beard.) And are you going to take your revenge,
good old mister stone-beard?
Sir?

CATALINON: That's one beard you can't pull out.
It's too strong for you.

DON JUAN: Tonight, I'll wait supper for you in my room.
And if vengeance is what you want,
we'll arrange a duel.
But it might be difficult
to fight with a stone sword.

CATALINON: Let's retire.
It's getting dark.

DON JUAN: This revenge will be long in coming
if you're the one who's fighting.
So be sharp and quick
and if you're waiting for my death
in order to revenge yourself,

then it's all but hopeless.
La muerte—tan largo me lo fiáis.
(They exit. Two Servants set a table.)
SERVANT 1: I want to get supper ready and right.
Don Juan is coming to eat here tonight.
SERVANT 2: The table's set.
But, my lord is late.
It's upsetting.
The drinks are getting
warm and the food cold.
But who would be so bold
as to order Don Juan
to order this disorder?
(Don Juan and Catalinon enter.)
DON JUAN: Did you close up?
Did you lock the door?
CATALINON: I locked it just as you ordered.
DON JUAN: You there, bring us our supper!
SERVANT 2: It's already laid out.
DON JUAN: Catalinon, sit down.
CATALINON: Why, I just adore dining on my feet.
DON JUAN: I'm telling you—sit down!
CATALINON: As you like.
SERVANT 1: That one must be traveling with him, if they're
eating together.
DON JUAN: Sit down.
(There is a knock.)
CATALINON: Someone's calling, I imagine.
Go see who's there.
SERVANT 1: I'm flying.
CATALINON: If it's the magistrate, sir?
DON JUAN: Whoever.
Don't be afraid.
(The Servant returns trembling.)
DON JUAN: Who is it? Why are you trembling?
CATALINON: He must have seen something terrible.
DON JUAN: I'm losing my temper.
Speak up, answer me—what have you seen?
Did some devil frighten you?

(To Catalinon.) You go and see who's at the door.
Quick. Immediately!

CATALINON: Me?

DON JUAN: Yes. You.
Fast now. Move those feet.

CATALINON: They found my grandmother dead, hanging like
a bunch of grapes and since then, it has been said
that her soul is walking around grieving.
I don't like so much knocking.

DON JUAN: Enough.

CATALINON: Sir, you know that I'm a little shit, and…

DON JUAN: Enough…

CATALINON: A grave risk!

DON JUAN: You're not going?

CATALINON: Who has the keys to the door?

SERVANT 2: Only the bolt is slid.

DON JUAN: What's the matter with you?
Why aren't you going?

CATALINON: Today is the end of Catalinon.
What if the raped and ravished
have come for their vengeance?
(Catalinon arrives at the door and comes back running. He falls and gets up.)

DON JUAN: What's this?

CATALINON: Good God!
They're grabbing me. They're killing me!

DON JUAN: Who's grabbing you? Who's killing you?
What did you see?

CATALINON: My lord…I…there…
I saw when…then I left…
Who grabbed me? Who snatched at me?
I got there, then…after blind…
when vile…
I swear to God, he spoke and said
"Who are you?"…he responded and then I answered…
ran into and saw…

DON JUAN: Who?

CATALINON: I don't know.

DON JUAN: The wine's addled your brains.
Give me the candle, you ass,
and I'll go see who's at the door.

(Don Juan takes the candle and goes to the door. Don Gonzalo enters as he was on the tomb. Don Juan backs away, holding his sword in one hand and the candle in the other. Don Gonzalo advances with small steps as Don Juan retreats in tandem until they are center stage.)

DON JUAN: Who goes there?

DON GONZALO: It's I.

DON JUAN: Who are you?

DON GONZALO: I'm the honorable knight
you invited to dinner.

DON JUAN: Well, there's enough for both of us
and if there are more with you,
there will be enough to eat.
The table's set.
Sit down.

CATALINON: God be with me.
San Anuncio, San Anton.
So tell me—do the dead eat?
You can tell me with signs.
Here's your seat.

DON JUAN: Sit down, Catalinon.

CATALINON: Thank you, sir.
I've already eaten.

DON JUAN: You're confused.
How can you be afraid of a dead man?
What would you do if he were alive?

CATALINON: Eat with your guest.
Since I've already had supper,
I need some rest.

DON JUAN: Are you trying to get me angry?

CATALINON: Oh, my God, sir.
I smell bad.

DON JUAN: Come here. I'm waiting.

CATALINON: I told you I smelled.
I thought I'd expired…but…
perhaps I've expelled.
(The Servants tremble.)

DON JUAN: And you?
What do you have to say for yourselves?
What are you doing?
Idiot! Trembling!

CATALINON: I never like to dine
with people from other countries.
I, sir, with a guest of stone?
DON JUAN: It's ridiculous to be afraid.
If he's made of stone, what
can he do to you?
CATALINON: Crush my head.
DON JUAN: Where are your manners?
Speak to him courteously.
CATALINON: Are you well?
Is it nice on the other side?
Is it flat or hilly?
Over there, is it poetry they prize?
DON JUAN: Hey!
Bring us something to drink.
CATALINON: Mr. Deadman, sir, do they
drink with ice?
(Don Gonzalo nods yes.)
CATALINON: So they have ice.
How nice.
DON JUAN: If you want some music,
I'll have them sing.
(Don Gonzalo nods his head.)
SERVANT 2: He said yes.
DON JUAN: Sing.
SERVANTS: *(Singing.)* Si de mi amor aguardáis
señora, de aquesta suerte
el galardon en la muerte,
que largo me lo fiáis!
CATALINON: They don't drink much there, do they?
I'll drink for both of us.
(He drinks.) A stone toast.
My God, I'm less afraid already.
(The Servants sing.)
CATALINON: Which of all the women you've seduced
are they referring to?
DON JUAN: Tonight, I laugh at all of them,
my friend
Isabela in Naples…

CATALINON: Ahh—that one, my lord, is no longer
"seduced"—
she's marrying you tomorrow as she should.
But you seduced the fisherwoman who
rescued you from the sea,
repaying her hospitality
with bitter coins.
You seduced Doña Ana…

DON JUAN: Shut up.
There's a party here who suffered
for her and who's waiting for revenge!

(Don Gonzalo makes a sign that everyone but Don Juan should leave the room.)

DON JUAN: You there—leave the table!
He's signaling that he wants everyone to leave
but me.

CATALINON: Don't stay.
By God, that's not good.
There's a dead person here
who could
kill a giant with one fist.

DON JUAN: Everyone leave.
You too, Catalinon.
Go on.
Here he comes.

(Servants and Catalinon exit. The two are alone. Don Gonzalo indicates that Don Juan should close the door.)

DON JUAN: The door is shut.
I'm waiting—what do you want—
shadow, illusion, or ghost?
Are you wandering in pain?
Is there some satisfaction, cure, or remedy
you hope to gain?
Tell me. I give you my word,
I'll do whatever you ask.
But then—
is God pleased with you
or did I kill you
while you were still in mortal sin?
Speak, I'm in suspense.

(Don Gonzalo speaks slowly like someone from another world.)

DON GONZALO: Will you give me your word as a gentleman?

DON JUAN: I'm a nobleman

I'm honorable and keep my word.

DON GONZALO: Give me your hand.

Don't be afraid.

DON JUAN: What are you saying?

Me afraid?

If you were Hell itself,

I'd still give you my hand.

DON GONZALO: By these words and your hand,

tomorrow at ten,

I'll be waiting for you

to come dine.

You will come.

DON JUAN: I expected something more serious.

Tomorrow then, I'm your guest.

Where should I go?

DON GONZALO: To my chapel.

DON JUAN: Should I go alone?

DON GONZALO: No. The two of you.

And keep your word,

as I've kept mine.

DON JUAN: I told you I'd do it.

I'm a Tenorio.

DON GONZALO: And I'm an Ulloa.

DON JUAN: I'll be there without fail.

DON GONZALO: I believe you. *(He goes to the door.)*

DON JUAN: I'll light the way

for you. Wait.

DON GONZALO: I don't need it.

I'm in a state of grace. *(He leaves.)*

DON JUAN: My God,

my body's bathed in sweat.

When he took my hand and pressed it,

I felt infernal fires.

I've never felt so much heat.

And yet my heart's like ice

and his breath, when he spoke,

gave off infernal fumes,
as cold as death.
But this is all a trick
of the imagination—
fear and fear of the dead is a
stupid and vulgar fascination.
Why, if one isn't afraid of a noble body,
alive with strength and reason and soul,
why fear the dead?
Tomorrow, I'll go
to his chapel.
Don Gonzalo will be the host
and all of Seville
will marvel at my bravery and skill
at facing what they fear most.

(He exits. Enter the King. Don Diego and Attendants.)

KING ALPHONSO: Isabela has finally arrived?

DON DIEGO: Yes, very displeased.

KING ALPHONSO: She hasn't taken well to the marriage?

DON DIEGO: She keenly feels the loss of her good name.

KING ALPHONSO: So then, her torment has other causes.

DON DIEGO: If her wedding is to be with Don Juan, Sire,
please command that he appear.

KING ALPHONSO: Yes.

Have him come before me,
nobly dressed,
and proclaim
this pleasurable event
throughout the land.
And let it be known
I've made Don Juan
Count of Lebrija.
He owns and rules it from now on.
Therefore Isabela should be content.
She's lost a duke, her equal,
but has gained a count.

DON DIEGO: I humbly kiss your feet
for all the kindness you've shown.

KING ALPHONSO: Nonsense.

You so honorably merit my favor,
that if we were to match kindness with
kindness, I would be your debtor.
But even so, you'd better warn Duke Octavio
about Isabela's wedding.
Poor Duke, he's unfortunate with women.
To him, they're all gossip and frivolity.
I've heard he's quite furious with Don Juan.

DON DIEGO: I'm not surprised,
especially if he's verified
Don Juan's crime
which has caused him so much harm.
(Enter Ripio.)

RIPIO: É arrivato il Duco Ottavio.

KING AND DON DIEGO: Duke Octavio!

KING ALPHONSO: Don't leave my side.
You're implicated in this crime as well.
(Enter Duke Octavio.)

OCTAVIO: Your Highness, unvanquished King,
give me your feet.

KING ALPHONSO: Rise, Duke, and cover your head.
What would you like?

OCTAVIO: I've come abjectly to ask
a favor at your feet,
something just and fair
that I'm worthy of being granted.

KING ALPHONSO: My good Duke,
as long as it's just,
I give you my word
I'll grant it.
Ask me what you will.

OCTAVIO: Sire, through letters from your ambassador—
and through infamous rumor,
you already know
that Don Juan Tenorio,
with Spanish arrogance—one night
in Naples—a night of terrible
remembrance for me—profaned
in my name, the sacred virtue
of a lady.

KING ALPHONSO: Go no further.

    I already know about your misfortune.

    In effect, what would you like?

OCTAVIO: Permission to fight it out

    with him in open country

    since he's a traitor.

DON DIEGO: No. Not that.

    His pure blood is as noble as…

KING ALPHONSO: Don Diego!

DON DIEGO: Sire.

OCTAVIO: Who are you

    to speak this way in the

    presence of a king?

DON DIEGO: I'm someone who's silent

    because the King orders me to be.

    If not, I'd answer you

    with this sword.

OCTAVIO: You're old.

DON DIEGO: I was young once

    in Italy.

    For your misfortune,

    they already know my sword

    in Naples and Milan.

OCTAVIO: Your blood's already grown cold.

    "I was" is worthless.

    "I am" is valid.

DON DIEGO: I was and I am. *(Draws his sword.)*

KING ALPHONSO: Hold it. Enough.

    Stop.

    That's it, Don Diego.

    You're showing but little respect

    for my person.

    And you, Duke,

    in this instance,

    Don Juan is a nobleman of

    my chambers and my creation,

    a branch of this trunk.

    Keep your distance.

OCTAVIO: I'll do as you wish, Sire.

KING ALPHONSO: Come with me, Don Diego.

DON DIEGO: *(Aside.)* Ay son, how badly you repay all my love
for you!

KING ALPHONSO: Duke.

OCTAVIO: My lord.

(Don Diego and the King exit. Enter Gaseno and Aminta.)

GASENO: Maybe this man will tell us where to find Don Juan Tenorio.
Sir, can you tell me if we can find a certain
Don Juan whose last name is
quite well-known
in these parts?

OCTAVIO: You must be talking about Don Juan Tenorio.

AMINTA: Yes sir.
That Don Juan.

OCTAVIO: He's here.
What do you want with him?

AMINTA: That gentleman is my husband.

OCTAVIO: What?

AMINTA: You did not know?
And you're from the palace?

OCTAVIO: Don Juan hasn't said
anything to me.

GASENO: Is it possible?

OCTAVIO: Yes, I swear.

GASENO: Lady Aminta is very virtuous,
quite noble herself.
When the two marry, he'll be getting
a descendant of the ancient
Christians right down to her bones.
And she owns
part of a hacienda,
much like a count or a marquis.
Don Juan is betrothed to her, you know.
He took her away from Batricio.

AMINTA: Tell him how she was a maiden
in his power.

GASENO: This isn't a trial or a complaint.

OCTAVIO: *(Aside.)* This is one of Don Juan's tricks.
Their telling me

will further my vengeance.

(To both.) So, what are you requesting?

GASENO: Time is passing rapidly
and we would either like the marriage
to take place or to take our
grievances to the King.

OCTAVIO: That's a sound idea.

GASENO: Right and just by law.

OCTAVIO: This opportunity fits my intention perfectly.
You'll have your wedding in the castle.

AMINTA: You mean my wedding?

OCTAVIO: *(Aside.)* We'll try a little invention and sport.
(To both.) Come here dressed as they do in court.
You'll enter one of the King's
rooms with me.

AMINTA: Give me your hand and promise
you will take me to Don Juan.

OCTAVIO: Thus
I'll be recompensed.

GASENO: This arrangement comforts me.

OCTAVIO: *(Aside.)* These two are giving me the chance
to take my vengeance
against the traitor Tenorio
for Isabela's offense.
(They exit. Enter Don Juan and Catalinon.)

CATALINON: How did the King receive you?

DON JUAN: More lovingly than my own father.

CATALINON: Did you see Isabela?

DON JUAN: Her too.

CATALINON: How does she look?

DON JUAN: Like an angel.

CATALINON: Did she receive you well?

DON JUAN: Her face was blushing pink and milky white
like the rose that bright dawn bursts
from its green prison.

CATALINON: And tonight is the wedding?

DON JUAN: Without fail.

CATALINON: If this had happened before,
you wouldn't have seduced so many ladies.

But you're taking a wife, sir,
with heavy responsibilities.

DON JUAN: Tell me, are you beginning to be
stupid?

CATALINON: You know, it might be better
to marry later.
Tomorrow.
Today is a very bad day.

DON JUAN: Why?
What day is today?

CATALINON: Tuesday—
Tuesday never take a bride,
nor travel,
nor leave your family's side.

DON JUAN: A thousand liars and lunatics
believe in that kind of nonsense.
The only bad day for me,
truly sad and detestable,
is the day I have no money.
Everything else is easy.

CATALINON: Well then, you better get dressed.

DON JUAN: We have some other business first.

CATALINON: What's that?

DON JUAN: Dinner with a dead man.

CATALINON: Stupidity of stupidities.

DON JUAN: Didn't you hear?
I gave my word.

CATALINON: And if you break it—so what?
Do you have to ask permission
from a granite statue?

DON JUAN: He could damn me with his voice.

CATALINON: The church is already closed.

DON JUAN: Call.

CATALINON: What good is it if I call?
Who could answer?
The sexton's asleep.

DON JUAN: Call at this portico.

CATALINON: It's open.

DON JUAN: Well, go in.

CATALINON: Let a monk with his stole and sprinkler
   go in.

DON JUAN: Follow me and keep quiet.

CATALINON: Keep quiet?

DON JUAN: Yes.

CATALINON: God in heaven,
   get me out of these invitations.
   (They enter one door and come out another.)

CATALINON: This church is extremely dark, sir,
   and very big.
   Ayyyy. Hold me.
   Someone grabbed my cape.
   (Enter Don Gonzalo.)

DON JUAN: Who's there?

DON GONZALO: It's I.

CATALINON: I'm dead!

DON GONZALO: I'm the dead man.
   Don't be frightened.
   I never believed you would really keep
   your word, seeing that you make fools of everyone
   else.

DON JUAN: Do you think I'm a coward?

DON GONZALO: Yes.
   You fled the night you killed me.

DON JUAN: I fled so I wouldn't be
   recognized.
   But now you have me here.
   Tell me quickly what you want.

DON GONZALO: I wish to invite you to supper.

CATALINON: Let's forget supper.
   It would only be cold cuts.
   I don't see a kitchen.

DON JUAN: Let's have supper, then.

DON GONZALO: In order to eat
   you have to lift this tombstone.

DON JUAN: I'll lift those pillars if I have to.

DON GONZALO: You're spirited, aren't you?

DON JUAN: I have valor and spirit in my very bones.

CATALINON: This table is like ebony,

it must be from Guinea.

So—perhaps you need someone to wash the dishes?

DON GONZALO: Sit down.

DON JUAN: Where?

CATALINON: Look.

Two pages in black are coming with chairs.

(Enter two Servants dressed in mourning, carrying two chairs.)

DON GONZALO: You. Sit down.

CATALINON: Me, sir?

I already ate this afternoon.

DON GONZALO: Don't contradict me.

CATALINON: I won't contradict you.

God in Heaven, get me out of here.

And what dish is this, sir?

DON GONZALO: That is a dish of

scorpions and serpent.

CATALINON: A nice dish.

DON GONZALO: That is our food.

Aren't you eating?

DON JUAN: I'd eat if you gave me as many asps and adders

as there were in all of hell.

DON GONZALO: I'd also like them to sing.

(The Servants sing.)

CATALINON: Good Lord,

This is terrible.

I understand those words.

It's miserable.

They're meant for us.

DON JUAN: Ice is splitting my chest.

(The Servants sing.)

CATALINON: Tell me, what's in this stew?

DON GONZALO: Fingernails.

CATALINON: Fingernails?

DON JUAN: I've eaten. Clear the table.

DON GONZALO: Give me your hand.

Don't be afraid.

The hand.

Give it to me.

DON JUAN: Are you saying I'm afraid?

(*Offers his hand.*) I'm burning!
Fire!

DON GONZALO: This is nothing to the fire
you've sought so long.
The miracles of God,
Don Juan, are now evident.
He wants your sins
paid for
at the hands of a dead man.
And since you didn't take
heed in time,
here's God's justice.
For what one does,
one pays in kind.
Quien tal hace, que tal pague.

DON JUAN: I'm burning.
I'll kill you with this dagger.
Ay! It's useless.
The blade rakes through this air.
I didn't seduce your daughter.
She saw through
my deception in time.

DON GONZALO: It doesn't matter.
You tried to deceive her.

DON JUAN: Let me call someone
who can receive my confession
and absolve me.

DON GONZALO: There's no escape.
You've thought of that
too late.

DON JUAN: I'm burning. I'm burning up. (*He falls dead.*)

CATALINON: No one escapes. It's true.
And here I am about to die
for having accompanied you!

DON GONZALO: This is God's justice.
Quien tal hace, que tal pague.
(*The tomb sinks noisily with Don Juan and Don Gonzalo. Catalinon crawls.*)

CATALINON: God help me.
What is this?

The chapel is burning
and I'm left!
Don Juan,
what remorse
to stand vigil
over your corpse.
Saint George, Holy Lamb.
I'll go tell your father,
crawling as best I can.
Oh…get me in peace
back to the street.
(Catalinon leaves. Enter King Alphonso, Don Diego, and Attendants.)
DON DIEGO: The Marquis is waiting
humbly to kiss your royal feet.
KING ALPHONSO: Bring him in
and tell the Count as well
to come so he won't be kept waiting.
(Enter Gaseno and Batricio.)
BATRICIO: Where sir,
is it permitted
that great events unfold
so that your men
offend the poor?
KING ALPHONSO: What are you saying?
BATRICIO: Don Juan Tenorio,
treacherous and detestable,
took my wife away from me,
on my wedding night,
before it was consummated.
I have brought a witness
to the truth of what I have stated.
(Enter Tisbea, Isabela, and Attendants.)
TISBEA: If Your Highness shows restraint
in punishing Don Juan,
I'll shout all my complaints
to God and all men
from now on!
For the ocean swept him
defeated to my feet.

I gave him welcome, life, and hospitality—
which
he repaid by lying, calling himself husband,
and seducing me!

KING ALPHONSO: What did you say?

ISABELA: She's telling the truth.

(Enter Aminta with Duke Octavio.)

AMINTA: And where is my husband?

KING ALPHONSO: And who is that?

AMINTA: What?! You still do not know?
I have come to marry
Don Juan Tenorio.
He owes me the honor.
He is noble and he
will not deny me.
Order us to be married immediately!

(Enter the Marquis de la Mota.)

MARQUIS DE LA MOTA: It's time the truth was known.
It was my friend, Don Juan,
who in a cruel malicious hoax,
fixed the blame on me
for crimes where I was
never guilty.
And here I have, Your Highness,
a witness to my innocence.

(Doña Ana enters.)

KING ALPHONSO: Have you ever seen such shameless impudence?
Arrest him and have him killed immediately!

DON DIEGO: For my services and my honor,
I ask solely one reward.
Take Juan and make him pay
for all his sins, my lord;
or lightning may strike me down
for having such an evil son.

KING ALPHONSO: So this is what my favorites do!

(Enter Catalinon.)

CATALINON: Sirs, all of you here—listen
to the most amazing event
ever witnessed by a Christian.

Then hearing it—kill me.
Don Juan Tenorio
making fun
of the High Commander,
after robbing him of his life
and honor,
his two most precious jewels,
further offended him
by pulling at the stony beard
of the statue on his tomb—
and worse—invited him to dine!
That he had never been so inclined!
That I was never born!
For the statue went and then
invited him in return!
And now—so as not to tire you,
I'll only say—
that after dining,
after a thousand grave omens,
he seized his hand and cried—
pressing it harder and harder
until Don Juan burned and died—
"God sent me to punish your crimes.
What one does, one pays in kind."

KING ALPHONSO: What are you saying?

CATALINON: The truth.

And before he died,
Don Juan said
that Doña Ana had been spared.
She didn't lose her honor.
She caught on to his trick
before he could seduce her.

MARQUIS DE LA MOTA: For that news,
I'll give you
a thousand rewards!

KING ALPHONSO: Heaven provides the true rewards.
And now, it is only just
that all of you are wedded.
The life that was so disastrous
has ended.

OCTAVIO: Since Isabela has been widowed,
    I'd like to marry her.
MARQUIS DE LA MOTA: And I, my cousin Ana.
TISBEA: The superb Anfriso will do for me!
BATRICIO: Now that the guest of stone has left—
    each should marry the other at last!
KING ALPHONSO: Transfer the tomb to St. Francis in Madrid,
    place it in a high vaulted chamber
    so the world will marvel at his deeds,
    take notice and remember.

END OF PLAY

THIN AIR:
TALES FROM A REVOLUTION

ORIGINAL PRODUCTION

Thin Air: Tales from a Revolution premiered at the San Diego Repertory Theater in San Diego, California in August of 1989. (Sam Woodhouse, Artistic Director.) The production was directed by Sam Woodhouse; music and music direction by Fred Lanuza; costumes and set design by Ernesto Díaz. The cast was as follows:

HILDA	Antonia Nero
ALEX	Leon Russom
ANYA	Tomasa Dominquez Gaetano
GEN. JUAN LESCOS	Jaime Sanchez
MODESTA	Roma Maffia
CARMEN	Roberta Mol
LUCAN	Michael Moran
JOHNNY	Ernesto Dorfman
SERGIO	Jaime Sanchez*
LITTLE GIRL	Lisi Myers
PRIEST	Leon Russom*
WAITERS/GUARDS/JOURNALISTS	Ernesto Dorfman*
	Roberta Mol*, Michael Moran*
	Tomasa Dominquez Gaetano*

* These roles were doubled.

Johnny may double with the Vice Consul. Don Sergio may double with General Juan Lescos Villanueva. Actors may play Waiters at the cocktail party as they are available.

CHARACTERS

VICE CONSUL, a man in his late twenties.

HILDA INEZ SANTA MARIA DE YOUNG, a well-born South American, forties

ALEXANDER BERTRAM YOUNG, a composer/musicologist, forties

LITTLE GIRL, casualty, memory, eight years old

CARMEN IZAGUIRRE, a guard at the Candaleria, Modesta's sister, early twenties

GENERAL JUAN LESCOS VILLANUEVA, powerful in the provinces before the revolution; late forties or early fifties

MODESTA IZAGUIRRE DE LESCOS, Juan's cleaning lady, then his wife, Carmen's older sister

ANYA YOUNG, student, midteens

JOHNNY, a guard outside the Candaleria, from the provinces, early twenties

LUCAN, guerrilla leader, later Minister of Interior; early thirties

PRIEST

GERMAN, little girl's dead brother

DON SERGIO, peasant, late sixties

ACT I

THE COCKTAIL PARTY

The stage is dark and quiet. A spot comes up center stage. We see Hilda asleep in a red cocktail dress, mirroring the cutout at the front of the stage. Magazines have spilled from her lap onto the floor. Perhaps one is still open on her lap. As Hilda sleeps, Alex walks into the spot. He is wearing a black T-shirt and tuxedo trousers with red suspenders. He looks at her for what becomes an uncomfortable amount of time as she sleeps. Slowly, another spot brightens on the piano, and one by one—like clowns emerging from a tiny car—the actors in dress generic to the characters they will play, emerge from the piano. First a Catholic priest emerges in full vestments followed by a peasant girl who fetches an armful of huge red flowers from a vase and stands next to the priest. As each actor comes out he kneels before the priest and is blessed. A flower is placed in his or her mouth. The actor then walks to an open area and greets someone with exaggerated emotion—joy or surliness, etc. Each actor uses the flower in a different way as an ornament, in a drink, as a gift or a punishment—the little girl goes to her brother and starts to dig. A pile of dirt starts to accumulate. Waiters grab trays full of champagne glasses and put towels over their arms and serve the guests. The chatter grows, the lights of the chandelier brighten, there is the sound of cocktail music. The party begins. The last actor out is the Vice Consul. He yells for the waiter and this awakens Hilda who begins to wander among the guests in amazement. Alex follows her.

VICE CONSUL: *(Holding his drink aloft.)* Waiter! Waiter!
(A waiter struggles through the crowd toward him.)
VICE CONSUL: *(The Vice Consul sidles up to a guest doing a soft shoe.)* Dadada dum dee dum dee dum dadada dum dee dum I love to dance—How about you?
(The guest turns away rudely.)
VICE CONSUL: Does she have a pole up her ass or what? Dadada dum dee— This part is a dream. I would *never* do this in real life! Dadada dum dee dum.
(Everyone ignores him studiously.)
VICE CONSUL: Ladies and gentlemen…Ladies…Your attention here for a moment. Ahem…if you have any eligible daughters between twenty-five and thirty-five please have them call the following number—

(Complete silence.)

VICE CONSUL: Just a little joke. At least you know I'm vulgar and inappropriate. What do I know about you?

(The waiter arrives.)

VICE CONSUL: There you are. Scotch. Please. Dewars. Neat. *No ice!*

(The waiter leaves to refill the glass.)

VICE CONSUL: I never have ice anymore. Though ice has been my teacher—ice—yes. In my vile youth I was a Vice Consul in a backwater tropical port in Latin America—of course I had been a near-eastern studies major—but what the hell! There I was. What a hole. What a job—visiting puking drunk American tourists in the lice-infested, cockroach-filled, vomit-encrusted, filthy, dark, foul, disgusting jails down there after they'd been beaten to a pulp for trying to pick up some respectable man's wife, thinking all Latin women were whores—no wonder I got the runs—you say. No wonder. I drank. I did like to drink. This much scotch over this much ice. It was hot and I sweated like a damn pig. I needed a drink now and then. I always figured it was a hangover—I mean—I boiled my milk, peeled my tomatoes, washed my lettuce in a slightly acidic solution, drank bottled water and never—but—never ate anything off the streets. But there I was—with the runs. *Seven years* of the runs. It was the ice. Never thought to ask what the ice was made from. That…shows to go ya…the unexamined life is a crock of shit—Dadada dum dee dum dee dum. *(He dances over to Hilda.)* What do you think of that, babe?

(Hilda ignores him. Perhaps she doesn't even hear him. The waiter brings the Vice Consul his glass of scotch. He checks for ice. The waiter gives Hilda a glass of champagne. She takes it and reaches out and pinches the priest hard. He jumps startled. But then decides to ignore it.)

HILDA: You must forgive me, Father. I feel compelled. I must tell who's real and who isn't.

(The waiter returns. Hilda pinches him on the ass. He reacts wildly and flees.)

HILDA: It's not subtle perhaps. But effective. How is the wine? No need to flatter me. It's not from my country. It's French. I'm not political. But I'll never serve our wines again! I was betrayed, you see. By my own country. Surely you heard about the coup? It was like a terrible storm. I lost my daughter—Anya. I rushed back. I tried. I was in Spain. My father was dying. I had to leave him. Cursing me. He was too sick to understand. He died hating me. What could I do? I boarded the first plane I could find. But the government closed our airports. There was no warning. We were turned away. We were so close. So close. I could see the lights of the buildings, even headlights. I could see the ocean churning in the dark. And Anya was somewhere below. Alone. In chaos. Oh Father, do you think she understood? *(She kneels.)* Father, forgive me, pray for me Father. Anya's only sixteen. Please pray for me. I couldn't stand her hating me and dying before she ever sees me again.

ALEX: Hilda. You've had enough.

HILDA: You're jealous.

ALEX: Sit down and turn pages for me. We're about to begin.

HILDA: You never used to be jealous.

ALEX: That was when you were sleeping with me. That used to make me feel quite secure, you know. Sleeping with you. Now come and sit down.

HILDA: I hate turning pages. It's boring. You can't listen. You have to watch. Who wants to *watch* music?

ALEX: Hilda!

HILDA: You think I'm drunk, don't you? *(To the crowd.)* Alex thinks I've had too much to *drink*. But it's not that. It's a bad day. You can't expect me to make *small talk* can you? Even under ordinary conditions it's beyond me. I wasn't brought up with small talk. My mother was a *saint*. She raised ten children—only six of whom she bore herself. My father was a *hero!* He cleared a thousand acres with one man and a machete. They killed fifty snakes a day and laid them out nose to tail in the plaza. When he wanted my mother, he went to her house and broke down the door. *That's what I expect from the world.* Not small talk!

(Alex leads her to the piano. The guests wait expectantly for Alex to begin.)

VICE CONSUL: *(Approaches some guests confidentially.)* Do you think Alex and Hilda will stay together? Really, you can be candid with me. God, I hope they do. I believe in marriage. *(He goes up to a woman.)* Would you marry me? How about a dance?

(Alex stands at the piano. He plays a chord softly. The crowd quiets. The little girl is very attentive, studying Alex. Hilda pinches the little girl who jumps and turns and stares at her with her hands on her hips.)

ALEX: Good evening. As you are probably well aware—I am Alexander Bertram Young—composer and musicologist—and this is my lovely wife, Hilda. We both thank you for coming to this series of concerts to help us raise money for our search for our dear, dear daughter... *(He can't go on.)*

HILDA: Anya.

ALEX: And as a tribute to your generosity, my wife's loving presence and my daughter's terrible, terrible absence, I want to play for you a concerto I was certain I had forgotten. A concerto I composed on a silent keyboard in prison— *(He whips it out. A wooden plank with a crude sketch of a keyboard on it.)* On the very board I drew with dirt and food and yes— blood.

(The audience murmurs again.)

ALEX: I had forgotten this concerto. But, now finally I remember it all! So— you will find this music like stepping off a cliff. I use only the extreme registers of the piano—the very highest—

(He strikes the plank. We hear the chord.)

ALEX: ...and the very lowest— *(He strikes a chord in the lower register. Then chords at both ends at once.)* Thus, I'm free of inessentials; I'm stretched temperamentally and philosophically. And—as a performer—the physicality of working the extremes is very free, very liberating. *(He sits at the piano.)* This is the music of the Twentieth Century!

(Wild applause. Alex raises his hands to attack the piano, but does not lower them to touch the keys. The music rises around him. Hilda wanders off to a chair in the hotel room. She picks up a stack of magazines and starts to thumb through them and falls asleep. Alex looks around for her. He rises angrily. The music continues and the crowd is in a rapt semicircle. He stalks off to find her. He stands over her out of breath and then vengefully, picks up some magazines and lets them drop with a thud to the floor. All the actors turn as one and stare at Hilda and Alex. Silence.)

HILDA: My God!

ALEX: Go to bed!

HILDA: You're angry with me.

ALEX: I can't stand it when you fall asleep in that chair.

HILDA: I don't sleep. I can't. I just close my eyes.

ALEX: Close your eyes in bed. Next to me.

HILDA: No. As soon as I lie down, I have terrible thoughts. Horrible visions. I just dreamt of a battle. A fight broke out and there was a barefoot little girl and a young woman stabbing someone with a long knife. And that stupid obsequious Vice Consul from home was there. Why would I dream about such an appalling man?

ALEX: Dream? How can you dream? Weren't you awake?

HILDA: Go to bed. Then you won't be angry with me. You won't see me here in the chair.

ALEX: Listen babe, I get really tired of you complaining you don't sleep. But you do. You doze off. I hear you snore. It pisses me off that you complain about not sleeping but you sleep sitting up. You do that for effect. It's some kind of reproof.

HILDA: Reproof?

ALEX: An accusation.

HILDA: I know what it means.

ALEX: Good. *(Alex starts looking into and on top of everything.)*

HILDA: What are you doing?

ALEX: Working.

HILDA: You're looking for something.

ALEX: Yes—an entire concerto.

HILDA: You'll remember it.

ALEX: Of course.

HILDA: Can I get you something? Some warm milk?

ALEX: Only if it's breast milk. Have you seen my pens? I hate it when I lose things.

HILDA: I know.

ALEX: Pens or little girls. It's really horrid, you know.

HILDA: Yes. I know. Alex.

ALEX: What?

HILDA: You should see a doctor.

ALEX: I find doctors boring, full of themselves. They think they know every— oh I see what you mean. I wouldn't worry if I were you. Not about me. So I'm a little obsessive about looking for things—you know it can be addictive, this search for just the right...right thing, the right word, the right moment, the right sound. The quest for perfection is never-ending.

HILDA: It was too soon to try and remember the concerto. Too soon—and in public.

ALEX: Damn it—it was there, flickering near my ear and as soon as I placed my fingertips on the keys—it sped away like a bat out of hell.

HILDA: That's what upset you tonight.

ALEX: Tonight? Well, yes and no. Actually—my whole life, that's what upset me! Honey—I'm upset because when I turn over in bed ready to hold you in my arms and whisper "Don't be afraid, I'm here"—you're gone. I'm upset because I'm on the brink of oblivion. I can no longer write a note of music. Not one note of my brilliant new concerto, not even a jingle for a deodorant ad. What's more—I know without a doubt that not one page of any piece of music I've ever written, not one scrap of melody will survive my demise by even one day. And that means not only will I be a forgotten failure in the future—but, oh God it also means all those crummy afternoons my mother chased me around the kitchen with a broom so I would practice were for nothing, naught, zero...oh yes and quite possibly I'm upset because I've lost my little girl and God only knows what's happened to her. And He's not telling. So you see I have had a few things on my mind—sleeping being the least of them. Where are my pens!

HILDA: When Anya's with us again, we'll be fine.

ALEX: When.

HILDA: When she is. Yes.

ALEX: Shall we try "if"?

HILDA: You listen to me Alex. I'm her mother. If anything were wrong, if she were hurt or dying, I'd know. I know I'd sense it. When I close my eyes—she's smiling.

ALEX: And when I close my eyes I see her hurtling by, twisting in the air. Her arms and legs askew—like a discarded doll. Her eyes were open. She was so frightened. Hildy—I dreamt she was falling.

(Hilda turns away abruptly.)

ALEX: Hilda, what can I do? My only hope was that she was with you. It was the only thing I could think of. After they opened the prisons, I searched everywhere. I couldn't find her. People would turn away. No one saw her. No one spoke to her. Houses were empty with the doors wide open. There were no lights, no phones. I prayed. I prayed she was with you.

HILDA: I knew you'd bring her with you on the plane. I knew you'd die before you'd leave her behind.

ALEX: *(He takes off his shirt. He has livid gashing scars over his chest and abdomen.)* I didn't die.

HILDA: You did for me.

ALEX: What do you want me to do? Do you want me to open up these again? Shall I bleed for you and for Anya? Will that help?

(Hilda touches his scar. Carmen leaves the party and signals for a waiter to follow. The waiter suddenly grabs Alex and forces him to his knees. He removes a watch and a lighter from Alex and passes them to Carmen.)

CARMEN: Welcome to prison. Welcome to the Candelaria. We're your unofficial welcoming party—we'd like to strip you of all foreign objects, right? *(She puts on the watch.)* Nice watch. Se-i-ko? What's that? French? Thanks so much.

HILDA: Hurt like I do. Suffer for Anya. Leaving her. *(She punches one of his scars.)*

ALEX: Don't!

HILDA: Do they still hurt? *(She presses one hard.)*

ALEX: Yes.

HILDA: Very much?

ALEX: Enough.

CARMEN: *(Lights the lighter under his nose.)* Oh wow. Look. Is this silver? I love this stone. Looks like a piece of sky. What is that—aquamarine? Great.

HILDA: Was she pretty?

ALEX: You mean the girl in prison?

HILDA: Yes.

(Carmen holds up a long knife with blood on it.)

CARMEN: My, my, my look, the garden's in bloom, I see. What does it look like? A rose, a carnation, Framboyan...A passion flower! I had a garden once—a shade garden and a sun garden. Vines in the shade, ivy, beans, squash. Flowers in the sun. We fed them both with trash. Garbage. They grew beautiful, just beautiful. Smelled like shit, you know. I didn't want any part of it, at first. But my father would slap me *(She slaps Alex.)* and say use whatever you got, even if it's shit. Look how good the garden grows. Another thing my father taught me—keep the dogs away. Not just the mean, bad ones that dig up all the roots, the happy little puppies too with floppy ears and wagging tails like you. They do the same damage. Good intentions and all. So you give them a good swift kick. *(Carmen kicks him.)* The harder the better so they never come back! Stupid foreigners! *(She stabs Alex.)*

ALEX: Pretty? Yeah, she was pretty like a meat cleaver.

HILDA: Yet, every time I touch this scar, you'll think of her. *(She presses the scar.)* Funny.

(Carmen exits.)

ALEX: Stop it.

HILDA: I want to hurt you.

ALEX: You can't.

HILDA: I will. You dog, you coward, you bastard!

ALEX: You can't hurt me, Hilda. Don't you see. As long as you're here with me—I can't be hurt. How stupid! Who would have thought I would be so tied to one woman. Your legs are too thin now, you have grey in your hair, you're filled with despair and bitterness—but—it knocks me out— you can still turn your head a certain way and break my heart. It's incredibly really. The only way to hurt me, really wound me, is for you to leave. *(Hilda is quiet. Alex takes off his wedding ring and puts it in her palm.)*

ALEX: Here.

HILDA: What are you doing? I don't want your ring.

ALEX: I don't either.

HILDA: But what does this mean? Alex?

ALEX: It means whatever you want it to mean. I'll know that when you give it back to me.

HILDA: When?

ALEX: Yes. When.

HILDA: Not "if"?

ALEX: Come to bed.

HILDA: Bring Anya back to me. Find her and bring her back.

ALEX: Come to bed.

HILDA: Why?

ALEX: We'll make love.

HILDA: I hate you.

ALEX: I love you more than ever. Hilda?

HILDA: We'll make love in the chair.

(The prison: Some guests at the cocktail party become vendors, beggars, relatives waiting outside the prison. They hassle Anya from time to time. The little girl is with her brother. She is slowly removing the flowers that cover him. Beneath each flower is a red wound. She makes a pile of the flowers next to her. Lights up. Anya comes running in. She is in her school uniform and is carrying some books. She goes to the gate of the prison, looks for someone to talk to, tries desperately to see inside.)

ANYA: Hello?! Hello?!

JOHNNY: *(Walking in on his usual tour.)* What do you want?

ANYA: My papá. He's in here. His name is Alexander Bertram Young.

JOHNNY: Don't know him.

ANYA: He was brought in. Today. Look. I know he's here. My neighbor followed the police. They grabbed him off the street and dragged him here. I swear.

JOHNNY: You can't stand here. Move back.

ANYA: Maybe you could find him. He's...he's not old, but he looks old. His hair is grey and he wears glasses. He's taller than you and...and I don't know what he was wearing but...

JOHNNY: I'm sorry.

ANYA: Papá! Papá!

JOHNNY: You can't stand here yelling like that.

ANYA: He'll know my voice. Is he in the courtyard? *(She strains to see.)*

JOHNNY: *(Steps between her and the gate.)* I'm sorry girl.

ANYA: He's an American. He'd be easy to spot. He's an American. I'm sure they made a mistake. They can't arrest him.

JOHNNY: Maybe he stole something. Maybe he killed someone. Even Americans do that.

ANYA: No. Not him. It's a mistake. He's a musician. A composer. He doesn't even have a penknife. Please.

JOHNNY: I'll be right back. What was his name?

ANYA: Not was. Is. His name is Alexander Bertram Young.

JOHNNY: I'm doing you a favor, you know. *(Johnny exits.)*

(Anya paces. She notices the little girl.)

ANYA: What's wrong?

(The little girl clutches her dead brother tighter.)

LITTLE GIRL: He's asleep. He's my brother.

ANYA: Is he hurt?

LITTLE GIRL: They covered him with red flowers from their magic wands.

ANYA: Those aren't flowers, little girl.

LITTLE GIRL: They are too!

(Johnny returns.)

JOHNNY: There's an American here.

ANYA: Is it him?

JOHNNY: I've already told you too much.

ANYA: Why is he in jail? What did he do?

JOHNNY: I don't know.

ANYA: Then let him out!

JOHNNY: I can't let him out.

ANYA: But he's in for no reason.

JOHNNY: Well he can't get out 'til we know why he's in. There's nothing I can do. Well, maybe you can give something. What can you give?

ANYA: I don't know.

JOHNNY: Do you have money?

ANYA: Why? What's it to you? Oh—I know.

JOHNNY: What?!

ANYA: You want a bribe. You people always do.

JOHNNY: You stupid girl, it's not for me. There are other people to pay off. I've seen it done.

ANYA: *(Goes to the gate.)* Papá! Papá!

JOHNNY: I told you. You can't do that.

ANYA: It'll keep his spirits up, if he knows I'm here. You tell him!

JOHNNY: *(Roughly jerks her away.)* No. Shut up.

    (She does.)

JOHNNY: They'll come out and put you in too. You're rich. I can tell. You expect everything to go your way. *(He hands her a handkerchief.)*

    (She blows her nose.)

ANYA: Thank you.

JOHNNY: And that uniform. Where do you go to school? I don't recognize it.

ANYA: The American School.

JOHNNY: It's a rich school, isn't it? Mostly foreigners.

ANYA: I'm not a foreigner. I was born here. My mother's from here.

JOHNNY: Well go to your mother and use your money to get your father out of jail. That's how it's done.

ANYA: My mother's in Spain.

JOHNNY: Well there's nothing I can do.

ANYA: You're from the provinces. I can tell by your accent. *(Looks at him closely.)* And you're only a boy. *(Disdainfully.)* There's obviously nothing a boy from the provinces can do. You probably still ride a donkey to work.

JOHNNY: You know if I really wanted to…

ANYA: What?

JOHNNY: You're spoiled.

ANYA: What would you do? Go ahead. I dare you.

    (He doesn't do anything.)

ANYA: See! So. You won't help at all.

JOHNNY: I don't pity you. If that's what you expect. I know girls who already have two children at your age, good mothers, hardworking wives. Go away from here. Go pull all those little strings you were born holding. You must know someone in the government. Get out of here!

    (Johnny marches off smartly. Lights dim except over the little girl. Stage right, Alex comes out and turns on the light near the piano. He plays a couple of notes with one hand. Then he starts writing. He plays a few more and writes and so on. Stage left, the little girl digs and the pile of dirt grows. Alex plays a little longer. He stops. The General's office: Meanwhile, stage left, the lights come up on General Juan Lescos Villanueva sitting in his white uniform at a large white desk talking on the telephone. Modesta is standing barefoot on his desk trying to make the ceiling fan work. The lights flicker on and off.)

GENERAL: Good! Livi would love to have you stay with us, I'm sure. However, our house was blown to bits. Just last night. Someone planted a bomb on our porch. In a brown paper bag. Half our living room is gone. And the porch—well you can imagine. Luckily we were out to supper. Yolanda had finally consented to go someplace with us. You can't trust anyone these days. How dismal.

MODESTA: Stupid idiots! How do they expect us to get anything done. This government's worse than the last. I don't care who hears me. There are stupid ugly electric wires all over the place, but you just turn on one little light and "poof," blackout. Modesta is good and fed up, let me tell you.

GENERAL: *(He reaches up her skirt.)* It's only a matter of finding the right outlet.

MODESTA: *(Slaps his hand away.)* You'll get a shock that'll rattle your teeth. *(She jumps down, the lights go on.)* It's about time. *(She takes up her mop.)* Lift your feet. Oh my God. Why do you put your cigars out on the floor? I keep the ashtrays clean! I tell you, Modesta has never seen such a mess, and if you're talking to the President, you tell him I said so. Tell him to get you those big silver ashtrays that stand on the floor. Move your chair.

(The General hangs up the telephone.)

MODESTA: *(Slapping his leg.)* Up. Up.

GENERAL: *(Puts his feet up.)* I know a few people who'd pay to see me taking orders.

MODESTA: Your wife for one.

GENERAL: I wasn't thinking of her. Are you done yet?

(Modesta brushes something out from under the desk and stomps it.)

MODESTA: There! Tell the President you need a fumigator too. But then, you don't talk to the President anymore—do you!

(The telephone rings. He answers it.)

GENERAL: Yes? What?!

MODESTA: So help me, if Modesta gets the tiniest hint this is one of your lady friends...

GENERAL: *(To Modesta.)* Shut up. *(Into the phone.)* Christ!

MODESTA: Modesta will tear her into pieces with her teeth!

GENERAL: Get rid of her. For God's sake. Keep her out!

(Anya rushes in clutching her schoolbooks.)

GENERAL: Oh, Jesus. *(He slams down the phone.)* Anya sweetheart. I thought you were in Europe.

ANYA: General...General...

GENERAL: You're upset. What is it, dear? Here. Sit down. Tell me what's the matter. Surely it can't be so bad.

ANYA: Papá's in jail.

GENERAL: Where's your mother?

ANYA: I don't know. Shopping in Madrid.

GENERAL: So your father's in jail. That's easily remedied, dear. I doubt he's done anything terribly serious—a lapsed visa perhaps.

ANYA: They beat him with clubs.

GENERAL: What?

ANYA: Oh General—

GENERAL: There must be some mistake.

ANYA: No.

GENERAL: I'm sure that wasn't ordered. Beat him? Who beat him?

ANYA: The police.

GENERAL: Are you sure? Perhaps something went wrong, come now. I can't help unless I know who arrested him. The local police? National guard? Special services? It could be the guerrillas. Who?

ANYA: I didn't see.

GENERAL: The uniform. Green? Khaki, Blue? Was there a uniform? The car then, a van, a jeep? Were there dogs? The national guard uses dogs. *(He takes out a piece of paper.)* A neighbor saw, eh? Give me her name.

ANYA: I can't remember. I know her so well, but I can't remember…Oh General…

GENERAL: Never mind.

ANYA: You know her. She has red hair.

GENERAL: Oh yes…her husband's a pharmacist…

(Anya nods.)

GENERAL: He has a mistress twice his age. I wouldn't give that woman much credence. She's an hysteric. She has visions. She talks to them in church. There. There. Don't cry. Everything will be fine, I promise. Modesta, bring the girl something warm for her nerves. Coffee?

(Anya shakes her head.)

GENERAL: Tea then. Hot tea. Go ahead.

(Modesta stalls.)

GENERAL: Quickly now.

(Modesta exits.)

GENERAL: *(To Anya.)* Now then…

ANYA: He's in prison. I went to the Candelaria.

GENERAL: Ahhhh good—but wait I can't believe they let you see him.

ANYA: I didn't see him. A guard told me he saw an American there.

GENERAL: A guard. Give me his name.

ANYA: I don't know it. I'm no help. He's from the provinces though.

GENERAL: They're all from the provinces. The only way to make them useful is to shove a gun in their hands…or in their backs. *(He laughs and checks himself.)* But it's only a matter of a simple phone call. I'll straighten it out in no time.

(Modesta enters.)

GENERAL: Here's your tea. Drink it up.

MODESTA: No tea. Tea is for grannies. I brought milk, warm milk with honey. Just the thing for little girls. Very little girls. Their bones are still forming. Here little one.

ANYA: *(Takes the milk.)* I'm not so little. I'm sixteen.

MODESTA: You look twelve. A man wouldn't think you were more than twelve.

GENERAL: See? I'm making the call to the Candelaria right now. *(On the phone.)* Yes. Get me Lieutenant Gutierrez. Justo Gutierrez. Now. All right. I'll hold. *(To Anya.)* That American might not even have been your father. Knowing him, he's wandering around the beach, setting up twenty tape recorders to get the sea's resonance from twenty different perspectives or something equally esoteric. How's your tea?

ANYA: It's milk.

MODESTA: Warm milk.

GENERAL: Sometimes these young soldiers—you know they're very patriotic, but very young—children really—they feel very macho, very complete with a gun. They might have thought your father was a spy—all that equipment he carries—who knows? And then, being a foreigner…you'd think he'd have lost his accent by now, wouldn't you, with that wonderful ear for music? I hold you and your mother directly responsible for him talking like a gringo after all this time. You cater to him too much. He has a terrible accent. Still. Abominable. *(Into the phone.)* Yes. I wanted Gutierrez. Gutierrez Hebrard! *(To Anya.)* You didn't tell them you were coming here, did you?

ANYA: No.

GENERAL: Does anyone know you were coming?

ANYA: No one.

MODESTA: *(To Anya.)* Move your feet please.

GENERAL: Modesta. Take your pail and mop into the hall.

MODESTA: I still have to finish here.

GENERAL: Finish later.

(Modesta hesitates.)

GENERAL: Leave! *(As Modesta is walking out, so she can hear.)* These girls from the provinces are impossible! Stubborn, dull-witted. You can't do a thing with them.

(Modesta slams the door.)

GENERAL: This is taking a long time. I'm sorry. Prisons aren't quite as organized as they should be, but then, we're not Germans, are we? *(He waits.)* We'll have this cleared up by tomorrow at the latest. What's one night in jail?

ANYA: Don't make Papa stay there overnight! Please.

GENERAL: What's so bad? I spent a night in jail once, in the States, when your father and I were at the University together. I studied agricultural management and he was in philosophy. That says it all, doesn't it? But I was more successful with women. I had an accent you know. That seemed to free them of constraints. And I drank to excess on occasion—so I was quite free of constraints. Your father never quite approved. But we were very close. He was the only one I called to bail me out. He took his time. He came the following morning. I always suspected he wanted me to learn my lesson. I did. I didn't drink for two whole weeks. But I tell you, it was difficult being a foreigner. You become quite literal and lonely in another language. But don't worry. I won't leave your father in jail overnight just for that. It's a slight temptation. I admit. Vengeance is sweet—but one doesn't play around with such things. *(Into the phone.)* Hello. Yes. Lieutenant Ortiz. Ahhh Carlos, it's you. Where's Gutierrez? Well where was he? No! Wait! Wait! All right. I'll hold. *(To Anya.)* How's your milk?

(Anya grimaces. The General fishes in his desk and pulls out a silver flask.)

GENERAL: Terrible cures for terrible times. Would a little of this help? What do you think? Yes? But—are you old enough? Of course you are. *(He pours some rum into Anya's milk.)* You must know Yolanda, no? She's a little older I think. Yes. Yolanda never learned to handle liquor. She gets tipsy with just a drop. It's the only time she's funny now. She's seventeen. She speaks to her mother and me through clenched teeth! Adolescents! *(Into the phone.)* For Christ's sake. Tell him to call me immediately. Immediately. Tell him he has five minutes or we'll use a bayonet to get him unplugged! Bastard! *(He hangs up.)* The director is temporarily indisposed. Actually he's in the bathroom. Don't cry. Don't. If he doesn't call back in five minutes, I'll go there myself. *(He takes a sip from his flask. He pours some more into Anya's glass.)* Here. Drink up. You'll feel better. I usually don't drink during business hours. But this news has upset me. Here we are suffering. Yes?

ANYA: Yes.

GENERAL: And your father? *(He shrugs.)* Oh to be like your father—footloose and fancy free wandering around the countryside recording his little folk ditties—

gathering them from patriot and rebel alike. Music not politics. That's what's important. Right? Let's drink to that. *(He toasts and takes a drink.)*

ANYA: I want to call my mother.

GENERAL: Why trouble your mother? You'll be with her in Europe tomorrow, sitting on your daddy's lap. Drink up.

ANYA: Mama knows everyone. She could call the Governor. She could call the President.

GENERAL: No, no, no—we can't have her turning the world upside down for such a small thing. I'll take care of it. You just relax and when you see Hilda—give her my regards. Ahhh Hilda, she always had me pegged... since we were very young. I knew her best then. We were neighbors. Did you know? Such a proud girl with eyes as green as new leaves. Those eyes. I was pitiful. She allowed me to walk her home. She had no choice really. I'd be there waiting for her. Joyfully. She'd always be late. Who cared! I was always there. What could she do? But she never kissed me. Not once. I was never meant for a girl like that. *(He bends over and kisses Anya roughly on the mouth.)*

(Anya jumps up. Her books drop to the floor.)

ANYA: Why did you do that?

GENERAL: A question. You're like your father. Your mother would have slapped me. *(He picks up her books.)* History. Latin. Latin's a dead language. Recite something. You could redeem a whole culture for me.

ANYA: I can't.

GENERAL: Would you prefer to wait outside with my secretary? *(He opens the book and shoves it in front of her.)*

ANYA: Hanc tibi, Fronto pater, genetrix Flacilla. Puellam
Oscula commendo deliasque meas,
Parvola ne nigras horrescat Erotion umbras
Oraque Tartarei prodigiosa canis.
Impletura fuit sextae modo frigora brumae.
(The general takes the book away from Anya.)

GENERAL: They should always have young girls teach Latin.

ANYA: You didn't understand a word, did you?

GENERAL: *(Reading rapidly at first, then with feeling.)* To you, Fronto my father, and you Flacilla my mother I commend my darling and my delight, my little girl Erotion. So that she may not be frightened at the dark shadows or at the Tartarean hounds' fearful jaws. She would have completed only six cold winters even if she had lived that number of days longer than she did.

"Mollia no rigidus caespes tegat ossa; nec illi.

Terra, gravis fuerris: no fuit illa tibi."

Do not lie heavily upon her, Earth,

She was not heavy on you.

How moving. Well... *(He clears his throat.)* I was a fair student, but a good soldier. And if your Latins weren't good soldiers, they wouldn't have left us a poem, not a scrap of paper. *(He takes a drink.)*

ANYA: You don't know if you can get Papa out. That's why you're drinking.

GENERAL: *(Holding the flask.)* Do you want some more?

ANYA: No. I want to call my mother.

GENERAL: You think badly of me now, don't you? Kisses are so dangerous. And I admit—I do jump into things. But then, I was never good at sitting back and admiring statues with blank eyes in museums. I want my hands in wet clay. And here I am with a pure heart and dirty hands.

ANYA: I don't care what you've done. I want to use your phone. May I?

GENERAL: Of course, of course, go right ahead...Oh—but my dear, perhaps you should consider something before you call? Yes? I didn't want to worry you before, you were so upset and frankly I've had a trauma or two—did I tell you our porch was bombed—pulverized really. No? Last night. You see it's dangerous times, quite dangerous. They're thinking of declaring a state of siege and all that. The guerrillas you know. Well, you see—perhaps your father did do something serious—I'm only raising the possibility. They did beat him. Perhaps he was capable of something much worse than we thought. Now, now I know it's unlikely. But what if the wrong person is contacted at the wrong moment do you see? It could be disastrous...for him...for you...for all of us. Understood? You'll see your father today. Right now. I'm making the call again. See? Why don't you go compose yourself. Run cold water on your wrists. Wash your face. That's a girl.

(Anya starts to leave.)

MODESTA: *(Stepping in.)* May I come in "mi General"?

GENERAL: All right. *(He dials a number.)* The bastards haven't returned my call. If they think because I had a tiff with that smirking bankrupt aristocrat who poses as Governor that...*(Into the phone.)* Hello. Yes lieutenant Gutierrez. At last. General Lescos. No excuses. Anya Young is in my office. Yes Young. Her father's at the Candelaria—correct? Good. She'd like to see him. Could we arrange this—immediately, teniente? I'm sure you can find a car and driver—perhaps the one who takes your wife to buy dresses. Yes. We're all in danger aren't we—so? Good. Thank you.

(He scribbles a brief note. To Anya.) You see? *(He hands her the note.)* Your pass. *(To Modesta.)* Take the girl downstairs and wait with her for the car. *(Into the phone.)* What color? *(To Anya.)* Dark blue. *(Into the phone.)* You will hold, Teniente, there are other matters…*(To Anya.)* Tell your father to take heart. Good luck.

(Modesta and Anya exit.)

GENERAL: *(Into the phone.)* Listen. Detain the girl. I need to know where she is at all times. Understood? Just keep her out of the way until I can get her father released. What do you mean? Of course I can get him released. Yes still! And so help me if there's one veiled threat, one wrong number in the dead of night, one mysterious paper bag left on my porch—you're a dead man. Understood? You owe me this. Yes. At the Candelaria. It's only for a few days, you bastard. I need her where I can get to her at a moment's…The Candelaria. There should be room enough. I hear you empty it out quite regularly. *(He picks up her schoolbooks. Opens one. Slams it shut.)* Who gives a damn what she sees. She's a kid not a spy. Well, sixteen. Look that won't be necessary. I'll have her out of there in a matter of… For Christ's sake, she couldn't tell a Marxist from your asshole you idiot! It's one little girl, you shitfaced, constipated little…Yes, she's pretty. No, she's nothing to me. Of course I know her father's a collaborator. Why do you think I had him arrested? They must be gotten out of the country. He's an American, you imbecile. Can you imagine the press!

(Modesta enters.)

GENERAL: The Governor would prefer he were beaten to death with a polo mallet but…It's politics not personal. No Yolanda and her barely…what do you mean? They would never think that. Impossible. Impossible! For the love of God, it won't come to that! Then don't let her out of the car! Send her back. I said send her back! I order you, Teniente! Why? Whose car is it? Mother of God. *(Defeated.)* All right. All right then. God…all right. If you have to dump her, dump her. *(He slams down the phone, enraged to the point of tears. He looks up and sees Modesta.)* What are you looking at? Take your clothes off!

End of Act I

ACT II

THE HOTEL ROOM

It is early the following morning. Stage right, bright light filters through the windows. Stage left is empty, but also brightly lit. Far downstage right the little girl enters dragging an immense rectangle of sod. It is quite heavy for her and she has to stop and rest. Once in a while she goes to the opposite end and brings it forward and then drops it and goes to the front and drags it again, proceeding to cross the entire stage. As she is doing this Hilda comes out and opens the blinds. She exits, and then returns with a tray of coffee and cakes. She exits and returns with a vase of large carnations. The little girl finally settles with the sod at the far end of the stage. The buzzer sounds long and insistent. Hilda comes out, extremely apprehensive, checks herself briefly in a mirror near the door and opens the door. General Juan Lescos, now called Juan, enters. He carries a small package wrapped in newspaper.

HILDA: Juan!

JUAN: Well…well…

HILDA: My…I can barely speak. Please sit down.
    (They sit.)

HILDA: It's good to see you. I'm glad you called.
    (They sit in silence.)

HILDA: Alex should be out in a moment. He's changed so. He can never seem to find anything anymore. His watch was under the bed. His keys were in an old jacket. He's looking for his wallet.

JUAN: How sad we should all have to meet like this.

HILDA: Shall I take your jacket? You must be hot. These rooms are terribly overheated.

JUAN: Yes. Yes of course. *(He stands and removes it.)* It's not the best quality, but I don't need jackets anymore.

HILDA: Yes.

JUAN: I'm in Miami now.

HILDA: On vacation?

JUAN: I own a restaurant, a cafe really. I always liked cafes. Now I own one.

HILDA: And Livi? How could I forget to ask for Livi? I tell you I don't know where my mind is. You should have brought her with you. Or perhaps you did.

JUAN: No.

HILDA: She must enjoy the warm weather there in Miami. She was quite a swimmer as I recall.

JUAN: She's not in Miami.

HILDA: I see.

JUAN: I've remarried.

HILDA: It's good you're not alone.

JUAN: Yes.

(*Awkward silence. Alex enters freshly showered.*)

ALEX: Johnny Lescos! God, I thought you were dead!

HILDA: You two must want some coffee.

ALEX: Coffee? Juanito—you want some coffee? I'd prefer some scotch myself.

HILDA: It's ten in the morning.

ALEX: With water.

HILDA: Alex.

ALEX: Well, don't think of it as scotch. Think of it as salvation. What do you say, Juan? Salvation or coffee?

JUAN: Both.

ALEX: A born diplomat.

HILDA: I can't watch. (*Hilda exits.*)

ALEX: Born to straddle fences—eh Juan? (*He pours the drinks.*) I hope you'll forgive this nasty bravado. That's just the way I woke up. I can never quite tell what state of mind I'll find myself in when I awake these days. You see, I don't need externals to make life unpredictable, I have myself. But you look well. And Livi?

JUAN: She stayed behind. Change was always difficult for her and…Thanks. (*He taxes the drink.*) We lost Yolanda.

ALEX: Yolanda?

JUAN: Yes. She…ah…went out to watch the rioting. One day. During the coup. She stood by the street holding her coffee cup. Like this. Watching the rioting as if it were parade…and a stray shot—perhaps it wasn't a stray shot, one never knows—she was killed by a stray shot. Yolanda was never political, you know. She wanted to have a good time with her friends. Not exactly profound, but now… (*He shrugs.*) Livi wouldn't leave her grave. So!

ALEX: I'm terribly sorry.

JUAN: Yes. Of course. Well, I have a restaurant. A cafe really. Coffee and hot milk. "La Parroquia." It's across from a church. The men sit and read the papers while the women are at mass. I read about your concerts. I saw your photos. I thought… *(He takes a long drink.)* We all got separated—imprisonment, the coup. It was like a terrible storm. I couldn't find anyone.

ALEX: I stewed in jail. Actually, I thought you were either dead or a son of a bitch. Letting me stew in jail. You hear the damndest things in jails—boots, shouts, pleas, prayers, tires screeching, shots. You know. And there was this one…this teenage Medea. She had big earrings, big earrings. They looked like they belonged in a bull's nose, and she had a knife, this teenage Medea. *(Pause.)* I shouldn't be so broken up. I apologize. It was only—what? Three months. I thought of all those heroic people—writing on matchbook covers and toilet paper. Bearing witness, you know. Persisting for years beyond all odds. And there I was quivering with fright. It was a thoroughly disgusting show of weakness. Really. And I blamed you. I was furious. There I was trapped in a room. Anya was God-knows-where. And you were the most powerful man in that province.

JUAN: You overestimated me.

ALEX: Did I?

JUAN: Yes.

ALEX: In any event, here we are.

JUAN: Yes.

ALEX: Who would think that some goons would yank me off the street like that.

(Juan is silent.)

ALEX: You know, I had these idiotic, terribly trite dreams for Anya. I thought she'd study, maybe law or nursing. Something significant, but then never use it. She'd marry instead and have babies. How sappy, how completely selfish. I never wanted her out in the world. Well. What can I say?

JUAN: Here we are.

ALEX: Most of us.

(Hilda enters with a tray.)

HILDA: Cream? Sugar? Aren't I the dutiful wife.

JUAN: Three spoons.

HILDA: So! What shall we do? How does dinner after the concert sound? Italian? French? Greek? Anyone for Greek? Cheese and olives sound perfect in this heat.

ALEX: What do you think, Juan?

JUAN: I brought you this. *(Juan hands Alex the book wrapped in newspaper.)*

ALEX: Thank you. I'd say "You shouldn't have"…but… *(He unwraps it.)* It's Anya's schoolbook. Her Latin book.

HILDA: Anya, my baby. *(She takes it.)* Sweetheart.

JUAN: We all got separated somehow...

ALEX: How the fuck did you get the book?

JUAN: Anya left it with me. The day she was detained.

HILDA: You saw her? Juan, what happened?

JUAN: She came to me for help. I couldn't help her.

HILDA: She was detained?

ALEX: Don't give me that bullshit. Christ of course you could help her. You were the most powerful man in the province.

HILDA: She was detained?

JUAN: That changed!

ALEX: Don't give me that shit!

HILDA: Alex!

ALEX: Alex what?!

JUAN: I should kill you. You betrayed me.

ALEX: I never betrayed you.

JUAN: You traveled under my signature, my personal recommendation. You were allowed to travel to all those squalid little villages infiltrated by hundreds of guerrillas. I stuck my neck out for you. I put my life on the line and you shit on it.

ALEX: Those villages were about to be wiped out and maybe hundreds, maybe thousands of years of musical history along with them.

JUAN: And so? So we lost a little music? So what? A clean slate. Life goes on. Maybe that's how it's meant to be—waves breaking—one crashes down a new one appears and then another and another and another. Everyone gets their chance to crash on the beach and so what? Would the world be worse if we lost some music?

HILDA: For God's sake!

JUAN: *(To Hilda.)* But Hilda, I ask you—what would you do with a man who invites one of the revolutionaries—one of the leaders no less—to record a little song for posterity? In front of the entire village? In front of the entire world? *(To Alex.)* What did you think that would do to me? To Hilda? To Anya? To my poor Yolanda? The only time you had a life-and-death decision in your hands and what did you do with it? You didn't even recognize it!

ALEX: You had me arrested?

JUAN: I had to order your arrest immediately. I was under suspicion. Your daughter walked into the middle of it. I couldn't protect anyone.

ALEX: You fucking had me arrested?

HILDA: You fools. Talking about yourselves. What about Anya? Please. Please. Tell me about Anya. Juan.

JUAN: She came to see me. But I let her go. I lost her.

ALEX: You lost her. What was she to you—a key chain? Didn't you even bother to find out what happened to her?

JUAN: I found out.

ALEX: Okay.

JUAN: *(Looks at Hilda then Alex.)* I really think we should talk privately.

HILDA: No.

ALEX: All right.

HILDA: No! I won't let you. Say it.

JUAN: I lost her.

HILDA: Say it.

> *(Juan is silent.)*

HILDA: You always have so many words, Juan. And now for Anya, you have so very few?

JUAN: I heard they threw her from a helicopter into the sea!

ALEX: Shit!

JUAN: The air's thin. She fell quickly. I hear the sea's like granite from that height. She never felt a thing, I'm sure.

HILDA: Oh Alex.

JUAN: The helpless can't help the helpless.

HILDA: She fell. Such a long, long way.

ALEX: Shhh. Now.

HILDA: She must have been so afraid. Tumbling. Falling. Over and over.

ALEX: No Hildy. Don't think of her falling. Not falling. Think of her later. Afterwards. Asleep. Think of her asleep. Shhhh.

> *(They stand embraced.)*

JUAN: Alex? Hilda? What should I do? Should I leave? Should I keep in touch? She was so light, you know. Her ribs were like little twigs poking through her shirt. I touched her when I showed her to the door. She was so light, but I can hardly bear her weight. Imagine. *(He hesitates to leave.)* I don't know what comes next. You can call the police if you like. *(Juan exits and joins the cocktail party. He takes a drink.)*

> *(The Village: Stage left Sergio, an old peasant, steps forward. A waiter holds out a microphone to him. People clap and move stage left.)*

SERGIO: You want me to sing into this?

ALEX: Right. Like this.

(He grabs the microphone and does a couple moments of an exaggerated Marvin Gaye type number. Everyone laughs.)

ALEX: Now you try it. When I count to three. One, two, three.

SERGIO: *(Sings.)* Maidens, beautiful maidens are worth gold

and young women silver.

Beautiful girls are worth gold

and young women silver.

A good widow is worth copper

shiny red copper

but an old lady's worth lead.

Yes, she's worth lead

and a separate bed,

a separate bed.

(People clap.)

SERGIO: That's an old song. Very, very old. I'm old and my grandfather taught it to me over the kitchen table a long time ago. He was having a fight with my grandmother. He'd sing loud and she'd come in, holding a chicken. He'd get to the part about old ladies and she'd twist the chicken in the air. Like this. Her thumb right here on its neck. Break its neck right there. They'd argue like that. He'd sing and she'd kill chickens. Kind of a threat, I guess. But what a party later. Lots of chicken.

(People applaud. A young man, Lucan, comes through the crowd with two other men carrying rifles. He hands his rifle to one of them and steps forward.)

LUCAN: I'd like to sing something.

SERGIO: *(To Alex.)* There's some folks who feel very strong about him.

ALEX: Who feels so strongly about him?

SERGIO: The government. A few women.

ALEX: So, is this song political?

LUCAN: Not at all. Except...

ALEX: Except?

LUCAN: I'm the one singing it.

ALEX: Why here?

LUCAN: It's for my wife. Two hundred kilometers from here.

ALEX: I don't get it. Oh. You want me to record it for her.

LUCAN: There's no need for that. You underestimate our primitive technology. We have no need of telephones or telex. We have gossip. Why did you know that if you stoop to pick up a dollar bill in the streets of one of these villages, within a minute and a half, four people will appear claiming they dropped it...And for an occasion like this—what can I tell you—within hours every gesture, every word, albeit somewhat exaggerated—will have traveled up and down this coast. This woman tells her brother who's mayor of that town who tells his wife and mistress who each tell their lovers and sisters and there you have it—an ancient miracle. Gossip. So I'll sing now and perhaps by tonight, my wife will be shaking her head and saying I'm a complete idiot. But then she'll smile. And I do want her to smile. So now—what do you say?

ALEX: You don't talk like a peasant.

LUCAN: And if I'm not?

ALEX: Yeah, sure. Sing. Why not? It's only music. Stand over there. *(To someone in the crowd.)* You. Hold the microphone here. Like this. Great.

LUCAN: I don't want this taped.

ALEX: I do—for my wife.

LUCAN: This is for my beautiful Ann-Marie. *(Singing.)*
>   I was nothing before
>   but now I'm a king
>   I'm guardian of her nights
>   and guardian of her dreams
>   and I love her.
>   I love her.
>   You can destroy all my hopes
>   You can crush me, but then
>   when she opens her arms
>   I'm made whole again
>   And I love her, I love her.
>   I'm far and away
>   in the night on the hills.
>   She's alone by a fire
>   she tends.
>   But asleep we can dance
>   through a forest of dreams,
>   my arms on her waist
>   my face in her hair
>   once again
>   and I love her
>   I love her.
>   I was nothing before
>   But now I'm a king
>   I'm guardian of her nights

and guardian of her dreams

and I love her I love her.

(He finishes. Clapping. The little girl approaches Lucan.)

LITTLE GIRL: *(To Lucan.)* Is my brother with you? His name is Germán. He went to the hills.

LUCAN: I don't know, little girl.

LITTLE GIRL: I just wondered.

(Lucan goes to Sergio. Hilda lowers her shawl and goes to the piano. She plays a note.)

ALEX: It was a love song, Hildy. He was lonely.

(Hilda exits. Bars descend. The crowd cowers. They take out paper and rip it into pieces and throw it in despair. They put ashes on their faces. Sergio stays close to Lucan. He kneels and Lucan blindfolds him.)

(A Prison: They are in the courtyard of a prison. The little girl is digging outside the bars. Sergio applies, with Lucan's help, blood to his temple, chest, and back. Lucan paces.)

LUCAN: "I play the night of the soldier, the time of the man without melancholy or extermination, of the type cast far from the ocean and a wave, and who does not know that the bitter water has separated him and that he is growing old…that he is growing old…uh… *(Races through.)* gradually and without fear, dedicated to what is normal in life, without cataclysms, without absences, living inside his skin and his suit, sincerely obscure. So, then, I see myself with stupid and gay comrades who smoke and spit and drink horribly, and who suddenly fall down, deathly sick. Because where are the aunt, the bride, the mother-in-law, the sister-in-law of the soldier?

SERGIO: Ahhh yes. Where are the women? Women.

LUCAN: Will you stop. This is a very hard poem to get through.

SERGIO: Why don't you remove this bandage from my eyes now.

LUCAN: These are just the early poems. When I get to the later ones.

SERGIO: He's Guatemalan?

LUCAN: No. Chilean. Neruda was from Chile.

SERGIO: Ahhh, to the south.

LUCAN: Don't play the canny old Indian with me. Chile's to the south of everything. Now…Now I've lost my place.

SERGIO: The women…sisters-in-law and so on…

LUCAN: I should cover your mouth.

SERGIO: Too late. I'm dead. You killed me.

LUCAN: I had to.

SERGIO: Yes. Yes. Yes. Yes.

LUCAN: How can you be in such good humor? It drives me crazy.

SERGIO: I like you. I liked you right off. I even forgave you for walking right into my living room that first time without knocking. You were so young and respectful. I mistook you for a son—perhaps the son who could see the future. I thought you were a liberator.

LUCAN: I am. You'll see.

SERGIO: You're not a liberator. And although you do see the future—a bright place inhabited by very happy people it seems—you always smile when you talk about the future...

LUCAN: Enough! We've been through this, old man. I warn you!

(A door is opened and shut. Anya is pushed in.)

SERGIO: Ahhh. I smell a woman.

LUCAN: What?

(The prisoners back away. Anya drops her schoolbooks. She is terrified.)

LUCAN: Take your clothes off. Slowly.

ANYA: No!

LUCAN: Open your books then, one by one. Move carefully.

(Anya opens her books in slow motion.)

LUCAN: Take off your clothes.

ANYA: I won't.

LUCAN: Then roll on the floor for Christ's sake.

(Anya lies on the floor. Very, very carefully she rolls over. She sits up.)

LUCAN: The last woman thrown in here was booby-trapped.

(Suddenly three women in black veils followed by two guards with clubs enter. The women point to one prisoner and then another saying things like "this one beat my son," "this one raped my daughter," "this one bombed my house," "this one robbed my store." The guards beat all the prisoners in a frenzy. As suddenly as they came, they leave. The prisoners groan, examine themselves and each other. Anya stands alone.)

ANYA: Who were those women?

LUCAN: The mothers? They let them in sometimes so they can point their fingers.

ANYA: Are you guilty?

LUCAN: None of us. We're political prisoners.

ANYA: Why do they do it then?

LUCAN: It's a function of despair.

(He looks at her. Anya sits on her books.)

LUCAN: You're a student. No. Don't explain. Spare me. *(Goes to the bars and yells.)* What the hell is this—a municipal holding pen? Why have you put a whore in here. I demand to see the director, the doctor, the door-keeper. I demand to see Amnesty International. The United Nations. The International Red Cross! My God, I haven't had my shots, my pills, a blood transfusion. What the hell's the matter with you assholes. Idiots!

ANYA: I'm not a whore.

SERGIO: You're acting like an idiot.

LUCAN: *(To Sergio.)* Shut up.

ANYA: I'm sorry.

LUCAN: *(Snaps.)* I'm not talking to you! *(He walks away.)*
    (Sergio follows on his knees. One of the prisoners, a priest, leads the others in prayer. Lucan is disgusted and walks away. Anya watches and then follows Lucan.)

ANYA: Will you help me?
    (Lucan doesn't want to notice her.)

ANYA: I didn't mean to offend you. Before. Whatever it is I did. Will you help me?

LUCAN: Help you?

ANYA: Protect me.

LUCAN: From them? *(He indicates the kneeling prisoners. He laughs.)* How about from me? I don't know who the hell you are and you certainly haven't the slightest idea who I am. And you ask me for protection? Perhaps I'm a maniac.
    (Anya backs away. Lucan walks to another place in the cell.)

ANYA: *(Approaches him.)* Then just your name. What's your name?
    (He says nothing.)

ANYA: Please.

LUCAN: Donald.

ANYA: Donald?

LUCAN: Duck.

ANYA: What?

LUCAN: Donald Duck. My name is Donald Duck.

ANYA: Donald. Is that what they call you?

LUCAN: You got it.

ANYA: My name's...

LUCAN: *(Shouting.)* Don't tell me your name!

ANYA: I won't. I promise, Donald.

LUCAN: And don't fucking call me Donald!
    (Anya begins to sob.)

LUCAN: Shit! My name isn't Donald. Look. You're a girl. This is a rough situation.

(He laughs.) A rough situation. But you have an out. Maybe. Fuck the Lieutenant. He's susceptible. Screw the guards; lick their boots, clean their asses. Anything might work. Just get the fuck out of here, get out, live, marry, have babies and start the world all over again.

ANYA: You're crazy.

LUCAN: *(To Sergio.)* How does that joke go? *(To Anya.)* I'm crazy but I'm not stupid. You could have a chance. Grab it. The guards will come back today. For roundup. Tomorrow at the very latest. Those poor devils over there are preparing themselves already. But you have other resources. What a shame you're not carrying any makeup. *(He laughs bitterly.)*

SERGIO: You've changed. You're not what I thought you were.

LUCAN: No shit.

ANYA: Who are you talking to?

LUCAN: Thin air.

ANYA: Well I won't do what you said. You are crazy. *(Anya looks at the priest and his group.)*

LUCAN: Are you a spy?

(Anya looks around.)

LUCAN: I'm talking to you! Are you a plant, a stool pigeon, a traitor, a spy? Never mind. *(He stalks away.)*

(Anya picks up her books. She is about to go to the priest.)

PRIEST: God is looking down
   from the height of heaven
   out of the blue where the stars are
   and He sees what is going on
   He is watching over us.
   And however powerful evil is,
   the night is calm and beautiful
   and in God's world
   there is and will be goodness
   as calm and beautiful as the night.

LUCAN: Don't go there. That crap saps your will. They're halfway across the black waters with their eyes closed. It drives me crazy. Well, they'll be closer to God soon enough—compliments of the regime.

ANYA: They're going to die?

LUCAN: You're all going for a little helicopter ride—perhaps God will catch you when you jump.

ANYA: Oh no. Me too? Me too? They'll throw me out of a helicopter?

LUCAN: Maybe I'm wrong. They did before, but... No. I'm not wrong.

ANYA: You've stayed alive. How have you stayed alive?

LUCAN: Me? I'm colored beads for the Indians. I'm currency, dear. One of me for two of them—if the tables turn. And turn they will and they know it… *(Yelling out.)* Don't you know it? Don't you?! *(Changes abruptly.)* They'd rather break me than kill me. It becomes quite a game—oh yes. These people have done all kinds of nasty things to make me a violent, vindictive fellow. But they won't succeed. They've only slightly increased my well-honed skepticism. Yes—I was trained in skepticism by a whole crew of quacks—law professors really—I received a full dose of incisive, deductive and inductive foresight and hindsight. So if you think I'm mad—what you see is not the work of our captors. No. It is the product of our universities. However, skepticism keeps me free of corruption. Of course, it does help that Fate has left me unbreakable in other ways. Ah yes—my misfortune is their bad luck. Every single person who was close to me—man, woman, child—has been wiped out, murdered, erased. So I'm quite free of entanglements and committed only to larger causes. Idiots! Long live the Revolution!

ANYA: I'm sorry. *(She kneels.)*
"Our Father, who art in heaven.
Hallowed be thy name." *(etc.)*

LUCAN: Drivel! *(He recites Neruda to drown her out.)*
"If at night, wildly alone, I could gather oblivion
and shadow and smoke,
above the railroads and the steamships,
with a black funnel,
biting the ashes,
I would do it for the tree in which you grow
and for the nests of golden waters you gather
and for the vine that covers your bones…
(He wrenches Anya to her feet.) Stop that! Get up!

ANYA: What? Why? What are you doing?

LUCAN: Anyone with a true understanding of God wouldn't talk to him all hunched over and mumbling in the dark. Christ. We're fighting a whole revolution to get women off their knees.

ANYA: I'll talk to God any way I want! Leave me alone!

LUCAN: Nothing should bring you to your knees! The peasants kneel and pray before they're shot, you know. They die on their knees! *(Pause.)* Look, nothing happens before it happens. Maybe they'll just torture you.

Maybe you won't die at all. Maybe there's another way out. *(Abruptly.)* Where's your mother?

ANYA: My mother?

LUCAN: Yes. Surely you have a mother.

ANYA: It doesn't matter.

LUCAN: You don't care for her I see. Well you're probably just like her. Where is she?

ANYA: Abroad.

LUCAN: She's rich, then. Good. Maybe they'll keep you for her money. And your father?

ANYA: He's American. Will that help? He's famous. He gives concerts. He has records. Will that help? Tell me!

LUCAN: *(Stares.)* Who am I to tell you anything. *(He walks away. Continues quoting with more difficulty.)*
"Cities of wet onions…"
No that's not it. Who cares?
Ahhh.
"Cities with the smell of wet onions
wait for you to pass singing raucously
and silent sperm boats pursue you
and green swallows nest in your hair…
in your hair…in your hair…
and also snails and weeks…

ANYA: *(Kneels.)* I'll pray for you too.

LUCAN: No.
(Anya prays. Carmen and a waiter walk in the courtyard by the little girl. A bell rings.)

LITTLE GIRL: What's that?
(Carmen and the waiter exit running.)

ANYA: What's that?

LUCAN: The guards.

ANYA: For me?
(Lucan shrugs.)

ANYA: My name's Anya.

LUCAN: Don't.

ANYA: What's your name? Tell me your name.
(He doesn't answer.)

ANYA: I'll give you a name in my prayers.
(Carmen and the waiter rush in with clubs.)

CARMEN: *(Swinging at Lucan.)* Back. Back.

WAITER: *(Pushes Anya in front. Drives the other prisoners with his club.)* Out. Out. Single file. Out.

(He kicks the priest. The priest falls. He kicks him again.)

WAITER: Bastard!

End of Act II

ACT III

THE COCKTAIL PARTY II

The scene should startlingly reflect the cocktail party scene at the top of the play—however the obviously dreamlike elements should not be there. The set is the same, the colors, the initial character speeches are isolated against the cocktail background and so on. Hilda is in her red dress. Alex is dressed as he was in the dream scene...Lucan will transform his appearance from jail to party with the help of Sergio during Hilda's first monologue to the priest.

ALEX: Good evening. As you are probably aware—I am Alexander Bertram Young—composer and musicologist and this is my lovely wife Hilda. We both thank you for coming to this series of concerts held in memory of our daughter Anya and of all other children who perished needlessly in prisons throughout the world. *(He continues silently miming his speech from the first act.)*

VICE CONSUL: *(To Hilda.)* Your hubby is quite a guy. You know I'm real sorry to hear about your little girl.

(Hilda goes to the priest, Lucan begins his transformation into the minister.)

VICE CONSUL: Waiter, Scotch please. Dewars, Neat.

(The waiter takes his glass and exits. Vice Consul tries unsuccessfully to get someone to listen to his spiel.)

VICE CONSUL: I tell you it took me years to figure out why I always got the runs down there after a couple of drinks. I was Vice Consul. I always had ice. Damn hot and I sweat like a pig. Always had the runs. Thought it was a fucking hangover. It was the damn ice.

(Everyone laughs. As Vice Consul is speaking Sergio takes off his blindfold and helps to dress and clean up Lucan who heads for the party.)

HILDA: *(To Priest.)* How is the wine Father? No need to flatter me. It's not from my country. It's French. I'm not political, not really. But I'll never serve our wines again. Some things are simply too much. My own country betrayed me—my little girl—Anya—is dead.

ALEX: Before I sit down to play, we'll begin with a recording of some folk songs I was able to snatch from the lion's jaws. *(He goes to the sound system and starts with the recording at the village.)*

(Lucan enters, reporters run up, flashbulbs flash, there is much "this way, Mr. Minister," "Mr. Minister" and jockeying for a place close to him. He looks around, spots Hilda, and comes over. He overhears her conversation.)

LUCAN: Señora Hilda Santa Maria de Young?

HILDA: Yes?

LUCAN: I must talk with you. Alone.

HILDA: Do I know you?

LUCAN: Too late! Here come the vultures. Help me out, will you? *(Loudly.)* You set the revolution back a hundred years. Mrs. Young. I'm making a public spectacle of myself trailing after the ousted aristocracy.

HILDA: *(Loudly.)* No one's forcing you! *(Whisper.)* You're crazy.

LUCAN: *(Loudly.)* Ahhhh. You deign to speak to me. How delightful!

HILDA: *(Turns to face him. Loudly for the reporters.)* My dear Mister Minister. I have nothing to say to you. The grocer is living in my house. That grocer! It's not that he's a grocer, mind you. It's that he's a cheat. He always put his finger on the scale whenever I bought fruit from him. Now he's living in my house!

REPORTER: Do you think you can stay in power? How about the flight of the middle class?

LUCAN: Oh, I can understand your—pique—it must be rather irritating to have a man like that living there. I admit. But you should meet the other family who's sharing your home. Extremely nice people. All seven of them!

HILDA: *(Loudly.)* You're going out of your way to offend me.

LUCAN: *(Whisper.)* Yes I am. Anything to get your attention. Turn your lovely face to mine. Ah…ecstasy. *(Loudly.)* You're right. I've misbehaved. *(He takes a flower from a vase.)* My apologies. *(He presents Hilda with the flower. To the press.)* You're very much like this cut flower—quite pretty, quite decorative, but with no roots. Without roots what you have to give will fade rather quickly, don't you think?

HILDA: *(Whispering.)* Why are you torturing me?

REPORTER: Is it true you were tortured? Mister Minister—I heard you had innocent peasants killed? Would you address that question?

LUCAN: *(To the reporter loudly.)* Torturing you? What a comfortable torture, don't you think? Champagne, flowers, glazed duck, lovely gowns, laughter. Why there's no blood, no screams, no rusty instruments. *(Takes a glass of champagne from a passing waiter.)* This is quite good. *(To Hilda.)* Did you choose it? It's French, obviously. Our vineyards have been destroyed. The owners doused them with gasoline and set them on fire. They preferred ruin to confiscation. How very, very selfish. I'm so glad you didn't burn your estate, Mrs. Young. War is hell, don't you agree?

HILDA: And you're spending it here at a cocktail party?

REPORTER I: Yes, why are you here?

REPORTER II: Mister Minister—

LUCAN: Ahhh—you see this as a cocktail party. I see this as my last battlefield. I'm here fighting for the souls of our expatriates. I need them to help me with this conundrum I find myself in—you see. I've been a successful revolutionary, which I love. However when you are a successful revolutionary, you then become a politician, which I hate. This is an insoluble dilemma. As a revolutionary I had to be unafraid of moral absolutes— indeed I had to kill for moral absolutes but now, as a politician, I must be unafraid of expediency. And whereas I spent my life as a revolutionary saying things which people did not want to hear. Now I'm the Minister of the Interior in a democracy and must say a little of what everyone wants to hear. This is tremendously wearing, and I will not compromise alone. Therefore I am here to enlist my expatriates as patriots of the highest order. And I shall begin with you, Mrs. Young *(To Hilda.)* Will you return to your country or will you abandon us? Will you be part of that exodus that throws us to the dogs; turns us over to foreign money, alien talent, or self-serving mercantilists who will hash out their foreign enmities on our soil at our expense? Will you be part of that? Will you turn your back and become American overnight? Or perhaps French? I don't deny things have changed. Change was long overdue. The country fell to us like ripe fruit. We barely had to shake the tree, Mrs. Young. But change is only change. It isn't disaster and it isn't success. The aftermath of change tips the scales. Will you be one of those who tips the scales? And which way will you tip them? Will you be a cheat, Mrs. Young? If you don't return—it will be your finger on the scale this time—not the grocer's!

HILDA: Jack—Jack—you there. Yes. Please get these people away from us.

VICE CONSUL: *(Herding the reporters away.)* In my vile youth, I was vice consul in that backwater tropical port in Latin America—of course I had been a near-eastern studies major—but what the hell…

(He continues his speech from Act I Scene I, but we can no longer hear him.)

HILDA: Now, with so many beautiful vowels to play with, shall I tell you what I think of you? I think you're very dashing. I can see why people follow you. And you're hopelessly rhetorical, our Latin curse, but you do speak well. However, you're like most revolutionaries—middle class and insensitive; just the type of person who doesn't notice the suffering of those closest to him. You're impervious. That's why you're ruthless. So I really have nothing more to say to you. You would have killed my father without a backward glance. He was one of those great landowners, we owned ten thousand hectares at one time. I loved him. He'd call the peasants "Señor" and shake their hands, but when he'd pass, the peasants would grab his hand and press his fingers to their foreheads and call him "patron." Was that his fault? Was it mine? Of course, it no longer matters. You can't kill him. He's dead. My daughter is dead as well, so as you can see there is no further reason for me ever to return to my country.

LUCAN: But there is. Your daughter's alive.

HILDA: What? What are you saying?

(Alex approaches.)

ALEX: Is this man annoying you?

HILDA: He's just told me Anya's alive.

LUCAN: There's strong reason to believe she escaped from prison.

ALEX: Have you seen her then?

LUCAN: No.

ALEX: I see.

HILDA: But you know something.

LUCAN: I have it on good authority.

ALEX: We have it on good authority that she died.

HILDA: Alex, for God's sake, let him speak.

ALEX: Of course I'll let him speak. I have to let him speak. We have no choice. *(To Lucan.)* You see, every time someone comes to us with unendurable sincerity and tells us "Anya is alive" or "Anya is dead"—then she becomes dead and then alive for us each time, over and over and over. And we'll always listen. But if you're lying, I'll kill you.

LUCAN: I knew Anya. We shared a cell. I was perturbed, perhaps insane. I turned on her. Afterwards...I felt abysmal. What can I say? I was haunted by her—in her little uniform, with her schoolbooks! When I was freed by the coup, I went back to see what had happened to her. I was told by more than one eyewitness that she was pulled suddenly from a line of prisoners who were waiting to be...

HILDA: Thrown from a helicopter. We know...

LUCAN: Yes. But Anya was led away. They all said that it was a man in uniform who pulled her out of the line and she was simply led away. That's all I know.

ALEX: You seem familiar...

LUCAN: Do I?

ALEX: Never mind. Go on. Where were we?—a man in uniform? What kind of uniform? Was it a soldier? A guard? An officer? With which force? The army? Do you know?

LUCAN: It's almost a clueless clue, isn't it? In a country where every man has a title and every title has a uniform. Perhaps it was a soldier, or a guard. But it could just as well have been a postman, a waiter. Perhaps a doorman. Perhaps it was someone with good intentions.

HILDA: Perhaps it wasn't.

LUCAN: Perhaps it wasn't.

ALEX: I have a strange feeling. If I know you, I'll know something else.

LUCAN: I promise you I'll find her. Soon. Very soon.

(Sergio comes over with a glass of champagne. Very chatty. He addresses Hilda and Alex, who don't see or hear him.)

SERGIO: Again. He's talking about the future. Such a bright place it seems, inhabited by very happy people. He always smiles when he talks about the future.

LUCAN: I'd shut up if I were you! Waiter.

SERGIO: We can't live in the future. Jefe—the future's a dream.

LUCAN: Waiter!

(A waiter comes over and wrestles Sergio to his knees. It appears as if his hands are tied behind him.)

WAITER: Jefe?

LUCAN: Shoot him. *(He turns away.)*

(The waiter drags Sergio away.)

ALEX: Ann-Marie. Your wife's name was Ann-Marie. You sang for me once.

LUCAN: Yes.

ALEX: A love song. And here we are. The composer who doesn't compose and the guerrilla poet who is no longer romantic. But that was a sweet moment.

LUCAN: A surpassingly sweet moment, that sweet little village with grass in the streets and that colorful old man—his name was Sergio—you know. He sang and danced for you. Of course that was the last time he danced. He never danced again. I had to have him shot you see—and I had to burn all the grass in those streets and the houses; and slaughter all the cattle and other little things like that—tactical necessities we call them— but that was later—after we met. When I sang for you, I was making a gesture. I wanted my wife to hear about my song and to smile knowing I was dreaming of her up in the hills. But that didn't quite work out either. Did you know? She never heard about the song I sang for you that day in the village. She'd been dead for two months

ALEX: Another lost paradise. I don't know what to make of you. I really don't.

I've always been apolitical—except when I was eighteen and called myself a Communist without the least knowledge of Marxism, Leninism, or of anything else. And here you are raised up like Lazarus, I suppose, all ready to help me. *(To Hilda.)* This man's the reason I lost Anya. Now he'll be the reason I find her. What kind of madman's joke is this?

LUCAN: I need a few days to arrange…

ALEX: We'll go to Miami and wait there. I can't be still any longer. And by the way, fuck you and the day I ever set eyes on you. *(He exits.)*

LUCAN: At least he has you.

HILDA: I suppose he does.

LUCAN: I loved my wife. Madly.

HILDA: I can't feel love right now.

LUCAN: I can. How strange. I'd like to see you again.

> *(Cameras flash. Guests surround him and move him away. A waiter approaches Hilda.)*

HILDA: Give me a drink. Something sweet. Terribly sweet. Anisette.

> *(Carmen comes up to Alex. She's wearing a party dress, long earrings and very, very red lipstick. She grabs his arm and jerks it toward her to look at the watch.)*

CARMEN: Do you have the time? Nice watch. Se-i-ko. Is it French?

> *(Alex jerks his arm away.)*

HILDA: Are you all right?

ALEX: Of course.

HILDA: It was wonderful news, don't you think?

ALEX: Not if she's dead.

HILDA: No. Not if she's dead. Alex…

ALEX: Look at him, over there. Lucan—isn't that his name? He's quite heroic and likable. I liked him quite a bit. You must like him too. You like heroes. You need people who are larger than life; who can fill a room because they're handsome or powerful.

HILDA: I know it's a failing. But why do you think I chose you? There you see. I love you. I adore you. And Anya's alive. She's alive. I believe it. Anything can happen. So forget that man, forget your concerto. Play a bolero. Play something sweet. Terribly sweet.

> *(We hear a bolero. Hilda lies on a bed. Lucan joins her. They caress. Sergio lies dead at their feet, his face bloody.)*

LUCAN: I'd like to see you again.

> *(They kiss. Lucan leaves the bed. It is an hotel room. Outside, a little girl*

places a rock underneath her brother's head like a pillow, she stands back to admire it. She steps back, looks at him, and crosses his arms on his chest.)
(The hotel room: Miami. There is a knock at the door. Hilda answers. Modesta is there in a cheap suit.)

HILDA: Yes?

MODESTA: Is this the...Young—

HILDA: Room?

MODESTA: Yes. Your husband, Alexander—Mister Young...

HILDA: *(Starting to shut the door.)* I'm sorry.

MODESTA: ...Modesta always forgets there's a Mister Young.

HILDA: What do you want?

MODESTA: So you're Hilda. You are beautiful. You're much more beautiful than I could ever be. But Modesta isn't as jealous as she thought. You have a husband. I never thought of you with a husband. And you're not young...

HILDA: How did you get up here? Who are you? *(She tries to shut the door.)*

MODESTA: I'm Modesta Izaguirre de...Lescos. Lescos. You know Juan. I'm his wife. *(She walks in the room.)* We live in Miami. Surely you haven't forgotten?

HILDA: Juan married you?

MODESTA: Why not? You know Juan well enough. As long as he knows it's chicken, he doesn't care if his meat's white or dark.

HILDA: I didn't mean that.

MODESTA: Didn't you? Well, you're the woman he dreams of, but I'm the one he's with. So I had to come see you for myself. I'm pregnant.

HILDA: You poor girl.

MODESTA: I'm not a poor girl. I feel more secure now. Modesta's been through hard times with him. She helps him manage his restaurant. She's more useful than he is now. Who wants an ex-politico who's fifty-five? Do you? Modesta can cook and clean. She's only twenty-four. She's got him to give her a baby too. Modesta doesn't have to be afraid of you anymore.

HILDA: And I'm not young.

(Hilda approaches Modesta, staring at her. Slowly she reaches out to pinch her hard. Modesta slaps her.)

MODESTA: Bitch! Why did you do that?

(Modesta moves stage left where it is a grey morning. A line of prisoners, including Anya, stands shivering. They don't speak to each other. There is a park bench to one side. Carmen, Modesta's sister, sits there taking a break, smoking.)

MODESTA: So what's up?

CARMEN: A break.

MODESTA: They give you all the cigarettes you want?

CARMEN: No. Prisoners bring them. I help myself.

MODESTA: You shouldn't smoke. It smells up your breath. *(She takes a cigarette.)*

CARMEN: I got a ring for you, look, real gold with stones. Take it. I got more.

MODESTA: I don't wear rings. My hands are always in water.

CARMEN: Come on. At least take this cigarette lighter. I like to give my big sister stuff. It makes me feel good. Take it. I sent Mom a watch. French. I don't approve of foreign stuff though. Makes money leave the country. It's bad for our workers too. Buy national. That's what they say. "Homemade is well-made." They're right too. But Mom can get more money for the one I sent. It's French, did I tell you?

MODESTA: Look at that girl!

CARMEN: Which one? Oh her. Why?

MODESTA: I thought I knew her.

CARMEN: Her? Where would you know someone like that?

MODESTA: No place. No place at all. I like her dress. With her blonde hair I mean.

CARMEN: Yeah. What a waste. Blondie's getting her wings today. Dress and all. So, how're you and the General?

MODESTA: Quiet!

CARMEN: Okay. So tell me.

MODESTA: We're fine.

CARMEN: Don't get knocked up. Not unless he marries you in the Church.

MODESTA: He's already married. But she's old. He's tired of her.

CARMEN: Maybe she's tired of him. He's old too.

MODESTA: Not so old. A civil ceremony's fine with me. Modesta likes her house, her little baby, a husband.

CARMEN: Not me. I like 'em young and full of vinegar. Like Johnny here. Hey Johnny. How're you doing? *(Elbows her sister.)* Watch this!

JOHNNY: Oh, hi Carmen. *(He bows to Modesta.)* Johnny Pacheco Orduñez, at your feet.

CARMEN: *(To Modesta.)* What did I tell you. They still do that on the coast. *(To Johnny.)* This is my sister Mode…

MODESTA: Modesta. Hi.

JOHNNY: Hi.

CARMEN: Sit down for a minute.

JOHNNY: Nope. I got to get a prisoner.

CARMEN: Loosen up. You're too straight. But cute…good-lookin'. Look, I got some cigarettes for you…and look at this… *(Lights a lighter.)* The lighter's real silver with a blue stone. I think it's aquamarine.

JOHNNY: I can't take presents from you.

CARMEN: Don't be a jerk. We're friends. We don't have to be engaged you know.

JOHNNY: But I don't got anything for you.

CARMEN: Another time. Another time. I like perfume. Just so's you know. Or silky things…You know. I'm a real girl.

(She elbows Modesta. They laugh.)

CARMEN: So?

JOHNNY: Yeah? *(He's eyeing the line of prisoners.)*

CARMEN: There's a dance coming up. You going?

JOHNNY: Yeah, probably. I like to dance… *(Looks at the line of prisoners.)* Where are they going?

CARMEN: Flying. To the ocean floor.

JOHNNY: Really? *(He laughs. Then he stops.)* They'll be killed. *(He takes a closer look.)*

MODESTA: I'd like to go to that dance.

CARMEN: Not with the General. What a bore.

MODESTA: He wouldn't go anyways. Johnny. Maybe Johnny could get me a date.

CARMEN: Yeah, Johnny. Where's your grandfather live? She likes 'em old.

JOHNNY: I've seen that girl in the red dress before. *(He goes to take a closer look.)* She's American, right?

CARMEN: She's nothing special. Plain as white milk. Hey, you got a girlfriend back home?

JOHNNY: Maybe a few.

(He looks at Anya. She looks away.)

MODESTA: Carmen. Let's go. I don't like to see these things.

CARMEN: Lucky you don't know 'em. Then it's really bad. *(She shrugs.)*

MODESTA: Nice meeting you, Johnny.

CARMEN: Friday, then?

JOHNNY: She's going to be killed, eh? Thrown out like garbage.

CARMEN: Like garbage.

MODESTA: Quit it.

CARMEN: I'll walk you as far as the gate. *(Checks her watch.)* I'm twenty minutes late. That rhymes. Gate. Late. I'm really something. You wanna come, Johnny?

JOHNNY: I'm going to have some fun. *(He walks straight to Anya.)*

CARMEN: I tell you men are animals. Some things are just too hard to take.
(She grabs Modesta and pulls her offstage.)
(Johnny pulls Anya roughly by the wrist. Anya resists.)

JOHNNY: Whore, puta, prostitute, filth! Would you like to serve your country before you go overboard, eh? A little fun for the homeboy?

ANYA: Let me go.

JOHNNY: Oh, you'll go all right. Are you in such a hurry to die—scum! *(He pulls her far downstage.)* Don't scratch me! Bitch! Traitor! *(He hits her.)* Shut up! Just do what I say!
(They move forward. The line of prisoners moves offstage. We see the pattern of clouds move across the back of the stage. Some birds. They are in a park. He throws her on a bench. Modesta is in the park eating her lunch.)

JOHNNY: There. Sit! See. I can talk to you like a dog. *(He looks around.)* Do you remember me?

ANYA: No.

JOHNNY: You asked me if I still rode a donkey to work.

ANYA: I don't remember. What do you want?

JOHNNY: I'm a man. You're a woman. What do you think I want?

ANYA: Do what you want then. I don't care.

JOHNNY: Have there been so many?

ANYA: There haven't been any. I just don't care.

JOHNNY: So, you're a virgin?
(She doesn't say anything.)

JOHNNY: You can't fool me, you know. I can tell the difference.
(She doesn't answer him.)

JOHNNY: I'm not a virgin.

ANYA: Who cares?

JOHNNY: Stupid girl. Don't you know anything. If you're a virgin, I'll marry you. If you're not, I'll send you to a whorehouse.

ANYA: What?

JOHNNY: I don't think they should kill you. Idiot. I saved your life. Yeah. They thought I was going to take you out and rape you and cut your throat. Didn't you? That was pretty good.

ANYA: And you want to marry me?

JOHNNY: Sure. Only if you're a virgin.

ANYA: Why? You don't even know who I am.

JOHNNY: Sure I do. Your mother was in Spain. I was at the gate when you were looking for your father. You said you went to the American school.

I know who you are. I thought of you over and over, but I never thought I would see you again. Girls like you don't look at me twice. *(He touches her hair.)* Girls like you with light skin and light hair and read foreign magazines and wear pretty clothes. But you're spoiled.

ANYA: You're right. I'm really spoiled. I can't cook. I can't sew. It would be completely stupid to marry me. I'd cry all the time. Why don't you just let me go.

JOHNNY: You'll have pretty babies. I want lots of them. My mother'd be pleased. She'd like someone else in the house. My sisters moved two towns away and she complains she hardly sees them. She complains a lot! She has arthritis, so she bends way over when she walks. She complains she knows every crack in the floor better than her own daughter's 'cause that's all she sees.

(He laughs. Anya doesn't.)

JOHNNY: You could give her massages. You could read to her too. She can't read. I can read, but I won't have time. I'll fish like my father. He was a good fisherman, but he bought a boat with a partner and they had terrible fights. My father had a bad temper and hands like hammers. People were afraid of him. Me too. So finally someone shot him in the back. I still own half the boat and the partner's old now. He had no sons. So I have something to go back to. I'll walk in with a wife. A beautiful wife. Can you imagine? We'll have a good life, as long as you're a virgin. Otherwise I can't promise you anything. If you start out with more than one man, you'll always want more than one man. I wouldn't stand for that.

ANYA: I don't want to go with you.

JOHNNY: Do you want to die from a helicopter?

ANYA: No.

JOHNNY: You'll be safe with me. There's only five hundred in my town. We don't let strangers in. My cousin's brother-in-law is mayor. We all call each other "cousin" whether we're related or not. We probably are. Not many new people around. That's why I left. But now with a new wife—it'll be different. There's dances in the park and you can swim in the river—that is—when I take you.

ANYA: Why get married? Why not just have a good time…for a while. You know.

JOHNNY: Once you have babies you won't think so much about leaving.

ANYA: I don't want babies.

JOHNNY: You can't stop that.

ANYA: I'll hate you.

JOHNNY: I saved your life. You won't hate me.

ANYA: It'll be so lonely for me, you know. And my parents—they'll think I'm dead.

JOHNNY: I know that. But I want you. Now kiss me.

ANYA: No.

JOHNNY: Don't act like that.

ANYA: You can kiss me, if you want. I won't yell or anything.

JOHNNY: No. I want you to kiss me. *(He slaps her.)*

ANYA: That's how you treat a wife?

JOHNNY: Oh, yes. Now kiss me.

ANYA: Fine. I'll kiss you, I'll fuck you, I'll lick your boots if you want me to, I'll clean your ass and I'll have babies and start the world all over again. That's what you want isn't it! *(She kisses him on the cheek.)*

JOHNNY: *(He grabs her.)* Who taught you to talk that way?

ANYA: Some guy in jail.

JOHNNY: If he taught you anything else, I'll know. *(He kisses her on the mouth.)* This is the best thing I've done in my life! I'll treat you like a queen. You'll see. I'll get you a dress and some sandals. We'll get my things. But quiet. If you talk to anyone but me I'll have to shoot you.

ANYA: I'm cold.

JOHNNY: Here. *(He gives her his jacket.)* Wait til Carmen sees I've run off with you. I'm glad I'll be out of reach. She'd tear my eyes out.

ANYA: Who's Carmen?

JOHNNY: A girl. Let's go. *(He pushes her.)* Move!

(They exit. Modesta watches as she returns to the hotel room.)

MODESTA: *(To Hilda.)* If you're nice. If you're civil, Modesta will tell you quite a bit about your daughter. Modesta can say anything she wants. I'm safe now. I have a baby. Maybe your daughter has one by now too—a dark little baby. Life is so different sometimes from what you imagine.

(On a roof we hear a helicopter nearby. Wind.)

VICE CONSUL: Mr. Minister—may I call you Lucan? I'm like you, ya know. I'm a misplaced person. I was born in Wisconsin. We had four feet of snow every February. And now, after the tropics, I can't tolerate winter anymore. The tropics changed me, man. I was a pretty light-hearted guy before that—now I can't rest till I check everything out. The unexamined life is a crock of shit—just a little lesson I learned there—you know what I mean. Don't get me wrong. I loved it there. Those dances you have are great—the huarache, the merengue. *(He does a couple of steps.)* Not bad for a gringo, eh? Wait. Don't leave. I was vice consul in your country before the coup—actually I was junior vice consul, but I had some important responsibilities, I really did. And I studied Spanish—and Quechua...well, yeah, that's a little farther south than you, but I did read some marxist history. You know Andre Guntar Frank—"The Development of Underdevelopment." He's a pretty shitty writer you must admit—but he did have a point about mono-economies and stuff...don't you think? I mean do you think he's right? I mean how do you know what's right? I hear you're really eliminating those death squads and you have a program for illiteracy and all that—but a lot of people don't like you. This could be just another flip-flop of power not a revolution at all. That's depressing. But how do you know? Who do you trust? I mean you look like a pretty nice guy and all...

LUCAN: I'm a butcher and a saint.

VICE CONSUL: Very good. That's funny. Well—guess what—I'm off to Tel Aviv. I'm reassigned. Near-eastern history and economics was my major field originally—of course it's been seven years since college...but look, I'm boring you so—will you sign something for me?

LUCAN: Sign something? What?

VICE CONSUL: A check. No. Just a little joke. *(He searches for a scrap of paper.)* Before you leave. Sign something. You know, like an autograph.

(A week later—a room with potted palms, a fan. Open boxes. We hear seagulls. Hilda is on the balcony.)

HILDA: Alex, come look. It's a beautiful stormy sunset. The clouds are red. Red. *(She looks up at the clouds.)*

ALEX: *(He comes up and stands quietly behind her.)* You have to pour water into the toilets to make them flush. And those damn crabs scuttling around the shower. This morning the largest and best hotel in the country ran out of butter.

HILDA: Oh God, it's beautiful. Alex—I want us to go right now. Down this beach, down any beach to find her. Oh Anya.

ALEX: Hilda, can you ever forgive me?

HILDA: We'll find her and all will be forgiven.

ALEX: How could I have been so stupid and pompous to have lost...Hilda, I always believed in extremes. I thought extremes were life. I searched for them—you know the razor cliff, the ravenous lion behind me. I hungered for the excruciating moment of clarity I'd achieve just before the world was being ripped away from me. That moment in art is worth everything. Everything. But in life—all I've done is plunge us into frantic darkness. Hilda, let's go to sleep and find this is all a horrible dream.

HILDA: I'm more awake than I've ever been. *(She kisses Alex.)*

ALEX: Please.

HILDA: Alex…

ALEX: You must be uncomfortable in all this jewelry. Take it off. *(Hilda laughs.)* Come on. Lie down with me. *(Hilda fumbles with her necklace.)* Here, let me do that for you. *(He undoes her necklace and kisses her neck.)* There. Is that better?

HILDA: Yes.

ALEX: And this earring. Do you want it off?

HILDA: Yes.

(Alex takes off the earring and kisses one ear.)

ALEX: And this other one? I can't imagine you want to sleep with one earring on. *(He takes that one off and kisses her other ear.)* Now, do we have bracelets? *(He takes her arm.)* Yes. Wonderful. Two! *(He takes one off and kisses her wrist.)*

(A loud knock at the door.)

HILDA: Who's that?

(Alex shrugs.)

HILDA: No one knows we're here, do they? Who knows we're here?

ALEX: I'll get it.

(A waiter leaves the party and gathers some of the red flowers and makes a bouquet. Alex opens the door. He gives them to Alex. Alex tips the waiter. The waiter exits. There is a card. Alex reads it. Suddenly we are aware of the cocktail party going on. Faintly. Alex is obviously stunned. He crumples the card and stuffs it in his pocket. He's unsure of what to do. He sits down.)

HILDA: *(From the balcony.)* Alex? What was it?

ALEX: Flowers.

HILDA: Flowers. Thank God. I thought it was something terrible.

(Alex gets up slowly and walks out to her.)

HILDA: Alex? Is something wrong?

ALEX: No. No. I just feel left out. They're for you.

HILDA: Who would send me flowers?

ALEX: Lucan.

HILDA: He wouldn't dare.

ALEX: Well he did. Here.

HILDA: I'm sure they're for both of us. Where's the card?

ALEX: You'll have to thank him. Oh yes—and mention the toilets.

HILDA: Was there a card?

ALEX: Yes.

HILDA: What's the matter with you? What did it say? Let me see it.

ALEX: It said "Good Luck." I ripped it up. I got jealous. I'm sorry.

HILDA: Well, I'll throw them out.

ALEX: Don't.

HILDA: I'm sure he meant these ironically. He once compared me to cut flowers...pretty but they fade quickly...

ALEX: Keep the flowers until they fade then—we should take advantage of everything beautiful for as long as we have it. Really. Keep them.

HILDA: All right. I will...they're not very pretty...they look like flowers those street children sell at intersections.

ALEX: Keep them.

HILDA: Do you still want my bracelet?

ALEX: What?

HILDA: My bracelet. My bracelet. The moment's ruined, isn't it?

ALEX: Ah yes. One bracelet left. *(He takes it off and kisses her wrist.)*

HILDA: Don't be jealous.

ALEX: I hate it when a lover sends my wife ugly flowers.

HILDA: Alex. We were never lovers.

ALEX: Really? Kiss me. *(He kisses her deeply.)*

HILDA: I wish these flowers had never come.

ALEX: Me too.

HILDA: I'll tell you what!

ALEX: What?

HILDA: Here. *(She takes the ring from a pocket.)*

ALEX: I can't take it.

HILDA: Why? Oh, the flowers.

(Alex doesn't say a thing.)

HILDA: You must take it. Don't you see. We have to be united when we find Anya. Oh. I see. You don't believe we'll find her. That's it isn't it?

ALEX: No, Hilda. By all that's holy. I know we'll find Anya. There's nothing I'm more sure of at this moment.

HILDA: Well good then. Fine. I'll seduce you then. You'll see. I'll send you magnificent flowers. I'll fill you with music. Again. Alex?...Maybe I will go to bed. This has all exhausted me. *(She kisses him and starts out.)* You know where we should start looking? Down around Nautla and Boca Andrea—there's this song stuck in my head. My maid used to sing it when she braided my hair. Those were such beautiful days. Everyone was alive then. *(Sings and half hums.)*
In a small wooden boat with a main sail
sailing, sailing on the sea

Nautla my love and lover
That's where I shall be
where I shall be.
You know, music can break your heart.

(Hilda kisses him and exits. Alex pulls out Anya's schoolbook from one of the boxes. He sits down on a chair. He takes the card out of his pocket. The Vice Consul approaches.)

VICE CONSUL: "Good Luck"?...The card I sent, didn't say "Good Luck"! Those idiots at the consulate must have botched it up, as usual. And did you see those flowers? I sent enough for half a dozen roses—and look what they picked! Flowers from a street urchin. I bet they spent the rest on booze. Let me see that card! *(He looks over Alex's shoulder.)* Hey. Wait a minute. You lied. They got it right! It says "My condolences on your dreadful loss"...was "dreadful loss" okay...I asked a couple of the gals at the office before I sent it...I mean I wanted the right word...you can't just say "dead" or "death" or anything. Jeez...I saw the news on the telex. What a shock! Exhaustion and exposure. How terrible. Whoa—don't tell me you hadn't heard yet?

(Alex opens Anya's book and starts to read. We see the little girl digging. She is tired.)

ALEX: Puellam oscula commendo deliciasque meas,
Parvola ne nigras horrescat Erotion umbras
Oraque Tartarei prodigiosa canis,
Intertam veteres ludat lasciva patronos
Et nomen blaeso garriat ore meum...

LITTLE GIRL: Hey you!

(The little girl is outside the prison. Carmen passes.)

CARMEN: *(Annoyed.)* What do you want?!

LITTLE GIRL: Could you help me?

CARMEN: What?

LITTLE GIRL: Tuck me in.

CARMEN: All right.

(The little girl brings Carmen to her brother. She lies down next to him and crosses her arms on her chest.)

CARMEN: There.

LITTLE GIRL: Okay. Now a prayer.

CARMEN: I don't know any prayers.

ALEX: Mollia no rigidus caespes tegat ossa, nec illa
Terra, gravis fueris, no fuit illa tibi.

Do not lie heavily upon her, Earth.
She did not lie heavy on you.
(Bits of the concerto come up. Then all of it. Lights dim to black.)

 END OF PLAY

THE REINCARNATION OF JAIME BROWN

ORIGINAL PRODUCTION

The Reincarnation of Jaime Brown was first presented through the New Plays Program at American Conservatory Theater (Carey Perloff, Artistic Director), San Francisco, California. It was directed by Craig Slaight; costumes by Allie Floor; lighting by Kelly Roberson; music composed by Lois Cantor, and Richard Taybe was the assistant director. The cast was as follows:

Jaime Brown	Stephanie Potts
Jimmy	Mike Merola
David Baldwin	Ryan Kennedy
San Bot Lhu (Sammy)	Sarah Hayon
Hudan Bot Lhu (Hughie)	Uri Horovitz
Tina, Marie, Joyce	Christianne Hauber
Boris	Brad Clard
Wilson Meredith	Jack Sharrar

CHARACTERS

In order of appearance:

JAIME BROWN, nineteen years old, street poet

JIMMY (James Hobarth III), nineteen years old, juggler, or other street performer, educated at Princeton

DAVID BALDWIN, twenty-three years old, singer, composer

SAMMY (San Bot Lhu), any age, all ages, expert in reincarnation, played by a woman, but appears as a man until the end

HUGHIE (Hudan Bot Lhu), as above, but a man, dressed identically to Sammy, always speaks in questions

MARIE, twenty, from Brooklyn, intermittent girlfriend of David's

JOYCE, twenty, Wilson's onetime date

BORIS (The Butler), twenties–thirties, strapping, handsome, blond Russian

TINA, forties, the Polish maid, Boris's wife

WILSON MEREDITH, late sixties, tycoon, literal, but cultured

> *All bits and crowd scenes should be played by cast members who are not in the immediate scene. No effort should be made to hide this fact. The same actress plays Tina, Marie, and Joyce.*

PLACE

All action takes place in the present at:

    Port Authority Bus Terminal in New York City
    Jaime's Apartment
    Wilson's Estate
    The Beach
    Kennedy Airport

ACT I

Jaime Brown enters in black. She carries a paper cup of coffee and wears a derby. She has obviously just awakened. Port Authority Bus Terminal takes shape around her. People wander by, pillars come down (obviously made of cardboard). They descend unevenly. One lands on a passerby who yelps and is extracted by two other people. Jaime dodges one.

JAIME: Construction in New York's a bitch. (*She passes a donut stand, hands the vendor a sheet of paper, and grabs a donut. He starts to protest.*) Don't sweat it, man—in a couple years that'll be worth a fortune. I sign all my copies. A small investment now could set you up for life, you know what I mean? (*People pass, she tries to sell them a poem.*) You want a poem, Miss...uh you there, Miss, how about a poem? Thanks a lot. And you sir...a poem, an adventure—

(*The man stops and looks her up and down lasciviously. Opens his raincoat and flashes Jaime. Jaime confronts him. As she walks forward, he walks back until at some point he turns and flees.*)

not that kind of adventure, man, but thanks for sharing.

I bet you and I are thinking a lot of the same things right now.

I'm out here selling poetry, but you're walking around naked under that raincoat with the same question burning between your...ah...ears.

"What's happened to poetry in America?"

Am I right?

I mean when was the last time a poem

rattled your bones?

Well here I am to remedy that.

Cast off, blast off

I'm the new wave poetry slave

I know what you're thinking—you have to study Elizabethan English to read poetry; you have to buy an arcane insane esoteric totally prosaic literary magazine available in only one bookstore on 47th street twice a year—am I correct?

Or you feel to hear a good poem you have to kneel at the knees of some MMP—Major Male Poet preferably facing his crotch.

Now tell me if that isn't true? Sad isn't it?

Well I say, no way

I give you your poetry straight

no rap, no rock, bee bop or hip hop

So how about five dollars, man?

You can afford it. Think of what you must save on clothes.

(*The Flasher turns and runs.*)

Yes, yes, yes

I'm the new wave poetry slave

the last living purist in America—

(*David walks by with an instrument case. She looks him over.*)

Well maybe I'm not all that pure,

Hey you—superdude.

Yeah you. What's up? (*She follows him.*)

You want a poem? A touch of culture, a touch of class

Love 'em and leave 'em right?

I have something just for you...

A road poem, a heartbreak poem, lonesome sexy blues.

DAVID: Are you trying to pick my pocket?

JAIME: Dude, those jeans are so tight

no one could pick your pocket without a surgical instrument.

Looks good though. Don't get me wrong.

Now, how about a poem?

I'm in a difficult profession here.

I'm a major if undiscovered poet

reduced to selling original works of art on the street.

I have hundreds of poems ready-made—for all occasions,

every mood, theory, relationship and philosophy of life.

Only two dollars. Five dollars will get you

an original, custom–composed on the spot, stirring, moving unique

work of art and for only one dollar—and this is an introductory

offer. I can write you a limerick as effective as a quick kick in

the butt.

What do you say?

DAVID: Sorry, kid.

JAIME: Signed. Dated, limited copy.

Think of it as an investment.

Or if you like, you can pass it off as your own.

You take the credit, I'll take the cash.

No problem.

DAVID: You're broke. (*He hands her a dollar.*)

JAIME: Totally.

But this isn't charity.

You get your limerick.

Now—who's this for? Sweetheart, mother, boss. The judge that let you off the hook, what?

DAVID: A girlfriend.

JAIME: Figures.

Her name?

DAVID: Marie.

JAIME: Catholic, round collars, flat shoes.

DAVID: Not quite.

JAIME: Okay. Forget it.

Marie…Marie…

Romantic, raucous, rancorous or vindictive?

I have a great vocabulary.

What mood do you want? I'm talking tone here.

DAVID: Romantic.

JAIME: Dirty or clean?

DAVID: Jesus.

JAIME: Okay, clean. Got it.

Where's she from?

DAVID: I have to meet her bus, all right?

JAIME: If I were making a suit, I'd take your measurements correct?

DAVID: She's from Arkansas.

JAIME: Nobody's from Arkansas…

Okay, Arkansas, the dude wants a rhyme for
Arkansas…

Arkansas *(She's writing.)*

I like a challenge.

All right.

DAVID: Shoot.

JAIME: I'll read it for free, but it's 50 cents if you want a copy.

DAVID: *(Hands her 2 quarters.)* Go buy an airplane.

How long've you been doing this?

JAIME: Eight months. *(Reads.)*

There's a sweet young thing
named Marie…

DAVID: Must be tough.

JAIME: No problem. *(Starts to read again.)*

There's a sweet young thing named Marie
Who I'm just dying to see…

DAVID: Have you ever thought of taking on a regular job?

JAIME: What are you talking about? I could get a steady job any day, but I
believe you are what you do, okay?

If I'm waitressing and waiting to be a poet—then I'm a waitress
waiting to be a poet. Simple, I cut the waiting.

Now let me read the damn thing, so I can get on with this.

There's a sweet young thing
named Marie.

Who I'm just dying to see

She's got what it takes

So I don't need no brakes

Cause Marie's just dying to "blank" me.

DAVID: Blank?

JAIME: As in fill in the blank…

I don't know you. So I couldn't tell how strong to make it…

so what do you want…hug, kiss, fuck?

Fill it in.

DAVID: You didn't use Arkansas.

JAIME: What do you want for a dollar?

(*Announcements of arrivals and departures.*)

DAVID: Here's five kid.

Keep the wolf away from the door.

JAIME: I got to give you a poem then. A real one. (*She finds one.*)

I personalize them.

What's your name?

DAVID: David.

JAIME: Hi. I'm Jaime Brown.

DAVID: Gotta go.

JAIME: Right.

You're a musician, right?

Guitar?

DAVID: Synthesizer. (*He exits.*)

JAIME: Musicians are cool.

(*A mugging is going on.*)

There must be a better way to make a living.

(*Jimmy walks by, also in black. Pale, thin. He carries a small bag. Stops
nearby, opens his bag. Starts juggling. He puts a hat on the floor. The mug-
gers come by. Stare and then throw him some money. The muggee comes by*

and takes it out angrily. Sammy comes in wearing a suit, tie, etc. Watches Jimmy and throws in a coin. Jaime starts her routine.)

JAIME: Okay, all right.

Poems for sale.

Poetry

the real thing

right from me.

Choose the topic, choose the tone

Buy a poem

that's all your own.

No rap, no haiku.

(*Sammy watches standing close, peering.*)

Look buster, if you don't want a poem, move on.

Okay?

SAMMY: You have a mole on your face.

JAIME: Mole! What mole? That's a beauty mark.

Get lost.

SAMMY: Are you an orphan?

JAIME: Look. I'm not a runaway. Okay? Or a crook, or a hooker.

There's no poster out on me no photo on a milk carton, got it?

SAMMY: I'd like a poem.

JAIME: Two dollars ready-made and five bucks made-to-order.

SAMMY: What do you have already made up?

JAIME: I have hundreds of poems.

I mean I have everything—suicide to seashells.

I have lots of love poems. People usually want love poems.

Do you have any idea what you want?

SAMMY: What kind of love poems do you have?

JAIME: Let's see. Ecstatic, dramatic, trivial, passionate...

SAMMY: No other kind of love?

JAIME: Right. Weird.

I should have known. Look.

I deal with heterosexual love.

If you want me to work it around a little

I'll have to charge you.

SAMMY: I see. No love of God, love of mankind, nature, beauty, truth, a rose and so on?

JAIME: Oh.

SAMMY: Yes?

JAIME: How about me writing you one on the spot.

SAMMY: Fine.

JAIME: Five dollars though.

SAMMY: Fine.

JAIME: You choose the topic, but I write what I want. And if it goes over 10 lines, there's an additional fee plus 50 cents for giving you a written copy.

SAMMY: Fine.

JAIME: So. You want one on love, right?

SAMMY: No.

JAIME: Okay.

What then?

SAMMY: *(Meaningfully.)* The number one.

JAIME: The number one.

As in one, two, three, four, five...?

SAMMY: Yes.

The number one.

(Jimmy has stopped juggling and has come to watch.)

JAIME: Half up front.

Don't wander off. This'll take a minute.

(Sammy hands her the money. Jaime scribbles, Jimmy juggles.)

JAIME: Okay. *(To Jimmy.)*

That beats it friend. Leave. I can't concentrate. Got it?

(Jimmy shrugs and walks away still juggling.)

Look, I have your poem Mr...

SAMMY: San Bot Lhu.

JAIME: Yeah. I personalize my work here. I put a dedication "to" and your name.

Now San Bot what?

SAMMY: Sammy, put Sammy.

JAIME: Great. *(Writes it in.)*

This is heavy. But I write what comes out, okay?

You ready?

SAMMY: *(Crosses his arms.)* Sure thing.

JAIME: *(Reads.)* To Sammy

One bears witness

disguised as the enemy

among us.

The burning stake

the bloody pike is his

the mother covering her
child's eyes.
One watches and remembers
One is the tower and the well.
the woman rocking in the street,
One is the empty house, the empty pocket,
the glass about to be filled.
  (A moment of silence.)

SAMMY: You don't look like you'd write a poem like that.
  (Takes the poem.)

JIMMY: Appearances are deceiving.

JAIME: What do you know?!

JIMMY: You're not a bad poet.

SAMMY: Are you here every day?

JAIME: When the sun's out I'm in Central Park. Rain, snow, frost, hail—I'm
  here.

SAMMY: I see. *(Sammy exits.)*

JIMMY: Are you all right?

JAIME: I'm fine. Why?

JIMMY: That poem was pretty depressing.

JAIME: Sue me.
  I've had a lousy life.
  Don't just stand there. This isn't a freak show.
  You make me nervous.

JIMMY: What?

JAIME: It's a big planet. Feel free to explore it.

JIMMY: We'd do better if we stuck together.

JAIME: No way.

JIMMY: *(Juggling.)* Who'd cross the street to buy a poem?
  Really.
  But juggling has high visibility.
  (Juggles high.)
  Get it?
  Juggling draws a crowd.
  Bingo. They see me, hear you,
  their hand's already in their pocket,
  voilà.

JAIME: It won't work now.
  Business is lousy.

JIMMY: So we'll go somewhere else.

JAIME: This place has always been lucky for me.

Just the last couple of days have been rotten.

JIMMY: Last couple of days?

JAIME: Yeah, the pits.

JIMMY: Mercury retrograde.

JAIME: Mercury retrograde. What's that? Metal pollution?

JIMMY: My dear, my dear...

Metal pollution.

You're a poet...think of the planets—Venus, Mercury;

think Romeo and Juliet; think star-crossed;

think getting into the bathtub and the phone rings:

think sending a letter and forgetting the zip code;

think bounced checks, stalled cars, accidents, strikes

misunderstandings—that's Mercury retrograde.

Mercury rules communications. When it goes retrograde—

miscommunications—thus people lose things or fight.

JAIME: Shit. That bad?

JIMMY: The only good attribute of Mercury retrograde is...

Finding lost objects and people from the past.

Mercury retrograde brings them back.

JAIME: So how long do I have to look forward to everyone fighting and striking and whatever—

JIMMY: It goes direct in three weeks. At noon I believe.

JAIME: Three weeks. No money for three weeks?!

JIMMY: Two hats are fuller than one.

James Hobarth III. Jimmy to you.

And?

JAIME: Jaime Brown, here.

JIMMY: Jimmy and Jaime...unfortunate.

But then, it could be quite vaudeville.

Jimmy and Jaime.

Okay, try Jaime and Jimmy...

(*Sammy returns dragging Hughie. They are dressed exactly alike.*)

Dear Heart, speaking of duos...

HUGHIE: This is her?

SAMMY: Ask her for a poem.

HUGHIE: Will you write me a poem? (*He holds out money.*)

Is this enough?

SAMMY: Look at the mole.

   (*Hughie peers at Jimmy.*)

JIMMY: (*Touches his face, he has a bandage on his cheek.*)

   How did you know I had a mole?

   I cut it off shaving.

SAMMY: Not him.

   Her mole.

   (*Hughie peers.*)

JAIME: Beauty mark, man.

HUGHIE: Are you an orphan?

JAIME: (*To Jimmy.*) Can you believe this?

   (*To Hughie.*) Look, tell me what kind of poem you want.

   (*Sammy and Hughie strike identical poses, identically dressed.*)

   (*Jaime looks at them.*)

   No. No.

   Let me guess.

   You want a poem about the number two, right?

HUGHIE: How does she know that?

SAMMY: What did I tell you!

JAIME: Just give me a minute.

JIMMY: I can do a routine about the number two. (*He juggles two balls.*) And number three. (*He juggles three balls.*) Number four.

   (*He juggles four.*) Should I go higher?

SAMMY: Yes. Yes.

JIMMY: Watch. (*He juggles the four balls very high.*)

JAIME: All right you guys,

   you dude…

SAMMY: She wants your name.

HUGHIE: Why?

SAMMY: This is Hudan Bot Lhu.

   Call him Hughie.

JAIME: To Hughie…

   Here we go.

   Two is always hungry,

   the double-barrelled shotgun

   propped against his chin

   the knock on the door

   the stillness of night

Two is the black horse and rider
the streak of horizon
Nose to nose and belly to belly
Two is always hungry
and in mortal danger.

HUGHIE: *(Excitedly.)* Did you hear?

SAMMY: Yes!

The shotgun!

HUGHIE: How about the "knock on the door?"

SAMMY: The stillness of night!

The suicide

That's just how it was.

Amazing.

HUGHIE: You wrote this?

JAIME: No I dreamed it.

Two fifty plus twenty-five cents.

SAMMY: *(Hands her the money.)* We need your birthdate.

HUGHIE: When were you born?

JAIME: Off limits.

Sorry guys.

SAMMY: We are experts in reincarnation!

We need information.

JIMMY: Reincarnation—a perfect Mercury retrograde activity. Finding lost people!

SAMMY: I assure you we are legitimate.

HUGHIE: Are there not wine connoisseurs who from the mere taste and appearance of a wine, can tell you the site of its vineyard and the year of its origin? Are there not antiquarians who by a mere glance at an object, can name the time, place, and individual maker?

SAMMY: And we, given certain details, can tell what your last incarnation was. We have clients.

We are searching for someone in particular now.

JIMMY: Give them your birthdate.

What can it hurt?

JAIME: February 25, 1976…

JIMMY: I was born on February 25th!

HUGHIE: And where were you born?

JAIME: On a farm in Missouri.

JIMMY: He needs the city.

JAIME: How do you know?

JIMMY: This is very exciting.

JAIME: I was born near Jefferson City.

JIMMY: What time?

HUGHIE: What time?

JAIME: How would I know?

SAMMY: *(Whips out cellular phone.)* Call your mother and ask.

JAIME: She's dead.

SAMMY and HUGHIE: Ahhhhhhhhhh.

HUGHIE: Are you an orphan?

JIMMY: Go ahead. Admit it.

  I'm an orphan. No big deal.

JAIME: Okay. All right.

  I'm an orphan.

  (To Jimmy.) What is this, a club?

  (To Hughie.) So how can I tell you what time I was born?

HUGHIE: Were you born in the morning?

JAIME: How would I…

  Wait—my mom always said I was born an early riser…

  (Sammy elbows Hughie.)

SAMMY: This has been very interesting. Thank you.

HUGHIE: What's your name?

JAIME: Jaime.

SAMMY: Jaime. James.

HUGHIE: You see?

JAIME: So who was I?

SAMMY: We'll be in touch.

  (They exit.)

JAIME: You can have this place. It's too weird.

JIMMY: We've seen the hand of God.

  We've just seen fate at work.

JAIME: We?

JIMMY: Now I know why we hit it off.

  We're both Pisces.

  Giving, sensual, sensitive.

JAIME: Are you hitting on me?

JIMMY: No. *(He turns abruptly and juggles away.)*

JAIME: Sensitive is right. *(Goes after him.)*

  So what's your problem?

JIMMY: I need a place to stay.

JAIME: Hey, I only have one room, no running water.

JIMMY: No problem. It's warm out.

Point me to a park bench.

I'm cool.

JAIME: You're crazy.

Where are you from?

JIMMY: Boston.

JAIME: In New York, you can't just sleep anywhere.

JIMMY: Don't worry about it. It's not your problem.

JAIME: Yeah. Sorry.

(*David walks by, arguing with a girl in a tight, short leather skirt, with tank top and spiked red hair. She has a heavy Brooklyn accent.*)

DAVID: I'm here, aren't I.

MARIE: So what? I'm supposed to be ecstatic?

I wake up and you left a note pinned to my chest.

You call that romantic?

DAVID: I knew if I said anything, we'd argue.

MARIE: And whaddaya call this?! (*She slaps him hard and walks off.*)

JIMMY: Typical.

Mercury retrograde.

Never leave a note.

JAIME: (*To David.*) Class act.

You always pick them like that?

DAVID: I like women who are hard to handle.

If they're too easy, I get bored.

JAIME: I guess she doesn't bore you, then. She seems like a three–ring circus.

DAVID: Actually, she's pretty predictable. She'll call me tonight between six and seven.

JAIME: So that's Arkansas.

DAVID: Via Brooklyn. (*Hands her back the limerick.*)

I didn't have a chance to give her this.

JAIME: Sorry. No refunds.

DAVID: Store credit?

JAIME: Read it to her when she calls.

DAVID: What if I'm not home?

(*Jaime shrugs.*)

What if I'm out with you, darling?

JIMMY: He's hitting on you.

JAIME: *(To Jimmy.)* Mind your own business.

(To David.) You're not going out with me.

DAVID: I like feisty women.

JAIME: You didn't ask me out.

DAVID: Will you go out with me?

JAIME: I don't know.

What would we do? Hang out?

DAVID: Sure. Go to the park, drink wine, listen to music.

JAIME: Your treat?

DAVID: Why not?

JAIME: Okay.

(To Jimmy.) I'm going to take your advice. Why fight the stars, right? The joint's yours.

JIMMY: Thanks.

DAVID: Do you have everything?

JAIME: Yeah.

Just a sec.

(Goes to Jimmy.) Look. You can't stay in my room. I need my privacy.

But you can stay in the hall.

The lady I take care of lives right across, but she won't mind.

Here's the address. *(She writes it out for him.)*

Ring the bell. I can see you from the window. Second floor, left front, there's tomato plants on the fire escape—and don't pick any!

I'm pretty sure you're safe, but I sleep with a knife, got it? So, keep out of trouble.

(She exits with David.)

JIMMY: I knew it.

Pisces are a soft touch.

(Wilson's Estate. Paneled room with many windows looking out over grounds. Sunlight. Wilson is listening to Gregorian chants. His girl of the moment, Joyce, in a two-piece thong bikini, with a bright luxurious scarf knotted as a skirt, jewelry. She's bored. Boris the Butler in white slacks and pale pink polo shirt is serving drinks. Boris is stoic, Joyce flirts outrageously when she thinks Wilson isn't looking.)

WILSON: Joyce—this music is magic, it's time travel, it's immortality, don't you think?

JOYCE: Divine.

WILSON: These Gregorian chants date from the eighth century. I can smell the damp ancient stone, the incense; I can see the brown-robed tonsured monks. Primitive. Extraordinary.

The eighth century experienced now in the twentieth!

Boris, Dewars please.

(*He holds out his glass. Boris rushes over and fills it.*)

JOYCE: *(Stretches so Boris notices. Wilson admires her too.)*

Mmmmmmmmmmmmmmmmmmmmmmmmmmmmmm.

WILSON: Do you know what they call these?

JOYCE: Sure. Gregory chants just like you said.

WILSON: Antiphonal psalmody. Plain chants. So many names. It reminds me of my son. He was a monk you know. The only way I can understand his calling is to listen to this music, ascetic grave. This music has given me hope through its own immortality. It expresses the possibility that my son is also immortal. Somewhere I believe his spark of life has been transferred to a new and startling soul—

just the way a song lives on by being passed from mouth to mouth down through the ages. My son too, lives on, reincarnated—and I will find him if it's at all possible.

Do you think it is, Joyce? Possible?

JOYCE: *(Runs her hands over Boris's thighs.)* Anything's possible. That's my motto. My mother said those were my father's first words when he saw me as a baby. What do you think he meant?

WILSON: Joyce dear—I'm a very rich man and I can afford to have the best— and the way I determine the best—is through a series of tests and you my dear…

JOYCE: Yes. Tell me.

WILSON: Have failed. *(He takes her glass.)*

The only reason I keep a butler who looks like a porno star is to separate the wheat from the chaff. There's a helicopter waiting for you on the lawn.

(Joyce gets up to leave.)

JOYCE: Wilson…

WILSON: Now. Now. Let's not spoil a perfectly superfluous weekend with attempts at insight.

A lovely weekend, Joyce.

(He kisses her cheek. She exits. He savors his drink.)

BORIS: Sirrr…

WILSON: No need to apologize.

I'm a capitalist. I believe in competition.

You can bring in the boys now.

(*Boris exits and returns with Sammy and Hughie.*)

WILSON: (*Without turning. Facing the ocean.*) Did you know that if you stay near the ocean and in the proximity of young women, you never get old? Passion—the elixir of youth!

HUGHIE: (*Very interested.*) Really?!

(*Sammy elbows him.*)

WILSON: Would you care for anything after your travels? Champagne, perhaps?

HUGHIE: (*Delightedly.*) Champagne?

(*Sammy elbows him.*)

Do you have something to eat?

WILSON: Of course, of course.

Bring some carrots.

SAMMY: We're starving.

WILSON: And some celery.

Would you like that with salt or plain?

HUGHIE: Salt?

SAMMY: Plain.

WILSON: And turn down the music as you leave. (*To Sammy and Hughie.*) Isn't it extraordinary?

SAMMY: Extraordinary.

WILSON: So gentlemen.

What do you have for me?

SAMMY: We have three candidates. All born within three years of your son's death. All orphans, discovered at the same latitude 40 North and longitude 73 West within a radius of 66 miles from his death.

HUGHIE: Don't you think it should be from his birth?

SAMMY: We've discussed this.

HUGHIE: Have we?

SAMMY: Yes. But we don't agree.

WILSON: I thought you were experts.

SAMMY: We always disagree over beginnings. But we never disagree at the end.

HUGHIE: Didn't we guarantee, no results, no payment?

WILSON: Yes you did.

No results, no payment.

HUGHIE: And weren't our references impeccable?

WILSON: You wouldn't be here otherwise.

SAMMY: The Dalai Lama himself and the Maharajah of Jaipur.

HUGHIE: Didn't we also get a prelate from the Orthodox Church?

SAMMY: No.

HUGHIE: Prince Charles?

SAMMY: Enough.

WILSON: Enough.

HUGHIE: *(Stage whisper.)* Could I have a mint julep?

(Sammy elbows him.)

WILSON: You two are my last hope of locating my son's reincarnation. I've already used psychics and numerologists and astrologers, white magic, black magic and psychotherapy. I've behaved like a dotty bereaved eccentric of the worst kind.

Yet I know, I sense that I can find my boy. I can find him.

But if I can't, if you two who are deemed the best in your field cannot find him, I'll accept defeat as gracefully as I can. I'm prepared to will my entire estate to a series of worthy causes—although to see my life's blood in the hands of lawyers and trustees is almost more than I can bear to imagine...

HUGHIE: *(Trying to be sociable. Holding a drink, slightly tipsy.)* Really?

WILSON: Does he always ask questions?

SAMMY: That's how he talks.

He distrusts reality. *(To Hughie, cueing a set speech.)*

Hughie?

HUGHIE: Why aren't questions enough?

Why do people insist on answers

if all answers fall short of reality?

Don't people see that questions are a journey?

Why must people insist we end the quest with finality?

BORIS: Another mint julep?

(Hughie takes it and smiles.)

SAMMY: Our candidates, sir.

WILSON: Yes.

SAMMY: Each candidate had a quality that was extremely pertinent to your son's life and character.

HUGHIE: Aren't there three?

SAMMY: Three. Yes three. The number of full expression; number one became a successful stockbroker at fifteen.

HUGHIE: Didn't your son take his vows as a novitiate at fifteen?

WILSON: Yes.

HUGHIE: How could an adolescent take a vow of silence?

SAMMY: Number two specializes in illumination of sacred texts in gold leaf. He also adores skeet shooting.

HUGHIE: Like your son?

WILSON: Yes.

HUGHIE: What about the girl?

WILSON: A girl?

Discount that one.

SAMMY: Unlikely perhaps, but your son did like men.

WILSON: Yes, he was a homosexual.

SAMMY: This girl likes men. She is also unusually attuned to mystical poetry.

WILSON: My son would never come back as a woman.

SAMMY: We think that this was his first incarnation as a man and therefore...

HUGHIE: We?

SAMMY: And therefore it was something of a shock to find himself a man and he left before his incarnation was completed...

HUGHIE: Wouldn't it be far more logical to conclude that his next incarnation would be as a woman and therefore he was preparing himself...?

SAMMY: In any event, finding himself in a man's body proved extremely agitating to him and before he could fully learn this life's lesson—what it is like to be a man who loves men—he...

WILSON: Propped a shotgun against his temple and pulled the trigger.

SAMMY: Yes.

HUGHIE: Perhaps we should look for someone suicidal?

(Sammy elbows him and Hughie doubles over.)

WILSON: Your conjectures don't interest me.

I want results.

No results, no money.

We have agreed on the criteria...

SAMMY: Yes.

The size of the cranium, slant of the ears, the mole, the nails with no half moons, coincidence of preferences, identification of your son's favorite ring, walking stick and mare.

HUGHIE: Mayor? Was he political?

SAMMY: (To Hughie.) Mare. Mare. A horse.

(To Wilson.) Moreover the person must be a Pisces, the ruling sign of your son's fourth house, the house of endings...

HUGHIE: Wouldn't you think...?

(Sammy covers Hughie's mouth.)

WILSON: I'm very anxious to see these people.

I'm actually nervous, can you believe it?

There are many strange and wonderful things in the world and yet...

How will I know—without a doubt—that this person is my son reincarnated? I can't imagine what proof could possibly convince me absolutely that I have found my son.

SAMMY: First,

discard the idea of proof.

Proof refers only to causality; results produced by an observable and logical sequence of classified and isolated phenomena.

The only thing proof gives you is objective correlation; statistical proof. So discard proof.

Accept—coincidence.

Coincidence is more than chance.

Coincidence is the interdependence of all events in a single moment in time. Synchronicity!

And we, who are trained in this field, will find for you the one detail in the moment of coincidence that reveals the absolute truth.

When you find the absolute truth—there is no doubt.

I promise you. It will be a true revelation.

WILSON: Shall we toast the truth?

(They hold their glasses aloft.)

To revelations.

HUGHIE: Revelations?

SAMMY: Revelations.

(They wait. Wilson is lost in thought.)

WILSON: My poor son died for passion,

while passion gives me something to live for. *(He exits.)*

HUGHIE: *(Takes more champagne from Boris's tray.)* Another toast?

SAMMY: To what?

HUGHIE: Passion? *(He toasts and drinks by himself.)*

SAMMY: You drink too much.

HUGHIE: *(Toasts by himself again.)* Isn't the body the tavern of the living spirit?

SAMMY: Temple.

The body is the temple of the living spirit.

HUGHIE: Ahhhhhhhhh.

(Later that evening, the street. Jaime and David returning from the park. A couple of bums are lying around as parts of Jaime's small room are being assembled. They grumble and are pushed aside. One bum grabs a bag from

the other. Bum One yells "Help." Police come. Bum Two yells "Stop, Thief"
and points ahead of himself. Police run off. Bum Two saunters across stage.)

JAIME: This neighborhood is the pits.

They always ask if it's affordable. No one asks
if it's livable. *(The apartment or rather room is assembled. Jaime points to
different corners.)*
No bathroom. But McDonald's is two doors down and
they're open all night.

DAVID: Starving artist, eh?

JAIME: Yeah.

I find it therapeutic to refer to different corners
of the same room as the living room, dining room, kitchen…

DAVID: Bedroom.

JAIME: Yeah. It's the bedroom. So?

DAVID: Nothing. *(Pointing to a poster.)*
Who's that?

JAIME: Rimbaud. The French poet.

DAVID: Didn't Sly Stallone do him? *(Imitates Rambo with a machine gun.)*

JAIME: You're thinking of Rambo you jerk—

DAVID: I know honey. I know.

JAIME: Well I like him. He did his best work by twenty-one, quit to run guns
and leave graffiti on the pyramids.
Great poets die young you know. I'm going to die when I'm twenty-
seven, maybe twenty-eight tops.

DAVID: Really?

JAIME: And this is…

DAVID: Let me guess.

JAIME: Shut up.

DAVID: My psychic energy, my spiritual guide tell meee…Bob Dylan. Greatest
rock poet ever born…

JAIME: And a great outlaw. I love outlaws.

DAVID: *(Checking out her windows.)* You must. These windows are an open
invitation to any outlaw who happens by. Put some bars on the windows—eh. Then you can chose which outlaws come into this pad.

JAIME: How sweet. You want to protect me.

DAVID: Do you bring just anyone up here?

JAIME: Do you go up to just anyone's pad—dude?

DAVID: You seem pretty sure I'm not going to jump you or anything.

JAIME: You seem cool. I'm a good judge of character.

DAVID: So was Jesus and Judas nailed him.

JAIME: Right.

DAVID: That was a joke.

JAIME: I know. It was good. Smart.

DAVID: Hey. What's up?

JAIME: Nothing. I'm great.

DAVID: We were having a great time and now you're like…

JAIME: Like what?

DAVID: Down, beat. I don't know.

Shall I leave?

JAIME: No.

DAVID: Fine.

(*They stand awkwardly.*)

JAIME: I'm nervous.

DAVID: What's the matter?

JAIME: I like you.

DAVID: (*Moving closer.*) Great!

JAIME: I mean really.

And now that I got you up here. I don't know what to do.

DAVID: What do you usually do?

JAIME: Usually? Are you nuts?

With all the disease-ridden, murderers, punks, pimps and perverts out there—do you think I'd be stupid enough to bring anyone to my room? Let alone have them know where I live?

DAVID: So I'm the first?

(*He moves away from her. Jaime nods.*)

JAIME: Don't sweat it. I've been deflowered.

Cowboys.

DAVID: Cowboys?

JAIME: (*Hooks her fingers in her jeans.*) Walllll ma'am, been real nice, but I gotta be movin' on.

Cowboys!

How about you?

DAVID: Me?

JAIME: Are you in love now?

DAVID: Let's just say I'm a cowboy, ma'am.

Better steer clear of me.

JAIME: Really?

DAVID: The only thing I know how to do is play music.

JAIME: So play.

DAVID: Right. *(Takes out his keyboard.)* Just happen to have my little keyboard.

JAIME: What kind of stuff do you play?

DAVID: Sorta post-punk, semi-funk, hillbilly-hardcore with a bluesy edge.

JAIME: Oh.

DAVID: *(Setting up.)* I have a new song.

JAIME: Groovy.

DAVID: Groovy? What's this sixties shit?

JAIME: I'm a purist. I'm trying to preserve classic language. Play.

DAVID: It doesn't have a title yet. *(He plays.)* So…what do you think?

JAIME: I think you're the real thing.

DAVID: Thanks.

JAIME: It's in your blood, isn't it?

DAVID: Yeah I guess. My dad was a jazz drummer. You know the kind in bars, plays, smokes pot with his friends—what people in jazz do.

Didn't really know him too well.

JAIME: My mom was into country. She was an Elvis freak.

We're pretty different.

DAVID: Very. *(He goes to kiss her.)*

JAIME: Do you believe in love at first sight?

DAVID: You're going to spoil this, aren't you?

JAIME: I thought that was romantic.

DAVID: Romantic? Love?

Love's a responsibility.

Now sex—that's romantic.

JAIME: I don't just go around saying that, you know.

DAVID: Why did you just say it now?

JAIME: 'Cause that's what I was feeling.

'Cause I thought you'd dig it.

I've never been in love before.

DAVID: And you're not afraid to tell me this?

JAIME: Well shit, yeah!

DAVID: Jaime, you're too open. You got to protect yourself. Look, I don't have a lot of experience with heart-on-the-sleeve kind of people. Maybe I should leave.

JAIME: Maybe you shouldn't take it so hard.

Maybe I was just trying to nail you against the wall to see what you'd do—rip your skin off a little before I decide whether to put salt or ice cream on you.

Do you want to leave?

DAVID: No.

JAIME: I could read you some of my stuff?

DAVID: No love poems.

JAIME: Right.

This one's great.

I based it on a man I overheard downstairs… *(Reads.)*
"I just like to see 'em fall, slow
like in the movies,
drops of blood spread,
sailing through the air
as if they don't belong nowhere
and land, spla—a—at, like rain
on the river…"

DAVID: Uh…no. I don't think so.

JAIME: That's just how he said it.

DAVID: I believe you.

JAIME: You said no love poems.

DAVID: You need a sense of humor.

JAIME: I thought that was kind of funny. "Spla—a—a—at, like rain on a river."

DAVID: But you're talking about blood, sweetheart,

What's this?

JAIME: Don't read it now.

DAVID: I don't like women who tell me what to do. *(He opens it and reads.)*
"When you are old"
When did you write this?

JAIME: In the park.

Look…

DAVID: When you are old
And mysterious to me,
a dim figure on a
fragile horizon,
Think back
Across the years,
That on one summer night
we broke out of ugliness

and fled
Two conspirators
with bottles full of
Wine and joyous music
on the radio
and remember,
if
you
can
That it was right and
fine and sometimes
More, and we left
Pain.
That interminable fire,
only scorching
Our heels."
(*Silence.*)

JAIME: It's not funny.

DAVID: No. (*He kisses her.*)

(*They move to the bed. A pale face appears at one of the windows. It's Jimmy. He taps on the window. David and Jaime spring apart.*)

JIMMY: Hey you guys. (*Taps.*)

JAIME: Just tell me, (*Covers her face with her hands.*)
Does he have a gun?

DAVID: It's the guy from the terminal…the little guy that juggles. Should I let him in?

JAIME: Oh God.
Mercury retrograde.

DAVID: What?

JAIME: Bad timing.
Crossed stars.
Romeo and Juliet.
Never mind.
Let him in.
(*Jimmy comes in through the window.*)

JIMMY: I guess you guys didn't hear me throwing pennies at the window.

DAVID: Guess not.

JIMMY: (*Looks at them, half-undressed.*) I'm sorry.

JAIME: Yeah. (*Starts dressing.*)
You want some wine?

JIMMY: I could use it.

JAIME: You have to drink it from the bottle...

DAVID: The bathroom's down the street.

At McDonald's.

Look. I better be on my way.

JIMMY: Don't leave on my account,

I'm really sorry.

I'm just not good on the streets.

I was juggling along the way...

attracted quite a crowd...only I looked up and

noticed quite a few were sexual deviants and psychopaths.

Not that I'm prejudiced.

It's live and let live with me, but I don't think we

shared that philosophy so I...uh...ran.

But I'll be out of here in a moment.

Just let me catch my breath.

Oh God, I can't believe I did this.

JAIME: David?

DAVID: I have a gig at eleven anyway.

I'm a disk jockey

Strangers in the Night on Staten Island.

Power pop and yuppie rock.

Best sound goin' round

etcetera, etcetera.

JAIME: He's really an artist—he writes songs.

DAVID: *(Gives her a light kiss on the cheek.)* It was sweet.

See you around.

Ciao good buddy.

JAIME: *(Following him to the door.)* Can I see you again?

Maybe I can come down to the club.

DAVID: I don't like women who pursue me. *(He leaves.)*

Be in touch, babe.

(Jaime stands at the door. Her back to Jimmy.)

JIMMY: Perfect timing.

James Hobarth III does it every time.

JAIME: You probably did me a favor.

You just don't have a one-night stand with someone you love.

JIMMY: Bad omen.

JAIME: What?

JIMMY: Wrong place. Wrong time.

JAIME: I thought we were just experiencing Mercury retrograde.

JIMMY: We are…it is but…

How can I have a fabulous new beginning under Mercury retrograde?

It does not bode well.

Here I was ready to strip my life to its barest essentials; to live without a past, without a dime.

Yes. I was going to be self-reliant, complete unto myself and what happens? I freak!

One look at that park—the black trees, the moonless night, the quiet pierced by occasional screams—

I couldn't hack it.

JAIME: Don't be so hard on yourself. A person doesn't sleep on a bench in a city where mugging's considered a rite of passage. You did the right thing.

Have some more wine and sit down.

JIMMY: Then I stumble over here and fuck things up.

JAIME: Just shut up and relax.

JIMMY: I'm not good on the streets.

I need a home.

It's okay if I sleep here?

JAIME: You're not going to rob or rape me, are you?

JIMMY: No really, I never…

JAIME: I'm joking.

Cool it.

It's fine.

I could use the company tonight.

You okay?

JIMMY: Yeah.

(*Jaime gets into bed.*)

JAIME: (*Sighing.*) I'm messed up.

Do you have an aspirin?

I have a monumental headache.

JIMMY: Cheap wine?

JAIME: Cheap date.

JIMMY: You know I bet you and I are a lot alike.

We need someone to love.

But we keep choosing crazy people, idiots, sociopaths,

the lame, the maimed, the married, right?

JAIME: Right.

JIMMY: If I make one more bad choice. it's over.

I swear. Plug pulled.

Lights out.

JAIME: Things'll get better I'm sure.

JIMMY: It's not a sure thing at all.

(Tragically.) I have Venus in Pisces.

JAIME: Oh, I see.

JIMMY: You don't.

If Venus is what you want

And Pisces is the sign of the martyr

That means I want to be a martyr. God!

Oh well, Good night.

(Next day. Wilson's Estate. We hear the helicopter taking off.)

JAIME: So is white slavery a possibility?

Will I wake up in Saudi Arabia in a duffel bag?

JIMMY: I doubt it.

JAIME: Man. I could live like this.

A helicopter, a pool,

the ocean.

I mean there's less bugs on this lawn than there

are in my apartment.

JIMMY: I must say, being airlifted is quite an experience.

JAIME: So is being paged at Port Authority. The only other place I've had my name called in public was at the dentist.

Can you believe it?

It's enough to make you believe in reincarnation.

(Boris walks in with a tray of champagne. Jimmy gives him an appreciative look that Boris returns discreetly.)

JIMMY: *(Checks his watch.)* It's ten o'clock and that's champagne.

JAIME: Shit. What a life.

BORIS: Would you care for a mimosa?

JIMMY: *(Looking at the label.)* Krug Brut '76...not bad...

terrific, actually.

I'd rather not spoil it with orange juice.

BORIS: Excellent decision.

JIMMY: Thank you.

BORIS: Do you know wines?

JIMMY: A little.

BORIS: I could sneak you a little "Taitinger Blanc de Blanc."

JIMMY: Fantastic.

BORIS: I know you'd appreciate it.

And you Miss?

JAIME: It's questionable whether I should drink given the
circumstances. Oh what the hell.

Sure give me a glass.

(Boris serves her and winks to Jimmy as he leaves.)

JAIME: So you appreciate good wine, eh?

JIMMY: Another life, dear

A previous life.

JAIME: Yeah, a life where you're fluent in astrology and wines.

JIMMY: Princeton '96…

Educated to ponder the universe and such questions as —

If the subways in New York are air-conditioned, but no one has ever felt
air conditioning, is the subway really air-conditioned? But not to worry.
I'm just folks.

I was summarily disinherited when I was fifteen.

My father caught me…let's say, he loathed my lifestyle.

Then he died and we were never able to patch it up properly…

Oh well… *(He sips his champagne.)*

BORIS: *(Enters.)* They'd like to see you now, Miss.

JAIME: If I turn out to be this man's son, all this will be mine, right?

JIMMY: Right.

JAIME: Groovy. *(She exits.)*

BORIS: We have 500 species of the rhododendron.

JIMMY: Lead the way!

BORIS: We have skeet shooting if you like.

JIMMY: *(As they leave.)* You're Scandinavian, aren't you? I'd say Danish.

The Danes have eyes the color of blueberries.

(They exit.)

(A half hour later. Enter Wilson, Sammy, Hughie, and Jaime, single file.)

SAMMY: Her ears are the right size.

HUGHIE: And did you see—she was missing part of the right lobe too?

JAIME: A dog bit me. I told you.

SAMMY: And she has the mole.

JAIME: Beauty mark.

SAMMY: Nails with no moon showing; she identified the cane, the photograph
of his mother, and his worry beads.

(Jaime wanders around the room as they talk. Flipping open books, opening boxes, etc.)

WILSON: And she's one in three chosen from the entire world's population as the probable reincarnation of my son. Hmmmmm.

SAMMY: You haven't seen the others.

HUGHIE: Do you think you should be looking through Mr. Wilson's things?

WILSON: No. No let her. I want to see what she picks out.

JAIME: Oh wow, you have Richard Wilbur. Great poet. *(She thumbs through the book.)*

WILSON: Yes. He was my son's favorite.

Do you know him?

JAIME: Oh yeah. He wrote the single greatest poem I ever read!

WILSON: My son was an avid reader.

JAIME: Oh I don't read much—it clouds your mind, but I do know Richard Wilbur.

WILSON: Is there a poem you'd like to show me?

JAIME: Are you kidding? *(She shows him.)*

WILSON: "Love Calls Us to the Things of This World"

Oh my… *(He takes out his handkerchief.)*

HUGHIE: What is it?

SAMMY: What is it?

JAIME: What is it?

WILSON: There's something here I tell you. There's something definitely here.

HUGHIE: Yes?

SAMMY: Yes?

JAIME: Yes?

WILSON: This was my son's favorite poem. His very favorite. My God!
'Bring them down from their ruddy gallows
Let there be clean linen for the backs of thieves;
Let lovers go fresh and sweet to be undone
And the heaviest nuns walk in a pure floating
Of dark habits
keeping their difficult balance'
(He turns away.)
Excuse me.

JAIME: Wow.

I'm sorry.

WILSON: No, no dear. You've brought my son to me. I felt him nearby today.
Gentlemen. I'm convinced she's the one.

HUGHIE: But the others?

SAMMY: I agree. You must see the others.

HUGHIE: Emotions might be clouding your judgment, don't you think?

SAMMY: I agree.

We must always offset emotional mysticism with mental balance.

WILSON: No. I tell you—intuitively, and by all the rules of your game—she is the reincarnation of my son. The percentages of correct answers are astronomical. I believe it was one hundred percent. Not one wrong guess, not one wrong move and now this…this… *(Holding up the book.)*

HUGHIE: Would you like a drink?

SAMMY: Hughie!

WILSON: You see? I have both intuitive and statistical proof, congratulations gentlemen.

I'm ecstatic.

Boris! Boris!

Of course there will be a longer period of examination, but I feel it.

I feel it just as you two said. A revelation.

Boris! Boris!

(Tina comes out.)

TINA: *(She is Polish.)* You called sir?

WILSON: Where is your husband?

TINA: I don't really know. I believe he's showing someone the grounds, sir.

WILSON: Never mind. Bring me my checkbook. It's on top of my desk. *(To Sammy and Hughie.)* You've earned your fee.

SAMMY: No!

HUGHIE: *(To Sammy.)* Are we refusing it?

SAMMY: Yes!

This is incomplete. We do not do incomplete work.

WILSON: I'll make out the check and you can do with it what you will.

SAMMY: It's not that we're so certain the girl is not your son.

We're just not sure she is.

JAIME: *(Haltingly.)* I have to tell you all something…

WILSON: Yes?

HUGHIE: Yes?

SAMMY: Yes?

JAIME: I don't feel like a man.

And I don't remember consciously anything about this place.

SAMMY: You wouldn't necessarily remember.

You share a soul with the old James. The soul is the unit of evolution.

The soul is old. But the personality is brand new and the personality is the unit of incarnation. So you wouldn't necessarily remember anything.

HUGHIE: Do you think that's quite true?

SAMMY: Of course that's what I think. I said it, didn't I?

HUGHIE: Not a trace of past lives? Not a preference carried over? Not a talent? Not an interest? What about the cane? The ring? The poem?

SAMMY: All right, a trace. There's a trace of previous lives.

WILSON: Why don't you wait for me in the library, gentlemen. I want some time alone with Jaime.

(*Sammy elbows Hughie. They exit.*)

(*To Jaime.*) So, what do you make of all this, my dear?

JAIME: Mercury retrograde.

WILSON: I beg your pardon.

JAIME: This could be a terrible mistake.

WILSON: Not so terrible.

Why don't we agree to give this a little time.

JAIME: All right.

WILSON: Three weeks?

JAIME: I guess.

WILSON: Anyone I should notify? Anyone you want to call?

JAIME: There's one dude…but no. Let him stew. It'll be good for his ego.

WILSON: Fine. Tina will show you to your room.

JAIME: What do I have to do?

WILSON: Be a poet, I imagine.

JAIME: I am one.

WILSON: Yes I know. So was my son.

JAIME: This is really spooky.

WILSON: It is eerie isn't it?

JAIME: It's too much. I can't see myself living here.

WILSON: Oh I see. You have a prejudice against money.

So did my son.

He couldn't imagine himself here either.

He went into a monastery.

JAIME: I'm different. I could never be a monk…I mean a nun. Whatever. I believe in sex.

WILSON: So did my son.

He was a Franciscan—of course.

Truly mystic. A fatal paradox.

He was a passionate boy who took a vow of chastity; a sensual person who lived in poverty; a romantic who engaged in affair after affair each sadder and more desperate than the last. He always chose someone inappropriate—a drunk or a married man. He was a homosexual who never made his peace—except with a double-barreled rifle at the end.

JAIME: I'm sorry.

WILSON: I loved him very, very much.

JAIME: I'm sorry.

WILSON: So—where were we?

Three weeks.

Give it a chance.

Immerse yourself.

Try an external approach to inner development.

Try the clothes, the food, the freedom, the richness

the color, sound, the perfume.

Let yourself awaken to the possibilities.

This is not preposterous.

Look at yoga—by adopting certain outer physical postures

a resonant chord can be struck in the inner soul.

JAIME: I'll do it.

WILSON: Just relax, let this experience wash over you—

money isn't evil, you know.

Lord, how many times did I say this to my son.

Money is time, space, loveliness—I can take money

and create a garden full of flowers and color and streams

and moss… I can take money and have musicians play

day and night, or have composers write music,

or architects build dream houses for the poor.

I can take money and change the direction of rivers,

or cure the sick…money is godlike in the right hands

It can even help poets…

That's why this money, this wealth I've

somehow impossibly accumulated, must end up in the right hands.

So stay. If you can't believe. Don't disbelieve.

And we'll see.

I feel this inexplicable tenderness toward you.

JAIME: Your son could've come back as a woman. Then he wouldn't be so torn up about loving men.

WILSON: You'll stay then? Wonderful. Go upstairs and see if Tina's around.

JAIME: I think your son had Venus in Pisces. (*She exits.*)

(*Hughie and Sammy march in very determined. Tina follows with the checkbook.*)

HUGHIE: Would you please listen to us for a moment?

SAMMY: Yes.

We want to talk to you alone.

(*Sammy pulls Wilson aside.*)

We feel what you're doing is wrong.

We feel quite strongly about it.

WILSON: Do you agree, Hughie?

SAMMY: We agree.

We always agree about conclusions.

We won't take the check.

HUGHIE: How could we risk our reputation?

How could we betray our gods and our talent?

How could we permit you to mistake passion for perspective?

WILSON: You needn't worry. I'm not about to hand over my

fortune to a charming little street poet—no matter

how charming.

If in three weeks Jaime has doubts, and I have reservations—I'll call off

the search and create a foundation.

HUGHIE: Why three weeks?

SAMMY: Three is the number of full expression.

WILSON: Because that's sufficient.

Now I must find Boris. We have some excellent recordings of the Tango,

Gardel himself, 1928, Paris.

The tango of course—it's a Latin American dance

in duple metre—much like the habanera. (*He exits.*)

HUGHIE: What about the other candidates?

(*Tina enters. Boris and Jimmy are outside. Jimmy is shooting at geese. We can't hear him fire.*)

TINA: Oh, there's Boris.

(*She taps on the window and waves. Boris waves back. She exits.*)

HUGHIE: Are you positive the girl's not the one?

SAMMY: I'm as convinced as you are.

We can't let him do this.

We must find the right person and bring him back here.

HUGHIE: And if we can't?

SAMMY: Fate.

This person is doomed to repeat his mistakes over and over and over until he is ready to redeem the qualities that destroyed him in his previous life.

HUGHIE: Does that mean, perhaps…?

SAMMY: Suicide.

HUGHIE: Ahhhhhhhhhh.

(*He puts his arm around Sammy's shoulders in comradely fashion. Behind the glass doors, in full view, Boris gently takes the rifle from Jimmy, leans it against one of the glass doors, and embraces him passionately.*)

END OF ACT I

ACT II

Three weeks later. Jaime's room. Also we see part of the street outside. Inside Jimmy has his juggling paraphernalia around. Jimmy is stripped to the waist, wearing sweat pants and juggling first three and then four balls. Rock music. In the street, David is walking. There is also another couple; the woman with a fur boa. A dummy falls at their feet. The Woman: "Quick Charles, up here. I do believe we've finally found a vacant apartment." She yanks him offstage. David steps over the dummy. He goes to the window over the fire escape and taps loudly on it, but Jimmy can't hear. He taps harder and shouts. Jimmy is startled and makes a big show of almost dropping all the balls, but then recovers. David indicates Jimmy should open the window. Jimmy still juggling, manages after several attempts to turn the radio down with one hand.

JIMMY: *(Yelling.)* It's open!

    Just lift it. It's open.

DAVID: *(Climbs in.)* Well what do you know. Jimmy the juggler.

    How's tricks?

JIMMY: Wonderful. I'm in love.

DAVID: I see. Congratulations.

JIMMY: I highly recommend it.

DAVID: Is…ah…Jaime around?

JIMMY: Oh no, no, no, no, no.

DAVID: Don't worry, I'm here for a signature, not a seduction.

JIMMY: She's not here. She's living with a millionaire.

DAVID: Hold on. I thought you were in love?

JIMMY: Oh, you thought Jaime and I…? No.

    She's hit an incredible streak of luck.

    For that matter so have I.

    We have a truly karmic connection. Both Pisces.

    Born on the same day.

    She has a mansion. I have this apartment.

    She's got Daddy Bigbucks and I—have a brand new friend.

DAVID: What's she doing with this millionaire?

JIMMY: I don't know—what time is it? Just kidding.

DAVID: Let's go find out what she's up to.

    I assume you know where she is.

JIMMY: My my, aren't we headstrong.

    What's the hurry?

DAVID: Here's your hat. Let's go.

JIMMY: I don't need a hat.

> Actually I don't wear it any longer. It weakens my hair follicles.
>
> Does it look like I'm losing my hair?
>
> I'm only nineteen, but the brush looks full...

DAVID: You look great.

JIMMY: *(Puts on a shirt—rather Hawaiian.)* I'm wearing colors now.

> I always wore black.
>
> But I feel like a prism these days.
>
> Light passes right through me...ah love...
>
> Are you sure my hair doesn't look thinner? I can see the scalp.

DAVID: Is Jaime in love too?

> Seeing as you have such a karmic connection.

JIMMY: If I'm in love, she's in love.

DAVID: Are you ready?

JIMMY: Wait!

DAVID: Why?

JIMMY: Sorry.

DAVID: What?

JIMMY: Today's out of the question.

> Momentous decisions are pending.
>
> She can't be interrupted. No. No. Impossible.
>
> I'll tell her you called.

DAVID: I have to see her now.

JIMMY: Now? After you waited three weeks, it has to be now, right this minute no matter whom you inconvenience or—destroy?

DAVID: Right.

JIMMY: Well you're no Pisces!

DAVID: Not on your life.

JIMMY: Don't tell me, don't tell me. Let me guess... *(Walks around him.)*

> Reddish tinge, brash, headstrong. Headstrong.
>
> You're an Aries, right?
>
> Aries rules the head.
>
> You're headstrong.
>
> Brash, romantic...
>
> If you want fireworks, take an Aries. Romeo was probably an Aries.

DAVID: So does that get me your recommendation?

JIMMY: No. Aries are romantic—but have no follow through.

> Give me a Taurus. Steady. Built.

I'm in love with a Taurus.

I have the most beautiful, sweet, exotic big blond Russian Taurus you ever laid eyes on.

Silver white hair, blue eyes, skin like a rosebud

And best of all—silent.

One of those one-word Taurus wonders like Gary Cooper—the original "Yuuup" man.

There was a Taurus.

They're so terrific. Like stoked fire.

Always burning and just stir them up a little...

But oh, I do go on...

DAVID: Where do we have to go to find this millionaire?

JIMMY: So do you love her?

DAVID: I like her.

JIMMY: "Like"... "like"...how paltry.

I don't even remember "like."

I've never been in love like this before.

It's a three-ring circus with four clowns

and my head going 'round like a four-ball shower. *(He does a four-ball shower and tosses the balls into a canvas case.)*

DAVID: This has got nothing to do with love.

We co-wrote a song together.

A major label is making interested noises.

I want to talk to her about rights and money.

JIMMY: Not love?

DAVID: Definitely not love.

JIMMY: Look, I know you're an Aries and it's hard, but think of someone besides yourself.

DAVID: Fuck you.

JIMMY: I shouldn't complicate things for her. Certainly not for "like." Now if you had been in love with her...

DAVID: I can say the word if that's what you want.

JIMMY: I'd do quite a lot for love.

I understand passion, but business *(He shrugs.)*

I mean this fellow is cultured, civilized, rich...

DAVID: And old. All that goes with old.

JIMMY: Seasoned.

Well I won't take you.

You'll queer the deal.

DAVID: I'm sure I'd have no effect on her.

   She's probably deeply in love with this man.

   Didn't you say you two were so cosmically attuned that if you're in love, her heart's going pitter pat as well?

JIMMY: Actually, I know for a fact she's in love.

DAVID: Good for her.

JIMMY: Well, it may not be. But she has a mentor.

   Poets need mentors.

   Us jugglers, on the other hand,

   we're independent—there's the street, the circus, bar mitzvahs— n'est-ce pas?

   But a poet?

   What can a poor poet do?

   You don't have a lot to offer her.

DAVID: I have a voice that can kill a cow at a hundred yards.

   I have talent, management ability…

JIMMY: And money?

DAVID: I don't buy into a billboard mentality—money equals happiness— buy this, buy that, own it all and you'll turn into a cougar, jump on top of a billboard, screw the girl in the black velvet dress and ride off into the sunset. However, if this deal goes through, they may offer me quite a bit of money.

JIMMY: But it won't help you. Sorry.

DAVID: *(Pushes Jimmy against the sill. He drops his juggling balls.)* Looking to get your balls busted, buster?

   Let's go.

JIMMY: All right. All right.

   I respond to passion as well as the next man. In fact I was going there anyway.

   Mercury goes direct today at noon.

   All this will be straightened out.

   No more Mercury retrograde.

   Thank God. *(He gets his things.)*

   I'm waiting until five past noon myself and then,

   I'll ask my Taurus to live with me.

   We'll walk by the ocean, hold hands, kiss, caress, embrace…

   My God,

   And I thought I'd die young, poor and

   alone.

There's hope I tell you.

There's always hope.

Well follow me, what can you do with an Aries?

(*David exits first.*)

Typical Aries—always has to lead even if he doesn't know where he's going! (*He exits.*)

(*Later that same morning. Jaime's bedroom on the second floor. A canopied bed. A desk piled with papers. A full-length mirror and a large glass door opening onto a balcony. We only see sky beyond billowy curtains. Hints of luxury. Tina the maid enters with a stack of lingerie. She steps out onto the balcony for a moment and catches sight of someone.*)

TINA: There you are you tomcat, you rooster.

I know you have a lover, you lovesick bull, you peacock,

I won't put up with this. I tell you...

JAIME: (*Enters wearing jeans, a T-shirt, a flamboyant headdress.*) What is it, Tina?

TINA: I will not put up with this! (*She puts the lingerie on the bed and preens in front of the mirror.*) I don't have to.

My father was a calvary officer in the Polish army and my uncle was a prelate in the Catholic Church.

I didn't have to settle for a Russian serf, a vulgar bulgar, a peasant always in heat!

JAIME: A love spat, right?

TINA: A love spat! I'll kill him.

No. I'll kill her!

The laundress found a note in his pocket.

signed your "adoring, worshipful servant," imagine!

In his trousers

And after all I've done.

I left my family, my country, my training for him.

I was trained as a lady's maid. A fine lady's maid. No one else could fold lingerie or arrange drawers the way I could.

My ladies never had a pleat out of place,

a button missing,

a spot on their lace—

and although I was always slimmer, taller,

more naturally elegant—

all of my ladies went out feeling like a million bucks.

And now?

Cotton underwear for Miss Bluejeans.

What's more—

I answer doors, announce guests, set the table—all to cover for...

(She shoves the note under Jaime's nose and quickly withdraws it and reads.)

You see, here's the note.

Can you believe...

"Never have I been so in love, so enthralled, so overwhelmed.

We'll meet on the beach at noon there is so much to say..."

Can you believe?

Well, she'll believe.

I'm going to confront her, this woman, this girl.

I'll tell her to her face that Boris is mine, married

in the Church in front of all the saints. I bet Boris the Bull did not tell

her that!

I betcha!

She'll see. And let her "overwhelm" herself someplace else!

Your lingerie is clean. *(She stalks out.)*

(Jaime is in a good mood. She sits at a table and puts her hair up. Tries it different ways. Then she puts on makeup. She is wrapped in a towel. She turns the radio up. There is a soft knock on the door. Another knock. Wilson lets himself in carrying a stack of books.)

WILSON: Jaime...

JAIME: Oh Wilson, I'm not ready yet.

WILSON: I'll stay here and wait. May I?

JAIME: Sure. *(She turns the music down.)*

Hope you don't mind rock.

WILSON: No as a matter of fact I was reading about rock and roll. Did you know it's a commercial amalgam of the styles of American White country music and Black rhythm and blues?

JAIME: *(Putting on some huge sapphire earrings.)* Yeah. *(She looks at herself. Takes another sip of champagne.)* Wow! Not bad.

WILSON: Yes. And Rhythm and Blues is particularly interesting. Did you know that the 12-bar melodic and harmonic pattern and the three-line stanzas are now common to much of the popular music of recent decades?

JAIME: Yeah. *(Wrapping a long piece of black silk around her until it forms a slinky dress with one strap.)* I'm almost ready Wilson.

WILSON: I think the idea about these get togethers to share interests is a splendid idea.

I wish I had been able to do this with my son—originally that is.

JAIME: *(Steps out.)* Ta Da!

> What do you think?

> Pretty hot, right?

> Watch out *Vogue*—here I come.

> I feel like a peacock.

WILSON: You look like a bird of paradise.

JAIME: These earrings are devastating.

WILSON: They belonged to the last Raj of Sinukhan who presented them to my mother who was a very beautiful woman.

> She'd be pleased to see them on you. She wanted them to go to a daughter if I had one, or to my son's wife if he married.

JAIME: Wilson. I can't keep these.

WILSON: We'll see.

JAIME: You're not treating me like a son.

WILSON: Like a daughter.

> I can't ignore the fact that you've come back to me as a girl. You look absolutely beautiful.

JAIME: *(Changing the subject.)* So our topic for today is…

WILSON: Oh yes—our topic of conversation for today.

JAIME: *(Taking the books.)* Emily Dickinson, Elizabeth Bishop, Ann Sexton—Women poets.

WILSON: Like you—blessed by the Greek literary goddesses Calliope, Erato, and Euterpe no doubt.

JAIME: No doubt.

WILSON: You make me want to show off.

JAIME: All women poets, eh?

WILSON: I wanted to do something of special interest to you.

JAIME: So because I'm a woman I'm interested in women poets?

WILSON: I suppose that is a bit simplistic isn't it?

> Well, I'm only a businessman puttering around in the arts.

JAIME: You're very kind, Wilson.

WILSON: Kind? Kind? I meant to be exciting.

> Well—in any event you really should read more. You have a fine untutored mind.

JAIME: I like being untutored.

> Every time I write, I'm an explorer.

WILSON: But you need heroes.

JAIME: My friends are my heroes.

WILSON: How gallant.

JAIME: You're my friend. My gallant friend.

I'm going to miss you.

WILSON: You know, Jaime—I was thinking.

JAIME: Yes.

WILSON: Although the three weeks are up at noon, I really think we should prolong this experiment. We both have doubts still and I see no reason why you can't stay a few more weeks. You should be here to see the ocean in the fall—it would inspire you. It's grainy and tempestuous. I've found I can learn all the seasons through the ocean's lens. You see—it even inspires me to wax poetic—'ocean's lens'—not bad. Just think what it would do for you.

JAIME: I don't know what to say.

I love it here. This is so decadent.

I grew up in the Midwest.

I shouldn't feel this way.

WILSON: Do you really think it's harmful for an artist to have money? Do you think you'd be the first? What about Baudelaire or James Merrill or Tolstoy? Do you think Bob Dylan's starving in a garrett or Baryshnikov is without a sinecure? Please—you sound like my son.

JAIME: Wilson…

(*David appears on the balcony and sees the embrace. He stays hidden. David enters.*)

WILSON: (*As he exits.*) Think about it. We'll discuss this at lunch. Today the three weeks are up in any event and we should discuss the future. I'll see you at noon then. Wear what you have on now.

(*He kisses her cheek and embraces her tightly.*)

There's a reason we've been brought together. Can't you feel it?

Fate is at work here, Divine Providence.

We should explore it together.

DAVID: Some outlaw.

JAIME: What?

DAVID: You look like you belong in a harem.

Have you fucked him yet?

JAIME: David? What are you doing here?

DAVID: Ditto.

JAIME: How did you find me?

DAVID: Cosmic intervention.

Stand up. Let me take a look at you. (*Whistles.*)

JAIME: Get out of here.

He'll hear you.

DAVID: Have you fucked him yet?

JAIME: You're really a limited person, you know that.

DAVID: Yes. How boring. I relate to life through my cock. They all say that. *(He languishes on the bed.)* But what's a poor boy to do?

JAIME: Did anyone see you come up?

DAVID: Not to worry.

All my years of seeing married women have paid off.

JAIME: What the hell do you want now?

DAVID: Now?

You sound hurt. Did I wait too long? Of course I haunted Port Authority in my off hours.

I climbed your firescape on several occasions.

You don't seem to have a phone or a fax—or a brain in your head. How was I to know you'd been reincarnated during the last three weeks?! *(He goes to kiss her. She moves away.)*

Well, I just dropped in to say "Howdy, Ma'am."

JAIME: David...

DAVID: Not to worry little lady—I'm here to complete your streak of luck. I have good news. I'm frontman in a new band, Harm's Way.

JAIME: So glad you dropped by to tell me.

DAVID: And our first hit single will be none other than "Conspirators."

JAIME: Great.

DAVID: You should be happier than that. It's going to make you rich— although I see you're quite comfortable already. And here I thought you were a waif shivering in the woods.

JAIME: Hold on a minute. I don't get it.

Why should this song make me rich?

DAVID: It's our song. The song we wrote.

JAIME: What "we" is this?

DAVID: As in you and I—we.

JAIME: What are you talking about?

DAVID: I took that poem you gave me. Did a little editing. Now it's a rock song.

JAIME: Are you kidding?

DAVID: Cut a demo with some of the guys at the club; sent it to Pacific Records. They loved it. Soooo we're gettin' a contract. All you have to do is sign on the dotted line.

JAIME: I didn't say you could use it.

DAVID: You gave it to me.

JAIME: It was private. Special. I wrote that poem just for you.

DAVID: And I wrote this song—just for you.

JAIME: Yeah, you and the guys had a good laugh, I bet.

DAVID: Will you at least listen to it for Christ's sake?

> (*He plays the demo tape.*)
> We are...we are...we are
> conspirators
> against the past
> armed with bottles full of wine
> lost for time
> with joyous music blast-ing
> on the radio
> so did you know
> we are conspirators
> we are, we are
> conspirators
> breaking out of ugliness and
> fleeing
> just you and me
> conspirators.
> We take what life deals
> take back what it steals
> we love and leave
> pain—that interminable fire
> only scorching our heels.
> We are conspirators...we are...we are...
> conspirators.
> (*Pause*)

JAIME: I didn't hear from you for a long time.

DAVID: You disappeared. What was I supposed to do—consult an astrologer to find you? At least, can I have your signature?

JAIME: No.

DAVID: Why?

> Revenge?

JAIME: It's not revenge.

DAVID: Look. I won't fuck with your karma, if that's what you're afraid of.

> I'll just copyright this song and send you some checks.
> You love my ass. You won't pass this up.

JAIME: Drop dead.

DAVID: I didn't need to come here to find you. I could've cashed in all by myself.

JAIME: I would have found out and sued your ass.

DAVID: So sue me. *(He holds her.)*

Call the cops.

You're really gorgeous, you know.

JAIME: You dig sapphires and silk.

DAVID: I dig skin like silk and eyes of brilliant blue.

Jaime—come on tour with us. We could write other songs.

I won't pressure you. If you want, you can be one of the boys.

JAIME: One of the boys with extra holes, right? Don't come on to me because you want to use my lyrics.

DAVID: Fine. Forget the come-on. Sign this, you'll have real financial independence. You won't have to lay around with an old geezer and eat bonbons.

JAIME: You're so stupid.

I've been working.

DAVID: Good. Let's see what you've been up to. *(He grabs some papers off her desk. He reads.)*

"Black ivy in a wasteland of debris…"

Hmmmm not quite…

Let's see. *(He reads.)*

"Her dreams are made of plasterboard and paste."

That's hearty.

Oh, yeah, here,

How about

"The faulty skein of sky and road has strung me out from place to place"

Glad to see you're so happy here.

JAIME: I always write sad stuff.

DAVID: You write sad stuff because you're sad and have sad things to say. Not much has changed here. On paper.

JAIME: I haven't digested this experience yet.

DAVID: Right.

Besides which,

you're his son.

JAIME: Jimmy told you.

DAVID: Son.

JAIME: Yeah. But we're going to talk more about it. Today in fact.

DAVID: Well there's nothing to talk about...it's perfectly obvious you're this guy's...this guy's...I can't say it, honest-to-God—

JAIME: Son.

DAVID: Whore.

JAIME: *(Slaps him hard.)* You asshole.

DAVID: I thought you were different than anyone else I'd met.

Free, open, out to conquer the world.

But I see I was wrong. You talk a good game

but all you're looking for is shelter, safety, a harbor in the storm. That's great if you're protecting babies—but not if you want to be out there—being an artist. Sorry.

You've lost your nerve.

(Tina knocks.)

TINA: Lunch, Miss.

DAVID: *(Falsetto. Imitating her.)* Are you coming, dear?

JAIME: *(To Tina.)* I'm coming.

DAVID: I'll be at Kennedy Airport. My flight leaves at five thirty-six for L.A.

JAIME: What? You snap your fingers and I jump? No way!

(Grabs the paper from David. Signs it and thrusts it into his hands.)

Here. Buy yourself another girlfriend!

And don't put my name on the song. We never met.

(She starts to leave. David stops her.)

DAVID: Now we know what love at first sight means, don't we!

It sure ain't love at second sight!

JAIME: You shit! *(She exits.)*

DAVID: Ditto my love. Ditto.

(He exits from the balcony. Empty room. Curtains billow. An exaggeratedly long dining table half set. Noon. Sammy and Hughie sit side by side. Boris and Tina come in and out arranging the table setting. Everything Boris puts down Tina rearranges.)

BORIS: Stop! Enough!

You think I am uncompetent.

TINA: Incompetent!

BORIS: *(Checks his watch.)* Ten before noon. I must go for a walk.

TINA: No!

BORIS: You do luncheons.

TINA: Don't go.

BORIS: I'm tired of your not founded jealousies.

TINA: Unfounded.

It's not unfounded!

I am not a fool.

BORIS: You are the only woman I ever love. I swear. I promise.

Boris is many things, a sportsman, a wanderer, a great lover but never a liar. You are the only woman I love. *(Checks his watch again.)* I must go.

TINA: Those are your last words?

BORIS: Yes.

TINA: Fine.

I will be right back. *(She flounces offstage.)*

BORIS: Where are you going?

TINA: Ahh, my big Russian bloodhound.

Don't worry so much. I only go to little ladies' room.

(She exits. Boris storms out and then returns. Throughout, Boris continues setting table and waiting impatiently.)

SAMMY: I'm glad we don't fight.

(Hughie says nothing.)

We talk things over.

For instance, there is the matter of failing Mr. Meredith.

HUGHIE: Have we failed?

SAMMY: We've failed.

The girl is not the right person...

HUGHIE: Ahhhhhhh.

SAMMY: You're no help. We've failed. Where are your suggestions?

HUGHIE: Where are your suggestions?

SAMMY: We've found the person.

We always find the person. But we haven't identified him!

HUGHIE: Or her?

SAMMY: We have the big picture.

Orphans, Pisces, midtown Manhattan, August.

Eighth house of legacies in a water sign.

HUGHIE: Wasn't it the fifth house of hidden karma
in a fire sign?

SAMMY: No! Well, maybe... But that's not it.

There is something we've overlooked.

HUGHIE: Do you really think we've failed?

SAMMY: We've failed.

It's the beginning of the end.

HUGHIE: Of what?

SAMMY: Of us, you nincompoop.

We don't work well together, we've run out of rope, out of ideas, out of steam.

HUGHIE: Are you kidding me?

SAMMY: I need someone decisive, energetic,
   Someone who can come up with answers, make statements,
   take the bull by the horns.

HUGHIE: Do you mean that?

SAMMY: Tell me something!

HUGHIE: What?

SAMMY: Something. Anything.

BORIS: *(Worriedly.)* Tina! Tina!

HUGHIE: What do you want from me?

SAMMY: Decisions. Action.

HUGHIE: Don't you know by now what I'm like?
   Do you know what you're asking?

SAMMY: Yes.

HUGHIE: Sure?

SAMMY: Yes.
   I'm asking for…

HUGHIE: What?

SAMMY: My needs are different.
   We're facing a crisis. I need someone who confronts reality. I need someone different.

HUGHIE: Haven't we always worked well together?

SAMMY: Until now.

HUGHIE: Why throw out a perfectly good partnership?

SAMMY: Is that all you can say?

HUGHIE: Do you want me to leave?

SAMMY: Do you want to leave?
   Answer. Yes or no. Do you want to leave?

HUGHIE: *(Crestfallen.)* Why are you doing this?
   Can't you see you're making me miserable?
   Aren't you miserable too? Don't you have any feelings?
   What's wrong with you?

SAMMY: That's it?
   All right.
   I can't stand it.
   Leave. Go. Get.

HUGHIE: Do you really mean it?

SAMMY: Fight for what you want, you fool!
   Can't you say anything?

HUGHIE: *(Leaving sadly.)* What's there to say?

    (Hughie exits. Sammy slumps in his seat. Jaime enters.)

JAIME: Hi guys…guy…what's wrong?

SAMMY: Nothing.

JAIME: Okay.

    Nothing's wrong with me either. *(She sits primly.)*

BORIS: *(Enters.)* Have you seen Tina?

JAIME: No.

BORIS: She went to the little girls' room. But

    now she's late…

    This is special lunch for you and Mr. Meredith.

    Big decisions. Big deal. BIG deal. Believe me.

    He wants everything special. And if there's no service, Tina and I both

    be fired. For sure. NO doubt. Kaput!

JAIME: Sammy?

SAMMY: I don't know anything about this. I'm no mind reader.

JAIME: I see. Well. Don't count on Tina being on time.

    (She sits. Boris stands. Sammy sits.)

    Nice day.

BORIS: Yes.

    No.

    Miserable day.

    People suffer.

SAMMY: Yes.

    People suffer.

BORIS: Why do you say Tina is late?

JAIME: I didn't say she'd be late.

BORIS: You know something. Tell me.

    It's your friend who will suffer.

    Your friend? *(He does juggling action.)*

JAIME: Jimmy?

    It's about Jimmy?

    Oh no.

BORIS: Tina is a strong lady, a very strong lady. Jimmy is tender, too tender.

    He will be upset, destroyed.

    Do you know what I mean?

JAIME: Yeah, sure I got it.

    You creep.

BORIS: Is Tina on the beach?

JAIME: She found a note.

BORIS: My God.

JAIME: The laundress.

BORIS: My God.

JAIME: I take it, Jimmy doesn't know about Tina.

BORIS: My God. *(He exits.)*

JAIME: My God. *(She exits after leaving her high heels on the table.)*

> *(Sammy sits dejectedly. Wilson enters. Pressed starched white shirt, blue-and-white striped pants, blue blazer. Perfumed, pomaded. Excellent.)*

WILSON: I see I'm early.

SAMMY: You might enjoy a walk along the beach.

WILSON: I'll just wait.

> Thank you...Hughie?

SAMMY: Sammy.

WILSON: Would you care for a drink?

SAMMY: No. Thank you.

> *(They wait.)*

WILSON: Yes. Well.

> Did you know the scale most typical of Chinese music is the pentatonic scale?

SAMMY: I see.

WILSON: You are Chinese?

SAMMY: No.

WILSON: I see.

> Well, I'll tell Boris.
>
> He'll find some books on it.
>
> Boris?
>
> Tina? *(He waits.)*
>
> How strange.

SAMMY: My highly developed intuition tells me

> you would gain great insight into your present circumstances if you went for a walk along the beach.

WILSON: *(Picks up Jaime's high heels.)* Why? Has something happened on the beach?

SAMMY: It will.

> *(Wilson exits. Sammy sits.)*
>
> *(Along the beach. We hear water and gulls. Jimmy is sitting on a dune, pant legs rolled up, bright sweater knotted around his shoulders. Picnic basket by his side. Peaceful. Tina awkwardly making her way carrying a rifle. Two*

tourists obviously from Manhattan by their dress, with some minor adjustments to the beach such as jacket slung over one arm, or carrying shoes. Perhaps they are a large woman and a small man. Woman speaks as they make their way across the stage: Woman: "You call this a beach? You call these waves? You call this is a vacation? Where have you been all your life?" Continues as they walk offstage. The Man meekly behind Woman: "You call these birds? You call this a stroll along the shore? You call this fun? You call this romance? You call this…" We hear a thud. The man returns alone. Tips his hat at Tina, who has now reached Jimmy, and exits.)

TINA: Excuse me. Do you have the time?

JIMMY: Yes. Certainly.

It's almost noon.

TINA: Good.

JIMMY: Aren't you from the house over there?

TINA: Mr. Meredith's. Yes.

I'm the maid.

JIMMY: I thought so.

TINA: You're a friend of Boris's and the young lady.

I've seen you.

JIMMY: Yes.

Hello.

TINA: Listen. I am looking for a young lady. Have you seen her?

JIMMY: No one's come by, but what's she look like? I'll keep an eye out for her.

TINA: No, that's all right.

Can I wait with you?

JIMMY: Sure.

Want a sandwich. Chips? A coke?

TINA: No. I have lost my appetite. Believe me!

JIMMY: You're upset.

TINA: So sensitive. Such a nice young man.

Too bad about your hair.

JIMMY: My hair?

TINA: A nice young man like you. But women don't mind baldness in a man.

Mature women don't, that is.

JIMMY: Thanks. That's good to know.

TINA: But yes. I'm upset.

Love is so sad.

JIMMY: You've had a fight with your lover?

TINA: My husband.

We always fight.

I love him and he loves me. But we always fight.

He's unfaithful.

JIMMY: You know how men are.

TINA: Yes.

I would make him jealous too.

JIMMY: Why don't you?

TINA: Too tired. *(She sighs.)*

I am ruining your picnic.

JIMMY: No. I'm waiting for someone.

TINA: A lover. Lucky you.

Boris and I were lovers once. My wild Russian bear, my love.

He is a bit younger than I am, twelve years or so…

JIMMY: Boris?

TINA: Boris. Your friend. My husband. The butler over there…

I cannot stand to have him running around so…

It makes me sad, so sad.

JIMMY: Boris.

TINA: Yes.

Do you have a tissue?

JIMMY: I. No.

Boris.

TINA: You are surprised.

I know.

He does not give the appearance of being married.

JIMMY: I have a napkin.

TINA: *(She wipes her eyes and nose.)* But he loves me. In his way. He loves me so much.

He lets me know what he is doing. *(She holds out the note.)*

(Jimmy takes it and gives it back, dazed.)

JIMMY: He gave this to you?

TINA: Yes.

We share everything.

He is loyal, but not faithful.

It is my cross to bear.

JIMMY: Yes.

TINA: No. I make you sad.

I'm sorry.

This girl has stood him up!

Hah!

JIMMY: It happens.

TINA: I say, Hah! on you my Soviet stallion.

Hah!

I leave you waiting for your lover.

And I give you advice, be firm, but quick too.

You're young, but you're losing your looks.

Even men need their looks. I'm glad I have a full head of hair,

not one grey strand. I really don't look so much older than my Boris, do

I?

JIMMY: No.

TINA: That comes from having a stallion for a husband.

My Russian stallion.

Well, you look like a sad boy, but I wish you luck. *(She exits.)*

JIMMY: *(Jimmy picks up gun to tell her she's forgotten it, but changes his mind.)* I

really must do something about my life.

I really must

I can barely breathe, all of a sudden...

The sky, the ocean, the wind is catching my breath...

He didn't even come.

Perhaps he sent her.

Jim you idiot, you stupid idiot. Be a man. Do something.

(He takes up the gun.)

Why don't you shoot something

Some poor dumb gull. *(He sights something and follows it.)*

Some poor dumb, dumb *(He lowers the gun sits down, holds it between his*

knees. He props the barrel against his forehead.)

creature.

(Jaime comes running up the beach.)

JAIME: Oh, Jimmy, stop!

JIMMY: Get away from me.

JAIME: Jimmy, please.

Put that gun away.

Nothing can be that bad.

JIMMY: Does the whole fucking world know?

What a laugh!

Everything I thought was beautiful and private

is a public joke.

JAIME: Hey dude, come on.

JIMMY: Dude?!

JAIME: Yeah, 70s, "dude." You're a major dude. You can work it out.
Man to man.

Talk to the guy, will you?

JIMMY: *(Gets up.)* Don't follow me.

JAIME: *(Follows him.)* This is no time to tune out. I mean you just turned a corner and ran smack into the love of your life. Who knows what'll happen next.

JIMMY: Just say I can't stand the suspense, all right?

JAIME: This is a minute in your life. It'll pass. Let it pass.

JIMMY: It won't pass. This minute resembles too many others.

I told you I either get them sick. Maimed or married. I'm stuck.

Next time around, things'll be different.

Now turn away for Christ's sakes. *(He kneels.)*

God's in his heaven and all's right with the world. *(He points the rifle at his temple and closes his eyes.)*

(Boris lumbers up, quite out of breath.)

BORIS: Jim, stop.

(Jimmy freezes but keeps the gun in place.)

JIMMY: Please.

BORIS: Tina talks with you. I know.

She exaggerates.

JIMMY: Exaggerates! How the hell do you exaggerate being married.

BORIS: Things are mixed up.

You don't understand.

We can talk.

You told me. Mercury is straight now. It's noon.

Everything be all right.

JIMMY: Mercury is what?

JAIME: Retrograde?

JIMMY: Not anymore. It's direct.

You're right. Mercury is direct.

That's why I came here.

BORIS: So now we get things straight. You know. We talk.

JIMMY: *(Opens his eyes.)* How could you give Tina my note?

BORIS: What note?

JIMMY: The note where I said I loved you.

BORIS: Ay...yayayayay

In my pocket. The laundress found it. *(He walks over and gets Jimmy up. Takes away the gun gently.)*

It was a mix up.

Come on. We can talk. Boris is a big man, full of feelings, but not smart.

JIMMY: I don't know, Boris.

BORIS: Boris is dumb. I love you. I love Tina and everyone is mad. How can love produce madness?

JAIME: That's the question of the century.

BORIS: *(Puts his arm around Jimmy.)* You see?

You explain it to me.

(They walk down the beach. Hughie comes running up.)

HUGHIE: Where is everyone?

JAIME: Walking down the beach into the sunset, Hughie.

HUGHIE: And your friend…?

JAIME: Jimmy?

HUGHIE: And Jimmy…is with…?

JAIME: Boris.

HUGHIE: He's with Boris? With a man? A man with another man?!

Delightful, no?

And this, Jimmy, is short for James?

JAIME: You got it.

HUGHIE: Ahhhhhh.

Don't you think that's perfect? *(He trots after them.)*

(Wilson comes up, perfectly groomed.)

WILSON: Jaime, Jaime dear. Wait a moment.

I've had an epiphany.

JAIME: Wilson, I have to talk to you.

WILSON: I know dear.

Oh I'm glad.

I thought you were leaving me.

Here—sit with me.

(They sit.)

The waves are pounding. How perfect. *(He presses her hand to his heart.)*

I must tell you, Jaime. I've made a mistake.

JAIME: Yes, I know.

WILSON: You're not my son.

JAIME: I know.

WILSON: Strangely I feel my son is near.

I feel his passionate presence. That sensitivity. But not in you. However, all those feelings I've had for you are real. Those stirrings. That tremendous excitement and tenderness.

It all became clear when you kissed me.

I tell you. When I saw you, it was love at first sight.

JAIME: Love at first sight!

WILSON: You believe in love at first sight too?

JAIME: Yes. Yes, I do.

WILSON: I knew it! What poet could resist it!

And this life, this opulence, this sumptuousness hasn't put you off completely, has it?

JAIME: No, but Wilson…

WILSON: There's hope…like a delicate bud…Oh forgive me—I sound like a greeting card.

JAIME: Wilson…

WILSON: And I haven't told you how magnificent you look. You can change so—wrapped in a bit of silk and those sapphires—you look so mysterious, a quiet fire…how's that? Less like a card. I think. My son would have been proud. He never knew me like this, you see.

JAIME: Wilson.

WILSON: Yes?

JAIME: This is all wrong.

WILSON: Oh I know it's doomed, but who cares. You don't have to love me. I love you enough for both of us now. I feel like a giant. I could straddle continents and oceans and lift mountain ranges and polar caps for you. Yes. Yes and I'm so much older. I'll die soon and you'll be rich.

If I can't find my son, I want you to have the money.

JAIME: I've got to be real careful here.

I can't take what's not mine.

It would make me weak.

What would my life be if I were saved before I've ever been in danger?

WILSON: You're right. You're right. Whatever you want.

No money. No things.

I understand that too.

You see, that's part of my epiphany.

How lovely.

I understand finally. The curse of things.

All these years in love with the beauty and power of money

the supreme luxury of it all.

But now, because of you

I understand the greatest luxury may be freedom

from the clutter of possessions, their care, the fear of their loss.

I understand my son. At last.

Because of you.

He was wise, not foolish.

He wanted to be free and let his spirit soar

and now that's what I want as well.

Jaime—you've given me a new life; nothing short of rebirth.

And you'll be my perfect companion.

JAIME: Wilson.

WILSON: I bore you. I terrify you. I disgust you.

JAIME: I love someone else.

WILSON: Oh.

JAIME: I'm sorry.

WILSON: Don't. Don't. *(He takes out a handkerchief.)*

JAIME: It was love at first sight.

(Hughie comes back nearly dancing.)

HUGHIE: And Sammy?

WILSON: We're talking.

HUGHIE: Do you have a moment?

WILSON: Not now. *(He turns to Jaime.)*

It is good-bye then.

JAIME: Yes.

WILSON: I see.

JAIME: I'm terribly sorry Wilson—that I wasn't your son and that I can't share your passion.

WILSON: Passion! Who wants passion!

I can see why it runs young people ragged.

JAIME: I would have missed a whole world if I hadn't met you. *(She kisses him.)*

WILSON: It's strange.

HUGHIE AND JAIME: *(Simultaneously)* What?

WILSON: I feel closer to my son than I ever have—although the search has failed and you're leaving me.

HUGHIE: Do you have a moment?

WILSON: Not now.

(To Jaime.) How will you get home?

JAIME: Your helicopter?

WILSON: Of course.

JAIME: Groovy.

(Wilson hugs her and then turns his back.)

Good luck Hughie. *(She exits.)*

WILSON: Stupid girl. *(He wipes his eyes.)*

Just delightful.

HUGHIE: Ahhhhhhhhh.

WILSON: What are you "ahhhhhing" about?

HUGHIE: Don't you see?

WILSON: See what?

HUGHIE: You have your wishes, don't you?

WILSON: Wishes? What are you babbling about?

The bottom has just dropped out of my world.

HUGHIE: Don't you feel young? Didn't you say young women make you feel young?

Didn't you say passion makes you feel young? Didn't you want passion?

WILSON: She doesn't feel passionate about me, you fool.

She walked away, didn't she? You saw it.

Passion. How can you babble on about me getting any sort of wish about passion when I'm the one who... *(Looks at Hughie.)*

Yes, I'm the one who feels passion.

Ahhhhhh.

HUGHIE: And you wanted to find your son?

WILSON: Please.

(Boris and Jimmy approach arm and arm.)

HUGHIE: And who's that?

WILSON: Boris?

No.

That young man?

HUGHIE: Can you guess his name?

WILSON: James?

James.

Ahhhhhh.

(Lights dim.)

(Kennedy Airport. The next day. Flights being announced. People walking to and fro. Jaime looking for David. A tour guide with some extremely foreign people huddled in a group walks by giving instructions. Tour guide: "When you get to New York, never establish eye contact with anyone. Babies are technically okay, but follow your instincts." David walks by with Marie. She is dressed for tropical weather and wears sunglasses. Jaime approaches.)

JAIME: *(She comes up behind Marie.)* Hey you.

Beat it.

MARIE: I can't believe it.

Are you talking to me?

Hey David, get a load of this!

DAVID: Jaime!

JAIME: Howdy, good-lookin'. Jus' thought I'd stop by and give my fondest
   regards.

DAVID: Jaime.

MARIE: You know this broad?

Great.

Terrific.

JAIME: Either of you have a quarter?

MARIE: *(Digs through her purse.)* Here. Call the zoo and tell them you escaped.

JAIME: Thanks…

Listen. I have the perfect limerick for you guys.

Half price. A real deal.

Are you prepared?

"There was a young dude name of David

Who liked all his women stark naked."

MARIE: This is offensive.

JAIME: "Who liked all his women stark naked.

When one of them balked

He got up and walked

And lost out on the best damn thing he ever had

in his whole life."

MARIE: Look sweetie…

handle this.

I got my ticket. *People* Magazine

I'm all set.

I'll see you at the gate.

(To Jaime.) You know sweet pea—

David and I have known each other for years.

We're steak and potatoes

and you're just a candy bar.

(Exits.)

JAIME: I like how you really step in and take over.

DAVID: I like women to fight over me.

JAIME: So?

DAVID: So what?

JAIME: So what should I do besides stand here feeling like a total idiot?

DAVID: Excuse me—but you did walk into the middle of my life unannounced and started making demands.

JAIME: Tsk, tsk, tsk. Do I believe my ears?

Are you talking double standard?

I thought that dialect was defunct.

DAVID: Marie's waiting.

JAIME: I thought you invited me?

DAVID: I thought you were otherwise engaged. If I'm not mistaken, your last words to me were— "We never met."

JAIME: Right. Well.

Great. We're even.

Nowhere together.

I thought you like women who give you a hard time.

DAVID: Sure. I like women who give me a hard time.

I couldn't love a woman like that.

JAIME: I should've seen this coming.

Lord have mercy—

You want a sweet young thing.

DAVID: Right.

JAIME: With a heart of gold.

DAVID: Helps.

JAIME: What other specifications?

DAVID: Gold…I like gold. Maybe some silver…You got fillin's ma'am?

(*Jaime nods.*)

Maybe some copper in her hair…

JAIME: Oh, I get it.

DAVID: You do?

JAIME: To find true love…

DAVID: Yes?

JAIME: You need…

DAVID: Yes?

JAIME: A metal detector.

(*David kisses her. People walk up including the tourist group of foreigners with their leader…all of whom are walking very carefully single file staring at their shoes. Suddenly a large cutout of a mountaintop descends. It should hit with a thud. Sammy is sitting crosslegged meditating. Hughie approaches.*)

HUGHIE: So how're you doing?

(*Sammy looks up then ignores him.*)

Are you deaf?

SAMMY: Only to counsel.

HUGHIE: What?

SAMMY: I thought we were through.

HUGHIE: Why?

SAMMY: After what I said.

HUGHIE: We solved the case, didn't we?

SAMMY: Yes.

HUGHIE: Aren't you glad?

SAMMY: Delighted.

HUGHIE: So?

SAMMY: We're not meant for each other.

HUGHIE: It comes to that?

SAMMY: Yes.

We have irreconcilable differences.

HUGHIE: Sammy, would you explain what's really going on?

Don't you know you're hurting me?

SAMMY: Not enough.

HUGHIE: What?

SAMMY: I said not enough! I'm not hurting you enough.

Now get away. You're ruining my meditation.

HUGHIE: What do you want?

Why can't you tell me what you want?

Isn't it important to discuss things, openly, fully?

Haven't we always treated each other that way?

SAMMY: If you ask one more question, I'll punch you in the face.

(Rises.)

HUGHIE: *(Backs away.)* Ahhhhh.

So, you want me to change my whole philosophy?

SAMMY: Tell me you love me.

HUGHIE: *(Pulls out a flask.)* How about a drink?

SAMMY: Hughie!

HUGHIE: *(Drinks.)* Do I insist that you alter your behavior for me? Change
your approach, your outlook on life?

Just for me?

Do I?

SAMMY: Coward.

Take a stand.

Express a belief.

Make a commitment.

HUGHIE: What's gotten into you?

SAMMY: I'm serious.

HUGHIE: Is it too much time in the West?

SAMMY: If you don't do it right now, this minute…

HUGHIE: *(Crosses his arms on his chest.)* Yes?

SAMMY: We're finished.

HUGHIE: Have you thought this through?

SAMMY: Life is change.

HUGHIE: But if I make a statement, don't I lose my posture as a seeker of truth, a humble observer and prober?

Don't I, with a simple statement, wed myself to a specific reality?

SAMMY: Yes. Me.

HUGHIE: Ahhhhh.

SAMMY: Life is change. *(Sammy takes off her cap. Her hair flows to her shoulders. Her mannerisms become more womanly.)*

We're changing. *(She faces Hughie, challengingly.)* So?

HUGHIE: Yes? *(He copies her stance, but takes a quick sip from the flask.)*

SAMMY: So tell me you love me.

(A long, long, very long pause.)

Hughie?

HUGHIE: *(Guiltily.)* What? *(He can't meet her eyes.)*

SAMMY: Never mind. *(She wipes her eyes and turns away.)*

HUGHIE: *(Taps her on the shoulder.)* I do love you, you know.

(Black out. Lights up.)

END OF PLAY

EDDIE MUNDO EDMUNDO

ORIGINAL PRODUCTION

Eddie Mundo Edmundo was commissioned and first presented by the Young Conservatory at the American Conservatory Theater (Carey Perloff, Artistic Director; John Sullivan, Managing Director), San Francisco, California, in August, 1993. It was directed by Craig Slaight; musical direction was by Maureen McKibben; costumes were designed by Callie Floor; design specialist was Cour Dain; music was by Jay Good; and the assistant to the director was Peter Glantz. The cast was as follows:

EDDIE	Paul Shikany
MUNDO	Devon Angus
CHELO	Carmen Caraballo
ALICIA	Kristine Juroiwa
NYIN	Jeffrey Bautista
THE WOMAN WITH BLUE EYES	Jennifer Paige
PIPO, HER BOY	Nicholas Kanios

CHARACTERS

EDDIE, seventeen-year-old boy from Manhattan
MUNDO, twenty-five-year-old "leper" in Nautla
CHELO, forty-eight-year-old woman who runs a restaurant, Eddie's aunt
ALICIA, sixteen-year-old girl
NYIN, fifty-year-old horse trader
THE WOMAN WITH BLUE EYES, late thirties, itinerant
HER BOY PIPO, eight years old, her son

TIME AND PLACE

All action takes place in the 1970s in the village of Nautla, Mexico, on the coast of the State of Veracruz.

ACT I
SCENE ONE

Shafts of light as if early morning through palm trees. Mundo by the river, washing himself. Back to the audience. His pole and bucket against a rock. He is singing. He is wearing bracelets of silver bells and bells around his neck.

MUNDO: *(Singing.)* Ay de mi, Llorona, Llorona
   Lead me to the river
   Ay de mi Llorona Llorona
   Lead me to the river.

   Wrap me in your shawl. Llorona
   The wind is cold as winter
   Wrap me in your shawl, Llorona
   The wind is cold as winter.

   Ay de mi Llorona, Llorona
   Llorona of the present and past
   Ay de mi Llorona, Llorona
   Llorona of the present and past.

   If once I was a marvel, Llorona
   Now I'm fading fast
   If once I was a marvel, Llorona
   Now my light is fading fast.
   (As he is singing, Eddie walks in, hiking, a backpack, sneakers, jeans; Mundo stops singing abruptly.)
EDDIE: Hey. Sorry.
   (Mundo is still.)
EDDIE: I'm looking for Nautla. The guy who dropped me off said to follow the river.
   (Mundo doesn't respond.)
EDDIE: Should be just up the road, right? *(He slaps some flies.)* Damn! Yeah, well. Thanks a lot. I'll be going now.
   (Mundo pulls up the muslin cloth he wraps himself in. He raises the hood and turns to stare at Eddie. His face is severely deformed. It looks as if it's made of melted wax. His skin has barklike patches on it. He says nothing.)
EDDIE: Shit.
   (Mundo gets up. He is tall and thin. He covers his face with a light veil and approaches.)

EDDIE: Look my name's Eddie Sanchez. Maybe you know Chelo Sanchez—
    (*Mundo stops.*)
EDDIE: She's my aunt. Maybe you knew my mother Tati?
    (*Mundo comes closer.*)
EDDIE: Yeah, well my Spanish ain't so good. I'll just be leaving now.
    (*Mundo raises his arm abruptly and points up the road staring intently at Eddie.*)
EDDIE: That way. I get it. She lives that way. That dirt road. Cool. Thanks.
    (*He starts off.*)
    (*Alicia comes with a bucket, calling.*)
ALICIA: Mundooo. Mundo—oh!
EDDIE: Hey—hi! Good Morning.
    (*Alicia stares at him. Turns to Mundo and ignores Eddie.*)
ALICIA: Mundo, we need at least a dozen claws. You know how Father Bernardo eats. And how many clams do you have, let's see.
    (*Mundo shows her the pail.*)
ALICIA: All of those. I'll come back at noon.
    (*Mundo exits.*)
EDDIE: (*After her.*) Don't let me forget to say good-bye. Man, what is it—no one talks around here? (*He starts off.*) This has got to be the fucking end of the world!

SCENE TWO

Alicia is on the bridge. River sounds. Seagulls. A little boy and a middle-aged worn-looking woman arrive.

BOY: (*Looking at the river.*) Ooooooooh.
WOMAN WITH BLUE EYES: Keep back you idiot. Do you want the current to gobble you up?
BOY: (*Looking way up and turning around.*) The trees are so green and so quiet.
WOMAN: That's all you know! Look.
BOY: What?
WOMAN: There's a boa constrictor in those branches just waiting to wind himself around your scrawny neck and crush you to death. And there!
BOY: Where?
WOMAN: In those leaves. There's a nauyauque hiding. He'll drop on your back

and bite you til you turn blue and die. Stay close to me. Things aren't what they seem.

BOY: I'm hungry.

WOMAN: *(Searches her bag and gives him a tortilla.)* Here.

BOY: It's so quiet. Do you like it? I like it. *(He eats.)* But Mamá, do you think…do you think. What about the wind, Mamá?

WOMAN: Keep your mouth shut. There's a village around here somewhere and I'll never get a days work with you hounding me with your gibberish.

BOY: You won't leave me?

WOMAN: If only I could.

ALICIA: *(From the bridge.)* Why do you talk to him like that?

WOMAN: Who are you to tell me how to talk to my boy?

ALICIA: Come here little boy.

(The boy goes to the bridge.)

ALICIA: I have a cookie for you.

WOMAN: Give him two. I need something sweet.

BOY: *(Snatches the cookie.)* Who are you?

ALICIA: Alicia.

BOY: I'm Pipo. Where do you live?

ALICIA: Here. In Nautla. And you?

BOY: Mamá?

WOMAN: We live on our feet and on our backs. And now, I need work girl. I need a roof and food for my boy.

ALICIA: What do you do?

WOMAN: I wash anything clean. So! Do you know anyone who needs help? A home, a store, a ranch, a restaurant?

(The boy is walking back very carefully. As if along an invisible line.)

BOY: Uh-oh.

ALICIA: *(To the boy.)* Are you afraid to walk back? Here—I'll help you. *(She walks with him.)*

WOMAN: Help me and you help him.

ALICIA: He doesn't look like your son. You have blue eyes—like a cat's.

WOMAN: An indian with blue eyes invites nothing but trouble. What about the work?

ALICIA: Well, we might need help at the restaurant—the rainy season's over and people come to the beach. Go down this road and ask for Chelo Sanchez. She'll know what to say.

WOMAN: What is this blessed place again?

ALICIA: Nautla.

(The boy clings to her dress.)

WOMAN: Idiot, you're tearing my dress. Move!

BOY: If it moves, mamá it'll sweep me away and I'll never see you again.

ALICIA: What's wrong with him?

WOMAN: How do I know? He's crazy, afraid of the air, especially the wind. *(She shoves him.)*

ALICIA: Don't do that!

WOMAN: He's no concern of yours.

ALICIA: Pipo—don't worry about the wind. Look at the birds. When the wind blows they face the wind and fly away. It helps them fly anywhere they want.

PIPO: No!

ALICIA: And today is a beautiful day. The sun's shining. Look at all the flowers. The air has never been so pure. *(She kisses the top of his head.)* *(The woman and Pipo leave.)*

SCENE THREE

Chelo's restaurant. Outdoor patio. Rough tables and chairs. Pots of flowers. Chelo sweeping, Eddie arrives.

EDDIE: Chelo Sanchez?

CHELO: Yes?

EDDIE: Aunt Chelo?

CHELO: Edmundo? *(She runs to him emotionally.)* Ay! Edmundo.
(They embrace and stay that way for a long moment. Eddie is moved too.)

CHELO: Only now that I see you I know it's true. She's gone. Poor Tati. Little Tati. I should have been the first.

EDDIE: She's gone.

CHELO: Did she suffer? Was she in pain?

EDDIE: Yeah.

CHELO: Did she die alone?

EDDIE: Yeah.

CHELO: Like your grandfather. Just like papá.

EDDIE: No one called. I walked in. It must have been right after she… It didn't even look like her, you know.

CHELO: In her illness—was your father by her side?

EDDIE: After a while he couldn't go in her room.

CHELO: Of course. *(She looks at him closely.)* You look like your father.

EDDIE: That's what they tell me.

CHELO: I pray you have your mother's heart. Here, sit. Do you want a beer? I want a beer. *(She disappears into the house and reappears with two beers.)* You like Mexican Beer?

EDDIE: Sure.

(She embraces him again and starts to cry.)

EDDIE: Auntie. Look. I brought you some things. She wanted you to have them. *(He opens his backpack and takes out a scarf.)*

CHELO: *(Takes the scarf and smells it.)* It still smells like her. Smell.

EDDIE: No. I got more pictures and a dress packed away. She didn't leave much.

CHELO: She didn't have much. But she had you.

EDDIE: Let's not talk about her okay? Oh—shit—one more thing. Here. *(He takes out a ring.)*

CHELO: She didn't want to be buried with her wedding ring?

EDDIE: Pop wanted to sell it. Maybe you could use it.

CHELO: I can use it. It's time me and your uncle got married. We've been fiancées for thirty years!

EDDIE: Thirty?

CHELO: You're a good boy. Stay as long as you want.

EDDIE: I don't know what I want, auntie. Mom talked about Nautla like it was paradise. Man, I could use paradise right now. Nautla—hey auntie—who's the man with the face like melted wax?

CHELO: Mundo. He's a fisherman. Why?

EDDIE: I'm here fifteen minutes and I've already seen the most grotesque human being and a girl who takes my breath away. Who knows what else might happen if I stay.

CHELO: You like girls.

EDDIE: Does the Pope pray?

CHELO: Edmundo.

EDDIE: Eddie.

CHELO: Eddie then—you should know—men here are…very excitable. Very proud. Especially about their women. So if one doesn't have a gun, he has a machete.

EDDIE: Sounds like home to me.

CHELO: I don't know New York City. But last week in Vega, your cousin, Ramon Flores, dragged his own daughter out of her house. Made her kneel and put six bullets in her head because she was unfaithful to her husband.

EDDIE: I get it.

CHELO: And that girl you saw with Mundo…

EDDIE: Yeah?

CHELO: Don't mess with her Eddie. She's our goddaughter. There's already a problem with her and a boy. She's very strong-willed. I promised her father I'd keep her here—safe—for a while. I don't want trouble in my house.

EDDIE: I'll respect your house, auntie.

CHELO: I'm putting the wood too close to the fire.

EDDIE: Who's the wood and who's the fire auntie?

CHELO: You're making a joke. It's not funny.

EDDIE: I can keep it in my pants.

CHELO: Did you talk like that to your mother?

EDDIE: *(Sings.)* In a small wooden boat on the ocean
sailing sailing out to sea
Nautla my love, my darling
That's where I must be
that's where I must be.
(En un barquito de vela,
Voga, voga por el mar.
Nautla de mis amores
Tendré que ilegar,
tendré que illegar.)

CHELO: Your mother taught you that.

EDDIE: Yeah.

CHELO: Your mother was too sweet. That was her trouble. And you—just don't be a bum.

EDDIE: Like my father.

CHELO: I didn't mean that.

EDDIE: Didn't you?

CHELO: Things happen.

EDDIE: Do you hate him so much?

CHELO: I'll tell you a little family history, Edmundo, your mother was carrying you while your parents were still down here. Our father was dying then. All the daughters, we took turns spending the night helping him sleep through his pain. Every night, our mother would give us five thousand pesos to buy morphine for our father. His pain was terrible. One night, your father volunteers "Hey, I'll stay so you girls can get some rest." So nice. So thoughtful. We couldn't thank him enough and mamá handed him the five thousand peso note as usual telling him what it was for. Your father kissed each one of us as we left and told us not to worry. That night, though, our papá never got his morphine.

EDDIE: What happened?

CHELO: What do you think? Your father met a local girl and wanted to play the big man. He bought tacos and chalupas and beer for her and her friends and guess who's money he used? Your grandfather lay twisting in bed with pain—all night. Now, do you still want me to answer your question?

EDDIE: No.

(Chelo kisses him. The woman with blue eyes enters. The boy and Alicia follow.)

WOMAN: Ah—an old woman kissing a young boy. I always thought it should be done in private, but what do I know—a poor ignorant woman looking for work. I can set tables, clean floors and dye them red once a month.

CHELO: I hope your work's cleaner than your thoughts.

WOMAN: I say what I see. I do what I'm told. A young girl—here she is—told me you might need a day worker.

CHELO: We could use one for a month or so. *(She winks at Eddie but puts her finger to her lips.)* Especially now that there's going to be a wedding. God help me.

WOMAN: God? God'll help you on your death bed. I'll help you now. I'm good. I'm not shy about what I can do. Even the saints want their candles.

CHELO: You can start now. You'll need to wash dishes. Bring the water in from the well. I like lemons in my wash water so the dishes smell clean.

WOMAN: That's easy enough.

CHELO: And there's a large basket of tortillas in the kitchen. When someone comes, you'll have to heat them four at a time over the burners without singeing them.

WOMAN: There should be good food at a restaurant.

CHELO: I'll give you forty pesos for two weeks and a bed for you both, and meals.

EDDIE: Hey—*(Stoops to see the boy.)* What's up midget?

ALICIA: His name's Pipo.

BOY: I like it here, Mamá. It's so still. *(He waits, listening.)* Will it last?

EDDIE: What's with this kid?

WOMAN: He wants to know if the work will last.

BOY: *(Happy, as if performing.)* The wind moves.

It's air. It's air.

The hot breath of animals

behind you

Beware.

I know. I've seen it.

WOMAN: It's nothing. Bad winds hit us on the road once. Trees fell and killed some people right next to us. Not this far away. There was blood I tell you. Now he's jumbled it all up in his head and he's cuckoo with it. *(To the boy.)* You're good at fetching water ain't you? *(To Chelo.)* He's stronger than he looks. Where do we put our things?

CHELO: I'll show you. The well's out back. You must want something to eat. *(She exits, they follow.)*

ALICIA: Who are you?

EDDIE: Eddie. Why didn't you talk to me before?

ALICIA: I didn't want to. Are you from New York City?

EDDIE: Yeah.

ALICIA: We have a saying—"Crazy as a goat in New York City." Is it like that?

EDDIE: What?

ALICIA: Crazy. Cars all over the place. Noise.

EDDIE: That's a pretty good description.

ALICIA: I'd hate it there.

EDDIE: I couldn't imagine you there.

ALICIA: Why not?

EDDIE: Give me fifty years and I'll tell you.

ALICIA: You think I'm ignorant?

EDDIE: No. No. It's just. Forget it.

ALICIA: Well. You don't belong here either.

EDDIE: Fine.

ALICIA: My name's Alicia. How old are you? I'm sixteen.

EDDIE: Old enough.

ALICIA: I have a boyfriend. My parents don't want me to marry him. I don't know why not. My mother married at fourteen. *(Waits for a response. There is none.)* That's why I'm here. He'll come and get me though. Soon.

EDDIE: Good. I wish you luck.

ALICIA: Doña Chelo told you not to talk to me, didn't she?

EDDIE: Sort of.

ALICIA: And you're afraid of me.

EDDIE: Give me a break.

ALICIA: You'd make an excellent priest, you know. Such self-control. And so handsome…I always wondered why so many priests are handsome. What a waste. And they're embarrassed by everything. Are you? *(She looks at him.)* It's fun torturing you like this. Making you talk.

EDDIE: I'm not talking.

ALICIA: I heard your mother died. I'm sorry. I was trying to cheer you up. I'll leave you alone. Your name is Eduardo?

EDDIE: Edmundo. Eddie.

ALICIA: Ooooooooooo.

EDDIE: What?

ALICIA: You have a namesake in the village.

EDDIE: Yeah, who?

ALICIA: I'll give you a hint. Neither of you speaks. But he sings.

EDDIE: Great.

ALICIA: Mundo.

EDDIE: You don't mean that…creature? He's Edmundo?…and here I thought Mundo was some deep nickname—you know, *mundo,* the word for world.

ALICIA: Ay, you make things so complicated!
  (Chelo enters.)

CHELO: Alicia—the crablegs, girl! We need them for the Father's lunch. Go ahead.

ALICIA: *(Hugs her.)* I love you, Doña. *(She exits.)*

EDDIE: So auntie—what can I do? There must be something I can help with around here.

CHELO: No. No. This is your vacation. Eat, swim, do whatever you like.

EDDIE: Maybe I'll go swimming.

CHELO: Yes—but maybe not in the river. It looks peaceful enough. But the current is very bad. It can pull an ox under in a minute and he's gone.

EDDIE: I'll fish.

CHELO: Fish. Good. But not a at high tide. The ocean rushes in and sharks swim up the river as far as a mile. They smell blood, it's all over.

EDDIE: Thanks. I'll just stay here for now. *(He gets out a paper and pen.)*

CHELO: You writing your father?

EDDIE: What?

CHELO: In the letter.

EDDIE: It's not a letter.

CHELO: Oh. *(She looks over his shoulder.)* English?

EDDIE: Yeah.

CHELO: It's so funny—a kid knowing so much English at your age. Look at that. Writing it as if it's nothing.

EDDIE: Yeah.

CHELO: Oh and there's a little matter I want to discuss with you.

EDDIE: She started the conversation, I swear to God.

CHELO: No, no, no. You gave your word. I believe you. This is about the ring and the wedding. Let that be our little secret for now.

EDDIE: No problem.

CHELO: Good. Oh—and Edmundo—we have to get your Uncle Nyin to confession. Soon. Maybe you could ask him to go with you sometime. Tomorrow.

EDDIE: I'm not religious, auntie.

CHELO: You can do me this favor.

EDDIE: I've never been to confession. I don't even know what words to use. Why don't you just ask him to go.

CHELO: I can't make that man see the need to. He's as full of sin as the next man. He spends half his nights and every Sunday drinking at La Ñapa's.

EDDIE: Maybe he feels drinking isn't a sin.

CHELO: La Ñapa is a prostitute. He has no business there.

EDDIE: Uncle Nyin doesn't know me. I don't think I'm the person to approach him on this.

CHELO: The fool. He only drinks there. His big feet are always on the floor when I go by. But he wants me to think differently. Other people do. They talk. I never hear the end of it. Now I'm only telling you this because you're Tati's son and I could always open my heart to her. But now…You see, it's urgent. Nyin must confess.

EDDIE: Why? Is he dying?

CHELO: Something sudden could happen.

EDDIE: Like a wedding?

CHELO: You never know.

EDDIE: Just tell him.

CHELO: He'll know…

EDDIE: Good.

CHELO: The day of the wedding.

EDDIE: This is fucked up, auntie.

CHELO: And what about being engaged for thirty years?! Nyin thinks it's romantic. I'll be fifty next month. I won't go to my deathbed unmarried and die in mortal sin for that man. And now with you children around, we have a responsibility.

EDDIE: I don't want to be involved.

CHELO: You're already involved. You're family. You brought the ring. I'm sure it was a sign from your mother.

EDDIE: Look…

CHELO: What? You think all family is, is a good meal together and that's it? You sit down, lick your plate and leave? No, no, no. If you want to be family, you're like snakes twisting together in a nest. You get warmth. You give warmth. If sometimes you're bitten, you take the poison and live through it. That way you all survive. So don't make me deny your mother's last wish for me. Take Nyin to confession. I'll make some excuse. Alicia'll go too. Nyin adores her. If she smiles, he has a good day. So you'll do it. Good. I'll have a talk with Alicia. *(She picks up a bridle.)* I'll make the bridal lazo. We'll have baked red snapper and a big white cake. I'll let out my lace dress. And one day, I'll just grab Father Bernardo and it's done. *(She looks heavenward.)* Tati, Tati—rest in peace. *(Chelo leaves. Eddie sits and writes.)*

SCENE FOUR

Later. The woman with blue eyes. She is cleaning the restaurant and her skirt is tied up revealing her legs. The boy is trying to hold on to her while she works.

WOMAN: A wedding, a wedding. What a joke! Stay out of my way boy. Can't you let go of my skirts! So young and wanting a woman's skirts.

BOY: But you're my mother. You're not a woman. And I love you.

WOMAN: I'm a woman, muchacho, and now I hate men. Hate them. Do you hear?!

BOY: Do you hate me then?

WOMAN: You're not a man yet. *(She pokes him in the groin.)* Though you've got the makings of a man. Anyway you're crazy and you're mine.

BOY: And I'll protect you. Always!

WOMAN: Right. The day a frog grows hair!

BOY: *(Happily he helps her straighten things.)* It smells like flowers here.

WOMAN: Flowers die too.

(Nyin enters dragging behind him the wired skeleton of a horse. He is a wiry

little man in old, shapeless clothes with a straw hat with a hatband on it. He rarely smiles, but when he does, it surprises his whole face into a wonderful, mischievous grin. The woman with blue eyes is bending over showing her legs. She does not see him. The boy goes directly to the horse and strokes it in wonder.)

NYIN: *(Coming up very close behind her.)* Now, what the hell do we have here?!

WOMAN: *(Jumps around and finds herself face-to-face with the skeleton. She shrieks.)* Jesus in heaven! What is that thing?!

NYIN: *(Taken aback by her appearance from the front.)* A walking rag.

WOMAN: *(Speaking of the horse.)* Ayy! A walking bone. And who are you?

NYIN: It's my house, damn it. Who are you?

WOMAN: I'm a hired woman.

NYIN: *(Examining her.)* You must have been a beauty once. Look at those blue eyes. I don't have to worry about you though. *(He takes off his hat and shows her the brim.)* That's snakeskin…see. Took it from the head of a boa constrictor.

WOMAN: So what's that to me?

NYIN: It protects me against the evil eye…blue, green, brown…even red ones.

WOMAN: If I had my eye on you, it would take more than a few snake scales to keep me away… Hah! *(She goes to touch him.)* You have dirt on your pants.

NYIN: *(Backing away.)* Don't touch me.

BOY: The wind ate the horse up, Mamá. But he's very clean. He shines…

NYIN: Strange child you got there. Where's Chelo?

WOMAN: Your wife?

NYIN: My fiancée.

WOMAN: Ahhh, I see. So this wedding is for you?

NYIN: What wedding? No wedding. Being engaged is the most romantic time of our life. We wouldn't ruin it.

WOMAN: Your sweetheart seems feverish. She's talking lilies and camellias and so much lace. None of it white. I thought for sure the wedding was hers.

NYIN: Our cousins from Vega and Orizaba. They marry here all the time. They even come from Fortín de las Flores.

BOY: Can I have a ride?

NYIN: No.

BOY: Please.

NYIN: He can't hold you now. Old Frijol. Poor old Frijol…look how they wired him together so I could bring him home…*(He sits down and cries.)* Poor Frijol. Black as a bean. He was a born leader… He looks like Archbishop Rinaldo, don't you think?
(The boy laughs happily.)
NYIN: All the horses respected him. They'd fall into line behind him, trusting as babes bobbing their heads all the way to the glue factory…Damn. *(He wipes his eyes and nose.)* But he was old and lame and this time I left him to go through with the others…he turned one last time…he couldn't understand why I didn't come take him by the bridle and pull him away like always. *(Cries harder.)* Trusting to the last. I betrayed him.
BOY: *(Comforting.)* He's quiet now and pretty. I like him.
NYIN: *(To boy.)* Well it's over and done…now where shall I put him?
WOMAN: In the trash heap!
NYIN: He's good as new. Looks younger than ever…*(He carries the skeleton near the restaurant door.)* Maybe here…hmmmmmm…*(He moves him near the altar.)* How about here?…eh, boy? I can stand him right here and he'll be a witness for the wedding. *(He finds the bridle with flowers worked in.)* Well, look at this. Good old Chelo was making something special for Frijol after all…*(He puts it on the horse.)*
WOMAN: That's the bridal wreath for the bride and groom.
NYIN: Poor souls. They'll be harnessed together like two beasts.
WOMAN: And when it's your turn?
NYIN: Don't look at me! Chelo's a strong woman, but I do as I please. I'm a free man.
WOMAN: *(Brushing up against him.)* I like free men. Even skinny ones. Rather have bones against me than nothing at all.
BOY: *(Coming to Nyin worried.)* What's that smell on the wind? Do you smell it?
NYIN: No boy.
WOMAN: I've never been married, but I've had all the men that have caught my fancy, I can tell you…
NYIN: Who would fancy a hag like you?
WOMAN: A hag, eh? You'll be sorry you said that!
BOY: Mamá…I think…the wind smells like blood!
WOMAN: Get away, boy!…

SCENE FIVE

At night. A full moon. Nyin and Chelo sitting at one of the tables.

NYIN: I don't like the woman you hired. The one with the blue eyes.

CHELO: I hired her for the boy's sake. And we need help with the wedding.

NYIN: So…

CHELO: Yes.

NYIN: Who is it after all that's getting married.

CHELO: You don't know them. A sweet young couple with stars in their eyes.

NYIN: I see. We'll make a lot of money on this…wedding?

CHELO: Enough.

NYIN: And what day did you say it was?

CHELO: My birthday. Don't you dare ask me the date. You better know it! Why are you so concerned?

NYIN: I don't like so many people in my house.

CHELO: One last time.

NYIN: I saw Frijol's bridal with flowers on it.

CHELO: I made it as an act of love.

NYIN: He'll never use it. Frijol was killed today.

CHELO: Today? Poor thing.

NYIN: I betrayed him. I betrayed him.

CHELO: We have more endings than beginnings at our age. Still…

NYIN: Betrayal is the worst sin of all.

CHELO: I'll be fifty on my birthday. Fifty. I feel everything I felt at eighteen. Bright colors make me cry and lovesongs sweep me off my feet.

NYIN: Yes. Yes. Time is passing. The bayou's drying up. My boat got jammed in the mangrove roots and I could barely get it out. I felt old.

CHELO: Do you want to marry me? Nyin?

NYIN: Of course I want to marry you. We're engaged, aren't we?

CHELO: When?

NYIN: When? Why? When do you want to get married?

CHELO: Before I die.

NYIN: You don't want to go and spoil it all, do you? After all—since when have we needed a church for what we want to do?
(He hugs her and she pushes him away.)

CHELO: There's children in the house now.

NYIN: You wouldn't want me to get married against my will would you?

CHELO: You were baptized, confirmed, and received communion against your will—that never stopped you before.

NYIN: I need to take a walk.

CHELO: To La Ñapa's.

NYIN: To someplace with barrels of pulque, and music. Somewhere romantic.

CHELO: Do you love me Nyin? I love you.

(Nyin walks away into the darkness.)

NYIN: I wish Frijol were here. The world's coming to an end.

SCENE SIX

Later the same night. Eddie writing. Alicia sitting at the other table. Pipo comes out.

PIPO: Who are you waiting for?

ALICIA: Ay!

PIPO: Couldn't you see me?

ALICIA: Yes of course, you silly. I was just thinking.

PIPO: My mother says she can't see me at night because I'm so dark. When I was little she tied a string from my wrist to hers at night so she wouldn't lose me. Why am I so dark?

ALICIA: Because your mother didn't wash you in a burra's milk—so you didn't lighten like some other children.

PIPO: I like your hair. It's springy. *(He plays with it.)* A man with a hat was here. He left his horse but you can't ride it.

ALICIA: You mean Frijol? It was that man's best friend. He told me.

PIPO: He told me too. Black as a bean, he said. My father was black too and my mother lost him in the dark.

ALICIA: You should go to bed.

PIPO: My mother's snoring.

ALICIA: Turn her on her side.

PIPO: Will you be here in the morning?

ALICIA: Yes.

PIPO: And the next one and the next one?

ALICIA: Yes you silly thing.

PIPO: *(He looks at Eddie.)* Are you two married?

ALICIA: No. Now go to bed. *(She kisses him.)*

PIPO: Good night.

ALICIA: Dream of angels so you'll dream of me. *(She laughs.)*

> *(Pipo exits. Eddie looks at Alicia. She glances at him. He looks down. Alicia stares at him.)*

ALICIA: Are you doing homework?

EDDIE: No.

ALICIA: Can I see what you're writing?

EDDIE: It's in English.

ALICIA: Oh. Is it a poem?

EDDIE: Sort of.

ALICIA: About me—sitting here in the moonlight, pensive and beautiful?

EDDIE: No.

ALICIA: Is it about your girlfriend back home with long golden hair and long golden legs?

EDDIE: I don't have a girlfriend.

ALICIA: Ahhh, Edmundo the priest.

EDDIE: You wouldn't be safe with the priests I know.

> *(They look at each other.)*

EDDIE: So—when's your boyfriend coming for you?

ALICIA: In a month. The next new moon.

EDDIE: Does he love you?

ALICIA: He adores me.

EDDIE: But he'll go a month without seeing you.

ALICIA: He pleaded with me to run off. He swore he couldn't live without me. He cried. He raged like a bull. He said he'd cut me or he'd die if I didn't leave with him. But it was too dangerous. And what's a few more weeks.

EDDIE: You don't love him.

ALICIA: How can you say that!

EDDIE: You're not that anxious to see him.

ALICIA: Well once we're married, we'll be together every minute. That's it.

EDDIE: Don't get married.

ALICIA: I'm not like that. Once we're together, we have to get married. That's the way it's done. Especially if your family doesn't like your choice—You run away, you sleep together—then everyone in the family is yelling and demanding you marry as soon as possible. The men really get mad. Machismo is nothing to fool around with. Men here are very jealous.

EDDIE: Men there too.

ALICIA: That bad?

EDDIE: Yes.

ALICIA: Are you the jealous type?

EDDIE: No. Not me.

ALICIA: Miguel is. My boyfriend. I sneak to the post office to call him. I told him about you.

EDDIE: Jesus Christ. Why?

ALICIA: To make sure he'd come.

EDDIE: Thanks a lot.

ALICIA: Can't you handle yourself?

EDDIE: I can handle myself and three others, with one hand tied behind my back if I have to.

ALICIA: Now you sound like one of us.

EDDIE: We're not so different.

ALICIA: Really?

EDDIE: Really.

ALICIA: Tell me—sometimes—don't you feel that when someone tells you not to do something—that's the very first thing you want to do?

EDDIE: Yeah. Sometimes.

ALICIA: Me too.

EDDIE: Don't play with me. I don't like it. *(He continues writing.)*

ALICIA: Write about me.

(Eddie ignores her.)

ALICIA: You and I are taking Nyin to confession tomorrow. Did Chelo tell you?

EDDIE: She told me.

ALICIA: Will you confess everything?

EDDIE: I have nothing to confess.

ALICIA: I do. Good night.

EDDIE: Dream of angels—

ALICIA: So you dream of me. Write about Pipo. Why don't you?

SCENE SEVEN

A college cafe. Two years later. Eddie taps a microphone.

EDDIE: Can you guys hear me okay? Great. Uh…yeah, well this poem's about a kid I met. I mean, I don't usually think about kids, but I always wonder where he is. I hope he's safe. The poem's called…uh… "Pipo gets well."
In a world so new
that many things had not

yet been named,
Pipo, the smallest,
almost died of delicacy,
every flutter of light
a heartbeat.
Once Pipo awoke delirious
and cried,
"Mamá, why am I
so much darker
than the rest?"
"Ah," his mother sighed,
"I did not wash you
in burra's milk
so you did not lighten
like the others."
And Pipo awoke again
and pointed to things
asking, "What's this,
What's this?" until
the world had a name
for all things
even the smallest
and the darkest.

SCENE EIGHT

Nyin, Alicia, and Eddie kneeling in a church pew. They whisper.

ALICIA: I can't believe it. She left. Hypocrite. She only took five minutes. I know for a fact she has more sins than that!

EDDIE: Maybe she just says etcetera.

NYIN: What? What are you saying?

ALICIA: Nyin—you can go now. That lady left.

NYIN: You go first.

(Alicia gets up. Genuflects, crosses herself.)

ALICIA: I'm going to light a candle for my grandmother. You go. Go on now. Then you can show Eddie what to do.

NYIN: I don't know why you can't do it just as well.

ALICIA: He's a boy. There's things he can't confess in front of me I'm sure. Now go on. *(She gets up and exits.)*

EDDIE: Well?

NYIN: Go ahead. Go ahead.

EDDIE: Aunt Chelo wanted you to show me how to confess.

NYIN: Priests make me nervous. Anyway, I have nothing to confess.

EDDIE: But Uncle Nyin...

NYIN: I'm not a hypocrite.

EDDIE: What about...that woman?

NYIN: What?

EDDIE: La Ñapa?

NYIN: Now that's where we should go for confession. You can talk to La Ñapa like a man and get an answer from a woman's point of view. She can keep a secret too. Don't look so shocked. There's nothing to it. Why don't you come to La Ñapa's with me? You're almost a man now—shit you're not a virgin are you? Ever had pulque—eh Don Edmundo? Bet not. You should try it. You'll like it there. I like it. I can take my shoes off and open my shirt. You'd get a kick out of La Ñapa—she's only a little thing—maybe four feet tall but can beat the shit out of most men. She stands on a table and beats her sons with sticks when they do wrong. They're big guys too, but they stand there and take it saying "No Mamá, I'm sorry Mamá." You have a lot to learn about Mexico, boy. Don't judge Mexico by all the poor people who come up to your country. We have skyscrapers. We have pyramids! We have blonds. Real ones. *(To Alicia offstage, gesturing.)* You go. You go first. *(To Eddie.)* That girl's an angel, what could she have to confess? Come on. We can leave now. She won't be but a minute.

EDDIE: It's important to Aunt Chelo that we all confess.

NYIN: Why?

EDDIE: La Ñapa?

NYIN: She's jealous? Good for her. It's part of romance, it keeps the heart alive. But I told you I have nothing to confess and I'll tell you why right now. For your ears only. In all these years—I've never touched another woman. Not La Ñapa. Not nobody. Don't get me wrong. I'm as hot-blooded as the next fella, but we're novios. We've been engaged for thirty years—why ruin a good thing? But shit. Thirty years without another woman. If you say a word—I'll deny it. I'll pull a knife. And if you think I'll go up there and admit that to some man in skirts—*(Nyin gets up.)* It's time to go.

EDDIE: You love Chelo—why are you ashamed?

NYIN: Are you stupid? For a man, virtues are vices! You coming?

EDDIE: No. I'll wait for Alicia.

NYIN: Be careful, boy. Don't start what you won't finish. In Mexico betrayal is the worst and only sin. Poor Frijol. *(He leaves.)*

EDDIE: *(Praying.)* It's not like that. I'm not like you, papá. I'm young. It's natural. Fuck!

SCENE NINE

By the river before dawn. Alicia enters with her pail and a stick. She waits. There's sound in the bushes.

ALICIA: Mundo?... *(Whispers.)* Mundo.

EDDIE: *(Out in the open.)* Pssssst. It's me.

ALICIA: Ay, you scared me. What are you doing here?

EDDIE: I saw you leave.

ALICIA: Go away. Mundo won't come out if you're here.

EDDIE: I thought you were meeting your boyfriend. From back home. The full moon...remember?

ALICIA: And what would you have done if I'd met him?

EDDIE: Watched. I needed to see what he was like and what you were like with him.

ALICIA: And then?

EDDIE: It didn't happen.

ALICIA: Go away then. I'm hunting crabs.

EDDIE: At first light.

ALICIA: That's when they come out and crawl around. Mundo helps me.

EDDIE: I could help you.

ALICIA: You have to grab them and pull off their big claw.

EDDIE: Then you let them die?

ALICIA: No. Their claw grows back.

EDDIE: I could do that. I've done worse.

ALICIA: You've killed a man?

EDDIE: No. But I've picked up cockroaches and let them crawl up my arm.

ALICIA: So brave.

EDDIE: Come here.

ALICIA: Why?

EDDIE: Hide with me. We'll spy on Mundo.

ALICIA: Why?

EDDIE: Why—why—why—why? Just come here.

ALICIA: No really. Why spy on Mundo?

EDDIE: To see what he has to make you sneak out to meet him.

ALICIA: I didn't sneak out. And I won't hide and laugh at him like a tourist.

EDDIE: You like him…or do you feel sorry for him?

ALICIA: I…I feel privileged. Mundo talks to no one. Sometimes he talks to me.

EDDIE: Yes. Have him talk to you.

ALICIA: No. He's not a talking dog. He trusts me.

EDDIE: And it's such a honor to win his trust?

ALICIA: It's always an honor to be trusted by someone who trusts no one else.

EDDIE: He'll trust me.

ALICIA: I don't think so.

EDDIE: Well, if he does, will you?

ALICIA: Yes.

EDDIE: So help me. Let me watch him. Then I'll know him better.

ALICIA: All right. We'll hide.

EDDIE: *(Slaps his arms.)* Damn flies! They don't even bite you.

ALICIA: Shhhhhh…

(We hear bells. Mundo walks along the river with his pole and bucket. He pokes around quietly for crabs. We hear a goat bleat.)

MUNDO: Goat. *(He digs in his robe and fills his hand with something and holds it out to the unseen goat.)* Baby come, come. Here. *(He waits, the goat bleats. He goes offstage.)*

(Eddie and Alicia look at each other. Mundo returns, wipes his hands on his robe and continues looking for crabs. He laughs.)

MUNDO: My goat. My goat. *(He pokes in crevices and starts to sing a popular lovesong. He wanders off as he sings.)*

I know I still have time
I know it's not too late
I know our love is true
That love will be our fate
And in all the years I live
Every heartbeat that remains
I'll live to give you love
I'll kiss away the pain
With kisses strong and wild
Like the passions you awake

I know I still have time
I know it's not too late.
(Alicia and Eddie wait until the song fades.)

EDDIE: Was he singing to his goat?

ALICIA: That was so sad.

EDDIE: I thought it was funny. All that for a goat…or maybe not for a goat. Maybe he's in love.

ALICIA: Ay no.

EDDIE: You pay him a lot of attention.

ALICIA: I talk to him.

EDDIE: And he talks back. Only to you. He could love you Alicia.

ALICIA: Don't say that Eddie.

EDDIE: Why?

ALICIA: It frightens me.

EDDIE: Because he's a leper?

ALICIA: No. Because he has those feelings—think how he must suffer. No. No. I think you're wrong. Mundo and I are like…like an old man and his niece.

EDDIE: Like you and Nyin.

ALICIA: Yes, like that. He'll be at the dance next week. I'll make sure he knows he can't…that he shouldn't…I'll talk all night about Miguel and our plans and about love…but I think he was singing to his goat. He likes to sing. He can't speak. But he can sing with no trouble. I don't know why. He's not a leper, you know. People think so, but Aunt Chelo told me some fungus ate his face. Something like that. The clinic in San Rafael sent someone out to see—so no one else would get it. But no— he's not a leper. I think it affected his voice though. You should ask him.

EDDIE: Man, you make me scared to talk to him. I feel like I should ask for his blessing, like he's a holy man.

ALICIA: No. Mundo's okay. He sings at dances sometimes. When it's people he knows.

EDDIE: Does he drink? Does he eat? Crack jokes? What's he like?
(Alicia shrugs.)

EDDIE: Will you dance with me at the dance next week?

ALICIA: Why not?

EDDIE: In front of Chelo?

ALICIA: In public at a dance there's nothing wrong.

EDDIE: And here? Now?

ALICIA: We shouldn't be here.

EDDIE: I know. Aunt Chelo.

ALICIA: My boyfriend. I'm forbidden. Or is that why you're here? Is it?

EDDIE: How about you? Why are you here?

(They kiss. Lightly at first and then fully.)

ALICIA: *(Steps away.)* What a fool!

EDDIE: Try not to look so pretty and I'll try not to be a fool.

ALICIA: I'm the fool not you. I wanted to kiss you but now, I don't know what I want.

EDDIE: I do. *(He takes her hand and kisses her again.)*

ALICIA: What?

EDDIE: What what?

ALICIA: You do that alot. *(Touches his face.)*

EDDIE: What?

ALICIA: What what?

(Imitates him. They laugh, kiss again.)

ALICIA: What do you want?

EDDIE: You. Now.

ALICIA: *(She thinks for a moment.)* All right. *(She unbuttons her blouse.)*

EDDIE: No. Wait. I'll be killed! You'll be killed! We'll be murdered in our sleep!

ALICIA: My boyfriend's two hundred miles away on an oil rig. Who would kill you?

EDDIE: It's a serious matter. Uncle Nyin...

(Alicia gives him a look.)

EDDIE: Okay. All right. Maybe he wouldn't kill me—but if Chelo ever knew. If she ever found out. I could never come back.

ALICIA: Were you ever going to?

EDDIE: No. I don't know.

ALICIA: Don't.

EDDIE: Why?

ALICIA: I could never be alone with you now if I ever thought you'd come back.

EDDIE: That's crazy.

ALICIA: I know. *(She touches his face.)* You have the face of an indian.

EDDIE: I have my father's face.

ALICIA: So smooth. It doesn't tell me you're American. It doesn't tell me anything—except when you smile.

EDDIE: What does it tell you then?

ALICIA: My magic worked. I bought three candles from La Ñapa and said some special words when a cloud passed over the moon and see, you're here! I conjured you up.

EDDIE: I don't believe in that.

ALICIA: I do. It works every time.

EDDIE: How many times have you done this?

ALICIA: Once. You're the first. Now swear to me you won't come back.

EDDIE: But why?

ALICIA: If we were together and you left I would be so sad. If you came back, but not for me—I think I'd die.

EDDIE: It's stupid to swear to anything.

ALICIA: I'll swear first. I swear I'll never follow you. I'll never search you out. I'll never know your street, or your father, or your room, or your friends, or your life, or your death when it comes.

EDDIE: My father betrayed every woman he ever knew.

ALICIA: So?

EDDIE: It would be so easy to promise you anything—everything right now. So very easy. *(He kisses her.)*

ALICIA: Then do it. It would be easy to believe you.

EDDIE: I'll stay this summer and never come back to Nautla.

ALICIA: Ever?

EDDIE: Never.

(They stare at each other.)

ALICIA: Maybe we shouldn't be alone here now.

EDDIE: Yes we should. *(He draws her to him.)*

SCENE TEN

The woman with blue eyes and the boy by the river.

WOMAN: *(Slapping herself.)* These flies. *(Looking around.)* How should I know where the girl is? She doesn't do half the work I do! Come here and give your mother a big hug.

PIPO: *(Finds Mundo's bells.)* What are these? *(He moves the bells so they ring. He puts them around his wrist.)*

WOMAN: Let me see those! Ayyy, take them off quickly. They're the leper bells. Take them off I say! *(She rips them off the boy and throws them in the river.)*

PIPO: No they're pretty. No.

WOMAN: I threw them in the river. I saved your life. They're leper bells.

PIPO: Do they call the wind up Mamá?

WOMAN: They're from a sick man with skin like tree bark and no face. A leper, a leper. Do you hear me?!

PIPO: A leper.

WOMAN: Child are you so backward you don't know what a leper is?

PIPO: No.

WOMAN: Why do you think they're run out of villages and made to wear bells? They're the walking dead!

PIPO: Dead?

WOMAN: Carajo! Do you want to marry?

PIPO: Yes.

WOMAN: No woman will touch you if you've touched a leper...do you want children?

PIPO: A hundred.

WOMAN: They'll be born monsters and their skin will rot and boil off if you're touched by a leper.

PIPO: *(Looking into the river.)* Mamá—the bells! I see them—spinning and spinning and spinning.

WOMAN: Keep away from there idiot. Imbecile. You could drown and I'd never know it!

PIPO: Mamá! Mamá! Look!

WOMAN: If you ever see a leper, call me. I'll chase him away. Let's go back.

PIPO: Mamá—look! The river's turning green.

WOMAN: *(Comes to look.)* The ocean's coming into the river. It's high tide.

End of Act I

ACT II
SCENE ONE

The park: a huge mural of Juarez and Zapata. Dance music: Merengue. We see Nyin and Chelo dancing. Pipo and Alicia. The woman with blue eyes is smoking. Everyone is dressed up. Nyin is a bit loaded. Eddie is standing there. Nyin comes over.

NYIN: Viva Mexico! Viva. Épale—*(He does a few dance steps.)* Come on boy— dance, dance.

CHELO: Come on, dance with me Edmundo. This old woman can dance.
(Nyin dances with Alicia.)

CHELO: You dance good. Dance with all the girls—see them whispering over there—Ay look, Diana elbowed the girl next to her and won't look at you now. Go. Give her a thrill. Ask her to dance.

NYIN: *(Staggers over with Alicia.)* This young girl is killing me—*(He takes Chelo's hand.)* I want to die in your arms. Come on Chelito. Leave the young ones alone.
(They dance off.)

NYIN: Slowly, but we'll get there.

ALICIA: *(Waves offstage.)* Adiós Pelon. *(To Pelon offstage.)* Me? Sure! *(To Eddie as she leaves.)* Dance, dance. They're watching!

EDDIE: I'm fine.

ALICIA: Coward. Then hold this. *(She gives him her sweater. She laughs and leaves.)*
(Eddie wanders to one side. The music fades. He presses the sweater to his face and breathes in Alicia's perfume. Chelo all perspiring comes over laughing.)

CHELO: Don't be so selfish. Give the girls a break!

EDDIE: I'm perfectly happy Auntie.
(We hear Nyin yell offstage.)

NYIN: Viva Mexico!

CHELO: Life is harder here than you think!

EDDIE: Viva Mexico! Ay Auntie—this music. There's no love songs like Mexican love songs. The States are dry as toast—my mother always said that. She said it's sad to be a Mexican without Mexico.

NYIN: *(Offstage.)* Viva Mexico!

EDDIE: She made my parents poor; she forced them out she broke their hearts—but they loved her. And I love her for them. Viva Mexico!

CHELO: Something's happened to make you feel all this "love."

EDDIE: I'm happy, that's all.

CHELO: Yes.

EDDIE: What?

CHELO: Tell me—why is it that you and Alicia chatter, chatter all the time and now, tonight you hardly speak. You never dance. You barely look at each other except for a short hot glance when you think no one's watching.

EDDIE: She's a beautiful girl.

CHELO: So is Diana.

EDDIE: I haven't asked her to dance either. Auntie, come on—don't worry...

CHELO: Nyin and I are to blame. We've set a bad example. We've been living selfishly. That has to end.

EDDIE: Dance with me. You dance like a girl of eighteen. You dance like you have stars under your feet.

CHELO: This is getting dangerous. You talk like an angel. Alicia's radiant and laughs too much. We have the ingredients for a tragedy. And how can I stop it if Nyin and I are living in sin? I'll settle this tonight. *(Chelo sees Mundo.)* Mundo—poor soul. You're invited to a wedding. Next week. There'll be lots to eat and drink. And two old people dressed like a bride and groom. *(She exits.)*

(Pipo and the woman with blue eyes dance by. Pipo goes up to Mundo curiously.)

PIPO: Are you a man? Are you a woman? I can't see your face.

(The woman with blue eyes steps between them. She forms a cross with her fingers and holds it up to him.)

WOMAN: Spirit be gone! Spirit be gone!

EDDIE: He's harmless.

WOMAN: He's a curse. *(To Mundo.)* Stay away from my boy!

EDDIE: Leave him alone.

WOMAN: I will if you dance with me. I used to be the best dancer in San Rafael.

(Alicia comes into view.)

EDDIE: Sorry. I have things to do. *(He takes Alicia's arm.)* Dance with me.

ALICIA: I thought we weren't going to be together tonight.

EDDIE: It doesn't matter. Chelo knows. Keep smiling.

ALICIA: What will we do?

EDDIE: To hell with everyone. Dance with me. Closer. Closer.

(They dance.)

EDDIE: Chelo doesn't know everything. Just a little. Kiss me.

ALICIA: No. Not here. Let's dance.

EDDIE: Kiss me. I'm dying to kiss you. I can't be this close without kissing you.

ALICIA: Don't. People are looking at us.

> *(Eddie whirls her around faster, closer. His face in her hair.)*

EDDIE: Who cares?! I'm crazy about you. Let them all know!

ALICIA: *(Pushes him away.)* Do you want to get us killed!

EDDIE: Come on. Who's going to kill us for a kiss?

ALICIA: My boyfriend's coming for me tonight!

EDDIE: What!? What are you talking about?

ALICIA: He's coming for me tonight. Look at the moon.

EDDIE: What about it?

ALICIA: It's the first new moon in August. He said he'd come.

EDDIE: So have you talked to him about us? Have you told him things are different now?

ALICIA: Are you crazy? Nothing's different. He'll ride up on a horse and I'll ride off behind him.

EDDIE: You didn't talk to him.

ALICIA: We arranged it a long time ago.

EDDIE: And you were just going to disappear?

ALICIA: Yes.

EDDIE: Alicia. You can't do this!

ALICIA: Why? Will you fight for me? Will you love me forever? Please!

EDDIE: You bitch!

ALICIA: We're engaged.

EDDIE: Have you slept with him?

ALICIA: And if I had—would you drop me as if I were a leper? *(She sees something.)* Ay!

EDDIE: What?

ALICIA: Miguel! *(She runs off.)*

> *(The woman with blue eyes approaches Mundo menacingly.)*

WOMAN: Get away.

> *(Mundo faces her.)*

WOMAN: You're filth. Disease. You're not a man. You're not even an animal, a beast. You're...you're the rotting bark of a tree! Do you hear me? A tree.

> *(Mundo reaches out to grab and shake her. She steps away.)*

WOMAN: If you touch me I'll cut your heart out and kill your little goat!

> *(Mundo exits.)*

SCENE TWO

Alicia walking. Mundo enters very agitated.

ALICIA: Oh it's you. Thank God. Walk with me a bit.
> *(Mundo goes in and out of the foliage ringing his bells and then listening. Finally he rings them and the goat bleats. He is relieved. He stands still and breathes deeply.)*

ALICIA: You lost your goat? I'm glad you found him. Does he have a name? He loves you. He follows you everywhere. Believe me—you're better off with goats.

MUNDO: *(Turns abruptly to face her.)* No.

ALICIA: I just meant—when you fall in love, people feel free to ask you to give up your entire life, as if they were asking the time of day. I don't know what to do. I'm stepping off a cliff. I'm dying. I'm lost. You must be past all that. Like Nyin and Chelo. You see things with a clearer eye and a calmer heart. I wish I could be like that now.

MUNDO: I'm twenty-five.

ALICIA: What is it? What's the matter?

MUNDO: *(Furious.)* I'm twenty-five.

ALICIA: Oh. You're young. How terrible. *(She reaches out to him to soothe him.)*
> *(Eddie rushes in. In the excitement of the moment, they forget Mundo's presence.)*

EDDIE: Alicia!

ALICIA: Why did you follow me?

EDDIE: Are you kidding? I'd follow you to the end of the world.

ALICIA: Fool! Do you have a machete? A gun? This isn't a game.

EDDIE: What are you going to do? Let Miguel come drag you away by the hair and fuck you so you have to get married. *(He grabs her.)* I could do that too.

ALICIA: *(Twisting away.)* You probably could.

EDDIE: You feel something for me. I know it.

ALICIA: Yes.

EDDIE: Don't go back. Stay here with me. *(He takes her hair in his hands.)* I'll stay here with you. I have to. I'm caught in your hair.
> *(They kiss. Mundo watches, then exits.)*

ALICIA: I never slept with him.

EDDIE: Shhhhhh.

ALICIA: He's nineteen.

EDDIE: I don't want to hear.

ALICIA: I want you to hear. You should know.

EDDIE: No.

ALICIA: His name is Miguel. You should know his name. He works in Poza Rica in the oil fields. He's thin. He comes to me after work, his shirt black with oil. His hands are rough and burned. We walk down the road and the back of our hands touch. That's enough. His house is one room with painted brick and he has a brand new stove. He'd tell me all about it. His life. He would share his whole life with me. And I know what kind of life it is. I would be his wife and stand in the mornings in a loose dress waving to him, the roof would be made of palm leaves and the floor cement. I could count on him and he could count on me. We know the same songs. He hardly smiles, but when he does—it's like the sun rising. He has an open smile. If I stay with you. I'll close it.

EDDIE: Stay with me. I want you so bad.

ALICIA: If I hurt him like this I can never go back.

EDDIE: Why would you have to go back? Do you love him?

ALICIA: How did this happen? A month ago I didn't know your name.

EDDIE: I know.

ALICIA: And a month from now?

EDDIE: I'll make you forget everyone you ever knew.

SCENE THREE

Chelo's restaurant patio. Tables and chairs overturned. Nyin stands near the skeleton of Frijol with a gun.

NYIN: *(To Frijol.)* I tell you Frijol. It's a good thing you're dead. You're free of all this craziness. Drink, girls, love, tears, rage. And for what? Shit. One boy a maniac waving a pistol over a girl he can't find; another chasing after a girl he can't catch. Now I have to worry about—let's see—*(He counts his fingers.)* Three people, four counting Chelo who'll have a stroke when she sees all this. And that boy is wild. He's crying like it's ripped out of his heart. Ay what torture it is to be young. If I were young again I couldn't live through it. Thank God Chelo and I are in our quiet years. Chelo's sturdy as a rock. And look at you and me. You're a bag of bones and I'm a sack. Ah well. *(He begins to clean up.)* How many days did we walk down these roads you and me with the sun beating on our backs like a live flame? I never thought those days would end. And you, my friend never thought at all. It was enough to be together with dust in our mouths taking one step and then another. Doing one thing and then another. I'd brush you, you'd spill my coffee over. If I felt bad, you knew it. You'd push me with your nose until I walked into a fence and laughed. I tell you—that's how things should be. Nothing is above the love of a man for his horse—so much is below. And then, then, I betrayed you, my simple trusting friend. I led you like a lamb to slaughter—except you were a horse. I miss you Frijol. But you're damn lucky—getting old isn't a bag of tricks either. The door closes. The tomb yawns open. *(Chelo enters.)*

CHELO: Nyin. What happened?

NYIN: Chelo?

CHELO: What've you done? Are you drunk? Why are you holding your rifle?

NYIN: Miguel was here looking for Alicia.

CHELO: What did you tell him?

NYIN: I told him he'd wear out his heart and no woman is worth that! But he wasn't in the mood to listen. He'd been drinking. First he wanted to shoot me. He kept saying "I might as well be dead. There's no greater glory than to die for love!." It would have been funny but he meant it. And he was drunk. Then he threw up and said "My love's gone to hell!" and left.

CHELO: Where's Alicia?

NYIN: I thought she was with you.

CHELO: No. No she left the dance a long time ago. And Eddie? Where's Edmundo?

NYIN: God knows.

CHELO: Ay no! Does Miguel have his gun?

NYIN: Yes. And he's furious.

CHELO: God in Heaven. You were merciful in never giving us children.

NYIN: I'll go find them.

CHELO: Hurry.

NYIN: *(Checking his rifle.)* I've never shot a man before.

CHELO: It won't come to that.

NYIN: Men have been shot over who goes through a door first. And if Miguel finds them together…the world's full of stupidity. *(He exits.)*

SCENE FOUR

Eddie and Alicia are lying on the ground kissing. We hear the bushes swish. Alicia sits up suddenly.

ALICIA: Did you hear that?

EDDIE: *(Gets up to investigate.)* Shhhhh.

ALICIA: Get a branch! Get a stone!

(Nyin enters.)

EDDIE: Uncle Nyin!

NYIN: *(Looks at Eddie, then at Alicia on the ground.)* Miguel was at the house.

ALICIA: *(Springs to her feet.)* Miguel? What did you tell him?

NYIN: He wrecked everything looking for you. Go help Chelo clean up. Now!

EDDIE: She's staying with me until he leaves.

NYIN: And you'll protect her?

EDDIE: Yes.

NYIN: Get out of my way. I don't have time for foolishness. You don't know what's going on here.

EDDIE: Careful Uncle. I know more than you think. A lot more.

NYIN: Get to the house Alicia. You've caused enough trouble with that poor boy Miguel, and now you've encouraged this little puppy here until he's pissing all over himself trying to please you. I've had enough. Go home.

ALICIA: Eddie—I have to. I'm sorry. *(She exits.)*

EDDIE: You can't deal with me like that.

NYIN: No?

EDDIE: No. I wouldn't let my father and I won't let you.

NYIN: We'll settle this in the morning.

EDDIE: Now. I mean it.

NYIN: All right. So?

EDDIE: I'll marry her. I'm staying.

NYIN: You're staying. In Mexico. In Nautla.

EDDIE: Yeah. What about it?

NYIN: And what will you do—find old horses and take them to the glue factory like me? Hunt for snakes and alligators in the swamps like me?

EDDIE: If I have to.

NYIN: This has gone farther than I thought. You must be completely crazy! Can you fish? Can you mend boats? Can you hunt? Can you trap? Do you have a gun or a net? Will a big American boy like you break your back for two centavos and a cold tortilla picking coffee or mangoes. Do you have a truck? A license to teach? Are you a magician creating jobs where no one else can find them. You want Alicia to be a maid while you look for work? Think boy—are we all so stupid that we head north for nothing? We give our work cheap to the gringoes for nothing? Tell me— who in your life do you know who comes south looking for jobs, for wages, for work, for life? Everyone goes North—to the States. Have you lost your mind? I don't know why I'm even trying to talk to you. When the post office opens in the morning I'll call your father.

EDDIE: I won't go.

NYIN: You're a boy—you'll go.

EDDIE: Who are you to talk? You ran away with Chelo at eighteen. I'm eighteen.

NYIN: I knew these swamps like the palm of my hand at eighteen. Rich men from Puebla and Orizaba knew my name. I'd take them for anacondas and alligators and turtles as big as truck tires. They paid me in cash. At eighteen I already had a name. People looked me up.

EDDIE: You have a name now too. And it's "Fool"...

NYIN: Take that back.

EDDIE: Ignorant fool.

NYIN: Even though you're American—I can't excuse that. Take that back, son.

EDDIE: No. You know—my father may be a fuck, but he had some good advice. He always told me—"If you throw a punch, make sure it hurts."

NYIN: Don't ever call a man a fool down here.

EDDIE: What would you call a man whose woman plans an entire wedding— invites the guests, orders the fool, calls in the priest without bothering to tell him he's the one to be led down the aisle to the altar as the groom?

NYIN: Wait. Wait. What's this?

EDDIE: Why do you think Aunt Chelo needs you to confess now—after thirty years? It's for your wedding mass.

NYIN: I can't believe it.

EDDIE: She's betrayed you.

NYIN: No.

EDDIE: Wake up. Everyone knows but you. And they're all waiting to laugh.

NYIN: What me the fool? Led like a lamb to slaughter. To hell with that! *(He exits.)*

SCENE FIVE

Alicia and Chelo at the restaurant. Cleaning up.

CHELO: Are you happy?

ALICIA: Why should I be?

CHELO: You have two men wild about you.

ALICIA: What good is that? I can't stop thinking about Eddie.

CHELO: And Miguel?

(Alicia shrugs.)

CHELO: It happened so quickly. Too quickly.

ALICIA: When the river rises it rises—whether it's from one storm or a week of rain. It sweeps you away.

CHELO: I tell you Alicia. These men. I don't know how they do it. It's something they're born with. They're so convincing. So sure. Even as little tiny things. Their dreams seem so powerful. We come to believe they're our dreams. They're always so clear about what they want; they want a horse; they want a shirt; they want hot peppers, but not the ones with veins; they want a new pistol and they want you all in the same breath. What do you want?

ALICIA: I want to see what happens, Doña. Whatever that is. I want to be swept away.

(Nyin enters. Angry. Strides by them both.)

ALICIA: Where's Eddie?

CHELO: Nyin?

NYIN: Where's my good shirt?

CHELO: Why?

NYIN: I want it.

CHELO: Now? Are you crazy?

(Nyin exits into the house again. Chelo follows. Alicia exits to find Eddie. The stage is empty for a moment. Nyin comes out, his white guayabera unbuttoned, putting on lots of cologne.)

CHELO: Nyin talk to me.

(He continues to splash on cologne.)

CHELO: What's wrong. What are you doing?

(He glares at her. He hands her the cologne. He starts to exit.)

CHELO: Where are you going?

(He goes to Frijol and kisses him.)

NYIN: Hunting. *(He exits.)*

SCENE SIX

Eddie in the dark. We hear bells. They stop.

EDDIE: I heard your bells. I know you're there. *(He waits.)* Why don't you cut the crap and come out? I could really use someone to talk to. How 'bout you? Look, I know you can talk. Me and Alicia heard you talking to your goat. That's right, me and Alicia. You ain't the only one that hides—you hear what I'm saying? *(Waits.)* Forget it! I ain't in the mood for your little games or whatever. You know, you should take a hint. Act human. I know you got a problem, but in my humble opinion you make it worse—you act so damn freaky. You dress like a swami or something. You don't talk. You just stare at people and make them damn uncomfortable. I mean, aren't you sick to death of being an outsider? A freakshow?
(Mundo steps into the light.)

EDDIE: Mundo. Man, I'm glad to see you. I was just saying. If you can talk to a goat, you can talk to people. What's wrong with people? *(He laughs.)* Right. The hundred million dollar question. People! Man, here I am giving you advice and I'm a punk wherever I go. I mean, at home, I'm a lousy spic. And here—? Jesus! I figured I'd be everyday people here. The mayor looks like me, the little bent guy who sells ice cones looks like me—you'd even look like me if you weren't so fucked up. But naaaah— Here I'm a dumb gringo who doesn't know his ass from a hole in the ground. It makes me think it ain't so bad back home, you hear what I'm saying? My neighborhood's pretty cool. More people in one apartment building than in this whole town, that's for sure. Hard to get my mind around that! One apartment building equals one town. Too much! Always people, action every minute. You go out four in the morning and the lights are on, people are walking their dogs, drinking whatever. If I'm short of money—hah! Big if—there's always someone who'll spot me a coke or a cigarette. New York, New York. It's got a bad rep, but it's great, man. You'd love New York. Nobody'd give you a second look there. You should see what's walking around. No offense. I could see you there…but Alicia? Forget it. Course, she'd never go. But if she did? What could I do with Alicia in New York City? First time someone looked at her cross-eyed, I'd go for their throat—which means I'd last five minutes before committing a homocide. "Crazy as a goat in New York City." You heard that saying? Can you imagine your little goat there—traffic zooming around, horns blasting. No way. No way. And Alicia with that face like a sweet fiery angel. Mundo, man, why do I have to be so young? I can't take her with me and I don't know how to stay.

(*He covers his eyes with his hand. Mundo approaches and pats his shoulder. Eddie jerks away embarrassed.*)

EDDIE: Look, the last thing I need is pity from you!

MUNDO: Yes. (*He leaves quickly.*)

EDDIE: Hey. I'm sorry. I'm sorry. You caught me off guard. Hey man, I'm sorry. It's not like that.

SCENE SEVEN

The bridge. The woman with blue eyes and her boy are coming home from the dance. The boy is humming. He holds up his fist.

PIPO: Look, Mamá—the stars are as big as my fist.

WOMAN: Then why is it always so dark on the road?

(*We hear bells and the bleating of a goat.*)

PIPO: Who's that?

WOMAN: He better not come close to me. I'll know what to do with him.

(*A dark figure, Nyin appears on the bridge.*)

WOMAN: Who's that? Can you see?

PIPO: It's the man with the hat.

WOMAN: (*Going up to Nyin.*) Well, well. Had too much to drink?

NYIN: Worse. Not enough.

WOMAN: You need to get drunk?

NYIN: Yes. Is the dance over?

WOMAN: The dance is over. The beer is packed. Of course—there's more than one way to get drunk and lose your senses.

NYIN: There is—eh?

WOMAN: You know it too.

NYIN: You mean mischief.

WOMAN: Well I ain't dead yet. Too bad you are.

NYIN: What do you mean?

WOMAN: Thirty years with the same woman. You're as good as married.

NYIN: I'm still a free man!

WOMAN: Not as free as all that.

NYIN: You'll be sorry you've spoke to me like this.

WOMAN: I think I'll be very happy that I spoke to you like this. *(She moves very close.)* And you'll make me even happier—isn't that so?

NYIN: What about the boy?

PIPO: Did you get married mother? Was it beautiful?

WOMAN: Shut up. Shut up. You're speaking nothing but dribble. Follow this path—straight and tell Doña Chelo to put you to bed.

PIPO: No.

WOMAN: I'll be right along. I have to make sure this man isn't dead. It's very serious business. Now get along.

PIPO: But the wind, Mamá! What if…

WOMAN: If you don't go I'll whip you till you can't sit down. You have to grow up sometime. Now git!

(Pipo leaves. Nyin grabs her arm.)

WOMAN: Wait. Wait up. God, when your blood heats up it boils.

NYIN: I've got the blood of conquistadors running through my veins. *(He pulls her along.)* Damn you're strong.

WOMAN: I'm as strong as some men. I wish I were a man.

NYIN: I'll make you glad you're a woman.

WOMAN: *(Holds up her skirts. Nyin is hidden. She looks like a bird of prey.)* Well get on with it. Get on with it. I like a good strong man who makes me feel like I've been hit by a thunderbolt.

SCENE EIGHT

Blackout. The boy walking in the dark. He hears a noise, stops.

PIPO: *(Looking around.)* Mamá? Mamá?

CHELO: Who's there?

(The boy comes to Chelo waiting on a dark patio of the restaurant. There is one candle lit in a bottle.)

CHELO: Ay Pipo. What are you doing wandering around alone? Where's your mother?

PIPO: She deserted me.

CHELO: No she hasn't. She'll be back. Don't cry. I'll take care of you as long as you want. Hush. Hush.

PIPO: She'll die without me. She always told me so.

CHELO: Was she hurt then? Where did you last see her?

PIPO: On the bridge. When the man with the hat came. He took her away. I heard her cry out.

CHELO: The hat?

PIPO: The hat and the horse of bones. I forget his name.

CHELO: Ay—my little boy.

PIPO: What shall we do?

CHELO: Wait.

PIPO: Shhhh.

CHELO: What do you hear?

PIPO: The wind.

CHELO: I'll sing to you—so you won't hear. Come here. *(She sits and holds him.)*

Ay de mi Llorona, Llorona
Llorona a field of flowers
Ay de mi Llorona, Llorona
Llorona a field of flowers

If you've never really loved, Llorona
You don't know pain and sorrow
If you've never really loved, Llorona
You don't know pain and sorrow

SCENE NINE

The next morning by the river Mundo is bathing. We see his upper body through leaves.

MUNDO: *(Singing overlapping with Chelo first and then continuing.)*

Ay de me Llorona Llorona
Llorona take me to the river
Ay de mi Llorona Llorona
Llorona take me to the river

Wrap me in your shawl, Llorona
The wind is cold as winter
Wrap me in your shawl, Llorona
The wind is cold as winter

(He hums a bit. He looks at his arms.) Not cold. No. *(He washes himself, he touches his skin.)* A tree. Bark. *(He starts scrubbing hard, then harder*

trying to make his skin smooth.) Off. (He looks closely to see if he has an effect. He touches his arm and then puts his fingers to his mouth. He pats his arm. He's bleeding.) Blood.

SCENE TEN

Alicia comes to find Eddie.

ALICIA: Eddie?
EDDIE: Shhhh. Can you hear Mundo's singing?
  (They both listen.)
ALICIA: He stopped.
EDDIE: You all right?
ALICIA: And you?
EDDIE: Come here.
  (She doesn't.)
ALICIA: What happened with Nyin?
EDDIE: Nothing much.
ALICIA: He was furious.
EDDIE: I guess the truth makes him furious.
ALICIA: You shouldn't have said anything.
EDDIE: He shouldn't have messed with me.
ALICIA: Nyin might leave because of this. They've been together for thirty years!
EDDIE: Hey! Are you blaming me? I didn't betray Nyin.
ALICIA: You betrayed Chelo.
EDDIE: What is this? I did it for "us," all right? I don't want to lose you. They've got their own problems to solve. Maybe we can solve some of our own.
ALICIA: If you were angry at me, would you betray me too?
EDDIE: Of course not.
ALICIA: How do you know?
EDDIE: Alicia what can I tell you. What I do now is all I have. I could die tomorrow.
  (A loud splash. A cry. The goat bleats.)
EDDIE: What's that?
ALICIA: Mundo—shame on you. Are you spying on us? *(To Eddie.)* Go see what he's doing.

EDDIE: *(Goes to the edge of the stage.)* It is Mundo. He's slipped. *(He holds out his hand and walks offstage.)* Here. Take my hand you idiot. Don't be stubborn! *(Eddie exits.)*

ALICIA: *(Watches.)* Eddie! Grab him. What's the matter? Eddie!

EDDIE: A branch. Get me a branch. *(Enters wet and muddy.)* Oh my God Alicia. He's gone. He wouldn't take my hand. He wouldn't take it.

ALICIA: *(Starts to run offstage.)* Mundo. Mundo.

EDDIE: You can't go in. There's a shark.

ALICIA: It's your fault. You talked about death.

EDDIE: Don't be stupid Alicia. Just saying a word doesn't call down the wrath of God. I held out my hand, but he backed away from me.

SCENE ELEVEN

At Chelo's restaurant patio. Chelo is sweeping. The boy Pipo is helping her. The woman with blue eyes walks in.

PIPO: Oh, Mamá. You didn't leave me!

WOMAN: What a stupid boy. How could I leave you? You're my son. *(She hugs him.)* Bobo. Frightened at every little thing.

CHELO: Where are you going? Your work's finished. Pack your things. Take some food from the kitchen and a beer. There's no place for you here. *(Nyin enters.)*

WOMAN: You promised me two months work!

CHELO: I don't remember.

WOMAN: *(Imploring to Nyin.)* And you…you there—what do you say?

CHELO: Yes, what do you say?

NYIN: I have nothing to say about this. This isn't my decision.

CHELO: No?

NYIN: No.

CHELO: I think this may be the most important decision you've made in your life. The woman with blue eyes says I promised her two months work. But I'm telling her I don't remember and I want her to leave now. So what do you say, Nyin. I need to know.

WOMAN: Well…husband?

NYIN: *(Bows his head. To Chelo.)* Fire her!

WOMAN: I see. All your talk of freedom for nothing. You might as well be married you two. You're acting like all men and their wives. Not a human heart between you. You both've used me and now it's out—eh? Well, I wouldn't stay anyway! Not me! Too much time in one place makes me itchy. Come on boy, we've learned our lesson here.

CHELO: You can leave the boy. You're always complaining about him anyway.

WOMAN: Would you like that? School? Other children? Meals till you burst?

PIPO: *(Holding her.)* Yes, Mamá. Please.

WOMAN: No, you can't have him. I need him…What would I be without him? Let's go.

PIPO: The air's green and the wind might get us on the road. Where will we go?

WOMAN: What do you care? Come on!

(They exit.)

SCENE TWELVE

Later that morning. We hear thunder. Chelo's restaurant patio. Eddie and Alicia enter.

EDDIE: Chelo? Chelo?

(Alicia sits heavily at one of the tables.)

EDDIE: I'll go look inside? Okay?

(Alicia says nothing.)

EDDIE: Do you want something…coffee maybe?

ALICIA: No.

(Eddie goes offstage and returns with a sweater.)

EDDIE: *(He goes to put it around Alicia's shoulders.)* Here.

ALICIA: I don't need it.

EDDIE: Okay. No one's around. *(He sits and then gets up immediately and paces.)* Pride killed him. Not me. Not me. I gave him my hand.

ALICIA: Maybe he wanted to die.

EDDIE: No. He stood up. He crossed his arms and looked at me. He never saw the sharks.

ALICIA: How like a man—not to back down, even when every leaf, every stone around him all but screams that he should. Machismo!

EDDIE: Why are you looking at me?

(Nyin and Chelo enter dressed up.)

EDDIE: Aunt Chelo—

CHELO: *(Ignoring him. To no one in particular.)* We've been to church.

NYIN: Last night the devil made his rounds. One night changed my life. Who am I to fight it?

CHELO: He's been to confession.

EDDIE: Uncle Nyin...

CHELO: You're not welcome here.

ALICIA: Doña Chelo! Mundo drowned.

CHELO: Ay no! May God rest his soul.

NYIN: Poor thing.

CHELO: What happened?

ALICIA: He's dead.

NYIN: *(To Eddie.)* High tide?

EDDIE: High tide.

CHELO: Poor sad thing. May he rest in peace.

NYIN: I'll take my boat and see if he was carried downstream.

EDDIE: There were sharks.

NYIN: If he's anywhere—he'll be at the river's mouth. Poor thing.

CHELO: Be careful, Nyin.

NYIN: I tell you, the Devil made his rounds last night.

ALICIA: He was so lonely.

NYIN: Maybe it was for the best. What future did he have? Creature like that. A man isn't meant to live so alone.

(Nyin exits.)

CHELO: He had a voice of an angel.

ALICIA: *(To Nyin.)* Bring his goat. He's tied by the river.

EDDIE: Auntie—

CHELO: No!

EDDIE: It's too new. It's too deep. I can't be away from her now. Auntie. Listen to me.

(Chelo avoids him.)

EDDIE: I'd do anything for Alicia. I'd do what I've already done all over again—and more! I'd lie for her. I'd take the clothes off your back. And if that makes me like my father, that's too damn bad.

CHELO: Ay Edmundo—don't you know yet? You're nothing like your father.

EDDIE: What do you mean?

CHELO: Your father loves no one but himself.

EDDIE: I'll marry her.

ALICIA: And what am I—a bag of beans you two are tossing around? I have my thoughts about this. Edmundo doesn't belong here. I don't want him. Mundo knew too. He wouldn't take Eddie's hand to save his life. He wouldn't owe his life to a stranger and neither will I!

EDDIE: How can you say I'm a stranger?

ALICIA: I look at you now and you're a complete stranger. A month ago, you didn't exist. A month from now you won't either.

EDDIE: You don't mean that. You're upset...

ALICIA: The first person you saw in Nautla was Mundo. Now he's dead.

EDDIE: So what's that supposed to mean?

ALICIA: You're released. You're free to go. God wants you to leave.

EDDIE: God wants me to leave?

ALICIA: It's a sign. I'm sure.

EDDIE: You bitch. Don't use God as an excuse to blow me off. Just admit it— you don't want me around. Go ahead. Now that you have a choice—all you wanted was a little taste of foreign fruit—right? Go on—admit it.

ALICIA: You're right. That's all I wanted.

EDDIE: No, Alicia.

(Alicia exits.)

EDDIE: My father said women were treacherous bitches—maybe he was right!

CHELO: Edmundo...Edmundo.

EDDIE: What?

CHELO: Men are so blind.

EDDIE: What!

CHELO: She's making it easy for you. To leave. That's what women do best. Now go get Mundo's goat.

SCENE THIRTEEN

Eddie looking for the goat. Thunder.

EDDIE: Come here. Come here. How the hell do you call a goat? Here boy... Here...*(He finds Mundo's pail and pole. He hits the pail and waits. He tries again and waits. He sings quietly.)*
I carry two kisses always, Llorona
very close to my soul
I carry two kisses always, Llorona
very close to my soul

The last one my mother gave me, Llorona
And the first kiss of yours I stole

The last one my mother gave me, Llorona
And the first kiss...
(We hear the bleating of a goat.) There you are little guy. Over here...*(He exits.)*

SCENE FOURTEEN

In church. Nyin and Chelo are kneeling. Alicia and Eddie slip the marriage lazo over their heads and go kneel in a pew.

ALICIA: Edmundo, Eddie—the priest told me—if you're ever in church and for some reason you can't pray—you should ask God to join your lazy prayers to the good prayers of the people around you.
EDDIE: Like you?
ALICIA: Yes.
EDDIE: Thanks.
ALICIA: Eddie?
EDDIE: Shhh. I'm praying.
ALICIA: Leave. Go. But don't forget me.

SCENE FIFTEEN

Eddie reading a poem to an audience.

EDDIE: This poem is called "Plane Ride Home" for obvious reasons.
Leaving Mexico behind,
letting it sink into the sea
while the great continents come
unmoored as they pass my window
stirring the ocean into flowers of
foam and widening their arms into
peninsulas; I leave forever,
foundering on the tusks of
a thousand green volcanoes;
memories
streaming from me like rain;
the bells of churches

echoing in my throat.
I am scattered
Blown north, south
into mystery like the unglimpsed
Peak of Orizaba mist-hung
in July. Summer guardian
you've betrayed me into carrying you
away with me. Wedge against my rib, are
you sword or are you shield?

END OF PLAY

ON SUNDAYS

ORIGINAL PRODUCTION

On Sundays was first presented at Arte Unido at Instituto de Arte Teatral Internacional Inc. (IATI) on April 15, 1983 in New York City. Production designed and directed by Manuel Yesckas, producer R. Perez-Ayala, sets and costumes by Isaias Rios, technical director Jimmy Rosado, choreographer Lynne Alvarez. The cast was as follows:

JULES . . . . Manuel Martinez
SYLVIA . . . . Yamila Constantina
THE BEAST . . . . Jose Angel Domingues

CHARACTERS

SYLVIA, a young dancer whom we see during one day of her life
JULES, a dapper man whom we see throughout his life beginning in his late twenties and ending when he is seventy-eight
THE BEAST

SCENE I

It is noon on a Sunday in a large, modern city. Traffic is heard, and people's voices as they pass. Downstage right is a large box with transparent sides. It is open at the top. Sylvia is in her bedroom; perhaps there is a pastel-colored makeup table and a mirror, a chair, some fluttery, transparent curtains. She is going through her morning ablutions. At her foot is the flipping tail of a beast. It lies still and then twitches as if to brush a fly away. She doesn't notice it.

Jules enters stage right. He is in his late twenties at this time. He has neatly combed, short, dark hair under his derby hat. He has a thin, neat mustache. He is wearing a summer suit and swings a cane. A newspaper is folded under his arm. He is dapper and charming, with a tinge of sadness. He whistles softly to himself and seems quite happy. He walks past the box as if it were a window. He catches sight of himself in one of the smooth sides and stops to adjust his hat, his tie, his mustache. He smiles, twirls his cane and continues. As he passes the side of the box, he catches a glimpse of Sylvia and stops abruptly.

JULES: Ooh la la! *(He is delighted. His actions are exaggerated, mimelike. He looks around cautiously to see if anyone is watching. He backs up and tries to see the entire figure. To do this, he gets down on the floor.)* Impossible! *(He gets up, dusts himself off, and using the smooth side, adjusts his mustache. He smiles to himself and tips his hat to himself.)* Ahh. C'est la vie! *(He tips his hat to Sylvia as he passes the door.)* And a good day to you… *(He looks around and adds softly.)* My lovely.

(He exits and immediately reappears. It is later in the afternoon and he looks wilted. His jacket is unbuttoned, his hat slanted over his forehead. He walks slower. There is something defeated in his posture. His newspaper has obviously been opened and refolded but not carefully. He walks very slowly across the stage, looking at his feet. As he approaches the side of the box, he lifts his head. He makes an effort to appear self-composed. He buttons his coat, straightens his posture. He adjusts his hat and walks very purposefully to the box, tips his hat, and starts to move past. He catches himself. He stops and pensively and hopefully addresses Sylvia.)

JULES: Roberta?… *(Pause.)* …Emily?… Blanche?… *(His tone becomes more pleading.)* Cynthia?… Diane?… Joyce?… Lillian? Rebecca?… Christine?… Aurora?… Daphne? *(He waits for a response, sighs deeply, and starts to proceed. He stops suddenly, snaps his fingers.)* Ah-ha! *(He returns to the door.)* Sylvia?… Sylvia, is that you? *(He almost collapses and rests his head on his arm, pressing against the box.)*

SCENE II

It is noon the following Sunday. Sylvia is now preparing breakfast, the Beast's tail is longer. Sylvia is careful to step over it whenever she crosses to set or clear the table. She is preoccupied. Jules enters, dressed as he always is, but he is carrying a bouquet of flowers. He approaches the box.

JULES: I'm sorry. I couldn't come before. I want to apologize. *(He looks around self-consciously. He moves closer so he won't be overheard. He faces the audience and speaks over his shoulder, trying to appear nonchalant to passersby.)* I brought you flowers. See?
(He tries to find a place to offer them to Sylvia. He holds them to the side, but they are not taken. He puts them on the ground and waits to see if she will reach out. Finally, he throws them over the top into the box. Sylvia finds them and puts them on her morning table.)

JULES: You look like Sylvia...but then perhaps you're not. *(Clears his throat.)* In any event I want to tell you that I am sorry I took advantage of your...unusual position...and poured my troubles out like that. I had no right. I'm sorry. *(He waits.)* Of course, I expect that you will hold what I told you in the highest regard and not disclose it to anyone. I hope I can trust you in this respect. *(He waits.)* You seem discreet. You appear to have that quality. *(He waits for a moment.)* In fact, Sylvia... May I call you Sylvia? You seem to possess more than discretion, much more. *(He becomes more and more passionate in his speech.)* You have an aura of calm. Self-possession, I'd say. Yes. But beyond that... *(He looks around insidiously.)* May I take the liberty...Yes, I will take the liberty of saying you project mystery and...and...
(He turns and kneels fervently before the door, his hands clasped together near his heart. The Beast's tail coils around Sylvia's ankle. She kicks it impatiently.)

JULES: Romance! Yes. Romance. *(He tries to embrace the box. Then he jumps to his feet and adjusts his clothing and his mustache.)* I feel foolish. Thank you for your patience. *(He is about to leave.)* I hope you will let me see you again. *(He takes out a date book from his pocket and flips through the pages, nodding and muttering. After some consideration, he adds.)* Let me see. Let me see...Ahhhh. Yes. I could come see you on Sundays. *(He tips his hat and exits.)*

SCENE III

Jules comes out with a paper bag with a handle, a Sunday newspaper with the magazine and comic sections, a portable radio, a folding chair, and a tiny, round table. He is wearing a flower in his lapel and comes out humming. He puts the table down near the box and opens the chair. He pulls a handkerchief from his breast pocket and flamboyantly opens it and uses it as a tablecloth. Next he takes a paper cup from the bag and a plate. He puts the paper cup in the center of the table and puts the flower from his lapel in it.

JULES: Good morning, my love. I've brought brunch and the *News*. The flower is perfectly formed. *Magnifique!*
(As he speaks and gets comfortable, eats and reads the paper, Sylvia will be getting dressed to go out. The Beast, which lies at her feet, switching his tail, raises a paw and tears whatever she puts on. She leaves the shreds on and continues dressing. Jules now takes out a thermos of coffee, another cup, a sweet roll, pat of butter, a plastic knife, sugar, a container of milk and strawberries. He begins to butter the sweet roll and eat strawberries while he chats.)
JULES: How fresh the strawberries are this time of year. The smallest ones are best, bittersweet. How fragrant this coffee is. It's Hawaiian and Indonesian. A blend. How crisp and sweet is this roll, and how creamy the butter is. It's a tender yellowish white. It makes me think of youth. *(Jules picks up the paper, glances through the comic section quickly. Once in a while he lets out a quick, sharp laugh. When he finishes, he folds it into a paper airplane and shoots it into the box. He sits down and reads another section, the Metropolitan section.)* My, my. Listen to this. "A wounded and lost whale wandered the shores of New York within forty feet of Coney Island beach before a police launch herded the forlorn mammal back to the open sea. The launch got between the whale and the shore and tried to steer him to the open sea as the disoriented whale repeatedly tried to enter several bays. 'He was injured,' the police chief said. 'You could see the cut marks on his back. He nudged the launch like it was his girl. We got worried he was going to try to have some fun with it, if you know what I mean,' the police chief continued." Ahem... *(He looks around nervously.)* ...My...my... *(Continues.)* "The police launch lost track of the whale but it was reported that the whale will most likely stay in the area for a while. The police chief added, 'They usually hang around. Sometimes they lose a mate and hang around waiting for it to return.'"

(Jules reaches out and touches the box tenderly. It begins to rain, light at first and then harder. He fishes in his bag and takes out a collapsible umbrella, which he opens. He sits sipping coffee, holding the umbrella over his head.)

SCENE IV

Sylvia, dressed now, tries to leave. The Beast blocks her way. There are several attempts. Jules comes rushing in. He carries his coat over his arm.

JULES: I hope you'll forgive that I'm late! *(He spreads his jacket on the ground near the door. He sits down there. He is animated, sparkling.)* But I went to the beach! It was delightful! Delicious. Three sea gulls circled the ocean and dove in. Seven women were having a picnic on a pink blanket. Nine couples were laughing on the boardwalk… *(Pause.)* I counted them. I like to know what is going on. The world interests me. No! It fascinates me! If only you were there.
(Sylvia taps on the glass and tries in vain to get Jule's attention. He stands up and takes out a piece of paper from his breast pocket. He unfolds it and takes an oratorical stance, half-facing the box and yet visible to the audience.)
JULES: I wrote a poem for you. *(He reads very grandly.)*
"The sea roars and swells
above me
my lone heart leaps
that dolphin part of me."
(He folds the paper and returns it to his pocket. He looks longingly at the box. Sylvia looks longingly out. He doesn't see her.)
JULES: That dolphin part of me.

SCENE V

During this scene Sylvia wrestles with the Beast who claws her. She bleeds. It is an overcast Sunday. Years have passed for Jules. This is noted by two things. First, the mirrored sides of the box are streaked with dirt; and second, some flowers, branches, pieces of paper; newspaper, and cloth have accumulated around the bottom of the box as if driven there by wind. Jules enters. He walks slowly, almost decrepitly, his hat in one hand, leaning on a cane. His hair is unkempt, with visible gray in it. He has a few days' growth of beard; his clothes are rumpled. He walks as if he is physically weak rather than old.

JULES: Well, I'm here. *(He pauses.)* It's been some time now. I don't know precisely how much. But it's been quite some time. You don't look well, I may add. You've changed. *(He pauses.)* Don't worry, though. I've only come…This will only be a short visit. For many reasons. *(His voice is tightly controlled.)* You may have noticed that I…don't feel too well. It's no wonder with all that's happened. In any event, you've failed to say anything about it. Is that your usual discretion? Well, let me tell you… your silence… *(He starts to lose control of his voice. As he talks, he absently starts to pick up the trash around the box or will wipe at a streak with part of his sleeve.)* is…more…than…I can…tolerate! I will not be treated… *(He loses his place. He clears his throat.)* I was ill, you see. A touch of flu. Can you see how pale I've become? How thin? My sources of revenue, my usual sources dried up, disappeared and I…I was…you might say, I was reluctant to leave my home. After all, it is my home, with all my special objects about me, little things I collect, a lifetime, if you wish. And I became afraid to step out. No telling who might come, and I hadn't a cent. Of course, in better health I would have set about…set about establishing new sources. Much more stable ones. I had several ideas in fact…and… *(He clears his throat.)* then these two men burst through the door. Unasked, uncalled for. It was humiliating. I was in my bedclothes…indeed, I had retired to my bedclothes some time before, days, perhaps a week…Needless to say, I was frightened but maintained a calm presence. "Please leave as you came in," I told them. But they ignored me, in my own house. I would have thrown them out, mind you, although I'm usually quite polite. They were uninvited. I don't know how they knew my name. They read it from a piece of paper and asked me if that was my name. "Why, yes, it is," I answered. "And now will you kindly leave. I'm very tired." But they wouldn't, you know. They looked official. Officious. *(He laughs.)* Like officious ice cream men, really. All in white. It made me laugh. Then one of them said, "Will ya look at this pitiful mess." Now, yes, I was very weak and may have had my eyes closed, but I heard that. *I heard that. (He is quite upset.)* "This pitiful mess" they called it, my home. Who are they to say that? What do they know about beauty, I ask you? But that wasn't the worst. They took me away. It took two of them. But I had worse to contend with. Yes. Your silence haunted me then. Your silence became a burden. All those days upon days. I worried about it. I fretted. Once or twice they told me I screamed out in my sleep. It was agony. *(He steps away from the box.)* And all that time. Not a word, not a note, not a sigh on my account. I paced, I cursed, I spit on you. Yes, I did, and several times. I vowed to come back and end this once and for all just as soon...just as soon as I...was able. *(He clears his throat and straightens his clothes. He empties his hat and pockets of trash and puts his derby on his head.)* I will no longer be humiliated. I will no longer be ignored. *(He raises his cane and beats the box until he breaks through one side.)* Do you hear? Some response is necessary! Some response is necessary! Some response is necessary! I will no longer tolerate...tolerate...emptiness!

(He stands back, satisfied with what he has done and stalks off without looking back. Sylvia is wrestling with the Beast. She takes its tail and wraps it around its throat and kills it. She lies there breathing heavily. Jules comes in carrying a paper shopping bag over one arm. He is dressed again as before, neatly, although not as precisely as at first. He leans more on his cane and is obviously older. His hair is white. He also carries a broom. He approaches smiling. The box looks in sad shape. It is even dirtier, and the glass is cracked. More debris is cluttering around its base. The dead Beast lies there, too, discarded.)

JULES: *(Looking at the box, walking entirely around it.)* Tsch...tsch...tsch...a little the worse for wear...tsch...tsch...But you know. It is time, time we made our peace. I have had you in my heart all these years...as if a sliver from one of these mirrors had entered it and settled there...My...my... *(He puts his bag down and begins to sweep away the debris.)* Yes, a sliver. So I have come back to you...my lovely. Do you remember how I called you that? There are many things I must tell you. There are things I must explain to you...Just a minute. *(He sweeps some of the debris offstage and returns.)* It looks better already. No one has taken care of you. Not the way I would have. *(He sweeps, walking all the way around the box. As he reappears, he looks older, perhaps more bent, slower.)* I have made mistakes. Incredible errors for a person who is basically careful, civilized sometimes to a fault. One of which I hope to expiate with you. There are so many things I never told you that would have perhaps...perhaps softened things between us...Just a moment... *(He sweeps the remaining debris offstage.)* There. Quite an improvement. But that is not all. Voilà! *(He extracts a large bottle of Windex and a rag from his bag. He begins to clean the glass.)* So many things I never ventured to tell you. Never dared to mention because I might disturb some imperceptibly delicate balance...But no matter. Now I can say...Now I will say what I please. *(He clears his throat and straightens his derby in the newly cleaned mirror. He makes a face at himself and smiles, tips his hat, almost forgetting his place for a moment.)* Now where was I? Oh, yes... Ahem. You see. You may wonder why I never approached you physically. It's not that I don't think that way. Quite the opposite is true. However, physical relationships are... I suppose you might say they are difficult for me, but that doesn't mean I haven't admired...ardently...the smoothness of an arm I have glimpsed... *(He tries to peer into the box, slants his hat roguishly.)* or the slenderness of a leg, a length of calf, the velvet flow of hair...why even now its perfume wafts, floats to me and makes me drowsy...

(He reappears, he has a slight wispy white goatee.)

(Sylvia steps out from behind the curtain. She is in tights and a leotard and wears a wreath on her head, streamers.)

JULES: And you have inspired me. I have often aspired to be as quiet and accepting as you, not to complain or exclaim, not to pile my emotions and desires against you here as if they were leaves and debris blown in by the wind. I have tried to emulate your steadfastness, your virtuous simplicity. *(He again turns the corner and reappears with a longer beard. Steps back and reviews his work.)* Aha. My lovely. You are once again nearly as I remember you.

(He steps close to wipe a speck away and catches sight of himself. He cannot see Sylvia, who steps up to the glass. She tries to find an opening in order to leave, but cannot. She is dejected because she can find no way out.)

JULES: Oo la la. I have grown old. Who would have thought... *(He shakes his head and puts away the Windex. Now he is removing small specks of dirt only he can see.)* But I must hurry to tell you more. Soon it will be too late. *(A strong wind comes up. We hear it. Then it blows Jules's hat away.)*

JULES: *(Talking over the wind.)* I believe...in fact I am sure that I have learned from your higher qualities. It has been painful, in fact at times it has been excruciatingly painful to never receive a word of love or feel your affection...but now I see that although one may never actually receive tokens of love...

(The wind almost blows him over. He holds on to the box. Sylvia hears the wind; she studies the opening at the top of the box and jumps. Large leaves, as big as he, blow onstage and settle against him or the box.)

JULES: *(Struggling physically and vocally against the wind.)* That doesn't matter. What is left, you see...oh, my dear, here is the beauty of it all...although you never receive the smallest hint, the vaguest gesture or the slightest trace of love... *(His voice rises.)* ...you can always...without fail...*give it* Voilà! That is a life! *(He laughs happily.)* C'est vrai, ma cherie...my lovely... *(He recovers himself enough to continue polishing the box. For a moment, poised to turn the corner, he tilts his head jauntily, twirls his mustache.)*

JULES: Now. Let me tell you a joke I overheard. It was quite humorous and I remember it perfectly...

(He steps around the corner and his voice is cut off by the wind. He does not reappear this time. The stage begins to fill with huge, gold, orange, and brown leaves. Sylvia climbs out of the box, looks around, and scampers behind it.)

END OF PLAY